Those Two Idiots!

Road Dog Publications was formed in 2010 as an imprint of Lost Classics Book Company and is dedicated to publishing the best in books on motorcycling, motorsports, and adventure travel. Visit us at www.roaddogpub.com.

ISBN 978-1-890623-66-1
Library of Congress Control Number: 2019945564

An Imprint of Lost Classics Book Company
This book also available in eBook format at online booksellers. ISBN 978-1-890623-67-8

Those Two Idiots!

Two continents. One journey. No idea.

by

A. P. Atkinson

Road Dog Publications

Publisher
Lake Wales, Florida

Many thanks to Coal for his tireless support in my journey and to Ade for annoyingly pestering me to get this written. Thanks to Saiem for giving me the world's best reason to never stop trying, to Chris for helping to make this happen, to Andrea for encouraging me when I was close to giving up, and to my publisher, Mike Fitterling, for believing in this book.

Thanks most of all to Marcin, the gigantic mess of scar-tissue that made this everything it could be and who, despite his many horrible, awful, terrible failings, I love like a brother.

About the Author

A. P. Atkinson, known as Jack to his friends for some inexplicable reason, was born in London in the latter part of the twentieth century. The majority consensus is that this was probably a bad move on his part.

Coming from a family of motorcyclists, he had an early interest in things with a wheel at each end. His father was an engineer and his uncle was renown for drunken bar fights and riding too fast, in no particular order. They encouraged him with a box of parts and the promise that there was a bike in there somewhere. There mostly was, and he built his first motorcycle at the age of sixteen and has built many more since; some even worked.

Several engineering disasters later, and a few drunken bar fights, he fostered a passion for not crashing through hedges while riding sports-bikes at speeds upon which the law frowns.

His other passion is writing, for which he discovered he had a little talent, at least more talent than he displayed at not crashing through hedges. At the age of eleven he grumbled to a friend about the quality of a story he had read. His friend challenged him to do better, which set him on a lifelong quest to live the life of an impoverished writer.

After creating a number of fictional stories that awkwardly blended science-fiction with motorcycles, he gave up and decided to find somewhere to quietly drink himself to death.

When he finally decided to leave London and discover what was actually out there, it all naturally came together: motorcycles, questionable ethics, a dubious grasp of grammar, a passion for telling stories, and absolutely no clue about what he was going to do next.

Table of Contents

1

An Itch that Needed Scratching

I'm an English motorcycle fanatic who's always had an interest in travelling. The enthusiasm for motorcycles has reached the proper level to be considered an obsession. I've owned hundreds of them and ridden hundreds more. I would hate to try and work out how much money I've lost on them over the years, but it's a lot.

I'm not a mechanic by any means, but I can find my way around an engine and probably slot in around the bottom end of barely competent. Likewise, I'm no engineer, but my dad was, and I grew up with a solid grounding into how things work. I'm not even a particularly good rider, but I crash rarely and can usually manage to get where I'm going, even with the odds stacked very much against me. I've taken sports-bikes to the edge of their performance and enjoy scrambling over unmade roads on machines that weren't designed for it. I'm the sort of person who will try anything and have been accused of being a thrill-seeker, but that was by a Canadian, so I'm not sure it counts. I wouldn't say that I am, but I do get bored easily and enjoy a challenge.

I had pretty much settled into the little spot just before middle-age and had reached a point in my life where everything had begun to change. My mates had mostly gotten married, started having children, and moving away from London. Slowly, my group of friends was dwindling away, until there was just a few of us left. Weekends were no longer the highlights of the week that they used to be when we were all younger and dumber.

Nightclubs had been replaced by bars, and bars had been replaced by coffee shops. My job suddenly had longer hours and suspiciously less money; my motorcycles were getting larger as my age allowed insurance bills to do the opposite. I was growing up, resisting it fiercely, but it was happening whether I liked it or not. I finally came to accept that no amount of dating younger women and buying sports-bikes was going to stop the inexorable march of time. I was going to have to come up with something even more stupid. Luckily, I am hugely resourceful when it comes to doing stupid things.

The whole idea of "middle-age" is difficult to define, in any case. I could get run over by a bus any time, and in London traffic, that's not just something we say in passing; it's a genuine possibility and not even unlikely. A friend of mine, a fellow motorcyclist, had a traumatised sister. She had been waiting at a bus-stop when a crashing sound caught her attention. She looked up just in time to see bits of motorcycle sprinkling themselves all over the road and the head of the rider rolling along past her. These things happen. On the other hand, I never expected to live this long, and not just because of the ever-present danger from mass-transit systems and my general ineptitude with motorcycle maintenance. I just never saw it coming.

When you're young, the thought of yourself ageing is a difficult thing to wrap your head around. Everything is of the moment, and consequences are something that happen to an unfortunate few. The concept of change is so far in the distance it fails to fully register as you wander from day to day, still learning the lessons life has to teach you. One day, you just find yourself in some place with bills over your head, a job you hate, a relationship with someone you don't really like very much, and a car in your front yard, where there should be a motorcycle.

While I'm essentially a responsible person by nature, I was never very good at growing up. There was always something about me that was somewhere between not quite right and not utterly, totally, and irretrievably wrong. Whatever it was, it left me feeling like a square peg in a round hole for much of my life, not quite fitting in, not quite being the same as everyone else. That wasn't much of an issue, as I had no great desire to be anything more or less than I was. I was fortunate enough to find enough other people with a similar inability to adjust to reality to make all this seem tolerable.

London is a big city, and I was born not quite in it. I lived most of my life skirting around the edges, trying hard to make enough money to survive on just the right side of abject poverty, and for the most part, I managed it.

Still, life in England, and in London especially, has always been hard on the soul. There's never enough money to go around, and struggling becomes such an established part of life that it's hard to imagine that anything could be any different. You work hand to mouth, never growing your resources, always checking and rechecking at the end of the month, and living in constant dread of a letter dropping on your mat that will remind you of yet another drain on your dwindling reserves of cash. I had a passion for motorcycles, which pushed my already stretched resources to breaking point and, sometimes, beyond.

I had my first motorcycle at the tender age of sixteen. It was a 50cc scooter and came in several cardboard boxes with some assembly required. I built it myself with a little help from my dad and my uncle, who had found the thing for me. It taught me a lot about bikes, especially how to crash them, which was something I did fairly often.

It was stolen, at one point, while I was working, but it was returned and rebuilt for only a few pounds and with surprisingly little swearing. Between the crashing and the joy-riding, I ended up losing all interest in two-wheeled transport and learned to drive a car instead. I became quite interested in cars and began to foster a passion for them that I had never found in the little scooter. Eventually, after a year or so, I had a Ford Mustang, a big American thing that was a rare sight in London; a car you couldn't help but notice and that was an absolute pleasure to drive.

Unfortunately, a sales rep did manage not to notice it early one morning and slammed into the back of it, causing enough damage to make it unsafe to drive and unpleasant to own. Off the road and with a job to get to, I was back to tiny motorcycles. This time, a 100cc Yamaha, borrowed from my brother.

But this time everything was different. I went to motorcycle rallies on it, I travelled, and it started to get under my skin. Before I had time to notice, the little 100cc machine had been replaced by a 250cc, a 600cc, and then a 750cc turbo-charged monstrosity of a bike that had a vicious little eye on my wallet. The obsession had begun, and there was no escaping it. I had no real desire to escape, in any case, which didn't really help.

I'd become hopelessly addicted to sports-bikes. I loved to twist the throttle and feel the barely contained insanity that a modern motorcycle unleashes on you. Unfortunately, the modern world hasn't managed to keep up with motorcycle development, at least in terms of power and performance. I had to face the distinct possibility of the loss of my license, freedom (such as it was in London), and my life on the back/front/side of a mass transit vehicle.

Slowly and reluctantly, I gravitated towards smaller, more sensible bikes, eventually developing a passion for 650cc singles. They don't have a high top speed, but they do accelerate nicely and are light enough to corner quickly. It was enough to keep me interested. At one point, I owned two Aprilias, an RSV1000 sports-bike and a 650cc enduro-style Pegaso. I found that I rarely rode the RSV, favouring the single for virtually all occasions. I still feel that a 650cc is probably the best compromise available and is largely the ideal bike.

This class of motorcycles also opened up the world of riding off-road. A short trip into the Kent countryside revealed green-lanes, and short tracks of dirt and rocks that it was just barely legal to ride on, if you were stupid enough to try. I like to think that I'm at least that stupid, and the evidence seemed to bear that out. Suddenly, it was more fun riding at low speed than it was riding flat out at speeds that bend the fabric of space and time and threaten the laws of everything, up to and including physics.

At that point in my life, my interest in street motorcycles was beginning to die off. Discovering the wonderful world of mud and finding a whole new side to two-wheeled life inspired a whole new wave of passion.

I had another interest too, and that was travelling. I managed to save some money, against all odds, and it finally seemed like that wasn't just becoming possible, it was becoming inevitable. My grandparents had all died off, my parents were young enough to look after themselves, my brother was settled down, and I had a burning itch that needed scratching, and not the kind you get from going to Thailand.

After round after round of depressing redundancies, this interest was becoming an obsession. I knew that I needed to get away, and as far away as possible. I was enjoying the weekend trips with my brother into the Kent countryside, but they weren't enough for me anymore. We would ride along the various trails, over rocks and mud, and through streams and woods, but I was finding it restrictive to the point of it being stifling. To stay on the right side of the law, the trails were narrow and short and increasingly repetitive. The roads I rode were familiar, and the life I was leading was feeling more and more like the lanes themselves.

I knew deep down that I just couldn't do it anymore. I lost my job, which ended up costing me a lot more than that. I did get myself back into work and actually quite enjoyed my new job. I was running around helping new stores to get set up, training staff, and meeting new people all around the town. The problem was that it was rapidly coming to an end; I would soon be put into a shop somewhere and would be managing it, and the prospect was not a welcome one.

I knew it was time to leave. The green-lanes suddenly became training, and I started buying motorcycles to test them; to decide on the right bike to get me out on the road; to escape the cage of a gruelling, thankless job with no prospects for the future.

I bought bikes with a purpose. I started with larger, faster bikes capable of devouring huge distances with ease. I rejected one after another—too awkward, not fun, not reliable—until my needs were met properly. I didn't really understand what I was looking for, so I researched, I asked more informed people, I spoke with dealers, mechanics, and men running scrap-yards. Slowly, I got a better idea of what I really needed. I started researching where to go, what prospects I had at the present, and what places were of interest.

I split up with my girlfriend, which left a vacancy in my life that was quickly filled by a Thai girl studying English in London.

She had a year left on her visa, and the plan was that, after that was up, I would go and try my luck in Thailand.

Of course, I had no intention of flying there.

2

Other Options

"Do you know they have flights now?"

I was sitting in a BMW showroom drinking a pretty good cup of coffee, which is served free to customers, or even people like me who have no intention of doing anything beyond getting mud on their carpet.

They know that people want what they're offering, so there's no hard-sell, no pressure, and free stuff on offer. The first time I went into this particular dealership, on the outskirts of a shopping complex somewhere in deepest, darkest Kent, they asked me if I wanted some coffee and what I wanted to watch on the TV. I was shown the magazine rack and told to help myself, and if I was hungry, they were cooking burgers outside that were, of course, free. Doing this to normal people is probably stupid enough, but doing it to bikers... Consequently, my brother and I spent a fair amount of time loitering without intent in their dealership. We ended up on first name terms with the staff, which was something they quite quickly came to regret.

I was sitting there with my brother one day, getting really quite a lot of mud on their carpet while trying to steal the larger notes from the bottom of the charity collection box. I'd not long returned from a light trip around Europe with my Thai girlfriend, and the bike was still in touring-mode, as was I.

"Touring mode" for the bike meant that heaps of junk were still bolted all over her, including extended tanks, fuel bottles, and spotlights. For me, it meant that my motorcycle clothing smelled like something had died in it. None of the modifications were technically quite legal by UK standards, and it all looked as aesthetically pleasant as a Bulgarian super-model. "Not for road use" was stamped all over my kit, and I sat there not caring in the slightest, until two police officers turned up on enduro bikes. They swaggered in to make use of the free coffee, a pair of blatant stereotypes from a poorly-made daytime drama.

One was a sidekick, barely capable of independent thought, and the other was bloated with his sense of arrogant self-importance, and of course, doughnuts. The staff seemed to know them and had clearly learned it was easier to let them be, rather than engage them in any kind of conversation. I didn't know any better, so I said hello.

"Is that your Frankenstein machine out there?"

You know you're not in trouble if they don't call you sir. Despite the condescension and strongly implied insult, there was no point denying it; she didn't look too pretty, as functionality rarely does. The modifications were awkward and uneven, based on my needs, and ignored pretty much every other requirement. I'd not had the time to build the ultimate touring machine that I had always dreamed of, so had instead settled for a touring machine that would get me home without catching fire.

It did actually catch fire twice later. And once before.

The conversation proceeded, and eventually the subject of what the hell I had done to it came up. I explained that I'd just got back from a month touring Europe with my partner and was now going to ride the same bike across the Middle East to Thailand. He laughed like he understood; it was the kind of laugh that the saying *we mock what we don't understand* was made for.

"Do you know they have flights now?" He cast a mocking smile to his partner, who replied with a blank stare.

He was right about one thing, but only one thing—I could fly to Thailand. I did, in fact, several times, and it was not a life-changing experience. It was fun, it was interesting, but I got back as still largely the same person, only with slightly more of a tan. This time was going to be different. This time I was going to stay there for a while; look into starting a business of some kind. I had an idea that I would like to work with bikes professionally, or at least not completely unprofessionally. Perhaps motorcycle touring, perhaps making parts for adventure bikes. I hadn't thought this all through properly yet, apart from knowing that it was time to leave England. What I had decided from the outset was that I wanted to take my bike.

Thailand seemed great, but it would be even better with my bike in it. Everything is better with my bike in it, except my living room; motorcycles take up more space than you might think.

After losing my previous BMW F800gs to local thieves, I'd needed to store my current motorcycle in my house. The police were able to later recover the BMW in the garage of a known motorcycle thief. Sadly, they were not able to make a case against him for some bizarre reason, and he was never charged with any crime. It's a good job for him that he hadn't managed to ride the bike at three mph over the speed limit, then he might have been in *real* trouble.

I liked having my own transport, and I liked my transport to have two wheels and slightly larger capacity than the tiny machines they had in Thailand already. Shipping my own motorcycle was an option, but one I rejected, so that only left the option of riding it there. Thailand is a long way, and there are certain inconveniences to deal with before the relatively simple task of riding a small, single-cylinder machine across a dozen countries. Paperwork is prohibitively complicated and expensive for a start, and preparation constitutes a mountain of it. That's without the real mountains you have to negotiate in a more literal sense, which are often covered in snow.

If Europe was anything to go by, it would also be littered with bits of broken motorcycles and smaller bits of bikers. You have to choose the right motorcycle for your trip and then make sure it's ready. You have to carefully select the equipment, the clothing, and the tools you're going to need, prepare the bike by upgrading all the things that need improvements, and ensure it all works properly with thorough testing.

I didn't do any of those things.

The trip was something I'd been planning for a while, but I use the term *planning* in the loosest possible sense. It had simply been an idea at the back of my head, an itch that needed scratching.

At first, I bought a few different bikes, to try them out long-term and see how well they suited me. I had owned a lot of bikes, enough that I already had a pretty good idea of what I was going to need. But adventure-bikes were still new to me, and I had a lot to learn.

I went through the process of rejecting the BMW R1200gs as too expensive and over-hyped to purchase the Triumph Tiger. There was something very satisfying about the idea of turning up in foreign countries on a British motorcycle, even if it was built in Thailand, with Japanese electronics and was based on a Kawasaki design. I had that for ten days before changing my mind and getting the BMW R1200gs after all. The Tiger was just awful anywhere other than in the mud. It was ungainly, top-heavy; it struggled to make a decent pace and just felt awkward and clumsy.

The BMW was better. It had been a nice bike in every way, except in the way of actually owning it, which was expensive and stressful, largely unrewarding, and left me with the feeling you get when you wake up after a night in the pub with an empty wallet and a sore brain. I'd bought it believing it to at least be reliable, but I was proved wrong even about that.

The fuel consumption was confused. Sometimes it was okay, other times it drank faster than an ageing blonde at her best friend's wedding. It had to be recovered twice by a man in a van who couldn't wait to tell me, with great enthusiasm, how many of these he had to pick up on a regular basis.

And then the battery died. The first time it stranded me outside a local supermarket. Simple enough, except when it dies on a BMW with a CANBUS system it sends the bike on a mad kind of seizure, spitting out diagnostic emergencies all over the over-informative dash. A new Odyssey battery not only fixed the immediate problem but made her a better and more reliable machine for the future. But it did leave me wondering why I had to part with £100 to make my bike work to even a basic degree. The bike was only a few miles from my house, but so heavy that pushing it was never an option. If a basic thing like the failure of a battery turned it from a motorcycle into a very large ornament, then it really wasn't much use any distance from my own home. If this had happened while I was in the middle of somewhere interesting, then I would be in real trouble.

The other time it had to be recovered was, granted, not entirely the bike's fault. I hit a pigeon head on. I guess it deserved everything it got, because it flew directly into an oncoming vehicle, at night, and with a fifty watt HID unit warning it that something large and unforgiving was coming directly at it. It flew into the front wheel, and the knobbly enduro tyre removed all the feathers in an instant, blasting them up through the headstock into my crash helmet, where they ended up sticking out of my nose, eyes, and mouth. Presumably, the stunned remains flash-fried on the engine, and some very happy local cats had a neat and convenient meal. This caused approximately no damage whatsoever, but it did make me stop to check and, of course, get the feathers out of my helmet while I coughed up the ones I'd been lucky enough to inhale. When I rode away, I had no brakes. The brakes were solenoid-operated and were really excellent, but when they fail, they leave the massive, lumbering bulk of the GS with the braking power of a Russian car from the 1960s. I rode defensively to my destination at around twenty mph and got it recovered again in the morning. I had to listen once more to stories of how often these things go wrong and need picking up.

Once I got it home, I Googled the problem, and it turned out to be, rather annoyingly, that the hand-guard had moved. It had touched the brake lever, sent the computer into diagnostic mode, and cut out the brakes. I moved it back. What I couldn't replace so easily was any faith in the machine. It was trouble, and I now knew it with a sense of certainty I usually reserve for my hatred of soup and all things soup-related. (It's not a food; it's just a drink that's showing off!)

So in the end, the message was clear. The R1200gs was just not built for the long haul, and I ended up offloading it onto a slightly brain-dead Belgian.

The next bike I tried was a BMW F800gs. Now that was a good little bike, apart from not being very little, or particularly good. After riding it through the woods and up some steps, I found the paint chipped easily, and the head was beginning to weep oil. In fact, all of the "known issues" began to manifest, and I had to conclude, once again, that it was too expensive and clearly designed to be ridden on the flat tarmac outside the local coffee shop. In the end, a guy who lived in the outskirts of Kent took that off my hands. I had not planned for that to be the case. I just woke up and found a gap where the bike had once been, and I never saw her again.

The situation eventually resolved itself when I got back more money than I paid for the bike, due to estimating the value accurately to the insurance, and wildly inaccurately to a desperate salesman who hadn't made a sale in quite some time. I had intended to sell it in any case, so it made little difference to me. By the time it went, I wasn't sorry to see it go.

Losing a bike meant I was temporarily faced with a large gap in my life that needed to be filled promptly with something that had a wheel at each end. I decided on something cheaper to run and smaller, as I used it off-road occasionally. This time, I thought I'd go with a single.

BMW made a range of single-cylinder bikes dating back to the early '90s, beginning with an experimental design to cash in on the sudden success of the Honda Dominator, which was an attempt to marry the comfy seating position of an enduro to a road-going machine. The Funduro was born. The name still sounds to me like a set of finger-nails dragging down a blackboard while something heavy swings from your balls, someone rubs chilli powder in your eyes, and someone else plays anything by Maria Carey as a background accompaniment.

The most recent experimentally over-priced single by BMW was the X-range, three bikes using the same engine and chassis but varying slightly in subtle ways, i.e. they had different sized front wheels. There was a seventeen-inch version road going super-moto, a twenty-one-inch off-road version, and a middle of the road nineteen-inch version, which happened to be the only one with a comfy seat and that was available in black.

My experience with BMWs, at that point, was that they break down often and are generally annoying, but I'd been assured the singles were truly reliable and were very economical besides. I bought one without riding it and travelled across London to pick it up. It was used, but in okay condition, low mileage, and was bearing no signs of abuse (yet!). Riding her home after the F800gs, she felt a little lacklustre in the power department and was noticeably slower. I only wanted it for commuting and basic use and liked the idea of it fitting in my house to frustrate the many people who wanted to steal it from outside. After riding it for a few days, I tried it on some green-lanes, and it was instantly far better than the GS and managed to be more comfortable while it was doing it. I gradually started to really like that bike, even though I never had any intention of using it as anything more than a routine commuter.

In casual conversation with my other-half, she more or less decided we should go travelling around Europe for a month on the bike after a throwaway comment I made; something about us going away to travel around Europe for a month on the bike. In a panic, I decided I needed to find an ideal bike for the trip that I could then come back and use to ride to Thailand and keep for fun once I was out there. After many hours on the Internet, I came to the conclusion that the Internet is rubbish for everything except looking at porn.

Everyone out there has an opinion, based on their own experience and personality, but nobody accepts that experience and personality vary wildly and thinks theirs is far more valid than everyone else's. I consider myself to be quite pragmatic and even tend to buy my bikes based on practical concerns, like how fast they are and whether or not they come in black. Now that I was trying hard to wean myself off my sports-bike addiction, I had to be even more pragmatic than ever and really couldn't find a better bike than I already had in my garage.

Actually, I didn't have a garage—I had a living room with a very dirty carpet and some odd scuffs on the doorway. I decided to draw out some cash and prepare that bike for touring, rather than just look for something better, because ultimately, I'm pretty lazy. The great thing about the consumer society we live in is that there is usually nothing better; there's only a facade, an illusion of improvement based on a manufactured desire, so people can sell you things you don't need. I actually had what I needed; it may have had certain drawbacks, and I may have wanted more power, but it was perfectly suited to my needs, rather than my highly dubious and unreliable "want" to ride far too fast in public places.

So preparation began by withdrawing money from the bank and basically throwing it everywhere aimlessly in the hope that some of it might make the bike better in some unfathomable way. Firstly, the most logical thing to me was to find out what had broken or failed on other bikes similar to mine. I found incidents of the rear subframe snapping and the rear shock absorber giving up, so I started there. I replaced the rear shock with a far better unit, which made a massive improvement as soon as I fitted it. It even looked better than the original one, which was carefully disposed of over the fence into the next door's garden. To avoid damaging the subframe, I fitted lightweight luggage, in this case, specially designed throw-over bags. They came with a nice set of rear bars to protect the exhaust, which came in very handy when someone kicked the bike over and left her lying in the road in a backstreet in London while I was working.

I had a number of friends who had expressed interest in joining me for various parts of the longer trip I was planning, but I didn't see anyone else preparing their bikes, so I was resigned to doing it alone. The planning took a fairly long while, and nobody seemed to believe I was actually going to do it. To me, the planning had, if anything, become slightly mundane, but when we left on our preliminary European tour, there seemed to be some surprise amongst the people that knew me that something was actually happening. Truth be told, there wasn't really any planning necessary on my part that first time, as a UK passport allows me free access to a whole lot of places that are worth seeing. Planning was no more complicated than looking at a map and getting the Euros from work.

The month spent travelling in Europe was a story all by itself. It certainly wasn't particularly challenging, but it served its purpose in giving me a far better idea of what I needed from my bike, what modifications worked, and what didn't. And on my return, I began an overhaul based on making her just as good as she could be, ready for the more gruelling trip ahead, which would test her to the limits of her endurance.

One loose end that needed to be tied up was that I had a job at the time. After a period of unemployment, I'd found myself working as a pawnbroker/money-lender/foreign exchange teller/auditor/area manager/consultant. The company I was working for was new and clueless about how to run a business, while I had done and seen it all before. Almost the entire management team had worked together selling shovels at a DIY chain, so how that related to this business I wasn't sure, and by studying the way they worked, it clearly didn't.

So when the time came to leave, it wasn't much of a problem for me to hand in my resignation. The area manager offered me a promotion, and after that insult, I resigned immediately, gave up my flat, and crashed on the floor of a mate's house as a temporary measure while we counted down the days until I left.

That was a good time that I look back on with fond memories. He had travelled himself, and we had many beer-fuelled discussions about things I can no longer remember, due to the sheer volume of beer we fuelled up on.

Thunderstick, as he's known, is a rather unusual person. His brain simply doesn't work like other people's, and whether or not that's a good thing is something I've never really put a lot of thought into; we're all just impressed that it works at all. Thunderstick was one of the friends that expressed an interest in coming along, but unfortunately, he had a job and a life he just didn't want to walk away from, something I had long since come to terms with.

I did some research on various forums and came across a Polish gentleman named Marcin who was living in England. And any kind of gentleman he certainly was not. He sent me a message saying that he was travelling all the way to Australia, so we agreed to meet at the Ace Cafe in London. He seemed like a decent enough guy with some travel experience under his belt and a bike twice as big as mine with a reputation for poor reliability. The trip would definitely be more interesting with a fellow traveller, I thought, and it would cut the costs too. Even though we barely knew each other, we decided to give it a go.

Marcin and I are very different people, in that he thinks exclusively in one dimension. If he wants to get somewhere quickly, he can only ride faster. The concept of slowing down and conserving fuel to avoid additional fuel stops blows his mind. If someone gave me a wrapped Christmas present, I'm the kind of guy who would shake it and try to guess what it was and then wait until the day to open it and see if I was right. Marcin would just eat it and hope it was food.

Marcin left a few days before I did. He needed to make some preparations to his bike in Poland and wanted to catch up with his family. I also still had a few things to do on mine before I left, so the situation suited us both. The plan was to meet in Wroclaw, Poland, in three days' time. So that was how long I had to take care of the remaining niggling loose ends, such as building my bike. And getting to Poland.

And, of course, there was the business of saying goodbye to my girlfriend . . . I'd been staying at her rented London flat for the previous few weeks, so I spent one last night there so we could say our farewells, and it was about this time the realisation dawned on her that this was actually going to happen.

The final few days I went back to crashing with my old friend and preparing my bike.

One of the biggest drawbacks at that stage was the lights. They were rubbish. It was just a plastic bowl headlight that threw out as much light as a mobile phone screen. It needed an upgrade, and while that sounds like an easy enough thing to do, it ate up a lot of my time. I also wanted to move the reserve fuel tank, which was another simple thing that turned into a major pain in the arse.

My bike was small, light, and nimble, and that turned out to be its biggest issue. It was so small and compact that finding space to mount everything was a serious concern. I spent much of my preparation time sitting down, staring cluelessly at the bike, and occasionally muttering swear-words as ideas fluttered in and out of my mind. Frustratingly for my Asian girlfriend, that was also how I managed my romantic relationships.

Finally, the time to leave was upon me, and I was as ready as I was going to get. Just like my previous trip, the bike was not quite what I wanted, but hopefully wouldn't catch on fire (again). Having made the best possible use of our last few evenings, drinking as late as possible and talking utter nonsense, I was ready to go, even if my bike wasn't.

3

Every Great Journey Begins with a Single Mistake

Date—October 19th
Location—London (not the nice bit)
Status—Stressed

Amazingly, I caught the boat to France on time. This would be an impressive achievement for me at any time, but it was made all the more special by a sequence of events that made me both glad to get away from that country and surprised to have made it, since everything seemed to be conspiring to make it almost impossible to leave.

The plan had been to be at my parents' house around 8:30 that morning to collect the rest of my gear and perform some last minute modifications to the bike. I hadn't been able to find a suitable way of mounting the screen, and my eventual solution, far from being suitable, involved me hacksawing lumps off the bike in the morning before leaving. Because of the high likelihood of dropping the bike at some point, I didn't want to mount the screen entirely on the headlight support, for fear of transferring damage to a critical part. My solution was two exhaust hanger brackets fixed to the bars with two galvanised steel roofing bolts, each holding on a threaded rod. Two light alloy strips held the bottom secure, in theory at least. In keeping with the theme of the motorcycle, it didn't follow any aesthetic style; it just essentially worked and had to be good enough to take some abuse. That was a common theme for many BMW motorcycles, other than the part about them not working. Style and elegance don't go hand in hand with German motorcycle engineering. If they can make something more complicated, then they're happy. If they can make it appallingly ugly while doing so, then their mission is accomplished.

Once, while travelling in the Black Forest in Germany, I visited a tourist shop for reasons that have since escaped me. They were selling sticks, expressly for the purpose of walking. These were literally sticks, and not really durable enough to take any weight, so how they were supposed to assist in the most natural human method of moving from one place to another was anybody's guess. Now, while the very presence of this stick actually complicated the act of walking, the German engineering had taken it an extra step further. A bell had been fitted, in addition to a small housing that contained a bottle of alcohol. This design ethos is probably why the BMW 1200s are the size of a tractor and look like a slightly drunk cartoon duck.

The next plan had been that Thunderstick would see me off, following on his own bike. To thank him for this courtesy, I nearly killed him when my number plate broke free and shot across the road at him, narrowly missing his head. Luckily for everybody, I had a spare. I had prepared in advance a more compact plate to take with me, which was technically too small to be legal in the UK but was just the right size for everywhere else. Of course, when I came to pick it up at my parents' garage, it was nowhere to be found. We wasted a valuable twenty minutes turning the place upside down, before finding it exactly where we'd been looking. It seemed that preparation was, indeed, everything, and this was a reminder that I was very, very bad at it.

So with time increasingly turned against us, we headed straight to the Oakdene Cafe for breakfast and to meet my brother on his shiny new bike. He sucks up motorcycles like I do and had just bought a brand new Triumph Street Triple, despite my warning him that all five Triumphs I'd had were total garbage. Naturally, his shiny new bike had broken down. Presumably, it was too shiny or too new or maybe one trip to the Oakdene Cafe the day before was simply too much for it, and it crapped out, rather than having to face another such indignity.

We chatted with the staff, who knew us well, and the stress of actually getting away from this country started to peel back to allow a slight regret of all the things I was leaving behind.

On top of my friends and family, who I knew I would miss a lot, there are a lot of little things I wouldn't be seeing again.

The Oakdene Cafe, a little biker's place in Kent I'd been going to for years, was one of them. Every Sunday morning the car-park would be filled with bikers showing off their machines, and on Thursday evenings there was a proper, organised meeting where several hundred motorcycles would show up on a good week. You could strike up a conversation with anyone—anyone who didn't own a BMW, at least, because those guys refused to involve themselves in conversations, despite us also riding "Beemers." Jap-bike riders were generally a much friendlier bunch, and I've been handed keys for a joy-ride several times.

The trip really starts to become real when your bike is piled high with crap, you're massively unprepared, and you start looking back on things you never really thought you'd miss.

A quick but substantial plate of healthy food was rejected in favour of a mountain of fried rubbish, and it was time to head off. My second coffee was a stark reminder of why I was glad to be leaving—it left a bad taste in my mouth; it was rather like being kicked in the head by a horse, only far less pleasant.

Thunderstick has a peripatetic job and travelled to the Kent coast regularly, so I told him to lead. We jumped on the M20 where we could head on down to the docks. I followed him as he missed the Dover turn-off and carried on in the opposite direction. I blasted my horn and shouted at him, but it was too late; he rode up the slip road and was gone. I circled back to the café and sent a text and then waited. I waited as long as I could, but finally, I had to leave.

I headed off to Dover, now with a heavy heart. When I stopped to refuel, I got a text saying he would meet me at the port, so with cautious optimism, I headed there and waited in the bookings car-park.

I checked with my ferry, and unlike SeaFrance and P&O, they offered a free transfer service, so at worst, I was facing having to wait until 4PM. That wasn't strictly ideal, as I was facing a long journey ahead of me on the other side through Belgium and into Kassel, Germany. I checked on the latest time I could board and found I had forty-five minutes, so long as I wasn't held up at customs control. I took my chances.

It was a tense time, indeed, and I jumped up every time I saw a bike, until eventually one of them was him. With just ten minutes to spare, he'd made it to the port, after a slightly over the limit blast along the M20 via the wrong port, apparently. If he hadn't made it then it would have been a real disappointment, as he'd been like a brother to me over the years. He's a through and through good guy with a laid back patience I'm envious of. If I could have chosen anyone to ride anywhere with it would have been him, with absolutely no reservations.

He gave me a set of slightly poorly thought-out gifts as a going away present—a compass and a telescope, which I had absolutely no space for. The compass got lost pretty soon after, and the telescope rattled to pieces, but it was a nice thought and was very much appreciated. He also gave me a badge, which is still attached to my jacket to this very day.

We parted ways awkwardly. I had wanted to do this trip, but I had to compromise, as pragmatists often do. He would have been the perfect travel companion, and that was always the dream, but he'd settled into his life with a girlfriend, a fairly decent job that he always seemed to hate, and a nice flat that was costing him far too much. Life had simply got in the way for him. We'd been friends for many years; we met selling mobile phones together, got drunk together more times than I can remember, and have been through some stuff together that people have no business walking away from. Saying goodbye to him was saying goodbye to my past. It was that moment that really brought home the fact that I was leaving, and leaving for good.

I got to customs control, and the officers only made eye contact because I stopped for them. They just nodded me through and carried on reading the paper, much as I had expected and exactly what I had hoped would happen. I considered that the first bit of good luck I'd had all day.

I got to the booking gate, and the code on my ticket didn't work. I was shocked that something might have gone wrong after such good fortune all morning! The lady told me that the code was not one of theirs and took my registration number instead. When she entered the code, she started to laugh—my ferry had actually been booked for 2AM, not 2PM. The free transfer came in handy, and I made the ferry with two whole minutes to spare.

All told, this is not quite the auspicious start you would hope for when heading out on a long trip into the largely unknown. I found myself sitting on a ferry, watching England retreat in the distance, on one of the last bright sunny days of the year. The stress levels for making that crossing were so high that I couldn't even begin thinking about the trip yet as something that should be fun. It just felt like something that I had to get done, an obstacle that I had to deal with.

On the other side I was facing a long afternoon ride, and I was hoping it would give me time to adjust myself to the trip. The stress of several months arranging visas, ordering parts for my bike that never showed up or were supplied wrongly, was still fresh on my mind. Everything going wrong was a daunting prospect, since leaving England was expected to be the easiest thing I was going to do for the foreseeable future.

A man came up to me to talk on the boat. He recognised me from loading and wanted to chat about the bike and what I was going to do with it. He was a little older than I was and had been thinking of doing the same kind of thing. It passed the time, and he seemed like a nice person. It's always reassuring how motorcycles, especially ones covered in everything a person owns in the entire world, attract a lot of interest and spark up some fun conversations. I hoped that would be true all the way around.

After unloading from the ferry, my Garmin sat-nav basically did its job, and I headed off for a town called Kassel. Needless to say, I ended up a fairly long way shy of my target. The roads were quite fair and my previous experience served me well enough, but when night finally fell, it did so with the subtle charm of a clumsy builder crashing through a roof. The roads were suddenly wet and icy with no warning, and the cold clamped down with a vengeance, as if it was picking on me personally. I carried on as best I could, but the cold got to me and forced me to surrender to my own better judgement. By the time I gave up, it was down to five degrees, and I was wearing only a summer jacket and summer gloves that didn't have a lining. To be fair, I could just about tolerate that, but the visor and screen were fogging up so much I couldn't see where I was going.

I tried to get some fuel along the way and found one miserable attendant who seemed to not like bikers. She grumbled about having to speak English and said I had to pay in advance. All protestations of not knowing how much the bike would take were met with a knowing grin and a shrug. I offered to leave cash as a deposit, but she said there was a queue and that I had to leave. Eventually, she said it was only that one pump and that all the others would work. None of them worked for me.

I went somewhere else, and the story was completely different. A nice girl was extremely helpful in explaining how the pumps worked. I don't know if my other experience had been a prejudice against motorcycles or because I was English, but it was just one more thing I expected to see more of as I made my way along.

In the end, I spotted an Etap Hotel, at Aachen in Germany, and I knew there was nothing cheaper or better nearby, because it was full of international lorry drivers, so I stumped up the cash and got myself a room. If you're travelling by motorcycle, truck drivers are a great yardstick of available facilities—where they gather you can be sure of a cheap roof over your head and available food somewhere.

I was disappointed in myself in that I didn't get farther, but Marcin had only made Hanover on his first day, and he had left at 7AM. I didn't even board the boat until 2PM, so making it as far as Aachen on my little bike, with half the power of his and no heated grips, was probably acceptable. The wind had been howling against me, but I kept up an average speed of seventy to seventy-five fairly comfortably, so the screen was at least doing its job for now. That was the national speed limit back in England, and I knew she could manage a little better, but probably not very much. The rate I was going was a good compromise between speed and fuel economy and was plenty fast enough for unfamiliar roads at night, even more so when you're likely to suddenly forget which side of the road to ride on and veer into the path of an oncoming car.

That only happened twice.

The work I'd done to the bike was definitely paying off. A month earlier she'd had a full service, with another oil change just before leaving. I'd replaced both the wheel and steering bearings as a preventative measure, as well as renewing the clutch cable and fitting a heavy duty set of chain and sprockets. The bike herself felt free and smooth. I felt anything but.

Once I had unpacked and set myself up for the night, I did my daily exercise routine and stretched out some of the stresses of the day, but I knew I still had to deal with another long, cold slog in the morning. I was facing a ride of roughly nine hours into Poland, but I planned not to leave until around ten. I knew that if I left any earlier it would still be cold—too cold for me anyway. I was hoping, with somewhat unrealistic optimism, that it might warm up a little after that. I was also hoping for my bike to transform into a totally reliable, 200 horsepower scrambler that did a thousand miles per gallon and to find a million dollars crammed into the mattress of my hotel bed. I find hope to not be very efficient, and sure enough, it let me down again.

So my first day on the road had left me wondering why exactly I hadn't flown after all. It seemed like everything wanted to go wrong, and all that after an incredible amount of work to make sure that myself, the bike, and the paperwork was all ready.

I had been told that the Pakistan visa was going to be the worst, so I got that sorted first. Sure enough, the embassy, in a very affluent part of London, had set up a tent in the garden and handed out numbered tickets to waiting applicants. It was quite funny, if not for the fact that my trip hinged on them doing their job; after realising that, it stopped being quite so funny after all. I finally managed to get past the first utterly incompetent layer of bureaucracy and got to the offices downstairs. I had my invitation and all necessary paperwork and was still rejected by a laughing, and slightly drooling, official, who couldn't actually provide any actual reason why he was rejecting the application.

I returned a few days later to try my luck once more. That time a woman dealt with my claim and simply asked me to explain exactly what it was I wanted. I told her I was travelling by motorcycle and that I wasn't sure of my entry time but could narrow it down to a few weeks. Once she understood this, she issued it without any hesitation at all.

The Indian visa simply wasn't worth doing in person. I paid a small fee to have it done for me, which was something Marcin later berated me up for on more than one occasion. The fee was less than the price of fuel and parking to get me to London, let alone the cost of the visa, so I considered it a bargain.

Iran was also quite needlessly complicated. The officials were rude, arrogant, and unnecessarily awkward, as many officials are. Getting that one was actually harder than getting my visa to Pakistan, but in the end, I managed to get it all done.

The bike herself also needed a "carnet," which was essentially a passport for the bike, an insurance document against you selling it or something. It costs several hundred percent the value of your bike, but you pay only a small amount of that. It's all hopelessly complicated. At the time only one company was allowed to arrange it, so the prices were prohibitively high. Paul, the one man who seemed to work there was very helpful, even when I estimated the value of my bike at one pound, which earned me a confused grunt from the other end of the phone. I told him it was a stolen and recovered bike and was so horrible to look at that seventeen people had been turned to stone while staring at it, so far.

I actually somehow managed to get away with all that.

I had spent time before in similar hotels to the one I was staying at. I had seen many almost identical ones in Europe when I had travelled with my girlfriend, and it seemed odd that she wasn't with me. I missed her more than I thought I would. I missed my friends too, who seemed to miss me more than I thought they would too.

When I left for my previous ride into Europe, I had my doubts then as well. The first few days were awful, and again, everything went wrong. My sat-nav had broken and sent me running in circles around the docks for two hours. After making up most of the lost time, I had then hit a storm that meant I'd had to head off and find a place to stay, some miles short of my destination. The next morning, my camera had dropped out of my pocket while riding along. I headed back for it and was lucky enough to find it lying intact on a quiet country road. Then, a truck hit it, just as I was about to step off the bike to grab it. It was so flat that even the card inside was useless.

My girlfriend had flown to Milan, so on my second day I rode for seventeen hours straight to get to the airport. When I arrived in the early hours of the morning, I was told that it was the wrong airport, and I had to loop back around fifty miles. I had accidentally left on my spotlights which drained my battery and killed the bike, so she refused pointedly to start. I needed a jump start, which meant stripping off half the bike. After all that, I discovered that she'd actually missed her flight and wouldn't be arriving until the morning.

After all that, things didn't seem all that bad, but then I had no idea how much worse things were going to get. How much worse could they get?

It's funny how naïve that thought was when looked back upon.

4

Some Dishes are Best Served Cold

Date—October 20th
Location—Germany
Mood—Wildly optimistic

I felt a lot better the following morning after a good night's sleep in a warm bed. I awoke knowing I had to face the horrors of the efficient German road system, which is not actually very efficient, and barely follows a system, but did seem to be a road—of sorts. The thought of that did take the edge off my massively misplaced optimism.

The big problem, as I saw it, was that the roads are were all over the place, and to get onto the main ones you need to go through random twisted lanes all pointing everywhere but where you'd logically expect. The result of this is that your GPS points one way and by the time you get on the road you think you want, you're pointing in a totally different direction altogether; if not totally, then largely at least, or perhaps more-so, if not less. If you think that sentence is confusing and frustrating, please feel free to drive in Germany, and then decide for yourself.

To make matters slightly worse, or perhaps to cause the aforementioned matters, my European map, Google, GPS, and the German authorities all have very different ideas regarding navigation and sense of direction. All of that meant that my progress was slow; so slow, in fact, that it barely qualified as progress. This wouldn't have been a huge problem if not for the huge problem that I had somewhere to be. That place was a very long way away on a freezing road almost entirely occupied by maniacs, albeit efficient ones.

I ended up having lunch at around 2:30 (European time) somewhere between Essen and Hanover. It was such an easy, comfortable ride according to the maps, that it almost seemed welcoming, but directions dried up as soon as I got onto the road in a most unwelcoming way. I was becoming used to that, and the shock to my system if it hadn't been the case might have been fatal.

Talking of getting on the road, even that had been a far from pleasant experience. I got out of a nice warm bed, wrapped myself up in multiple layers, and even added my wet-gear over the top as a precautionary wind breaker, but by the time I actually reached the main road I was already horribly cold. The wind cut through my gear like it wasn't even there, and I was shaking inside my laughably inefficient German motorcycle clothing. At around 9:30, I headed out onto the road feeling like a man fresh out of the shower, with no access to a towel, who was standing in a wind tunnel in winter. It was only a scant, and somewhat intimidating, four degrees, and by lunchtime, it had risen to a more tolerable twelve. Add the wind blast to the equation (which German weather did for me, most efficiently) and the outcome was a very miserable little adventure-motorcyclist freezing off all of his favourite bits for hours on end, wishing he would die quickly, or at least efficiently, ideally after crashing into a bakery that served strong alcoholic spirits.

On the plus side, if there is such a thing to slowly freezing to death, I was carrying bottled water, and it was like getting a bottle fresh out of the fridge. Actually, it was a little colder than I usually like it, with ice-crystals floating around in it and penguins screaming to be put out of their misery. There were a few places with no trees by the sides of the road, and some of these gaps even had sunshine breaking through, a comfortable warming flicker of natural light warming my dulled senses. But without the cover of the trees to break it up, the wind blasted across the relatively flat fields and right into me. It almost felt like Germany was picking on me for some reason, and doing it most efficiently.

It's funny the things that go through your mind when you're travelling by motorcycle through even remotely hostile conditions. The foremost is not, "I should get out more." It's true, most people's idea of a fun time is probably more like lying on a beach surrounded by semi-naked, highly attractive members of the opposite sex while sipping on cocktails and waiting for gigantic portions of food, covered in cheese, to arrive. Very few people would list sitting on an uncomfortable, vibrating slab of noisy metal inside an industrial fridge while feeling like you're being blasted by the propeller of a WWI bi-plane running at full throttle as their ideal kind of day. I did find myself questioning whether I was mentally retarded or had ingested some kind of mind altering substance that had skewed my perspective rather drastically.

In the end, the fact that I was doing this entirely of my own will and expending my own resources to do it led me to the conclusion that I was either so certifiably insane, or so stupid, that I should never be allowed to operate machinery. The fact that, whichever was true, led me to be operating that very machinery just confused me even more. I find that with a brain like mine it's best not to use it too much. Someone could get hurt.

The German drivers were being arrogant to the point of it being ridiculous. They seemed to have an almost complete absence of empathy for other people, especially those travelling slower or who were just smaller than they were. They see you indicate to pull out after a truck decided to pull out on top of you without looking, and they just head straight for you, with no consideration of your continued survival. This happened more than once; more than several times, in fact. After a while, it got annoying.

My first encounter with the police on this trip was a mostly positive one. The police were not like they were at home in London. I pulled in to check my map and got chatting with some locals, and an officer came over to help. He filled out a list of directions, shook my hand, and stayed to chat with a pair of local builders in a way that seemed just friendly and without any tension on either side. In England they would have tried to arrest me for crimes against humanity, just for the horrific offence of owning a motorcycle. The only drawback was that his directions were almost, but not totally, incorrect. They did get me back to the main roads, and after that a mixture of common sense, directions, maps, and the GPS pink arrow got me heading in mostly the right direction.

After hours of heading in the what I hoped was the right direction, the cold was starting to get my mind wandering. I was having a bit of trouble focusing and remembered I hadn't eaten yet. I resolved to stay on the road until I found a place with something to eat and fuel for the bike. There was never any point making more than one stop when there were more miles ahead of you than there were behind. By then, I was wearily resigned to making an early stopover in Hanover at the local F1 hotel. I was faced with an arduous ride into Poland lined up for me in the morning, an effort that looked set to stretch my resolve even more than the German roads.

When I stopped, I took the time to work out my position, and I looked set to make Hanover by late afternoon, if my GPS was telling me the truth. I decided that was the best option for me, better at least than freezing to death. It would give me a chance to unload my heavy gear into a small hotel room and head out for something to eat. I was facing an early night and was sorely in need of it.

Motorcycle travel is tiring; the wind is in your face, even with a screen to break it, and your whole body is in use all the time. It's physically difficult, and it takes a toll on your ability to stay alert and focussed. It certainly took a toll on mine.

If all went to plan, then I could make an early start on my journey towards, and then around, Berlin. I was hoping to make it through there as fast as possible since, a month previously, my girlfriend and I spent three days there exploring the city. While that was barely enough time to scratch the surface, I felt like I'd "been there, done that" and had no burning desire to be there and do it again. Big cities are generally very similar, and Berlin was a very big one. Getting through it was incredibly tough, so going around was probably the better choice.

So I found the F1 hotel with no real problems, despite my Garmin sat-nav having now completely packed up, again. It had played up badly during my first trip to Europe and was up to its old tricks once more. The touch screen had failed, the maps came and went, and often it said I was riding on a completely different road to what I was actually on. One time before, while in Poland, it had led me to a hotel. When we arrived, it was actually a dead horse laying in a ploughed field.

The next day held an almost straight ride into Poland, so I wasn't particularly concerned at that point, but I wouldn't recommend that brand of GPS to anyone I liked or might meet ever again.

The weather added some intermittent showers, because the freezing cold and blasting rain clearly wasn't fun enough. After I arrived at the hotel, the weather actually got a fair bit worse, so I was lucky to have missed most of it while cowering in my room, gibbering to myself nonsensically. Once the sun went in it got worse by a significant degree; the roads got icy in a matter of a few minutes, and riding on them would have been a hopeless task, interspersed with the inevitable act of dragging my bike out of bushes and checking for broken bones. When winter properly takes hold, this route would not be a fun one to take. I dreaded to think about what was up ahead in terms of the weather.

Behind us was Damon, an Australian adventure biker I met in London. He was set to follow us out, travelling a few weeks behind us, but the journey was going to get harder every day. Winter was coming, and it looked set to take hold with a ferocious grip, making two-wheeled transport nearly impossible. But then, I guess, that was why they called it adventure-riding and why you couldn't find a travel agent that would help you to book a few weeks doing it. It wasn't for the faint hearted, it was for people filled with bottomless reserves of self-hatred and severe mental-health issues. At least in that respect, I was properly prepared.

I asked for directions to find something to eat and was told there was a supermarket. Sure enough, I found a local Aldi. I grabbed some bits, and they told me, with a smug grin, that they didn't take Visa cards. I queried the fact that they had a card machine on the counter to take payment, and yet they didn't accept the most common form of payment on the planet. He didn't speak the most common language, either, so that particular conversation was going precisely nowhere. I went on and found a Penny Market, which turned out to be more or less the same thing. Of course, they didn't take it either! I was told there was a cash machine somewhere, and then a guy found me struggling on the street and showed me where it was. My faith in humanity was a little strengthened, if not restored to previous levels.

Try as I might, I didn't like Germany. I always found it too much like England, but with all the bad things amplified. Riding there on the motorways is like circling the M25 but with never ending German-made estate cars flying up behind you at 130mph. I was riding at an average seventy-five mph and was a slow-mover by their standards, but not as slow as the endless trucks they weave around. Still, they seemed to regard me as something of no worth, cutting too close by me and even forcing me out of lanes.

What has a Yamaha Virago 535, a BMW R1150gs, and a black R6 got in common? They were all on the road with me. With no exaggeration, they were literally the only motorcycles I had seen all day, a stark contrast to the summer, when Europe is swarming with them. The R6 was on a trailer being towed to a warm garage (I imagine), and the Virago was parked around the back of a petrol station. I guess the cold relegates them to being stored somewhere while their owners go and vent their frustrations by trying to knock over weary travellers with the sporty family cars driven flat out until the top ends burst.

Presumably, at least, they probably burst efficiently.

5

A Change Is as Good as a Rest, But a Rest Is Better

Date—October 21th
Location—Somewhere near Hanover, Germany
Status—Cold. Really cold. Really dreadfully cold

I made an early start and got on the road around 7:30, and it was a whole hour earlier than that by the clock my brain was still set to. I was fairly proud of myself for that one small victory against the German roads.

To say it was pretty cold there at that time of the morning would be like saying that to ride a motorcycle through it was a little bit ill-advised. Consequently, I was the only one doing it. My instruments were showing a meagre four degrees, and even the bike started only with a minor hesitation and grumbled at me for pressing the big red button than normally made her rattle to life enthusiastically.

I pulled straight into the petrol station at the end of the road and was nearly wiped out by a van who didn't bother to look as he took a shortcut by driving through the forecourt directly across my path. Luckily for me, I had dialled into the German attitude by then, so I'd already given him space to perform his psychopathic demonstration of a near total lack of humanity, and no harm was done. He just looked at me and drove on, no emotional impact whatsoever from his act of arrogance and stupidity that could easily have left me dead.

This lack of consideration of the potential consequences was horribly apparent in the entire spectrum of German driving, as well as in other areas of the culture. As I passed briefly through, it was a rare thing to get smiled at for holding a door open or nodded to for some other act of courtesy. There was very little of what the English consider basic manners; most people there seem only bothered with their own personal concerns. On the other hand, there were often moments of genuine human warmth.

Clearly suffering from the weather conditions, a petrol station attendant offered to pour me some coffee to warm me up, free of charge. On another occasion, while unloading my gear from the bike, a truck driver ran to help me with the door (although he was probably Polish, to be fair).

In England the manners are maybe more superficial, and many people, once you scratch the surface, have little substance. In Germany the manners are virtually non-existent, but there is some empathy with some of them, which makes up for the shortcomings of the drivers. Perhaps it's a social difference and nothing more, but Germans seem more closed off, more tied up in their own little world, disconnected from the outside of their cars. The English are a polite society, almost to the point of it being annoying. Perhaps simply growing up in a different culture left me judging others I meet with an impossible standard, but that wasn't the impression I got. I just felt like people should simply care a little more about the feelings and safety of others.

Once I got out on the road, the temperature climbed to six degrees, but the wind-chill made it feel like a lot less. I still hadn't really gotten into the right mood for the journey, and the constant voice in my head asking what the hell I was doing this for was nagging away at me like my girlfriend in front a pile of unwashed plates. My muscles burned, like a million red-hot needles were being poked into my joints, and I could feel my reactions slowing as the cold robbed my fingers of mobility. I could sense the controls were becoming sluggish and awkward, or at least I was.

The sunrise before me painted the canopy a dull effervescent orange, as the brilliant light caressed the few white clouds that dotted the morning sky. The orange faded to yellow while growing brighter and then to white as morning broke on the horizon before me, lighting my way with the optimistic promise of whatever might lay ahead. It also hurt like hell as the light dug into my eyes like burning knives. Unlike a car or truck, the only sun-visor I had is what nature saw fit to equip me with, so I managed an hour on the road, squinting like I was fighting out a gut-full of German sausage.

I made good time, averaging around seventy-five mph, but I was a slow nuisance to the other users on the crazy German Autobahn. I, more or less, lived in the middle lane, the right being packed with a convoy of never ending slow-driving trucks on a journey to everywhere and the fast lane full of old German drivers belting past in cars with so many electronic gadgets it was a wonder that they even bothered with a driver at all. Even at seventy-five, cars were flying past me like I was an old woman driving a clapped out green Nissan Micra up the hard shoulder of the A2 back home.

I stopped for a passable coffee at a petrol station at 9AM and let my gloves thaw out on the exhaust pipe. I hoped, against reason, that ten minutes might warm my fingers through and allow the sun to take a little of the edge off the weather.

I bought a pair of fabric working gloves to wear under my unlined summer gloves, and while it made it a bit tight, it also made the weather far more tolerable on the road ahead. I made good time for the next few hours and proceeded without anything of interest happening. I even started to enjoy it, now that progress was being made and I was acclimatising to the conditions. Perhaps frostbite had simply killed off every nerve ending in my body—I certainly hoped so. The roads were clear, and the route couldn't have been much more straight forwards, because it was, quite literally, straight forwards. There were no turns, no deviations, I just had to keep going until I reached Poznan. It couldn't have been much easier, but that didn't mean that there were no mistakes I could make if I really, really tried being really, really stupid.

I stopped again for more coffee, and by then the daylight was warm and fresh, but at ten degrees it was still not ideal weather for motorcycling, and few people would be doing this for fun.

Before a journey I routinely avoid anything with sugar in it, and for as long as I can tolerate it, I don't drink coffee at all. The reason for this is, once on the road, I know I'll frequently need a shot of energy, and a hot coffee will have a much stronger effect if I'm not used to it, and at a pinch, a bar of chocolate will give me a sugar-rush that will put me back on the road when the road has already taken me off of it.

For the whole ride so far that day, I had not seen one other bike on the road, so only the crazy and the stupid were out on two wheels, and I knew I had to fit in there somewhere, and probably not where I hoped.

There was a stark contrast to the English roads that I couldn't help but notice. No matter what you say, the English are year-long bikers; they don't give up just because there's rain or snow or insanely high taxation or the most hideously oppressive test criteria known to man or beast. Certainly, it was never quite this cold, and not for very long does it get really awful, but no matter what, you'll see another motorcyclist struggling along somewhere. Not in Germany, where struggling is apparently considered inefficient or too polite for some reason.

I was starting to get into the spirit of my mammoth road trip by now. It wasn't warmer, but I was used to it being colder. I'd found ways to deal with the useless GPS and overly complicated road system, and thinking of what was up ahead was spurring me on. By the evening I hoped I'd be meeting up with Marcin and planning the first leg of our onward journey.

A day off the road to work on the bike would also be nice, just to check her over and see how she was holding up to the real world. I'd been considering moving the auxiliary fuel tank to the front, where it was before, only this time directly drilling the mounting holes to the bash plate. I was hoping that doing so would free up enough space to safely clear the wheel in an emergency stop.

One of the major drawbacks of the BMW G650x was a tiny ten-litre fuel tank that only gave around 130 miles of range from completely full to hopelessly stranded at the side of the road. I knew this from being hopelessly stranded on the side of the road.

Consequently, I'd looked for ways to massively increase the range without violently decreasing my bank balance. My options were limited to a very expensive Touratech tank, which added a great deal of fuel to the front of the bike and didn't actually fit my version without even more money spent on parts I didn't want. There was also a metal tank that bolted to the rear, made by an after-market company somewhere in America. Either option added a lot of weight and were very expensive for things that essentially removed any advantage the little bike had in being so light. I'd settled on a very cheap plastic box of a tank that was universal and could be fitted anywhere, so long as you could find the space. Originally, I'd bolted it to the front of a tough bash-plate, but it had stood a few centimetres forward on the mounting bracket. While I'd had absolutely no trouble with it, there was a small black mark leading me to suspect that on heavy braking, the front tyre might have touched the tank.

I considered drilling into the plate and mounting it directly. That should have worked, but I ended up going with a hopelessly complex array of twisted alloy that took the same tank to the absolutely ideal position at the side. Of course, in practice it was slightly less absolutely ideal but did look kind of cool.

There was a slight vibration showing in the medium rev range, and it worried me that it might stress the alloy mounting bracket, which I had made myself even though I had virtually no idea what I was doing. I had tested it, but never with days of use on a fast road at a constant high speed. All that seemed to be exactly the perfect conditions to cause problems.

I had experimented with moving the tank bag to the rear of the bike. It was actually a tail pack, anyway, and it seemed to be working, giving me more space up front without making the bike feel heavier at the back than it already was.

I worried for the subframe. Apart from the small tank, the bike had another issue that needed addressing. The rear subframe was very lightweight alloy and couldn't take much of a load without snapping. I had rejected large metal boxes, partly for that reason, as well as thinking they might be dangerous in a fall. Despite my misgivings, all the weight was balanced on the crossbeam, where it's designed to take the weight of a pillion, and it had done this very thing successfully for thousands of miles. I went around Europe with my partner on the back and her entire wardrobe loaded behind her with no problem, so my worries were tempered with cautious, yet abundant, optimism.

It was a relief when I finally crossed into Poland. Everything was cheaper and easier there, from the women, to the lives of adventure motorcyclists. Poland is also not really Europe; it's different, different enough to be genuinely interesting. Riding through it is an experience—a life-threatening experience The people, the buildings, and everything else looks a bit unfamiliar, and it was a welcome and refreshing change to the ceaseless, endless drone of monotony on the motorways. I made good time in Germany, and seeing as how I was following the exact some road called the exact same thing, I foolishly expected the same thing would follow. Of course it did not.

The road into Poland was superb, or at least it would be if they ever got round to finishing it. Until they did, the road was just a narrow country lane behind endless trucks with blank fabric covers that, if the clichés are anything to go by, are either coming back for some more illegal migrant workers or unloading stolen goods. In any case, they didn't move fast unless they were overtaking and coming straight at you on the wrong side of the road, which continued to be a disconcerting experience.

Eventually, after many disconcerting experiences, I arrived at Poznan via a toll booth for a few miles of unfinished road that charging money for using seemed cheeky, at best. Poznan was a nice little town with plenty to look at and do. My spirits were high since I had escaped Germany. It had been a very expensive place to be and not particularly fun. The roads were stale and monotonous and riding on them was a gloomy and repetitive drudge.

Marcin was held up with something he was doing, and he couldn't meet that day. I agreed to meet him the next in Wroclaw, instead, and hunted around for a hostel or hotel, anything that might give me a bed for the night and something to eat. There was no space anywhere, and even more worrying, the bike went to reserve after only 115 miles, when normally it delivered close to 200 with the auxiliary fuel-tank filled. Even in town, and with a hell of a lot of sitting at traffic lights, I was still expecting 160 at the absolute worst. I discovered the breather hose was twisted, and the additional tank was mostly full, so there was some relief that at least it was just the reserve tank not feeding, which was an easy fix, unlike a malfunctioning injector system, which was not.

I eventually ended up in a slightly upmarket hotel outside of town and was warned it was expensive. It ended up costing me £35 with free Internet and breakfast, so everyone who thought that was expensive should ride through France and Germany . . . and England, come to that.

So that evening, it would be fair to say I was exhausted. I had managed only 330 miles, plus three hours of searching for a hotel, and all that on a 7AM start. The next day promised an easy ride into Wroclaw in the morning to finally meet up with Marcin and see where the road ahead would take us. The journey was properly about to begin, and I was finally feeling like I was ready for it.

6

Tied Up and Down

Date—October 22th
Location—Poznan, Poland
Mood—Generally happy

As breakfast was free, I filled myself up with it. You can be sure of one thing on the road and that's that you can never really be sure of anything. You're never sure when you might find a good place for food and generally settle for whatever you can find at the petrol station you fuel up at. It's even worse when you've got a deadline.

There is a dark secret, an unspoken fact, that the adventure motorcyclists of the world share. It's something that we're loath to admit, even to ourselves, and the truth casts a shadow over our very being. That secret is that under the cold, harsh reality of the world, with the piercing light of honesty shining on us, we're actually not really very adventurous. We ride from petrol station to petrol station, and that's the sad reality of life on a bike. In some more interesting places the petrol station might be a robe-covered man at the side of the road selling suspicious yellow liquid from a plastic bottle or it might be a huge complex resembling an airport with a restaurant, clean toilets, and security guards to protect our beloved motorcycles. Whatever and wherever we are, we're essentially slaves to the fuel our bikes run on, and our routes eventually tie us to fuel stops. We can push the range of our machines, but there are limits imposed by fuel efficiency versus weight. We're stuck on a path that has to take us somewhere to get fuel in only a few hundred miles. When faced with that reality, the delusion of far flung unexplored places, discoveries of hidden pockets of unspoiled humanity, is as remote as the possibility of finding a respectable petrol-station sandwich.

The hotel had laid on a buffet with cold meats and cheese, bread, and some fried stuff I couldn't even identify. Actually, being Poland, it was a lot of fried stuff, and I could come nowhere near to identifying it, even as food in some cases.

Hot dogs seem popular there; you rarely see a guy walking around at night without some phallic snack sticking out of his mouth, but I was just an adventure motorcyclist. I wasn't there to judge, merely to consume petrol as I struggled to find adventures in mundane things by approaching them with a near complete lack of common sense.

There were fried eggs, but they'd been fried with bacon, so the meat was right inside the egg by some wizardry I couldn't quite understand, so I stuck to boiled eggs and cheese, which was enough to get me on the road with a full stomach. There was some kind of potato salad, which was rather good, and the coffee was decent, which is obviously the most important thing in the world, possibly more important than having petrol in the fuel tank, unless you need petrol in the tank in order to ride somewhere to find coffee.

I was deep inside the real world now, in a part of Poland where just enough normalcy had settled in to make it essentially civilised, by Polish standards at least. I had much yet to learn about that side of things, and for now I simply hoped for the best. The time on the road passed quickly; the directions were easy to follow, and the weather was treating me gently. Whether I had gotten used to the driving or it was genuinely lighter I couldn't say, but I noticed far less anti-social and horrifying instances of trucks driving straight at me on the wrong side of the road, blasting their horns as if there was anything I could do to avoid them.

By lunchtime, I had reached the city; Wroclaw, where Marcin was now staying. Perhaps calling it a large town was more appropriate, but it was definitely large enough, the road system was logical, and the driving was easy. I circled around several times to get my bearings and then searched for something to eat. I found a kebab shop while riding around, and was lucky enough to find a girl who could speak almost perfect English.

I have never been gifted in terms of foreign languages, but I've formulated a mixture of points and grunts with loud and slowly-spoken English words that seems to allow me to communicate my needs to almost everyone I've met on the road. Still, it's a relief when I meet someone who's better with languages than I am and can actually understand the subtleties and nuances of my language beyond me grabbing at things like a hungry chimpanzee.

She watched in horror as I grabbed at things like a hungry chimpanzee.

I checked the bike out and was thrilled to discover I was having minor troubles already. The crush-washer on the sump bolt was already crushed long ago, and it had decided not to hold up to the rigours of its incredibly difficult job of not allowing oil to drip out of the bottom of the engine. That left me needing to find one and replace it, without losing all the oil in the process. That was not going to be easy or fun, but probably more fun than ignoring it and wondering when my engine might blow up. That was assuming I could find a new washer at all, which seemed eerily unlikely. I had a big spanner and tightened it up, hoping it might stem the problem. The drip did slow down and then seemed to stop altogether, so I hoped for the best.

I hope for the best a lot. The best rarely delivers.

In preparing the bike, I'd taken the time to upgrade all the moving parts, all the consumables had been subjected to preventative maintenance, and where possible, replaced with something more durable (or at least more expensive). I never thought to replace a washer, a thing that squeezes very slightly into place to make a more secure oil seal, which was pretty stupid of me, as it was meant to be replaced at the last oil change. It's comforting to know that motorcycles have a way of testing your patience and surprising us with their creative alternatives to running smoothly.

To add to my minor worries, the new auxiliary tank side-mount was causing me some concerns. I had eventually decided to fit it in the perfect mounting position, instead of finding the simplest method. I wanted it low down and off to the right-hand side, on the opposite side to the exhaust and tucked in beneath the radiator. It sat in a perfect little spot, freeing up space for tools to be attached to the bash-plate. This had been a stupid mistake, and I should have known better than to make it.

Fitting it had involved complex mounting brackets that I'd had to make myself. The vibrations were stressing the side support, and a small crack was starting to form at one of the bends. It hadn't done anything like that before, but the constant higher speeds were something I'd not tested it with, because it was impossible to replicate days of motorway driving in my living room. I had tried.

And there was more . . . The fuel hose had gotten bent somehow and had taken on a permanent crease, so I needed a new length of hose. Currently, the fuel was unlikely to feed very reliably, since the entire set-up was essentially a hack and wasn't meant to work at all. The fact that it did was a triumph of obstinacy over common sense. I had based the design on the other, more expensive options but came up with a way to do it on a much cheaper budget. When it worked all that was great, but it when it didn't it left me feeling like maybe I should have stretched the budget a little further and opted for something made by someone who actually knew what they were doing.

None of these were major problems and were actually little more than nuisances really, and certainly nothing that would keep me from moving forwards. The biggest piece of preparation I had done was getting to know my bike. I knew what her tolerances where; I knew her strengths and weaknesses. I knew where to look to make sure things were holding up and when they really were falling down. I had researched my bike thoroughly, so I knew exactly what to expect, and I'd done all of the preparation work myself, except for one service by a qualified mechanic, as a way of checking over everything else that I'd done.

Once my stomach was full, I managed to contact Marcin. He was tied up with his bike, having booked it into KTM for a full service. I'm not quite sure how it works with KTM; presumably there wasn't enough wrong with it, so KTM's team of crack engineers added some new problems for him?

Marcin was a big man; a huge, highly motivated force of nature, who could only be diverted from his horrendously destructive path through a country's food-supply by a quantity of beer. Usually, quite a large quantity of beer. His bike was chosen along that very philosophy; a KTM 990 Adventure, chosen purely because it had the biggest engine and made the most power. He'd done no research, no preparation, and put in no thought beyond finding a bike that would go faster.

While that sounds short-sighted, there's a school of thought that says you really should be able to buy an adventure bike and go on an adventure, without spending tons of money modifying it and getting it ready. That was actually once possible, but things changed when manufacturing technology was turned from building things well to building them as cheaply as possible, in order to maximise profits. Now, conventional wisdom tells us that there's not a bike in a showroom anywhere you could expect to provide trouble-free long range travel just as soon as you ride it out of the showroom. To me that seems insane.

With Marcin otherwise occupied doing who knew what, I was left to my own devices. A lone adventurer exploring a new and exciting town, infinite possibilities stretched out before me, a universe of possible experiences. Consequently, I ended up in McDonalds, sipping coffee and using the free Wi-Fi. I couldn't really enjoy wandering around a strange town on my own when I couldn't walk more than ten metres from my bike. My luggage system was a pair of soft panniers; they had no locks since a good pocket knife would go straight through the fabric in any case. Everything I owned was literally strapped to the bike. I had a separate bag clipped to the back that held everything valuable, while everything vital, such as passports, carnet, and bank-cards stayed in my pockets. Even so, I couldn't stray far and spent the afternoon anchored to the bike, avoiding alcohol like a normal person.

The level of English around the town was not particularly good, and the standard of driving could suddenly get even worse. Several times, drivers honked at me to get out of their way, simply because they wanted to turn in front of me.

It started to get a bit demoralising. I was tired and feeling drained after days riding on unfamiliar straight roads, and sitting around on my own for hours with nothing to do but think about it was making me realise just how tired I really was. There was a stark contrast between a run during summer, when spirits are high and every face has a smile painted on, and winter, when smiles are much harder to find.

For the first time, I felt like turning round. As I sat waiting with nothing to occupy my mind, I really began to wonder what the hell I was doing.

7

And So It Begins

Date—October 23th
Location—Wroclaw, Poland
Status—Insensible to external stimuli

By the time my brain was capable of registering such things, we were in Slovakia! How that happened is partly shrouded in mystery, since my memory of that entire time remains wrapped up in a nice, soft, cold blanket of beer to this very day. Whatever terrible things happened the previous evening, my brain was now quite happy where it was and didn't want to come out and play. I didn't particularly want to either.

I'd finally met up with Marcin during the afternoon before in Wroclaw. He'd brought along a friend, and the three of us went out that night for a few quiet beers and for him to show me around his home town, a place of which he was immensely proud. We'd only met twice in London for an hour at a time and exchanged a few emails. Beyond that, we knew virtually nothing about each other, so this was a good chance for us to get to know our respective riding companions.

We started out in a traditionally Polish bar, where we shot back a few vodkas and put away some salted cucumber. It was a traditional Polish drinking snack, something like a gherkin, only instead of pickling it they salted it, but it tasted pretty much the same to me. The vodka seemed to be the Polish staple, so I prepared myself for a brutal hangover. After that, we went on to an Irish place and had Guinness while chatting with some guys from Ireland who were there working as builders, bending several of the popular clichés.

They were already slightly over the limit when we found them, and we were well on the way ourselves. A more accurate description might be that they were so completely hammered-drunk that standing up was becoming an issue for them, and bladder control was only achievable with an effort of pure will. One of them started stripping in the bar, and the staff cheered as he ran around naked, beating his hairy chest and making monkey noises. That wouldn't happen in London! My home town is pretty up-tight, and even going out at weekends to burn off the stresses and strains of the week is a reserved affair, limited to a fairly strict routine. Outbursts of humanity simply aren't tolerated. I liked Wroclaw.

After that, we went from bar to bar, and the rest of the night is a bit of a blur, even more so for Marcin, who didn't get back to the hostel until around 9AM. At some point, there was more salted cucumber, a nightclub with a car halfway through the wall (which might have been decoration or another example of the driving), and a kebab. Almost definitely a kebab.

I woke up in an obscenely early hour of the morning to the sound of my own name, whispered on the lips of a young woman. I woke and then widened my eyes in surprise. Someone had said "Jack" followed by some kind of good morning thing. In my bleary, not quite alive but wishing I was a little more dead, state I lay there for a moment just thinking about all this.

Presumably, she had a name as well, but I had other things on my mind, like worrying why she was in my bed and how I was going to get her out of it. As I came to my senses, such as my senses were, I came to the realisation that I absolutely couldn't have actually done anything with her, as I had been so drunk that breathing had been something of an effort.

We quickly established that nothing had happened, but we'd got talking and must have wandered back to the hostel together, chatting and drinking beer, vodka, white spirit, or whatever else Polish people put down their necks. In any case, she said she had to go home, as her parents would be worried about it. Suddenly, that was even worse.

I escorted her to the train station, where I finally plucked up the courage to ask her age and was happy to hear that she was in her early-twenties.

I asked her if she had my phone number, and she replied that she didn't. I told her that was perfect, turned, and left as quickly as I could to head back to the hostel and snag a little more sleep before we headed out.

No amount of water and grumbling was helping with the complete carnage that Polish vodka had wrought upon my body. Marcin, a shadow of his former self, shuffled in and collapsed into the hostel bed, his friend holding him just barely upright until his face smashed into the plastic-coated mattress. I distinctly remember hearing a faint gurgling sound that might have been a death-rattle and just quietly lay there hoping that it wasn't me that had died.

At 11AM the receptionist was banging on the door telling us to leave. Considering that standing up was asking a lot, we informed her politely that she had no hope of getting rid of us just yet, so she gave us another half an hour to recover. Somehow, we managed to get ourselves up and sorted, our luggage packed, and even recovered the ability to speak, at least to some degree.

She accepted our apology, and we had some kind of conversation about how aggressive some of her guests were, and we took pity on one another; her, because we were us, and us, because she had to deal with people just like us. She assured us that there weren't any people like us, which did make me feel a little better.

Too tired to move any great distance, we shuffled next door to a Japanese restaurant and ordered some food. It seemed oddly inappropriate somehow. Greasy, heavy food was the order of the day, and Poland does that exceptionally well, so the delicate Japanese food didn't quite fit. Marcin compensated by ordering a lot of it, essentially everything on the menu. We spoke about the ride that we had to look forward to, but most of the conversation regarded food and drink, and how we shouldn't have had so much of it the night before but probably would again that evening.

With some food inside, I felt a bit better, but it was accepted that progress would be short that day. Eventually, we ventured out onto the motorway and headed towards the Slovakian border to see how things went. Borders are unpredictable—every country has their own version of rules, and every official interprets them slightly differently. Officials are often bloated with a sense of completely misplaced importance and seem to take a perverse pleasure in stamping their authority with a smug grin.

We had no problems on the few miles that we did manage to cover that day, which surprised both of us. My GPS by then was essentially useless; it had given up completely, the touch screen had died, and it wasn't tracking properly. Marcin took the lead because his unit, the same model as mine, was still working. The pace was quick, and my bike didn't like it, so she drank far more fuel than normal in a kind of mechanical protest. The road was fairly clear and easy going. It was every inch a boringly modern motorway, and we made good time as we trudged along it.

The cold was not getting to me as badly as it did at first, and oddly, my seat was feeling comfortable this time. I assumed I must be getting used to it, my muscles giving up and just accepting their fate, pummelled into new and unnatural shapes. I was evolving into the perfect motorcycle touring human, perhaps, or just hadn't fought off the Polish vodka yet.

The standard seat on the bike was terrible and, over a sufficiently large bump, was probably capable of forcing your sphincter up into your throat. It was little more than a conservative layer of foam on top of a lump of very liberal plastic. There were times I would have been better served with a plank of wood with nails sticking out of it. Consequently, I changed it. The G650x Country is a little short for me, so adding a load of extra padding was a benefit. I'd taken it to a place in Kent with a good reputation for quality work. I asked for a gel-seat, as I had been told that they were far better than padding. What nobody had told me was that in cold weather they're fine, but when it gets hot the gel basically turns into concrete. I was beginning to work that out for myself by now, and realised I had made a terrible mistake, which I was going to pay for at the other end.

The only problem we had was that the road suddenly stopped, so we had to divert from the motorways to the main roads, which suited me better in any case; my 650cc was not built for speed. Strangely, I went onto reserve at about 135 miles, and that was far less than usual. The pace was quick, but not that quick. There was some fuel in the bottom of the reserve tank, so my guess was that the hose wasn't reaching the bottom, but even so, there couldn't have been all that much petrol in there. The bike seemed to be running well, so I wasn't too worried, just yet.

It was nice to be on the road and finally on the way out into the unknown. My mood had changed, and it felt like the trip had really begun. We were riding now into a part of the world I had never been; familiarity was behind us, and the road stretched out before us offering endless possibilities.

And we'd got all that stupid stuff out of our systems now, hadn't we? It would be plain sailing from here on.

8

The Rain in Prague Falls Mainly on the Adventure Motorcyclists

Date—October 24th
Location—Ostrava, Moraskoslezsky Kraj, Czech Republic
Status—Highly motivated (to find beer)

We started out our day in an almost entirely charmless village somewhere in the southern part of the Czech Republic. It was the kind of town that neither they nor Slovakia really wanted, but the Czech Republic appeared to have lost the coin toss, and so they were stuck with it. It was grey and ugly and framed with rusty iron pipes and faces that hadn't smiled in many years. There was nothing on the streets but bars and signs of industry and not really very much of anything else. This was the kind of place where people who have no choices left go to work; not to have fun, not to have families, and certainly not to live their lives. It was a town based on economy, and the needs of human beings were quite low on the list of priorities.

We passed through as quickly as we could and began heading outwards when we had our first GPS glitch. Not mine, of course. Mine was already more useless than a well-conceived argument for moderation, presented to Marcin around lunchtimes. This time it was Marcin's turn to deal with an error with his updated maps. We came to a small roundabout, and the sign showed two turn-offs, but there was only one, and the sat-nav couldn't make sense of it. Nor could Marcin, and for a while he strongly considered driving off through the field where the road should have been, had it actually existed.

Charitably, I'd like to assume it was a new road that was planned, but more likely it was a typical situation where the maps and roads don't quite agree with each other, a known Eastern European issue, and one we expected to get at least moderately worse. It was also a known issue with Marcin, which would also prove to get at least moderately worse.

The roads out of the Czech Republic were bordering on the appalling. Their version of a motorway was like riding over a cheese-grater with cheddar tyres. It also had the dubious pleasure of being beset with freezing fog, so it was a little like riding through a batch of particularly foul-smelling potato soup, served straight from the fridge in an old sock it had been stored in. When we started out in the morning, we were experiencing temperatures around four degrees, and it showed. It was cold! We grumbled and moaned quite a bit, but now I had the luxury of having someone to moan at who was just as fed up with his life as I was.

This motorcycle adventure touring stuff was great. For the price of a holiday in the South of France, we were now driving through stale water particles mixed with pollution with our visors open for long enough to stain our eyeballs grey. Yesterday we had hangovers that can only be compared to slamming a car door on your head, and we were so cold that we were both considering soiling ourselves to warm us up a bit. Why wasn't everyone doing this?

On our way out of town, we stopped to get a picture in front of the only nice building we could find. Instantly, a police officer told us off for riding on the pavement, appearing from nowhere and wagging a tiny finger at us as if we were naughty children.

To be honest, it was a bit disconcerting to be told off by a very attractive four-foot-tall woman who weighed less than whatever Marcin had let in the toilet after breakfast. I can't mention her name here, because like most very attractive women, she refused to give it to me. But at least she kept smiling at us and laughing, so we didn't take all this too seriously. In fact, I got her to take a picture for us, and she seemed to forget she had a job to do and was happy to snap some pictures of us before we rode away.

So we motored on through the freezing fog until we found a petrol station, the true natural environment of the adventure motorcyclist. We filled up, ready for the journey ahead, wherever and whatever might be waiting for us around the corner, amidst the infinite possibilities of the world before us. We assumed that it was quite likely that it would be more freezing fog and roads that didn't actually exist, until we ended up in yet another petrol station.

We weren't wrong.

My fuelling was playing up still, and it was starting to bother me. The fuel just wasn't being sucked from the little reserve tank into the main unit. A quick check on the fuel tube showed it had started to melt. I looked and quickly found the "Made in China" notation that explained why a fuel hose would turn to jelly in under a week. I removed it and flushed the system out with Redex EFI cleaner, which would hopefully remove any traces of hose that had liquefied and found their way into my injector.

After that, we powered on as best we could, and the weather seemed to be mostly on our side. We had a few showers along the way, but nothing I would call rain, at least not the kind of rain that made suicide feel like the better option. We crossed into Slovakia and stopped for lunch, because Marcin eats like a horse, and if we hadn't, then there was a distinct and troubling possibility that he might actually eat me. Just to clarify, he ate the quantity a horse might eat. I don't wish to imply that he was eating straw, nor that it was from a large bag strapped to the front of his head.

Slovakia, or at least Bratislava, was very tidy, friendly, and cheap, for the most part. We stopped for pictures and got moved on by a fat secret police officer who seemed to appear from nowhere and probably had nothing better to do. The very fact that he announced that his work was secret meant he was either having a slow day or his English teacher had skipped the lesson where they studied irony. In case we weren't sure, he also had a badge on his coat with the words spelled out in fake gold letters.

Lunch was served up in a little café we found while driving down a small road that was meant to be a field, or a field that was meant to be a road. The distinction was hard to make at that point. Marcin ordered something with meat. I asked about vegetarian options and was told I could have chips. Then the chef came out and offered to bake me a broccoli gratin, which turned out to be excellent and around half the price you'd pay elsewhere in Europe. I was impressed and well-fed, and Marcin was so well-fed that I was impressed that he didn't explode.

So with full bellies and the strong prospect of beer ahead, we motored on and finally reached the Hungarian border. This time it was a proper border, with security and everything . . . everything except people, so we just drove on through it and wandered into yet another new country.

Then the winds kicked up, and they kicked up hard. It was sudden; we were lashed with cross-winds while winding down a steep hill as the sun began to melt away into darkness. We were managing an average speed of around seventy-five mph, and that dropped down severely as my little bike struggled to hold a straight line. Then, to make matters worse, the rains hit us as hard as I'd ever been hit, and this time it wasn't a shower, it was more like a judgement from some angry, drunken Norse god. It hammered down on us, soaking through my waterproof gear in minutes, obscuring the road ahead into a mist of rain and blurred tail lights.

There were certainly many things for which any higher being could choose to judge me. While essentially falling just short of being a criminal, my behaviour over the years wasn't always the absolute best that could be hoped for. In fact, if god chose to exist, and to then take offence at anyone, I was a pretty good choice. I certainly wasn't in the league of every American president, every religious leader, or anyone from Poland, but I was getting there.

My speed dropped and dropped until I lost Marcin altogether. He faded from a glimmering red tail light, into a pin-prick of red light somewhere ahead, and then finally he vanished as my glasses fogged up and were so covered with driving rain that I could barely see my own hands. I just couldn't keep the pace any longer. I was virtually driving blind, and the wind was battering me like a Bulgarian scrotum-faced prostitute after I'd complained about the smell.

He waited for me in a petrol station. I had a feeling he would, so I caught sight of him, waved, and he caught me up back on the road. Finally, after a reasonably miserable stretch of pounding rain and heavy traffic, we got into Budapest, where I found I had a busted tail light and no fuel again. My consumption was way up, probably due to the pace and the blocked fuel pipe, which had caved in on itself and had closed off the breathing tube. The tail light was actually more of a concern, since it was a solid state LED unit, which shouldn't technically be capable of burning out. Anything was possible with BMWs—they had the most complex and advanced technology it was possible to imagine, and if any motorcycle could find a new and inventive way to break down, then you could be sure it would be one of theirs. Not for the first time, I thought to myself, "Why didn't I just buy one of those Hondas that everyone says are so good?"

We got some more food and then headed for a hotel we had found on the Internet; a place where standards were lower than the price and which was ideally suited to a pair of riders who were cheaper than the room. The hotel didn't have the cheap room we had hoped for, reserved, and booked online, but they found a double room with separate beds, which was cheap enough and had parking off the main road, ideal for our bikes. We settled in, ripping our luggage from our bikes and checking to see if everything had survived the storm better than we had.

My blown tail light problem, as suspected, was caused by a dodgy cheap HID unit which had only popped a fuse by some miracle, and not done any real damage. I had swapped the standard light out, since it was essentially garbage. It was barely as useful as holding a candle in my teeth and put out just enough light power to charge a solar pocket-calculator. That was just about a barely tolerable situation for a sluggish 650cc enduro, but the same unit was also fitted to a tuned, 1200cc, top-of-the-range bike. BMW had every right to feel ashamed of themselves for fitting this to anything larger than a scooter, but it was unlikely they did, since Germans didn't appear to think that basic emotions were very efficient, and engineers even less so.

In any case, I felt ashamed for them on their behalf, and so I eventually swapped the whole thing out for a Buell unit. Buell is a motorcycle company that I want very much to love. They have a Harley-Davidson motor, rebuilt by Rotax, the best motorcycle engine manufacturer in the world, give or take. Their bikes not only look insanely brilliant but have tons of common-sense innovations crammed into every inch of the design. Unfortunately, they just don't seem to work very well. They're a lot like KTM, I suppose, but without such a strong focus on being hideously unreliable. I've never actually owned one, because their bikes look great on paper, but only look great on paper, and don't really work in the real world. They're a bit like democracy in that respect, except Buell doesn't go round to other motorcycle dealers blowing up their showrooms.

My headlight was a double-bowl arrangement in a very sturdy plastic housing, and I fitted HIDs to both bowls. The lighting was immediately impressive, but the quality of the units was less so, and one had self-destructed just two days before I left. I replaced it with a cheap one from eBay, which had also now self-destructed, thanks to its in-built Chinese quality. I often wondered if KTMs were all built in China. BMWs now certainly were.

I decided that in the morning I would shut off the full beam switch and replace the fuse. That would mean I would then only have dipped lights and no full beams.

I had broken one of my own rules—whenever you do an upgrade to a motorcycle, do it a long time before you leave so you have time to test it. I had screwed up and was going to have to pay the price. Still, my lights were much better than Marcin's. He had fitted an LED bulb without realising that LED and HID are very different things, so his barely glowed bright enough for him to even be seen by things heading straight for him. I wanted to swap out the fuel line too; that way normal service should be resumed, the fuel should feed normally, and the breathing issue should resolve itself.

My life had become an ocean of things that should be true, but probably wouldn't be, and issues that should resolve themselves, but were very unlikely to do so. There were still other issues that shouldn't resolve themselves, but would likely respond favourably to being left on their own until they went away all by themselves. In any case, after a day like this, the answer to, and largely the cause of all my problems, was beer, and lots of it.

We had experienced an odd thing that day, just odd enough to catch my attention. The place we stopped for lunch and the place we stopped for dinner were hundreds of miles apart and in different countries, but they both had the same salt-shaker. Even weirder, the hotel we stayed in that night and the one previously both had the exact same toilet paper. You can judge the quality of our adventure so far by the fact that we had noticed this, and that we found it remarkably interesting.

So, we were now in Budapest. It was wet and cold, but a quite stunningly beautiful city. Everywhere you turn is another pristine example of real culture and history lit up proudly, a monument to their achievements. It was clean, people were happy, and the food was good.

Hopefully, if time allowed, we would get a chance to get some snaps in daylight. Tomorrow was meant to offer better weather, so I was hoping that held true, but I wasn't expecting it. As a biker who had spent more years of his life riding motorcycles than not, I was used to the indignities of riding through harsh conditions.

That didn't mean I enjoyed it.

9

A Difference of Scale

Date—October 25th
Location—Hungary
Status—Starting to settle into things

The morning saw us waking up in Budapest, and I can think of plenty of worse places to be. The evening had been spent in the hotel bar where beer flowed a little too freely, and many of my brain cells had given up and walked out in protest. This must have been what it felt like to be Marcin.

I woke fairly early and went out in search of SD cards, as someone had stolen the one out of my camera and I chose to blame my girlfriend, largely because it had to have been her. I also needed a length of rubber hose, because my fuel line had collapsed and was making my bike misbehave. The SD card was needed in the somewhat vague hope that I might coax a little life out of my failed Garmin GPS.

I went for a ride to a shopping mall I had spotted on the way in and found a different one on our doorstep, so I went there instead.

Inside, it was familiar territory; shops lined the tiled floors, tinny bland music filled the air, and the sounds of dozens of muted conversations buzzed all around me. While walking aimlessly around, I found a Euronics store that could provide for my SD needs but nothing on the rubber hose front, rather disappointingly. It was hardly surprising really—not many boutique shops stocked motorcycle parts, which is largely what I blame for the collapse of Western society.

I waited for the store to open and asked random strangers about a length of rubber hose while patiently biding my time. Nobody spoke English at all, which I found a little surprising. My unsophisticated grunts and pointing motions served me poorly, and nobody seemed to understand what it was that I wanted. In hindsight, I was lucky the police weren't called.

In the end, I drew a blank. I got my SD cards after considerable difficulty, but my bike was still running like a sack of shit, or worse, a KTM. She was grumpy with me for some reason; probably that reason was that BMW had designed her to be a "Cross Country" motorcycle but not equipped her to actually be one. Motorcycles like this were usually just made for infrequent visits to a local coffee-shop, and now she was being asked to live up to her name. It was like asking someone called "Colin" to be interesting at a party.

When I actually thought about it, perhaps BMW hadn't meant her to be designed for crossing countries but more for across countryside conditions. They really needed to put more thought into their names before another thing like "Funduro" happens.

I assumed I had done bad things to her by fitting her with a petrol line that had gone hard and then melted, dripping blobs of pink chemicals into the intricate and delicate injection system. She wouldn't stay running at all, which was reminiscent of the troubles I had with the spark plugs some time ago. BMW, in their wisdom, had fitted odd plug-caps inside their coil-packs, and the plugs were required to have a screw-on adapter. If that adapter became slightly unscrewed then contact was poor and the bike would begin to misfire and eventually run like a KTM.

I got back, packed up, and hoped for the best; my mechanical expertise wouldn't stretch much further than that anyway. It was raining when we left, so I expected another day of abject misery interspersed with Marcin devouring everything that wasn't quick enough to escape his gaping maw. I stuck one of the SD cards in my GPS, and mostly it started magically working, as if Harry Potter himself had rubbed his magic wand all over it. We plodded on, and I noticed that the engine stayed running, which was a pleasant and most welcome surprise. It showed that my mechanical fortitude really was up to the task and hoping for the best really was an efficient way of dealing with problems like these.

We stopped at a little alley with dozens of bike shops so I could get some hose, but all were closed. We found an open scooter shop thing, and they apologised that they could not accept cards and didn't have rubber hose. All they had was proper fuel lines. This was one of those rare times when what you find exceeds your expectations. It's even more rare when travelling with Marcin.

They offered me a length of absolutely perfect stuff, but the price was just under two Euros, and all I had was a note for five. I was happy, and we were in a rush, so I told them to keep the change, which made them slightly excited, and they accepted my terms with childlike enthusiasm. In England that hose would have cost me over £15 and most likely would have dissolved on the spot and completely clogged my injectors, turning my bike into a very expensive hat-stand.

So we rode off, my bike running fine. For now . . .

After some time on the road—a mostly dry road—we stopped at a petrol station for some food. I had a small cheese pasty, while Marcin ate pretty much everything that I hadn't. They didn't understand us well enough to get the order right, which was, again, slightly strange. Whenever it didn't matter everyone spoke flawless English, but when asking for things that did matter we completely failed to find anyone who understood anything we said. It didn't really matter very much, since Marcin's appetite was as discriminating as American machine-gun fire. It's a miracle that he left behind place-mats and cutlery.

Marcin had a bowl of soup that he assured me was a genuine Polish delicacy made from boiling down the insides of a dead cow. It had the foetid aroma that lines the roads along cow farms that pile dung along the pavement. He was welcome to his cow-stomach/turd soup, and I leant as far back as I could while he slurped it up noisily enough to annoy other customers and set off nearby car alarms.

We had two choices on how to proceed in terms of what route to take towards Turkey, and both seemed exactly equal in terms of distance or conditions—Romania or Serbia. Romania was my choice, as I was hoping to have an adventure involving vampires. Someone on the HUBB had said he was scammed for insurance in Serbia, and that was the opposite choice of Marcin after the advice of a man we met in a bar. So with no reliable information and Google just toying with us, I did the most reasonable thing possible—I asked some lorry drivers, figuring they did this trip often enough to know best which way we should go. They sided with the man in the pub—Serbia was safer, faster, and easier, they told us with no signs of sarcasm.

We were sold, Marcin especially so, since he rarely gets a chance to be proven right. An hour later, we crossed the border. In all it took fifteen minutes. It was very straightforward, friendly, and simple, much like Marcin himself, in fact. We offered our passports, got them back, and moved on to customs. Customs looked at the passports, shrugged, handed them back, died of boredom, and we were then free to enter. It couldn't have been much easier. We hadn't known quite what to expect, as we were now officially leaving the European Union, so that was our first actual border crossing on this trip.

The roads were, indeed, pretty decent, as we'd been advised, but in a few places they were in a fairly bad state of repair. It was interesting how unfinished lengths of road were already collapsing, and telling of the economy that stretches of motorway were open with cones along miles of their length and already having a patchwork quilt or repaired sections before even being completed.

Driving there was actually pretty respectable as well. We were able to relax and enjoy the view, and that view grew more interesting and impressive as we went along. It was a country of farmland stretching to the horizon, a tapestry of rolling green hills with clear skies above. The roads may have been a little rough around the edges, but there was none of the rampant arrogance of other drivers in Europe that we'd started to become accustomed to. These people might have simple tastes, but the accidental killing of bikers wasn't one of them.

We made it into Belgrade, after being lashed by winds for several hundred miles, but I'd started not to really notice that any more.

Hours spent on the bike quickly accustom you to anything, and I found the changing conditions were getting increasingly easy to adapt to. I felt like we had gone from being two very different people who moaned at each other a lot to realising that as two people who moan at each other a lot we really weren't all that entirely different at all. We were certainly now moaning a lot less and enjoying things a lot more. A few days on the road had changed everything.

Belgrade was a charming town, and spirits were high. There we were after our first proper border crossing into a strange, non-European country. The city was huge, vast in fact, and the architecture was interesting, but muted, and without the flair of some we'd seen. The outskirts ranged from ploughed dirty fields with Russian cars being used as tractors to little alcoves of children running amok. The city centre was a patchwork of grey buildings that looked just different enough to be interesting to look at without being entirely unfamiliar.

We stopped off a few times to take some pictures. After all, how often do you ride through Serbia, assuming you're not a truck driver? We were stuck in traffic several times, which was understandable, considering the sheer size of the place. A lot of people still paid attention to the bikes, but we were getting used to that too. We'd come to accept that we were a novelty, overloaded with luggage and with foreign number-plates from a country hundreds of miles behind us. We were a beacon for people to stare at while stuck in traffic, a break from the endless tail-gated cars that stretched on ad-infinitum. Once we were in the centre, we got trapped in a huge mass of stationary vehicles because, with our gear, we were just too large to filter thorough the tiny gaps between them. We heard a beep, and a young man on the back of a scooter was waving to us; just a cheery person happy to see the odd spectacle of foreign bikers in his home-town. Even when we stopped to take pictures people came up to us to offer to take one of us both. We were made to feel welcome, indeed; the town had an open heart and was much warmer than the winds that had reddened our faces and swelled our fingers.

Once into the heart of Belgrade all was good; traffic died off, and the road ahead led us out onto wide open roads, but Marcin wanted to plod on for a few more miles. I didn't mind, but when we left I just couldn't keep up with the pace. As darkness fell we were doing over seventy-five mph, and he was pulling away into the shadows, with no street-lamps to light our way. I had repaired my fuse problem but couldn't go to full beam, so had no way to flash him and let him know he was going too fast. At that speed, I couldn't even over-take and let him know I just wasn't going to keep up. The horn honked impotently, and the speed kept tracking upwards until the gap between us grew and grew, and I was increasingly aware that I had no means to let him know he was pulling away, unless he happened to glance in his mirror, something I suspected he wasn't going to do any time soon.

Eventually, I just slowed down to a leisurely fifty and let him catch on that I wasn't there. He eventually slowed down, and I overtook to lead us to a motel. He was hoping to do ninety miles outside of town, but we made only another fifty. I said we needed to talk about the pace and his constant need to always push the mileage beyond what was reasonable and into what was utterly retarded, dangerous, and illegal.

He was burning rubber to get to Sydney by Christmas, but my plans were different. I didn't see any way an extra day or two made much difference in the overall scheme of things. Through Turkey there were reportedly no motorways past Ankara, I had heard; Iran had a poor road system; and then in Pakistan we would have to wait for escorts. We were led to believe that India was a joke of international proportions, in terms of the driving and that we would make poor time there. We chatted briefly about it over some food and beer, the best time to discuss anything, really.

There are few things in life more frustrating than riding a motorcycle and watching as someone pulls away from you and knowing there's nothing you can do about it, and I told him so. Marcin was driven, always pushing faster with no consideration of any possible consequences. I had thought the trip through and decided a 650cc single was ideal, bearing in mind the rough roads ahead. It was a good choice, but it wasn't a fast one. It was a bike that could stretch to 100 mph for brief stints, but wasn't happy much above seventy. This was all made worse with the heavy luggage and equipment she was also carrying. We'd discussed this before agreeing to make the trip together, and he had agreed to accept the shortcomings of my bike for the greater good. It had been my main concern about riding with him. My bike made around fifty-four bhp, perhaps a little more with moderate modifications I had made to her, while Marcin's made nearly twice the power. Damon, the other traveller we were both hoping to ride with, had a Yamaha Tenere 660cc single, which made even less power than mine. We talked it through in London, and Marcin and I had agreed it wouldn't be a problem, since we'd be riding at the speed limits anyway.

On a previous trip, while in the Black Forest in Germany, I had been ambling about, wondering why the Germans were so obsessed with giant clocks, when I'd found a black BMW R1100gs parked up on the roadside. The R1100gs is widely considered the point where BMW perfected the enduro-touring motorcycle. It earned its reputation for reliability by actually being reliable, instead of being paid for by sponsorship deals in motorcycle magazines. It was a fine, capable bike, with just enough power and easy manners. With the miles leaving their mark on me, I had felt at the time that this was the bike I probably should have gone for, and I was feeling that way again.

Certainly, the 1200 version suffered from too many compromises in terms of build quality and over-complication, but the old one would have been a solid choice; perhaps even the later R1150gs, which also had a sound following. I had seen a black 1150 at an auction and had come very close to buying it on the spot. And this was after my current bike had been prepped for action at a considerable cost. Also, storage would have been a serious issue, as the old BMWs are not particularly compact. I ended up talking myself out of it, but never quite managed to shake the feeling that I might have made a mistake.

I didn't know how bad the roads ahead might be. Perhaps the KTM would falter, the weight might be too much to carry, or perhaps the legendary bad roads would be paved, and we'd both be better suited on Suzuki Bandits. I had chosen a bike capable of anything the world might throw at it, but so far, the only thing I was needing was more power, and it was the one thing the bike simply couldn't give me.

We sat briefly in our motel room and checked emails. We sat in silence for a while, both using the free Internet and lost in thoughts. Then I noticed he was searching the motorcycle forums, and I knew exactly what he was doing. He was looking for other people on the same trip we were doing so he could dump me and carry on with a new riding partner. I knew, because at that time I was doing exactly the same thing. We both exchanged awkward glances and closed the forums down with guilty looks at one another.

I really quite liked Marcin, and we were mostly happy riding together so far, so we put it behind us and arranged to compromise the next day. We intended to slow the pace so my little single could keep up more comfortably, and we would leave earlier and ride a little longer. That way we all would get what we wanted. He needed to see the miles clock up, and I needed to set a pace my far smaller bike could more easily manage.

The hotel/motel was just the right side of good, and at a price Europe can't compete with. The waiter had a real sense of purpose and brought us plate after plate of local delicacies and drinks, which was still cheaper than eating out in France, for instance. He took a real pleasure in recommending things to us and seeing our delighted reactions to everything he brought.

We spoke at length about our bikes as we ate. With my partner on the back of my bike in Europe, my fuel system delivered 180-190 miles per tank. Now it was giving me 135 miles. That was a marked drop in range and a considerable concern. Marcin agreed that he was noticing a similar drop in his range too, so we were optimistically suspecting that the fuel was of a lower octane than advertised. Both bikes were running fine and had normal power, it was just that they were delivering poorer than usual mileage. We hoped, me especially, that the fuel injection systems were compensating for the poor fuel, and we were both suffering the same minor problem, which would hopeful go away when we went away.

In the meantime, we spent the evening sampling local adult beverages until we collapsed somewhere.

10

Oh Dear

Date—October 26th
Location—Serbia
Mood—Enthusiastic, but unrealistically so

Amidst the cold, the speed we never agreed to (or agreed not to), the emotional high and consequent lows, Serbian alcohol, and animals killed unceremoniously at the side of the road, it was a long, arduous, and difficult day.

The motel we stayed at was nice, very nice in fact. The sun in the morning lit it up and brought warm smiles to our faces. Coffee was available and set us up ready for a day of who knew what? Not us, because not knowing was half the fun, and most of the problem.

But all good things come to an end, such as breakfast, and it was eventually time to do what riding motorcycles is all about—riding them for as long as possible, between stopping for petrol, until your arse feels like a lump of wet clay.

We agreed with some old gentleman, who seemed quite dubious on the matter, to push our bikes from the front to the back, so they were safer and closer to our room. Our emotional attachment to them was foremost on our minds for most of the time, even more so than our emotional detachment from one another. He said it was no problem but had to think about it first, eyes were rolled, and shoulders were shrugged. Later we realized that his reluctance to let us move our bikes was because the hotel was built on the side of a toll road. Moving them allowed us to get back on our way without going through the barriers and thus we wouldn't be paying the full toll. We did it anyway, and thanks to our deviousness, we enjoyed a saving of around twenty pence, or essentially nothing, in real money.

Yes, the motel was nice indeed; extremely warm and friendly, and the evening had recharged our batteries, or mine at least. Small dogs wandered around in the morning playing, and everyone smiled honestly back at us. I like dogs, and the friendliest of them followed us around, yapping playfully and begging for a little of what we had.

Once we made it out on the road, we found this very same dog covering a small section of it with what used to be his spine. There was considerably more of that to follow.

The road broke from the drudgery of a motorway into a main road—a dual carriageway for the most part, and the scenery grew better as we trundled along. The wind was still not going to be our friend and lashed at my little bike like an angry inner-city dweller trying to get through a car window to your wallet. Even Marcin felt it that day; his bike was aerodynamically designed to alleviate the pains of wind, weighs twice as much, and has twice as much power, but at one point we were riding pitched to roughly ten degrees just so that we could manage to hold a straight line. Of course, straight is subjective, and I managed to barely keep between the lanes and crossed them more than once as my little bike wobbled about like I was riding drunk and with my eyes firmly closed.

Suddenly, about fifteen miles on from our start, the scenery turned into . . . *scenery*! Burnt black fields peppered the horizon, as dimly apparent mountains warned us of their presence like ghosts in the far recesses of the distance. The rocky, barren land stretched on imposingly as far as we could see, and while not quite beautiful, it was striking and impressive. The ride went on for around a hundred miles and never stopped being impressive the entire time. The rolling hills blended into a barren landscape of hardship and drudgery that, while it was a privilege to see in passing, must have been a burden to be tied to, and we felt for the people making a life from it.

Ancient tractors moved dirt from one place to another, occasionally Russian cars were seen in distant fields, and sometimes whole families tended the land in exchange for barely enough to survive on. Towns gave way to rows of wooden and rock-made shacks, crumbling away on the horizon. There was an unmistakable Mediterranean feel to the architecture, but with the unplanned, run-down look of the small, painful Asian slum-towns. It was a place of hard lives and tough people, a people recovering from a past that was rockier than the terrain. If people who had suffered like this ever decided to take that suffering and visit it on the real people who were actually behind it, then the world would undoubtedly be a better place.

Finally, we stopped for fuel, and we noted with relief that our range was improving. We stopped around 145 miles, and I had several litres left; that meant that things were working properly down below, and who doesn't like it when things work properly down below? We grabbed a second breakfast in a motorway service centre, and it turned out to be both excellent and cheap as well. Unfortunately, we didn't have enough money to pay for it after he refused our cards. Marcin and I exchanged awkward glances, as our pockets were stuffed with Euros, which weren't an acceptable currency. We had assumed our cards would work, as they had before, but out here that didn't seem to be the case. Eventually, even that wasn't a problem. He took what local money we had with a smile and told us it was enough. In England that wouldn't have been the case—there would have been shouting, and threats of police and violence, or police violence, and certainly, violent police.

After we left the petrol station, somewhere around the town of Nis, we headed out to follow the road, and there was an instant dramatic shift as we entered the mountains. We were now in a truly foreign land. Craggy peaks of rock oversaw us as we wound our way through narrow paths claimed back from the awesome natural beauty of this region. The roads were amazing, clean, clear, and trustworthy, and they wound through some truly spectacular views. We were lucky enough to even have good weather, with temperatures around seventeen degrees, which were comfortable, even with the winds.

Even after we passed the initial outcropping of rock, the barren, rugged landscape kept us entertained for miles, until eventually we found the Bulgarian border. We had to climb to reach it, and grey clouds darkened the sky.

The views closed in until, eventually, an ugly scar of human nature blighted our view with a border crossing. Nobody seemed to care, and we had to ask someone to come and check our passports. We were allowed through straight away, of course; Bulgaria is Europe, and we held passports that allowed us in without fuss.

Between the Serbian exit and Bulgarian entrance was a no-mans-land of empty nothing, where nobody had any right to be... except a small market full of shops. I guess that speaks volumes in a philosophical sense.

The entrance was pretty straightforward too. They checked our stuff, and we were quickly allowed into Bulgaria. Suddenly, the trappings of war-torn poverty were swept aside. The roads were clear and smooth, and the edges were tidy and clear. We made good time towards Sofia, a large city along the way and a place we wanted to see. From the last ten miles until we reached it, we were able to see the outskirts, so we knew this was going to be a big and impressive place to visit.

I could write a diatribe on my initial impressions as we crossed the border and entered the town, but Marcin said it in words that surpassed anything I could imagine and eloquently summed up our thoughts and impressions. We stopped at a set of lights, he looked around at the town sprawled out before him, and then he turned to me and said, "Oh dear."

On the right was a shanty town full of a minority people that had been thrown to the wolves. Tiny ramshackle huts lined the length of a small river as far as we could see. People, darker than the average and different looking, were laying on the pavement smoking and drinking things that had no business in the human body, while the passers-by locked their windows and twitched nervously at every sound.

One of them approached Marcin and made a strange gesture with his fingers over his mouth that looked as though he wanted to offer him oral sex. Marcin showed remarkable restrain in not punching him, but eventually the individual staggered off, collapsed, and probably died somewhere, his body vanishing as he rolled into a bush.

A local rolled down his window nervously and shouted at us in English not to give them money. If we had, they would come in force and try to steal everything we had. We exchanged glances and raised eyebrows.

We rode into town and struggled to find something worth taking pictures of. Even when we left the bikes for an instant, people began to head to them, eyeing up our stuff like vultures. There was a strong unease about the place. We felt unwelcome and that we were a target. Eyes peered through us; groups clustered and pointed, moving furtively towards our bikes as soon as our backs were turned. It was a stark contrast from Serbia, and from anywhere we'd been so far.

We left in a hurry. With the traffic, the grey and unpleasant buildings, and even greyer and more unpleasant people, the entire city was the visual equivalent of a punch to the throat.

The roads in and around the place were polished smooth by the wheels of the vehicles, so they looked strangely like they were wet all the time and behaved as if they really were.

At one point, Marcin braked for traffic lights and carried on for four to five metres, after his ABS thought he was lying about really wanting to stop and switched off the brakes. At first, I thought he'd jumped the lights and expected me to follow; it was a surprise that he'd do something so stupid, but not really that much of a surprise. I winced as he narrowly avoided being smashed to pieces by oncoming cars. He then wheeled the bike back clumsily and explained what had happened with a wide, but relieved-looking grin. It was a tense moment. He could easily have been hit by oncoming traffic and avoided doing that by far too short of a margin. Even he seemed shaken for once.

Neither of us trusted ABS, and it was something we could both agree on. Too often things like that happen. On an excellent, smooth, straight, and decent piece of tarmac it might work fine, but on anything else it can conspire to kill you. Off-road it was a liability, but many modern "adventure" motorcycles had it fitted with no option to turn it off. I had got into the habit of turning mine off unless it was raining, and now, Marcin did the same.

Outside of town, the roads were a mixture of being perfectly fine for a few yards and like riding on an overturned truckload of spilled dildos for a few more. The bike vibrated all over the place, but we did get used to it after a while, and both of our bikes took the abuse in stride.

We motored on towards the next biggest town at the best speed we could manage over the rutted, fine, and then ever more rutted roads, then Marcin insisted he wanted to do another fifty miles. As it was still light, I agreed that we should. I was in no great mood to stay.

I had seen even better fuel economy than last time as we filled up, so we were assuming that our bikes had suffered from no more than a few tanks of crappy petrol. I put in some higher than usual octane gas and hoped she would continue to be even better until she returned her normal economy.

There was a strange rattling noise coming from the front of my bike, a kind of eerie tapping that was remote and distant but loud enough to be heard right through my helmet. I assumed it was my screen, which was only held on by stupidity, but it turned out to be coming from the back of the bike in front.

Marcin's bike was over-loaded, which was no mean feat on a bike essentially the size of a small town. Things were shifting around, his chain was loose, and the whole bike, in fact, was not in the very peak of operational efficiency. In fact, if the bike were a person, it would be a large person, a person putting little thought into planning ahead, a person blundering from one beer to the next while gorging itself on everything edible around it. In fact, if the bike were a person, it would be Marcin.

Just as had happened earlier that day, as soon as we left the station, the scenery changed, only this time the main road became a back-street, and the warnings about the Eastern part of Europe not being accurate on GPS took a pointedly apparent turn for the worst.

We spent the next three hours riding through pitch darkness, utterly lost, and with our GPS proving to be as accurate a method of navigation as asking a Magic 8-ball where it thought we should go. The night was punctuated by small regions of civilisation, lights in the darkness, but nothing available to weary travellers in terms of a place to spend the night. We tried, but prices were disproportionately high. I was ready to camp, but in the end, we found ourselves in a pretty large town and found a hotel within our minimalistic price range. We managed to unpack our bikes and somehow shoehorn all of Marcin's gear into a double suite, which was actually quite a good deal harder than it sounds.

We parked at the rear, gingerly picking our way through concrete bollards spaced to stop cars and small trucks from entering. My little 650cc bike made it with no problems, but Marcin's clipped the side and did some damage to his huge alloy boxes. It was nothing that couldn't be beaten out with the heavy end of a spanner, as it turned out.

Food was served, but we stood out, singled out for aggressive stares, as we sat eating our dinner. The place wasn't welcoming at all; nothing much about the country was. It was the last place we would ride before leaving Europe altogether, and we had hoped it might be more than it eventually was. Still, for all that, it was an interesting experience. Surprises are better than a monotonous drone of similarity, and the differences between countries was a welcome relief after the monotonous drone of my motorcycle as we swallowed up motorway miles.

At least beer was easy to find, and that came as no surprise to anyone.

11

The Rules of the Road

Date—October 27th
Location—Bulgaria
Status—Seemingly unwelcome

The mornings in Bulgaria are a grim thing indeed, mostly because all the windows there show views of Bulgaria. From the hotel window there was a scene of pealing grey banality, darkened windows, and the occasional sound of a clapped-out car being driven to such degrees of excess that they achieved speeds of nearly fifty miles per hour. It looked like the movie set of a Cold War thriller, set in some dark alcove in the deepest depths of some communist hell. Shady characters crept around, their beady eyes flashing everywhere with furtive intent, and travellers were stared at, treated with suspicion and contempt.

The day before, I had seen a Vauxhall Kadet, the precursor of the Astra. 1980s Vauxhalls were seemingly everywhere there, usually being driven flat out with collapsed suspension, no windows, and a patchwork quilt of different coloured panels. The driving was, to be fair, pretty decent compared to most of what we'd seen so far, and we knew there was worse to come.

Of course, travelling as fast as we were, we saw relatively little of the places we passed through. Our impressions were mostly made up from the way people drove around us, the food, and the all too few human interactions we managed to get along the way; usually while buying food, if you are unfortunate enough to travel with Marcin. We were seeing snapshots of places, barely lingering long enough to get an impression.

Most people we'd seen so far had been respectful drivers, giving us space to be a minor nuisance on their roads, and most bikers, even on scooters, were taking an interest in a friendly way. A guy on a scooter had come up beside me only the previous day and asked me to rev the engine, then nodded in appreciation and drove off quite happy. My bike had a slightly loud exhaust. It was all part of my strategy to save weight and increase fuel range. Still, it had seemed a slightly strange request, but one that I was more than happy to oblige. It had left both Marcin and myself laughing at the world.

Most groups of people in Bulgaria gave us the impression of being more interested in stealing our stuff than anything else. We left the bikes for a moment, and shabby looking guys would start heading towards them, nudging each other and looking around furtively. It was annoying. This was Europe and the last leg of our journey through the Union, and we'd hoped for a more uplifting experience; at least a happier send-off as we embarked on our journey towards more interesting places.

That day we were aiming to go somewhere for breakfast and then undertake an easy ride into Istanbul. When I say "easy," I mean we were theoretically on an easy schedule, but we had to guess what direction to take because sat-nav was no longer any use to us. We were riding on blind faith, compass pointing, and best-guess. Intelligent guesses were asking a little too much for these two idiots.

We were set to find ourselves travelling down narrow roads, sometimes with single lanes, but they were full of Turkish trucks, which meant we couldn't have actually have been all that lost. It was just that the country was a bit broken in terms of the design of the roads.

We had to have a light and flexible schedule, because we were facing a border crossing. This time, we anticipated a more intense experience, and everything we'd read backed up our worst suspicions. Turkey had rules beyond those of Europe, I had read ahead, and we were warned that all our equipment would have to be unloaded and inspected. That prospect was daunting, since I wasn't entirely sure how I'd managed to pack it all in there in the first place. Even more so for Marcin—his luggage was ridiculously huge and dense, much like himself.

Talking of broken, we had some trouble getting into the car park the previous evening, and Marcin had clipped his side box. The boxes were insanely massive, and the pucks that held on the huge slab-sided chunks of alloy took quite a hit. In the cold light of morning, the damage was slightly worse than we thought. The screws on the plastic mushroom that held on the whole weight of the box had sheared off completely on one of the connectors, and the whole thing had completely fallen off. That morning, we surgically repaired it after a trip into town for coffee and food. Surgery was performed by Marcin with a big spanner until the alloy was straight again, and I had some nuts and bolts in my bag of junk that were probably better than the original screws, so the problem really turned out to be no problem at all. Another successful roadside repair and a victory for my spares kit, which was little more than a random selection of nuts, bolts, and screws scooped up into an old bag.

The town we had left behind us was . . . different. People stared at us like we were the outsiders that we actually were. They stared at us even more when we bought postcards and walked around taking pictures of them, while they blinked back at us with curious incredulity. It had been an interesting visit, but we weren't sorry to be leaving Bulgaria, Europe's dustbin. The road beckoned, and now that we were pretty much in the gutter, we could see the stars.

Rule of the road, number one: Do not follow Marcin into a bathroom.

Rule of the road, number two: DO NOT FOLLOW MARCIN INTO A BATHROOM.

I had heard the warnings and heeded them, but something happened that day that lit up my senses in the worst possible way imaginable. To this day I wake up screaming, my sheets drenched in sweat, my eyes wide in terror, at the very thought of the horrors I witnessed back then. While loading the bikes outside in the open air, he farted, but the word *fart* barely comes close to describing the horror of that smell. It was like he'd cast a demon out through his trousers. It was as if evil itself was clawing its way out of his foetid innards. It was a moment that will forever darken my very soul, leaving me rolling around on the floor in agony while he chuckled like a movie villain and asked if I'd like another.

We wandered into town that morning and had breakfast, of sorts. Marcin got a plastic tray filled with grilled meat, and I had the worst cup of coffee in the known universe. He exclaimed in disappointment that it was just a sausage, after all. We were keen to try everything, and most countries had their own unique twists on the foods we were used to. The fact that it was something familiar slightly annoyed him. It didn't stop him eating it, though, and ordering more. Nothing stops him eating anything. With my cup of wretched coffee, I had a nice savoury biscuit thing, and then we were ready to go. You never really know what to expect, so it would be more accurate to say we were ready to be ready to go.

We knew the roads ahead were going to be lacking a certain quality, specifically, a smooth and flat quality, but we headed on anyway at a good pace. My bike might not be fast, and being German, it might not be conventionally attractive, but it was good at roads that lacked smooth and flat qualities.

Police offices were wooden shacks with broken windows, roads were pitted worse than the face of a McDonalds employee, and the sky was an oddly muted grey, as if an artist had painted it with a dirty brush. From the moment we'd entered the place, everything seemed to be on fire. Every dustbin or suitably large metal container had a fire burning in it, and that continued as we went along the road.

Finally, after what seemed like a disproportionate length of time, we made it to the Turkish border. We endured what we thought was a fairly good crossing, but it still cost us around an hour of pointless messing about. Back then, we thought an hour was bad!

At first, they told us we needed a visa, which we knew. We were able to buy one on the border for £10 and a few minutes of waiting around. I had heard it was £130 if you booked it in London before you travelled, and consequently, the advice was not to do so. I don't know if that information was true, but it wouldn't surprise me; my limited experience with visas and the government operatives that issue them were almost exclusively negative, and not just negative but hugely and massively so. Doing it at the border was certainly easy enough. Apart from ourselves, the border was largely deserted, so everything went quite smoothly.

After that, and three passport checks, they wanted to check our bike documents. They noticed, quite rightly, that we didn't have "green card" insurance beyond Europe, because we didn't and had no idea what it was or why we needed it. Marcin argued that we did have it and was actually insured all the way to the lunar surface, and I asked what would happen if we promised to drive really, really carefully.

They seemed very friendly after a quick chat and a joke, and said they'd turn a blind eye and we could go, so long as we only stayed a few days. It turned out that saved us £50 each, so we both promised to drink the savings, and thus inject the money directly into their economy! It's a good example of how being basically decent to people goes a long way. I have heard a great many stories of people achieving the impossible, just by asking nicely and hoping for the best. Hoping for the best was certainly continuing to serve us well.

We then moved on to a luggage inspection, and while we were unstrapping the gear, Marcin managed to cut his forehead on a chair. I'm not sure how that happened, or even how it could have happened. It was far from a lethal wound, but he bled quite impressively, and everyone looked quite worried.

We patched him up with my pretty hopeless, but legally-required, medical kit bought from Poundland, and the sympathy we gained sped us on our way. The Internet had told us we would be required to unpack all our gear, but in the end, we just asked what to do, and were told by people with big smiles on their faces that it was all done and we were free to go on our way. So we went.

This was another example of how being decent makes everything go smoother. It also doesn't hurt to accidentally injure yourself, especially in a part of your body that has never worked and you have no possible use for, in this case, Marcin's head. Nobody could argue that border crossings aren't annoying, but keep smiling, make jokes, be friendly, be helpful, and remember people are just doing their jobs, and most problems seem to go away all by themselves.

We also went away all by ourselves, which was probably what they wanted to happen too, since Marcin's blood might have been corroding a hole through the floor by the time we were back on our bikes.

The roads forward were decent enough, and we made good time. Turkey got increasingly windy, so towards the end of the run I was struggling to keep control, just for a refreshing change. My clutch had begun to feel like it was slipping, although the problem appeared to be the clutch cable, as adjusting it temporarily alleviated the problem. It felt solid enough to finish this trip, even if the slipping got worse and the plates were in need of replacing. My fuel economy was lousy again, which was a gigantic pain in the arse now that we were paying £1.85 per litre for petrol.

If anything, the roads were a little boring. They put me in mind of the better roads around Europe and seemed a little too familiar; a little too easy. We were outside of Europe now and wouldn't be going back. We wanted things to be different, and they weren't. The scenery was almost German, rolling green hills lay on either side of the light grey tarmac lanes, all maintained to an excellent standard.

We stopped to grab some food and empty out the bottles of water we'd topped up on while sitting around the visa office. We pulled in to a large petrol station with a white hut out to the side. It was large, with enough seating for over a hundred customers, but we were the only ones there. It was basic, like a school canteen, and the food came served in metal trays that were barely keeping the food warm. The food was alright but just as basic as the building, and it was pricey after what we'd been used to, even in Europe.

I had expected a little more from the food, although to be fair, this was just an unspectacular café at the side of the road, attached to a petrol station. Maybe I should have expected high prices and low standards. Nobody dines in economic excellence while filling up with petrol at the side of the road.

I had once been engaged to a Turkish girl, and the food had been the best thing about that relationship, with literally everything else being the worst. The food had mostly been very good, her mother especially being a very good cook. As a human being she wasn't quite so good. On my first time being invited round for dinner, she had been told I don't eat meat, so she served just that, stuffed into a bell-pepper and mixed with rice. My girlfriend complained, and her mother replied, "It's not meat, it's lamb."

For some odd cultural reason, I was asked to hide if Turkish people came round, since she didn't approve of her daughter dating a white man. All of this was especially confusing since we all lived in London, where her mother, herself, was dating a man who was even whiter than me. To put it mildly, over the course of the relationship all respect was effectively lost. It was lost highly effectively, in fact.

It had been one of those relationships where afterwards all your friends come up to you and tell you they always hated her with a "we told you so" look on their faces, even though nobody told me anything of the sort. This might be part of the reason I like bikes so much, you never sell one of those and have your friends come up to you and tell you that they're relieved your got rid of it because it gave them dirty looks behind your back and then made threatening phone-calls to your next bike for two years afterwards.

Another pair of European bikers joined us briefly, pulling up behind us, attracted by our bikes with the EU number-plates. One was riding a BMW R1200gs Adventure and the other an older litre-class Honda CBR. The BMW was gleaming, spotless, and immaculate, dripping with evidence of money thrown at it. The CBR looked like it had worked for a living, but had been well looked after, and it was clearly a rider's bike.

They had come through Romania, and like us with our journey through Serbia, they thought it was great. We had both followed different advice and ended up crossing through different countries, and ended up with almost identical and positive experiences. It's a fact of life that people more freely discuss the negative, so the forums were filled with the downsides of various options, and there were fewer remarks in the positive. I did enjoy those Serbian roads, so I had no regrets at our choice. Sadly, they had no experience with vampires, so I didn't feel that I'd really missed out on anything important.

They did look at me funny when I asked.

We rode out together, all four of us. The others, with larger bikes, went off as fast as they could, roaring away into the distance, and I could almost hear Marcin's thoughts about having to keep his speed down to mine. As a sports-bike fan, the speed we were making was just as frustrating to me. I had planned the bike for the much harder, more challenging roads ahead and knew that she would be less ideal for roads like these. But things were changing, and in this country, the little BMW would soon show herself to be the better choice.

Turkey was full of Turkish people. We met a few on our stops off, and they seemed generous, warm, friendly, and welcoming. They were also lethal behind the wheels of a powered vehicle. The driving was far beyond anything we'd seen so far, and calling it stupid was selling the scale of it somewhat short. Stupid is losing your keys; this was more like insanity on a national scale. We suspected that things would get worse as we went along, so we just did our best to get used to it.

Istanbul is a truly beautiful city, slightly disjointed and a bit cluttered, but was charming and with amazing architecture and a rich cultural history. Also, you can ride your bike anywhere and the police just look at you apathetically. All of these were huge benefits, and we took advantage of them. Things did feel different—the sky was warm and blue, and the hazy grimness of Bulgaria was long since forgotten. The city was perched on a hill, and from most angles, at sufficient distance, it was spectacular to see. It had water running through it, giving the air a cool, gentle, and salty freshness.

A couple of guys pulled up next to us on BMW F800gs Adventures. They asked us if there was anything we needed; just trying to help out a pair of fellow bikers. That was a very welcome change and brought smiles to our faces. We didn't need anything from them but felt, as we did all around the town, very welcomed. A new clutch, better fuel economy . . . more power might have been nice, but I wasn't likely to find that anywhere around.

People there were among the friendliest we'd met so far, when out from behind the wheels of their cars. Walking around the town looking for somewhere cheap to eat was a challenge. Some overly-friendly young men jumped out and introduced themselves, trying to drag us kicking and screaming into their bars. One guy said he was from South London, just like me. I asked him whereabouts, and he said "Birmingham . . . in Kent." Nice. It's always nice to meet someone with inferior navigational skills to my own, and that was a rare treat.

Food was around the same price as at home, but they tended to throw in starters and tea, and were far, far nicer about everything.

People there still seemed like people, not mindless automatons emptily serving a profit-making system, and there was a sense of humanity about them and a refreshing lack of fast-food chains. Put them behind the wheels of a car and they turn into blinkered, self-serving maniacs, but at least they were smiling while they were doing it.

Beer was available, but only with certain limitations—their only beer was Efes, and it sucked. It tasted like water mixed with beer, mixed with piss, mixed with pissy, watery beer.

We had arranged to meet up with the bikers we had previously met at lunch and share some of the afore-mentioned beer, enough hopefully to stop noticing the many, many drawbacks that came with it. We found them easily enough, and rather against the odds, which always seemed heavily stacked against us. Their own guest-house was full, and the area was a little rich for our blood, in any case. The owner very generously offered the use of his Wi-Fi to help us find something in our price range and brought us tea while we did it.

We found a hotel online, a kind of hostel, with private rooms lined with beds that were good enough. Sleeping is no great challenge after a day on a motorcycle, and that is especially true with sufficient Efes in your system to kill a mature donkey. Basic it may have been, but we were pretty basic people when you got right down to it. Tomorrow we would be heading onwards, onwards towards the other part of Turkey, towards the Muslim area, where the opulence of Istanbul would be left behind us. Marcin seemed better informed in that regard than I was and was convinced that standards were set to plummet.

If the weather, the traffic, and the roads were on our side, then we should be able to reach the next large town before dark the next day. Of course, we didn't know what to expect and expected our expectation would be wrong, no matter what it was. Between my inability to navigate, and Marcin's inability to do anything else, anything could happen and probably would.

A friend emailed to ask when we'd next be back in civilisation, and the truth was we wouldn't be, not until we made it to Thailand, and that was civilisation of a very different kind, indeed. Motorcycle repair shops with diagnostic computers, adequate medical facilities, and even a decent supply of alcohol were things that would be left behind as we forged on into the unknown. Unknown to us at least, thanks to our avoiding the Internet as much as possible.

We didn't want to spoil the surprise.

That turned out not to be a clever move.

12

Live Life Till You Die of It

Date—October 28th
Location—Istanbul, Turkey
Status—Gridlocked by carpet salesmen that failed basic geography

We were lucky enough to experience a near perfect day on the road. There were no disasters, no emergencies, nice weather, great scenery, food that we could just about identify as food, and Marcin not trying to ride so fast that we ruptured the fabric of the universe and risked arriving two hours before we left.

We started out in Istanbul. I had a few expectations from Turkey, since my forner girlfriend had come from that very country. After that miserable experience, (it might come as a bit of a surprise that it ended appallingly badly and even more of a surprise that it wasn't my fault), I figured that there was little left there that could possibly shock or repulse me further. Istanbul was a pleasant surprise in that respect—it was a bustling and vibrant city with interesting and varied architecture and friendly people. More importantly, the toll roads weren't guarded, and the police let us drive wherever we pleased. Well, that's not entirely true—they did try to chase us, but they were on foot, and we were faster.

That morning, we stopped along the way for a few snaps to remember passing through, and it all began to wear a bit thin after a surprisingly short amount of time. This was clearly a place ideally suited to small doses, and more than a weekend might begin to grind on your nerves quite badly.

The friendly people started getting a little irritating as the paper-thin facade peeled back. They were clearly after something all the time, and their hopelessly unsophisticated attempts to appeal to our western mentality was just grating after the novelty of the first few had worn off. The streets were lined with endless carpet shops, and they grabbed at you to stop and chat, eventually trying to sell us something that couldn't be more useless to a person whose entire worldly possessions were strapped to the back of a motorcycle.

That day, a girl started trying to engage us in conversation after we parked on her tourist attraction. She proclaimed loudly that I had a perfect bike. I loved my bike more than any man has a right to, but for that moment, she was covered in scrappy bolt-ons that were less attractive than my own armpit, and she was as dirty as I wished my girlfriend was (my girlfriend wasn't even close).

She then told Marcin that he had a perfect bum. We looked at one another and didn't know how to reply to that one; even Marcin, who deals with every situation by meeting it head on and then eating it/trying to have sex with it or driving as fast as he possibly can at it, was a little thrown by that one. In the end, I took the moral high-ground like an Englishman would and asked the only sensible question—what was wrong with mine? I suppose that in the grand scheme of things having a perfect bike is still pretty good, even if only a slightly insane Turkish girl thinks so.

People asked to be allowed to clean our shoes, others asked if we'd like to take pictures of them, for just a small amount of money. Everyone used a friendly smile as a way to get your money out of your pocket and into theirs. That was the only thing that seemed to matter to anyone we met. After a while, it was just time to move along, and we hoped that things had a bit more depth to them out of the city.

Before we left, of course, we had to face the ritual of packing the bikes. Mine was easy, and I was getting good at it—it only took a few minutes for me to be ready for the road.

Back inside the hostel there were two toilets available, but someone seemed to have moved into one of them and declared it as their own. The Turkish practice of leaving food in tepid metal cans all day before serving them had made my stomach feel slightly unsettled, and there was no waiting for the troubled individual in the normal, Western-standard toilet to finish. As it was an emergency situation, I had to make do with the other one.

To call it a toilet was a compliment; it was a hole in the ground, incapable of flushing, or of accepting toilet paper. The easiest thing in the world in this position is to shit in your own underpants, but I avoided soiling myself and mostly hit the target. I was rather proud of myself that I had succeeded on my first attempt and that my underpants were no more soiled than they were before. Marcin came back from the shower and told me someone with real power had been using the toilet next to his. I admitted it was me, and he seemed oddly impressed for once. When we packed the bike, I made the rookie mistake of sniffing the air, and there was a foul, sickly aroma wafting around the entire hotel lobby.

"It was me. Don't you recognise?" he said with a grin. He was insanely proud of himself for ruining several people's days, and in some cases, lives.

After a number of encounters with various Turkish people who were offering every imaginable favour as a special gift, and the constant rush-hour traffic that seemed to last all day, we finally got on the road out of there.

We headed for a major bridge; Marcin was very keen to get on it in a horribly touristy way. I was a bit disappointed, because it was just a bridge. It might have been a big bridge, but it was still just a bridge. I'm not a good tourist, apparently, and he grumbled and moaned at me and called me things that questioned the nature of my parentage. I called him an idiot, and we both seemed satisfied that we'd made our point, and then we got on with our lives.

It took us close to forty miles of travel to get out of the city sprawl. It seemed that Istanbul was just that massive, and it seemed to reach on forever. It was a city of fourteen million people, of whom roughly half own or work in the mindless, endless, mostly identical cafés and carpet shops that all have the same thing at the same price, and the rest just drive around, bumper to bumper, until they crash into something. Presumably, the rest are driving around with their carpets or are on their way between lunches and toilet emergencies.

The wind was still fairly strong, and I was buffeted a lot, although Marcin seemed fine, as usual, because he is just a force of nature and immune to such things as reality.

We stopped to gas up and have some lunch at a petrol station on the motorway as we trundled along on the outskirts of the city. The station was the biggest I have ever seen, with a mall literally attached to the petrol station. It had half a dozen restaurants, shops, cafés, and bars, all inside the sprawling, cavernous interior. It was just utterly ridiculous in terms of scale, even more so since we had the entire place to ourselves.

The toilets were even more ridiculous. The urinals had TV screens above each one, and everything was so clean that there was just about no way to get any kind of infection, no matter how hard you might be willing to try. Luckily, there was far more opportunity with lunch, and you didn't have to try that hard.

The food was expensive and second-rate. I had some macaroni cheese, some beans, and a little salad. Marcin had everything else, as usual. Even after four bowls of food he was still hungry, but we carried on regardless; with the wind, at least I couldn't hear his anguished moans, and the drone of our engines blotted out the rumbling of his cavernous stomach as he tried to ingest passing birds.

He was literally a one-man famine waiting to be afflicted upon the countries ahead of us. He was a monstrous, ravenous plague devouring its way from continent to continent. I'm sure it must have made the news—a few months after the terrible earthquake, now Marcin is coming and . . . he's hungry! A truly horrifying prospect.

For whatever reason, the weather seemed to improve, and we weren't going to moan about that, since we were busy moaning about everything else, mostly each other, and usually bickering like a pair of kids who want to play with the same toy. The wind died down, so I could comfortably add a few extra miles per hour, and the trip was far more comfortable in terms of holding a straight line.

Even though it was warmer than we were used to, it was still cold to ride in it. The wind blasting over us and the slight humidity meant we were effectively experiencing the same conditions as the inside of a fridge, and for those that want to know, it appears that the light does, indeed, stay on.

Soon after that, the terrain changed. Even though we were on a motorway, the scenery went from ordinary to spectacular in a matter of seconds. Green hills took hold of the horizons and rolled into infinity around us, and then the mountains ahead began to lumber our way. The ground flattened out into a barren rocky wasteland peppered with yellow bushes, and stretches of water glistened a deep blue beside us under a perfect, cloudless sky. The ride was everything you could ask of a road trip, and we enjoyed every second of it.

Somehow, Marcin lost a catch on his helmet, but my handy box of spares put that right quite quickly. He was still struggling with a £300 video camera that came supplied with a 50p fitting clip that had failed completely. We had successfully recorded several hours of wobbly, blurred video of the sun so far, and not much else. As we travelled towards Ankara, we bodged him up with double-sided tape and a power lead running from a hastily assembled collection of wires and plugs. Once we'd disguised him as an evil cyborg from a bad sci-fi movie with Evil, Death, or Killer in the title, we made on for the last hour or so of our trip that day, while I quietly contemplated writing a book called *Evil Death Killer*.

The petrol was a higher quality there; my fuel economy had returned to pretty much normal again, and Marcin was having none of the running problems he had outside of Bulgaria, where his bike was threatening to give up and go home. They had a strange system where someone has to unlock the pump before it works, but invariably, there's never enough people working, so everyone stands around waiting to pay twenty percent more for a litre of fuel than England, and not be able to actually buy it.

We reached Ankara after duelling with several coach drivers who drove with their accelerator buried in the carpet in practically all conditions, as well as several myopic ones who shouldn't be allowed to walk on their own, let alone take control of a vehicle. To say the driving mentality there was a little bit unsophisticated is a bit like saying Marcin smells a little bit when he farts.

Our GPS took us to the heart of the town. Anatomically, it put me in mind less of a heart and more of an organ lower down in the human body where things are disposed of. This was meant to be the capital city, but it struck us as run down, battered, and decaying as we rode around it. There was no style there, it just seemed to be barely functional, and nothing was barely functioning quite right.

It left us both with the impression that it had been designed and maintained by a small, but gifted, dog. The people just apathetically shuffled about sneering at one another, and the buildings did well to remain standing if it rained. Some parts were little more than huts, others were, at the very best, only a pale imitation of Istanbul. How this was the capital of the country was something of a mystery to us after how impressive Istanbul had been. Granted, we were seeing a small part of it, but it was hard to imagine there was a shining enclave of unbridled beauty hiding away somewhere, shyly peering out from behind a crumbling curtain of dissolving grey concrete.

It was an ugly little town, with the style and facilities, noise, smell, and comfort of a two-stoke enduro motorcycle, but without the ability to ride over curbs. All this came as a surprise after the vibrant and lively city we had left behind. Where that would have been impressive anywhere in the world, Ankara would barely have been acceptable anywhere in the world. The place just didn't seem quite right, not quite right at all. Standards had dropped like a gigantic sink-hole had opened up and swallowed up the world.

We found a hotel at a price that we felt was right enough, but to say it was basic would be selling it short. It was cruder than a complaint letter written about an English teacher by a student who had to be forced to do his homework. We knew conditions ahead would be increasingly basic, but it came as a surprise that after a single day's ride from a city to the capitol city of a country it could plummet so rapidly.

I went inside to negotiate a price, while Marcin waited outside with the bikes. By now, I was the designated speaker, since I was pretty good at dealing with people, while Marcin just pissed everyone off. We hoisted them up on the curb illegally, hoping the police would leave us alone, and presuming they had better things to do, such as drink themselves into a stupor out of crushing depression.

I had a look around the place before agreeing on a price. The toilet was just a hole and didn't have any mechanism by which to remove leftover waste. I was confident Marcin would personally see that there would be plenty of that to remove, so the whole thing was a bit troubling. To get to the toilet itself was going to take some effort, as a large amount of junk was piled up between the door and the hole. The room itself was a box with crumbling walls and a single electrical socket that was nailed to a plank of wood and stuck to the wall. Other luxury facilities included most of a floor.

I got the price down to a reasonable level, even though I felt like they should be paying me to take this kind of risk. The previous night we'd stayed at a low-end hostel, but the standards it maintained put this place to shame, and it had been cheaper besides.

As I came out, I was greeted with the odd spectacle of Marcin sitting on his bike, quaffing free tea that was being served to him from a silver tray by some random passer-by who had taken a friendly interest in our bikes. Everything in Turkey comes with free tea apparently, including illegal parking.

We unpacked our gear, and I had to come up with a rota for charging our electronic devices, since the one socket really was the only one available in the room. We then wandered out for something to eat, but that was frustrated by the complete lack of anything being open. By 8PM, everything had closed up for the night; the shop-fronts were bathed in darkness, and the doors were boarded up to keep the outside world on the outside. It was like the place was experiencing a zombie apocalypse.

We walked several miles in the vague hope of stumbling across a pocket of civilisation, chatting about our relative experiences, still really getting to know one another. We talked of Marcin's experiences in Australia, mine in Europe, and argued about whose bike was best, although we both knew that his was a disaster waiting to happen. I suspected we wouldn't have to wait long.

Eventually, we came across a kebab-shop that didn't have any kebabs. They were happy enough to make us something to eat, so long as having a crowd of locals pointing and laughing didn't bother us. It didn't. Beer was hard to come by with such a strong Muslim influence in effect, so we settled for some bottles of purple liquid that we were told was fermented beetroot and carrot. It sounded disgusting, so I ordered two. After all, you have to try everything.

It was by far the most vile thing that had ever been on the inside of my skin. It was quite literally like drinking bile out of a tramp's shoe. We challenged one another to see who could drink the most without vomiting, and Marcin beat me by a small degree, but neither of us managed to finish a glass.

Luckily, the food was OK, even though it was just a very expensive cheese sandwich, served with a side-order of being pointed at by men with spectacularly huge eyebrows.

13

The Descent

Date—October 29th
Location—Ankara, Turkey
Status—Managing our expectations

Ankara proved to be such a monumental disappointment after Istanbul that we just didn't feel any particular need to stay in the country any longer that we absolutely had to. The room in which we were staying was grim—to this day, one of the grimmest things I've ever seen, up to and including Marcin's underpants. Waking up in it was a depressing experience and only spurred us on to the road, which was really where we truly belonged in any case.

That or prison.

I was dialled into the journey now—we both were, and each morning was a small adventure in itself, filled with optimism and excitement about what the road would throw at us. The places we saw were merely fleeting snapshots, places to experience briefly as we passed through on our way forwards. It was the road now that called us; the ride itself was the point, the twisting stretch of grey tarmac which held the unknown up ahead. Ankara was a city that would soon be left behind, and with no regret about it.

We packed up without the slightest glimmer of hesitation and happily rode away to find out what the rest of the country had in store for us. We felt like we'd seen the two sides of Turkey now; the affluent European part and the run down side with the strong Islamic influence. We were ready to leave it behind us, since Iran was ahead of us and was one of the jewels in the crown of our trip.

We avoided doing any research, as we wanted Iran to be largely an unknown; we wanted to experience it with an open mind, without the influence or the opinions of others. We were excited about what lay ahead, and as we threw our legs over our cold motorcycles, and with the weight of our gear dragging us down, our enthusiasm dragged us onwards.

Unfortunately, there were seventeen hours (according to the Google-machine) of roads to negotiate between us and Iran, and Google is notoriously untrustworthy on such matters. Marcin wanted to press on to a completely unrealistic degree, but I was more tempered with realism, since I used my brain as more than just a compost bag for the hair on my head to grow out of. So I came up with a more realistic target for the day and called him something insulting, to which he laughed like he thought I didn't mean it.

Erzincan was pretty far at 450 miles and a projected travel time of ten hours but seemed a good size, a place where we would undoubtedly find a place to sleep and a hot meal. What Google failed to mention was that the temperatures were going to hit zero degrees and that the wind would blast us off the road. It also failed to mention the roadworks, crazy Turkish drivers, and the fact that we had to climb 2,000 metres above sea level into the mountains, where the ice would cling to the roads like whatever came out of Marcin did to toilets. Even the water in our eyes was going to freeze. As a rider who has commuted in London, this was neither a new experience, nor one that I was looking forward to.

Many times, in the depths of winter, I had ridden in such conditions. Snow is not a firm favourite of any motorcyclist, but for those of us who wear glasses, we often have to open the visor to avoid fogging up and going blind. That means that very often my eyeballs have set frozen in my sockets with the little coloured brown bit on the front getting locked by ice-crystals in a fixed position. That is usually fine, until you stop and try to move them or focus on something other than the road. Then a searing hot stab of pain reminds you that you're making terrible choices in life.

So we set off from the hotel. To call it a hotel was to apply an unreasonably grandiose title to it. We had tents and sleeping bags with us, and in fact, we'd slept in our bags the night before to avoid being eaten by rats. We had hoped to camp along the way, but guesthouses outside of Europe were so cheap and the weather was so cold that, for now, the thought of it hadn't been taken very seriously. We were pushing ourselves hard in terms of hours spent on the bikes. Anyone who hasn't travelled by motorcycle might not realise what a punishing and physical experience it actually is, especially on a small single, and even more especially, doing it with Marcin. After a day of fighting the elements, a warm shower, a quiet room, and a place to eat were like a beacon of promise and sometimes all that kept our mental wheels turning.

The previous night we had gone out to dinner and struggled to find anywhere open after 8PM. We ended up walking several miles into a region of town where life looked to be worth less than a carton of cigarettes. We managed to find a place that was open, but they wanted us to eat what looked like washing-up water with bleached chicken parts floating in it. The second place was more promising, as there were people still alive in it. I got them to understand that I was a vegetarian and that Marcin would eat anything that had been killed, the more brutally the better.

We were stared at, laughed at, and the mood was generally sombre. We felt clearly unwelcome. Not that this particularly bothered us, or even made us keep our voices down. Marcin really enjoyed it when people didn't like him, and went around taking pictures of the scowling faces of people glaring at us disapprovingly. I just smiled and thought about how I was coming to really like that guy, despite the smell and pretty much everything else about him.

As we rode out, the place left us feeling a strong sense of disappointment. We'd done very little research, as we were looking for the road to reveal itself to us without the spectre of preconceptions to colour our experience, but after the bustling Istanbul, it was hard to believe that Ankara was the capital, with it being so run-down and grim.

All that just made it easier to leave, and we made our way out of the city and onto the road ahead. Marcin did his usual trick of trying to get me killed in his excitement at the prospect of taking pictures as we struggled to find something worth taking pictures of. He would swerve across the road, braking wildly to pull over, without a hint of warning, forcing me to lock up the brakes or slam into him.

The town looked even worse in daylight. Interestingly, we passed the military headquarters building in the centre of town, where young soldiers were playfully pointing Heckler and Koch HK33 rifles at one another, like young children with sticks. The building was painted bright pink! I guess you should never pick on the Turkish army—these boys clearly aren't afraid of anything.

It was a bit of a relief to be back on the road, as I knew we had a pig of a journey ahead of us, and I was stealing myself to deal with it. You never know what lies before you, but you come to have a good idea what to expect. The surrounding towns quickly thinned out, and we ended up on a single carriageway. It was the first clue of what we were going to see, and the road was actually very decent and respectful of our battered arse-muscles. It had a slightly odd texture, like toffee with gravel in it, but it stuck to the tires like glue, and for the most part, and was a pleasure to ride on, leaving us feeling very sure-footed in corners.

Within twenty minutes, a Turk tried to kill me. It wasn't personal or even that he didn't see me so much as that the thought that he should look seemed to not even occur to him. He swung in a bus from the outside lane, right through the traffic and into me, forcing me to actually swerve off the road. I saw him and accelerated onto the gravel path and through the bus queue, literally forcing the crowd to scatter as I aimed for the largest gap between people, pulled my brakes, and waited to collide with something firmer than my own bones. Marcin came back and asked where he hit me; I guess in his mirror it had looked even closer than I thought it was, and I thought it was very close indeed.

No harm was done, and I promise that I will never mention Turkish driving again. If I did, I would fill too many pages with this depressing nonsense. I'll talk about other depressing nonsense from here on instead. Promise.

Nobody in the crowd seemed to actually notice what had happened. The crowd went back into position like a liquid settling after a rock was thrown into a puddle. The bus-driver continued to be oblivious that he had come close to causing my death and had forced me to swerve into a crowd of pedestrians. It was all quite routine to them.

From there we made time into the freezing cold, ignoring the challenges, and facing the future with optimism, and a degree of resolve I usually reserved for dealing with customers back when I had worked as a pawnbroker.

Nothing is truly depressing after being a pawnbroker, even Bulgaria.

The sky was a fixed canopy of grey, and if sunlight glinted through, it was a very temporary thing that bore no warmth onto us. The temperature reached about seven degrees, and it felt like we were freezing. We had no heat in the hotel the previous night; everything was broken, so our gear was still cold before we had even started. The chill of my own clothes was pressing on my skin, making my muscles heavy and my reactions slow. We stopped briefly at a traffic light, and Marcin looked over as I was furiously rubbing my hands together in a desperately futile attempt to warm up.

"Heated grips, you no have?" he said, pointing to his own bars with a vicious grin on his smug lips.

I grumbled that I had testicles instead and suggested that the size of his bike might be making up for other shortcomings. He grinned even harder. Insults don't work on Marcin. I've never worked out what does, or if anything does.

We didn't get far before my tank ran low, so we had to make our first stop for fuel. We'd actually covered around eighty miles by then, but the freezing morning conditions had got to us both. We filled up, and I was irritated by how few miles I'd done on a tank, until it turned out my auxiliary tank was still full, and somehow the cold had stopped the fuel from feeding. This was hardly surprising, as the cold was having a similar effect on me.

We had some soup to warm us through. I couldn't say what was in it—maybe some carrot and potato, but there was a hint of coriander and mint. It was really quite good, and it warmed us through well enough that the shivering subsided temporarily. It's still not a food, though, and should have been served in a mug. Soup is not a food.

Like everywhere else, we enjoyed instant celebrity status because we were bikers, foreign, and cold. Everyone asked us where we were from or what we were doing. One guy wanted to know if Marcin's bike was a Kawasaki and if my GPS was a television. Marcin frowned grimly and began muttering the word *Kawasaki* like his parentage had been questioned in the most insulting way imaginable. I just laughed at the prospect of catching up on some movies while riding along and tried to explain it was a very sophisticated and expensive navigation tool that didn't actually work.

Perhaps this explained a few things? In any case, aside from the out-of-control vehicles, they were friendly and engaging, and the darkness of Ankara was forgotten. The road had again recovered much of its appeal, even though we were dying of exposure, and me more so than Marcin.

So we headed off, resolved to ride until my tank went dry again, which was about 125 miles we guessed, more than enough before we could take another break. The scenery switched from the outer city to a craggy, foreboding mass of rocks and mountains and terrain that looked awesomely uninviting. The scenery smoothed out at times, and then suddenly, we'd go round a corner and be surrounded by rocks, hills, or rocks and hills, occasionally hills and rocks, hilly rocks, and rocky hills. Although there were green coverings to the landscape, there was no doubt we were in a desert region, and humans were not entirely welcome there.

It stayed cold, but to the freezing temperatures were later added high winds. They were not too bad at first, enough to slow us down slightly, or enough to slow *me* down slightly anyway. The portly KTM weathered it easily, while my little single wobbled like a drunk at a funeral.

Along the way, we saw our first tumble-weed and our first man riding a donkey. Things like that really bring home the fact that we were moving towards the desert and into the Middle East. Things were changing, and they were changing fast. People and faces were looking different, and people were behaving in ways we hadn't seen before.

This was the reason I was doing it—we were out of Europe now, out of our world, and heading into a place we had no experience of. Riding a motorcycle means you're travelling quickly while seeing everything. Even at lower speeds, we were overtaking weather fronts, passing through and onwards past communities, and the world was passing along as we were passing through it. It was something special to see, and the cold, the wind, the rutted surface, and Marcin's appalling personal hygiene couldn't quell our love of it.

A hearty breakfast perked me up, but after about an hour I was feeling tired again. The cold was eating into me, my muscles were numb, my fingertips were burning hot with pain, and my face was on fire from the constant blast of the wind howling through my helmet. I had a growing sense of fatigue. My chest was burning with every breath as freezing air was drawn into my weakened lungs. It passed soon enough, but it was a worry for a while that perhaps my health was falling prey to something lurking with hostile intent, some nasty bug infesting my body with its sinister touch.

Eventually, my tank ran dry, and we pulled in for some more fuel, thanking the gods of motorcycling for the brief respite. We had made around 130 miles that time, and although we were behind the schedule I had set myself, it was time to eat, and we both welcomed the break. Even Marcin was ready for some of the free tea everyone offers, and something to eat besides. There was a restaurant next to the petrol station, so it seemed a good place to stop and refuel not just our machines but ourselves besides. As usual, we attracted a crowd. People came out of nowhere, and prodded and poked the bikes like they'd never seen such a thing before. In such a barren place, it wasn't outside the realm of possibility that they actually hadn't.

We paid the guy who clearly ran the place. He spoke boldly in Turkish and seemed irritated that we couldn't understand what he was saying, but the fact remained that we couldn't, and no amount of irritation was going to suddenly change that.

We found the restaurant closed but were offered free tea, which for once, was pretty lousy, but it was hot, so I welcomed it for that. They seemed apologetic that they couldn't feed us but could manage to make us bread with cheese and sausage in the petrol station kiosk. We were past caring what we ate at that point; a break from our bikes was all we really wanted, so we agreed politely to their offer of hospitality. The local produce was actually delicious, warm home-made bread and cheese that packed a ferocious bite. They brought us more tea and treated us like we were something far more special than we really were. The owner's son seemed very excited, like we were the most exciting thing to pass through there for quite some time, which to be fair, we probably were.

Marcin didn't eat all the sausage, so the boy was allowed to have it, which made him even more excited at his odd visitors. In a town with four or five agricultural supply stores and a petrol station there couldn't be much money for luxuries. I paid for lunch and was charged the equivalent of a few pounds. We paid for the kid to have some sweets and left to a fanfare like we were old friends of the family. Even with no language to share our thoughts, connections between humans are easy to forge. A smile is all you really need for most occasions, which is ideal if it's all of you've got, and my language skills don't extend much beyond that.

So we rode on again until my tank drained down. Now that it was only going to run for around 120 miles with no reserve tank giving me any extra, it was ideal for a quick break and to warm up. We powered on as best we could, but the day was dragging on by then, and we were increasingly tired and in need of a rest.

The conditions were making it harder as the seconds ticked by on the clock and the tarmac beneath us was stretching on infinitely into the distance. The scenery was impressive, but I had been impressed four hours ago, and now thoughts of beer, a shower, and hot food were nudging all other concerns right out of my brain. Worse yet, we'd only made it to the halfway point and were already cold and tired. When we'd hit around 130 miles, we stopped again to fill up. That time, my tank had drained, so I could have made it a lot further. The cold seemed to have an effect on the tank and the ability of the drain hole to feed fuel.

I remembered reading somewhere that a thin layer of Vaseline and a really tight seal were crucial to feeding petrol the way I was doing. It had never occurred to me that the temperature might have some effect on it, the way it seemed to be doing, so once it worked, I had stopped tweaking it.

In any case, we were cold, and Marcin suggested tea. There was none at the petrol station, so we went to the restaurant that was attached to it. They had no coffee, and I was devastated. Needing a perk, I looked for something with sugar in it and got us some things that looked like honey-combs. It turned out that was exactly what they were. They were very good and gave me a little wake-up jolt of energy, making me ready for the next leg. Marcin poked at his suspiciously and glared at me like I was trying to poison him. Had we found something he wouldn't eat?

The place was a simple construction, like an old English motorway café—plain plaster walls, bare alloy window frames, and white counters. The windows offered a teasing glimpse of a mountain range with snow tipped mountains off in the distance and grey, threatening skies beyond.

We still had about 110 miles left to cover by that point and were told it would take us at least a few more long, arduous hours. We'd liked to have believed we could move faster than that, but we both knew that even that was going to be a challenge. The truth was, we'd both had enough for one day; we would have stopped there and slept on the floor if we could have, but we'd made a promise to ourselves—an arrangement—and neither of us wanted to be the one to suggest letting the other down.

We headed off, and it had dropped to eight degrees, and the sun was beginning to set. We were both shaking visibly while we got on our bikes, so we knew it was going to be a hard last slog into town.

Night came in fast in the mountains, and the cold ate us alive. By then, the wind had decided it wanted to be more than just a nuisance. The blasts were more of a constant push, forcing me off towards the edge of the road, so that I was having to fight for control. Even Marcin was being pushed, and neither of us could quite hold a straight line. It was even worse when a truck passed us in the opposite direction—the shock-wave hit me and sent my little bike reeling, and Marcin's often did the same. The darkness was beginning to encroach on the mountains, but the scenery didn't relent. All the while, the conditions showed no signs of taking any pity on us. It was Turkey's revenge on us for not liking Ankara.

By then we were at 2,200 metres altitude, and the sunset was casting a red glow in the cloud cover that clung to the tips of the massive, rugged peaks all around us. The temperature was showing at a dubious six degrees and dropping rapidly, but it felt colder than that. With no choice, we just went as quickly as we could, covering the miles as fast as we were able. It just wasn't fast enough, though, and didn't seem particularly fast at all. Seconds were precious when the cold was deadening both our senses and reactions. The road ahead offered challenges that would be tough on a good day, and we were past the end of a good day and riding into the oncoming bad night.

The roads themselves were actually amazing. They snaked through the peaks as they led us on a powered descent through winding paths, on a surface that clung to our tires like an alcoholic to a bottle of meths.

Although it hardly felt so at the time, it was funny how the best roads in Turkey could turn into the worst with the absence of light and the further absence of warmth. It was the kind of funny where nobody was actually laughing, much like the experience of watching an American sitcom.

We turned a corner, and instantly the light was gone. One minute it was dusk with a warm orange glow behind our heads and a setting sun blinding us in our mirrors, and then instantly it was darkness as a peak cut us off from the last lingering shreds of light. That was the last we saw of the sun as we began down the mountain-pass towards town, with over an hour still left to ride.

We cut a dangerous pace, but it was a calculated risk, as the dangers of staying out in the dropping temperature were definite, whereas the risks of the velocity were acceptable to two experienced riders who desperately needed some beer.

The time dragged on and on as we cut through the blackened night. We virtually had the roads to ourselves; they were occupied by only a few scattered lorries and idiots in people-carriers, risking their lives to go just a little faster than we were, cutting past us with engines revved beyond their limits.

When we finally saw the lights of a town it was a relief, and the biggest one of our journey so far. We headed directly to the centre and set the sat-nav to lead us to a hotel, any hotel. We had a further eight-tenths of a mile to go, and directly forwards. The town was strikingly modern, clean, and immaculately tidy, in shocking contrast to the disaster that was Ankara. It looked oddly out of place dropped, as it was, in the middle of a rugged desert.

We arrived at the hotel, and sadly, it was full . . . except for one last room that was 100 Turkish Lira a night. I discussed it with Marcin, whose turn it was to pay, and he spotted another one that he hoped might be cheaper. I tried there. They had only one room left as well, but it was only forty Lira, and went the further step of having somewhere we could safely park our bikes, which turned out to be the hotel lobby. I was sold, and his wallet was over-joyed. We turned ourselves around at the roundabout and headed back across the road to our destination.

We unpacked and settled in very quickly. It had been an exhausting day, and my modest estimates of how much land we could cover had forced us quite far outside of what was comfortable. I thought about all this while I showered and let the warm water sooth some of the freezing cold and tension from my weary muscles.

Pretty quickly, we decided it was time to go out for some food. We paced up and down a short while, idly looking out for a place to eat, when I noticed something a little odd. It didn't quite register at first, it began as a nagging sense that something wasn't right and grew to be a more pointed realisation.

There were no women! There were none anywhere, nowhere to be seen. There was not a single woman on the streets anywhere in town. After eating some very decent food, which was a bit cheaper than the night before, we went and bought some beer. Still, there were no women to be found anywhere—not walking on the street, working in shops, buying tampons or perfume, campaigning for equal rights, or heading out to book-clubs to discuss gender-bias in literature. None. It was very weird and slightly disconcerting. Marcin didn't notice, because it wasn't related to anything he could legally eat, but when I pointed it out to him, he began looking around, and he grumbled grudgingly that I was right.

We had only one more day of riding before we made it to the Iranian border. That would be our first country under Sharia law; a country ruled by a religion that held things we held sacred in contempt. Women being treated as equals and alcohol being served in abundance would be gone once we set foot on the other side of that border, and the influence was showing with every mile we rode. Things were changing fast, and we both knew it—even Marcin, who generally knew nothing and was proud of it.

14

Values

Date—October 30th
Location—Erzican, Turkey
Status—Worn out/tired/knackered/used up/fatigued

We experienced another amazing day on the road, but this time, the amazing thing is that we survived it. By the evening, we were officially in a war zone, and the place looked every inch of it. We stopped off in a little town called Doğubeyazıt, which probably translates to "the toilet of Turkey." If the country got an enema, this was where they'd stick the hose.

We checked into a highly questionable hotel in this highly questionable town, and all the lights in the town went out completely while we were doing it. Then the generator kicked in, and the place was bathed in sickly yellow light. That was the moment that the protests started. Cars drove up and down the main street honking horns and flashing lights, rocks were thrown, gunshots were heard in the distance. We were warned in the restaurant that there were political problems, and they might be closing the town tomorrow. So that was all the perfect end to what had been a perfect day.

It all started in Erzican, where we'd finished up the night before, cold and fatigued. Erzican was a very nice little town, modern and friendly; people couldn't do enough to help us out. As it turned out, we got a hotel for forty Turkish lira, that equates in real money to less than £20, and it came with breakfast. Breakfast was also very respectable, a nice spread of things to choose from, or there would have been if Marcin hadn't got there first.

Rule of the road number 3—If sharing a buffet with Marcin, make very sure you get there first.

I went to the local shop and was relieved to see two women working there, so this probably wasn't some science fiction town where the women had been replaced with robots who had to be recharged at night. But you can never tell about these things! My relief was tempered by disappointment, as I often felt that this story needed more robots, especially since there were no vampires and we hadn't actually seen any proper zombies either.

I bought some bread and some toilet roll, or as we had now come to refer to it, Turkish survival kit. I was short of some cash, so was told to drop it by later. I shamefully admit that I forgot and now owe a guy four Turkich Lira, which is especially bad, since he was only trying to do me a favour. I only realised many miles down the road.

We dragged the bikes out of the hotel; well, I walked mine out—Marcin had to heave the mighty bulk of the KTM out with some fair degree of difficulty while I laughed, mocked him, and threw toilet rolls. We enjoyed instant celebrity status—adults stood watching our every move, children came and stood in awe to gaze in amazement as I performed the seemingly impossible tasks of checking my oil level and lubricating my chain. Even more exciting, Marcin put a new screw in his handlebars, and this was met with rapturous applause.

All this seemed beyond fascinating to our audience. I chased the kids with a camera, and in the end got them to sit on the bike for pictures, which they were itching nervously to do. They chased us down the street waving as we made our way out of town. I was wearing the same gear as I had been yesterday, and I was worried that I might be massively over-dressed, as the temperature was reading twenty-two degrees, and I was beginning to sweat inside my expensive winter-ish clothing, which was actually just multiple layers of cheap summer-ish clothing.

Warmer weather would have certainly been a welcome change, especially to those of us who didn't have heated grips, a large squared-off fairing, and Marcin's inability to be bothered by such trivial things as reality.

As we made it out of town cars pulled up next to us, the drivers waving and wearing pink shirts for some unknown reason. In Turkey, the Fiat Tofas is the weapon of choice for the ambitious boy-racer. I'd seen them before in other countries, but they had not been called that, or at least not that I'd noticed. In any case, it seemed to be a car built to make other cars look good. It was a poorly-designed box with a wheel in each corner and the headlights arranged around a gaping square grill that gave them a sad expression.

But in Erzican they suffered the indignity of being modified in every way imaginable, unless you can imagine a way which actually employs any degree of good taste. Most commonly it was seen lowered to the ground and sporting massive chrome wheels, which battered the standard wheel-arches until the lips were a wrinkled mess of twisted metal. They are also decorated with all manner of things hanging from the mirrors. Also, they're generally brown and try to race you from the lights, somewhat hopelessly. We saw many, many of those that day, and not one beat two heavily loaded bikes on a fun ride through Turkey, and we never once tried to beat them.

The horse-play, however, was clearly well-meaning, and the modified cars were just a sign of bored young men wanting to show off. The cars, I supposed, must have been manufactured locally and probably used some older design to keep costs manageable. Personally, I love modifications and think they're often a sign of creativity and individuality. Just as often they're a sign of horrible taste.

I have been to Italy.

As we made our way out of town, it became quickly apparent that I was not over-dressed but was, in fact, probably not wearing enough clothes. The temperature dropped to thirteen degrees in a few minutes and kept sinking, curiously the opposite of the rest of our ride, where the morning set the lower end of the tone. Thirteen degrees, to us, felt very comfortable after what we had grown accustomed to, and we carried on with unreasonable optimism that we found from some unknown place deep within us. The roads had moments of spectacular, awe-inspiring scenic impact, interspersed with hours of staring at rocks that had none of that whatsoever.

Along the sides of the road I noticed a good many people selling fruit and vegetables on the verges from ramshackle wooden frames with makeshift plastic covers.

The first we saw was a tired-looking old man, broken into a folding chair in worse shape than the twisted timbers of his ageing shack. He was quietly smoking his life away, watching us pass without interest, his eyes were dead to a world that had long since passed him by, taking his hopes and dreams right along with it.

Soon after, we passed a man in a suit jacket and mismatched trousers, fat and balding, his white hair trying to cover his thinning scalp but actually just drawing attention to his age and the fact that he was dealing badly with it.

Next, we passed a young man who was maybe in his mid-teens. He watched us keenly, his eyes fixated on the unusual spectacle of two motorcycles passing along the battered road in front of his produce stand. All of these people were the same, just separated by the illusion of time. One would invariably become the other. The young man full of hopes, still fascinated by the world; the man who has learnt who he is and where he fits in, his dreams put to the side so he can usher in the next generation to the life he knows; and then the old man, broken by the passing of time, in a role he now knows served nobody less than it served him.

There I was, riding through Turkey on my way to the Middle East. I was in an incredibly fortunate position, and I knew it; and never did I know it more keenly that at that moment. Even among my friends and family, who live in an affluent country, I was privileged to have this opportunity to ride my dreams, but amongst people with nothing, the realisation of how lucky some of us truly are was incredibly pointed.

This is the failing of the system we live in, and the system we have allowed to take over our lives. The need to consume has turned the world into a resource. If there's no incentive to profit from a thing, then the thing is deemed to have no value. There, in Turkey, education was not guaranteed, and people worked because they had absolutely no choice. There's no money in helping them to find their potential.

How many scientists have we lost because they were born in impoverished nations? How many artists? Has the next Nicola Tesla died after a lifetime of selling giant cabbages by the side of a road, instead of moving the entire human race forward in its understanding of the universe? How much talent is wasted because there's no profit in harvesting it? Every day, we're losing the human quality that might manifest as the next artist to create a world-changing perspective; the cure for cancer could be lost, because someone with the ability to find it is wasting their life in a tin hut. Perhaps the creator of a system that leads mankind out of the shackles of wage dependence under the greed of the politicians and bankers is somewhere rotting away at the side of the road.

In any case, those people seemed hopeless. They just sat there, knowing their aspirations will go unmatched by their actions or their experiences. Nobody was out there helping them achieve their potential, because to do so would serve nobody that controlled the flow of money. We need to start growing up as a species and see that things that don't necessarily profit us personally can still be worth doing if they profit us all. This will never happen while money is the blood of our society, pumping around a bloated, decaying body, with a hopelessly unused brain.

Everything in our world is based on the idea of consumption and growth, perpetual growth in a finite world and consumption of things that aren't infinitely regenerated. It's short-sighted, but most people never think about it. We're not taught to think about it in schools, and most of us are happy to just let other people do our thinking for us.

But that all means that everything has to be profitable, and profitability means getting the most and spending the least. Overheads must be cut, while charging the most for whatever it is that you're selling. Consequently, quality suffers.

I was careful not to fall into that trap when I chose my bike for this trip. Of course, it's a consumer product, so there's no point in my claiming I have a totally elevated point of view, but I chose a way to limit my entry into the abyss of humanity-swallowing consumerism. I was using a BMW G650x that I bought second-hand. This bike was a rare breed in the motor industry, because it wasn't built just to make a profit. Most bikes, along with essentially everything else, are designed to be built as cheaply as possible, create the maximum amount of desire in the consumers, and then be sold for as much as they can get. The X-range was built with a slightly different end-result, that being to give BMW something to race in enduro competitions that year, including the Dakar rally. It was based on their previous Rotax 650cc singles with uprated engines and better electronics, but it came with a high price and people didn't want it when it arrived in the showrooms.

Now, they can be found relatively cheaply on the second hand market, which was where I found mine. The manufacturer earned nothing from me, I bought the bike for around thirty percent of the new price, and it had been built to a higher standard than you'd normally expect. In fact, if things were built to accommodate needs, instead of to accommodate the incentive for profit, then this is what bikes would generally be like. BMW certainly cut some corners, but I stuck those corners back on, and now the bike was just as good as it can be, within the considerations of the value and resources available, which is precisely how everything could be built if that was what we actually wanted.

Young men at the side of the road have no value and are not considered a useful resource, and we need to change that. People's lives are the only thing of value, and the hopeless, endless waste of the most precious, and in the end, the only real thing of value on the planet has to be addressed. It only can be if we see how useless money really is as a way to measure someone's worth.

That is what happens when people like me have too much time to think.

The roads carried on endlessly, just growing colder and colder and colder. We stopped for fuel, first in a place that worryingly, didn't give us any free tea. It gave us a chance to get some nice pictures, something we'd not taken particularly seriously on this leg of the trip. In fact, on that day we stopped a few times. We were on a looser schedule than usual and had a bit more time to make our daily target, so we had a chance to play around a little bit. I'm glad we did—there was just too much we would have missed otherwise. We stopped off the road on a wide gravel beach along the side of a fast-moving stream. Off in the distance the horizon was dominated by an imposing mountain with a mine burrowing into the face of it. Green hills rolled up the sides up to the freezing pinnacle where it was too cold even for grass to grow.

Eventually, we made it to the next big city, but the sat-nav took us at least ten miles out of our way. There was nothing there, in any case, we wanted to see. In fact, there wasn't much of anything. We stopped for a quick drink in a truck stop, but then we realised we had no domestic money. Luckily, they accepted whatever we had, and we paid them with a Euro coin, and they seemed more than happy.

After that, we plodded on into snow-capped mountains reaching to a recorded height of 2,400 metres. We probably made it higher, but I had other things on my mind at the time. The temperature dropped to four degrees, and we stopped at some roadside things to snap some pics and warm up for a bit. The landmark object that we'd stopped to look at turned out to be a shaped mountain of farmyard poop.

As we were suiting up to leave, another pair of bikers passed the other way on BMW singles. They stopped, and we met up for a chat. They were a German couple, Mark and Esther, who had to sort out paperwork to enter Iran, so we chatted very briefly about what we each might find up ahead. They told us it was cold where we were going, and we told them the same thing. There was another English couple a day ahead, so we planned to try to find them tomorrow, if our border crossing went as well as we hoped it would.

We carried on to the next petrol station, and my bike managed 170 miles before reserve—not too bad and a sign that the dodgy Hungarian fuel was now completely out of her system. It was still not quite her normal form, though, but I could easily put that down to keeping up with Marcin on his mad quest to go very slightly faster. So far our bikes were doing well, and it was a tough job we were asking of them. The roads toward the end of Turkey ranged from very good to hardly being roads at all. We were shaking and pushing them pretty hard, but they seemed to take it well enough.

I spotted a slight leak from the side of the engine—the breather tube had coughed out a lump of dirt and oil. Marcin looked horrified and asked how much longer I'd be able to ride in that condition. I checked the oil—it was still full and was a clear yellow colour, so I told him she'd make it all the way, so long as I kept an eye on things, in case this was a warning that something else wasn't right.

After our final fuel stop, the weather got darker. Night doesn't fall there as much as collapse on top of you in an instant with a crushing sense of doom. We had only forty-five minutes ride left ahead of us, but the darkness hit us like a blanket of ice had dropped on top of us, biting into our senses and burning our fingers and joints. We went on as best we could. Marcin seemed happy to just ride flat out, but I slowed down a bit, as the road conditions were increasingly poor, and in the dark I could barely see in front of me, even with my uprated headlights.

When we finally made it into the town, we went around looking for the hotel we'd heard about. We found one, which might have been it, and got a room for fifty Turkish lira, which we thought was a respectable price, until we saw the room. It had the odd fragrance of a broken toilet, even before Marcin started on it.

There were no roads, just brickwork laid unevenly over bare sand. The people stared at us like we were aliens, and this time, not in a friendly way. The bikes had also attracted a great deal of attention, which didn't seem welcome at all.

We found some food but got ripped off. That was the first time it had happened in Turkey, and we felt let down. We asked for a kebab, some salad, and some beans. We got served half the restaurant and charged 110 lira, way above the normal price in any other part of the country. We took it on the chin with good grace and made light of it, leaving without the smiles leaving our faces. Then Karma struck, and they only charged me eleven lira. I queried the price, but the young man serving hurriedly assured me all was well, grinning at me like a man knowing he'd be putting my money in his pocket. Well, if he thought it was right, I was happy, and we paid the tiny sum and left without a fuss.

The news was reporting terrorist attacks up and down the border, and that wasn't remotely hard to believe. There was a palpable tension there, an ugly atmosphere of a people ill at ease.

I'm glad we'd taken this route. We'd challenged ourselves to keep going through the cold, and we'd seen some amazing sights—things we'd never have seen anywhere else, as well as having some experiences we couldn't otherwise have had. We talked and agreed that we'd both enjoyed this leg of the trip and had a good time along the way, but we'd seen enough of Turkey. I was ready to leave and was keen to move on; we were both ready to go and see what the road ahead would bring us.

Iran was ahead; one of the key attractions of the journey. In fact, from now on, things would only get more interesting.

Turkey was not a place I wanted to stick around in. We had been there long enough to catch the vibe, and it hadn't always been a good one. This was clearly a country of clashes, not compromises. People, styles, religions, politics, and philosophies seemed to grind against one another, never settling, never quite meshing together. Istanbul was a Western place with Muslim influence, an essentially European city based on a totally different culture, and as you move on poverty clashes hard on the outskirts. Further on, the capital plunges to a lower standard, and you plunge harder as you press on.

People are usually friendly and want to meet you, but they are more interested in showing you how nice they are; there wasn't much genuine interaction to be had. Of course, this might have been the language barrier, but the interest seemed cursory, not genuine. As we had sat drinking beer, there had been no interest in us; we'd fired no conversations with them. In Istanbul we'd been a target for touts with something to sell, beyond that we were often a target of suspicious, angry glaring.

The driving was an example of how they often were, and they didn't drive with the intention of taking prisoners. They didn't seem to care if other people were hurt or killed; they put on blinkers when they take the wheel. There was no interest in the welfare of others or the outcomes of their own actions.

Never overtake a slow-moving Turkish driver. They behave like you have just stepped on their dick. They have to come back and overtake you twice as hard, which invariably means they have to push their clapped-out car far too hard and fall back later, hovering just behind you, armed with poor reactions and worse brakes. I'd rather have them in front where I can keep my eye on them any time.

Moving so quickly, we just got an impression of people and cultures based on the very few things we had seen. We saw the driving, we tasted the food, and we met people in highly social places like bars. Perhaps the easiest way to judge a people is the driving. The truth of a person is exposed by the way they act when they think nobody is there to judge them. In that respect, the country came off poorly. The food was okay, but wasn't at all what I'd expected. Having shared meals with a Turkish fiancée and her insane, racist, and totally self-obsessed family, I have to say I was impressed with the food. My expectations in that respect were high, apparently slightly too high.

The next morning we would face a border crossing, and nobody likes border crossings. I was keen to get out of Turkey but far more keen to enter Iran. In only eight days we had come this far, and I was excited to see what would happen during the next eight.

15

Never Believe the Touts

Date—October 31st
Location—Doğubeyazit, Turkey
Status—The Two Idiots are about to prove it

We woke up in the dingy little hotel where we stayed on the Turkish side of the Iranian border crossing. Waking up anywhere else would have been suspicious under the circumstances. I slept approximately no time at all, thanks to the continual noise of praying, crapping, farting, and clearing of throats. From the sound of the throat-clearing, I assumed they were doing it with a toilet brush or several excited rats tied to a plank of wood. For much of the night, the noise was like someone sexually bothering a cat and trying to mute the noise by shoving a rolled up newspaper down its throat. I hadn't seen any cats, which might provide additional evidence for or against this possibility, depending on how you think about it.

We thought we'd managed to arrange some breakfast, and against all the odds, we actually had. The downstairs lobby was filled with old men, all chatting and drinking the weak Turkish tea that everyone seemed helplessly addicted to. I've never been a huge fan of tea, in any case, but real coffee was just a distant memory now, and anything warm was pretty welcome.

There was no space for us, but we were invited to join a couple of men over by the door, which is what we did. Then we got some tea, eggs, olives, bread, and cheese. All very simple stuff in a big city, but I got the impression they had gone to a lot of trouble and were quite proud of themselves for it.

There was broken English, and I was told that the old man who ran the hotel was considered locally to be someone very important. Another older man joined us later on, a Kurd, he told us, but I couldn't make out his name. The other, who had spoken to us first, was a Turk, we were told. They joked about one another being trouble, but it was all very friendly. These men were grown up and were old enough to see the wisdom of getting along and the foolishness of not.

Not everybody in that town was, and there seemed to have been some real trouble the night before. We heard and saw some of it, but they didn't seem to like talking about it. People waved their hands and changed the subject when we asked.

Something happened outside while we were talking; there was shouting, and the old man went out in a hurry. I followed him with a camera and saw nothing but a market stand setting up, and maybe that was all there was to it. Certainly, when we asked, nobody wanted to talk to us.

A small child did something that I wasn't quick enough to catch, and so the old man threw him to the ground with notable ferocity. Then the kid spat back at him, laughing with an ugly, twisted grin on his face, his expression one of someone who had so much abuse that it meant nothing to him any longer.

It was a minor act of violence, but seeing it still managed to surprise me, but honestly, the child seemed like he deserved it. He was clearly looking to provoke the man into giving him the response he got.

That morning we didn't invite the children to chat and play on the bikes; we just packed and left as quickly as possible. I settled the bill and gave the old man a tip, barely £3, the price of rounding the bill up to the nearest note. He seemed embarrassed, probably because we had already paid three times what the room was worth, but we knew that already.

In the end, we were very lucky to come from a country with a strong currency, and all we had to thank them for their hospitality was a little cash. He took the tip, and we made sure they knew how much we appreciated what little they'd done for us. I felt that visitors were a rare thing, and they'd welcomed us with all the enthusiasm they could muster, mostly enthusiasm at the prospect of over-charging us, but enthusiasm, nonetheless.

Istanbul might be a beautiful city, but it was a place with its hand out, grasping for some of whatever you might have. The further you went the more you noticed a change. The Turks are warmer, more welcoming, and friendlier. There are parts with real poverty and places with hardships that are tough to describe, even after seeing it. Only someone living that life could really explain or really understand it, certainly not some idiots motorcycling through as fast as they could.

It seemed it was the European influence that had caused Istanbul to be what it was. The burning need to make you spend your money, the glowing lights, the flashy facade. It was all just too much lipstick on a pretty girl. When you moved further into Turkey, they were a simpler people who hadn't adapted well to any of that and the two extremes left the country feeling like two very different places. Simple the people may be, but they had mostly been approachable, welcoming, and warm.

Ankara had the big-city mentality and was disappointing after what we'd seen before. Marcin had read ahead, and yet what we found was more surprising to him than it was to me. But the smaller little towns we visited along the way had something you can't hold a price to. Maybe the people were harder, but the country was hard too, with icy winds and rugged stretches of rock where life struggled to take hold. What else could you expect?

We were told on the road that the upcoming town was a toilet. It was. It was a ramshackle, crumbling mess of a place, but the people partly made up for it. A town isn't made out of bricks but of the complex interpersonal relations of the people living in it. There were strong, proud family connections and a history that had a wealth of culture the people were proud of. It was a pleasure and a privilege to visit the place, and we left feeling it was a great part of our trip, even despite the constant rip-offs, mob violence, and sudden acts of child-abuse.

The GPS took us on a slightly different road out of town along the perimetre of a military complex. A van full of young soldiers blocked the lane, perhaps trying to force us to stop and not making a very good job of it. We went round them, and they laughed, not bothered at all that we had outsmarted them. Perhaps they were used to that. The camp, or base, or whatever it was, looked pretty unpleasant. It looked more like a concentration camp than anything else, and it was clearly armed to the teeth.

This shed a little more light on the troubles and the now obvious reason behind them. In that part of the town the tension was even more palpable. You could feel the antagonism in the air, the callous disregard and arrogance of the young troops, bloated with their sense of importance once a loaded gun had been handed to little men not yet ready to deal with such responsibility. They were pitched against unarmed civilians, who seemed set on doing nothing more than surviving in their home. It was an ugly place and a dark scene to be riding through.

The track led us out to the main road, where we joined a long, straight path to the Iran border. It was bleak, a place where nothing but the odd wanderer reside, and a few flocks of future-kebabs, blissfully unaware of their fate to wind up slowly rotating on a sharp pole while a fat man with a huge moustache would charge tourists too much to eat bits of them.

We met up with a row of lorries around the same time as a sign that said it was six miles to the border. They were stationary, and the drivers' doors were open. That told us that they had been waiting for some considerable time, and that didn't bode well for us. We skipped onto a supply lane, like bikers do, and just rode up it, filtering on past until we were told otherwise. We were stopped briefly at a military checkpoint, but just waved through on our way. They seemed to be wondering why we stopped more than why we were there.

Finally, we got to the border control area where, like the military base, no pictures were allowed. The Turkish border had been a modern and businesslike structure, but this was more run-down and quite basic; in fact, it was crude by comparison. We didn't know yet if that was a good thing or a bad one.

Passing out of Turkey was very straightforward. We accidentally picked up a pair of helpers, who set about making everything far more difficult than it actually was. They latched on and pretended to be officials but clearly weren't. The final clue was when we asked to see ID, and they just ran away. By then, of course, it was too late, but we didn't really know that yet.

They offered to swap money for us, but we told them we didn't have any and were just going to get some out later from the cash-machines like we always did. They offered us all sorts of stories about there being no cash-points in Iran. They told us we had to give them our Euros, and they'd give us the best price.

We'd read some details on the Internet—the number one piece of advice on every website was to ignore the helpers. We were told that they lie and lie and lie again; they'll say anything to get you to hand over your money to them. With that still firmly in mind, we ignored them and headed up to the Iran entry gate.

Passport control took just a few moments, and then we were invited in to have our books stamped. That was also pretty straightforward, friendly even, compared to the office in London where I'd applied for the visa. There was a big queue, but they opened another booth, just for us, and we went right to the front. I got the impression that we weren't treated as being special, we were just not commercial travellers, and the rest were the drivers of the loaded lorries outside. Their paperwork was therefore more difficult.

After that, we took our bikes through and into the country, amidst a sea of people offering to swap money for us and shouting in a very loud and hostile way that we were their new best friends. Everyone in Iran seemed to want to shake our hands that day, so much so that I was slightly concerned about early onset of arthritis.

On the day I got engaged to my Turkish ex-girlfriend I was suddenly allowed to meet the family and had to run the gauntlet of literally hundreds of unusually hairy hands shaking mine with a little too much enthusiasm. It had been a long day of wearing a fixed smile while people barked their names in my face while trying really hard to crush every bone in my hand. The Iranian border reminded me of that.

Carnets were similarly straightforward. Photocopies of our details were made, and we breezed through customs control with the minimum of fuss. The only slight issue was checking VIN numbers on the bike—mine was up by the headstock under the handlebars, but Marcin's was a bit tricky to find. Eventually it turned out to be under the seat, but Marcin had got to know his bike so poorly that even basic details managed to escape him.

When they found it, they didn't check it against the paperwork; they just said it was OK and turned to leave. We tried to ask about what else we needed and were told twenty Euros for each bike. We didn't have any but negotiated it down to the 25 UK pounds we did have. They gave us sheets with green stamps and figured we had sorted out our insurance, which we'd been told was a legal requirement. Looking back, that was incredibly naïve of us.

We moved on down a steep hill, along a lightly twisted dirt track to another office, where a guy asked us to pull in. We were taken to yet another office where papers were stamped, and the locals took pictures of themselves on our bikes. All seemed well; smiles were plastered on every face, not entirely genuine ones, but beggars can't be choosers, and we were happy to take what we could get.

The offices were run down, but the complex was large, at least as large as the border into Turkey, if nowhere near as nice, and at least ten times busier. We cleared customs, and the gate opened to let us into Iran. We were finally there.

My initial impression was that it was a total shit-hole.

It always amazes me that these border towns are so run down. It seems to me that they're the principal trade routes and the place that gives travellers the first glimpse of what their country has to offer. With that in mind, I always expect them to be better maintained, but the truth seems to be almost totally the opposite. It was like a modern retelling of a Wild West frontier town. Dogs were dead and rotting away on the sides of the streets, open sewers ran along the pavement, people crashed cars into one another, buildings were crumbling and old, dishevelled people staggered around in ragged clothes, begging for money, ideally in folding, paper form.

By no modern standard was this a good face to show the world of what Iran had to offer. People were also far from friendly, and those that were friendly were motivated by a quite robust degree of self-interest. It was a bleak start to the next leg of our journey and left us wondering what Iran was really going to be like.

A man who called himself a customs official found us and told us that we needed insurance. I argued that we'd paid it. This went on for some time, mostly with him grinning widely and laughing at me. Finally, I went back into the enclosure and found the missing pieces of stamped paper we had been given at the border. They turned out to be customs papers and nothing more—our money had vanished into someone's pocket. I explained that we'd paid, and the official just laughed, since corruption is clearly hilarious.

It's a strange thing and is very hard to accept as someone coming from Europe that the officials on the border are the first ones to try to steal from you, but it's something you get used to as you plunge headlong into the Middle East or the Third World, where it's actually far worse. Everyone is trying to steal from you all the time, sometimes boldly asking for a tip and at other times lying to your face about the hundreds of dollars you need to give them for a service they've completely made up.

So we bartered and got the insurance down to fifty Euros, which we didn't have. In fact, we didn't have any Euros whatsoever. We went off to a small cluster of general stores and tried getting money out at all the local ATMs. All of them rejected our cards, and we began to get alarmed that maybe the lying touts were actually telling the truth about that one, very important point.

It seemed pretty obvious, after half an hour of trying, that indeed they were.

The ATMs wouldn't give us money, and our cash-point cards were as useless as trying to reason with an Iranian official. So now we were in need of legal documents, fuel, food and hotels, and we had no cash or a way to gain access to any of it.

We only had single-entry visas, so if we left the country to go back into Turkey, we weren't going to be allowed back in. Even worse, our visas for Pakistan were time-sensitive, and if we missed our window, it would be almost impossible to get them extended or replaced. We had no choice but to move forwards.

Suddenly, I remembered the two travellers we'd met on the road in Turkey. They had problems on the border, although we hadn't had time to discuss what they were in any length. They had been forced to turn around and go back to the nearest Iranian embassy and apply for a second set of entry visas. That now made a horribly, ugly kind of sense, and it seemed we were now sinking right along with them in precisely the same boat.

Marcin wanted to leave and just ride off without insurance, but I had done enough research to know that we needed it if we wanted to get back out at the other end.

The seller, of course, wouldn't accept my card but grabbed my papers and headed off to his office, presumably to hold me there until I paid him some money. I took the documents back off him and collected both mine and Marcin's passports, papers, and carnet, and went outside, back into the compound, with the idea of trying to sort something out.

I failed.

In fact, nobody seemed to know what I was talking about when I mentioned the insurance, even though everyone spoke passable English. All I could get was directions to an office down the back of the same alcove between two buildings where the very same tout was lurking that I'd tried to deal with before.

I went back to see what options we had. Could we send money back after getting some later on in a bigger city? Could we do a bank-transfer? The man waved the insurance papers in my face and grinned at me, pushing the price up to now twice what we had been told it was meant to be.

The officials loved to take our documents and wander off with them, so this time I did the same—I took the insurance documents he was waving at me and headed off towards the bikes with the intention of working out a way to pay for them after discussing it with Marcin. The official, or probably not so official, followed me around, grumbling and looking confused. I pointed back to the bikes, where Marcin was waiting, and went off to see if he had anything constructive to add to all this.

When I got to him, Marcin was in possession of a $100 bill, for some reason. I asked him where he got it, and he said someone had given it to him, a passing stranger had simply handed it over out of sheer kindness.

I had dealt with foreign exchange professionally, so I had a quick look and decided immediately that it was a fake, and a very obvious one. It was printed on totally the wrong kind of paper, and it looked like a very primitive effort. I told him it wasn't real and had to remind him that people don't just come up and give you money, even if you were far, far prettier than he was. Well, perhaps they do, but you would have to be far, far, far prettier.

The official came out saying he now wanted fifty Euros. He caught sight of the dollar bill and began to froth at the mouth with excitement. He worked out a deal in his head so the money covered the insurance, even though the bill would have been worth far more than he offered. He grabbed the bill greedily without asking, and just handed us back the change before I could explain.

I told him firmly he couldn't have it, but he snatched it up and refused to listen, turning his back on me and beginning to walk away. This went on for several minutes as I tried to explain to him that he couldn't take it. After being ignored while trying to explain it was a fake for some time, I thought, "You know what, keep the bloody thing. You deserve it." I left him to find out in his own way what he'd done. We rode off with enough money to fill our tanks and then break down somewhere in the desert, some way outside of town.

For the first time, we knew we were in trouble. We'd been in trouble before, but for the first time, we actually knew it. We stopped to formulate a plan, as if thinking about things might make a difference to the fact that we were stuck in a potentially hostile social climate with no money and no means to acquire any. Several people offered to take our cards over the border, withdraw cash, and come back and give it to us. We had to decline for reasons so obvious I don't need to put them here.

Marcin just wanted to ride on and see what happened, while I wanted to organise something. There was a lake where we knew an English couple on bikes was staying, and we could make it there with the fuel we had. Better yet, the same German couple were following in a day or so, and the ride to the lake took us very close to another different border crossing. According to the maps, the lake was near a big tourist town, so we thought it was worth a try to head there. We followed the main road, and then things got worse . . . as usual.

The main road dissolved into a town, the town dissolved into mud, and the mud dissolved into an enduro track. Clearly, the maps weren't entirely correct. Marcin powered on angrily like the terrain was his enemy, and I barely kept up, even though my bike was weighing only half as much. We stopped and reconsidered our options, as if we actually had any.

There was another, bigger town along the main road, Tabriz, where there was a good, or at least better, chance of getting some cash. I preferred the other choice. We had enough fuel to cross back into Turkey, if necessary, and apply for new visas to get back on our way, but it would hold us up for a few days if we chose to do that.

In the end, the missing road only gave us one option and that was to drive forwards. We carried on reluctantly. My fuel system had not been reliable, maybe due to the temperature, so my fingers were crossed that we'd have some luck in at least one area. There was a slight pinking noise, but we plodded at only fifty mph to wring the best range out of the big KTM Marcin was riding, and we dragged our sorry selves into Tabriz.

The roads darkened quickly, as expected, and even though the road conditions were poor, we kept up the pace as best we could. As it got darker, it got even worse. The main roads were a truly terrible place to be at night.

Cars didn't have any respect for motorcycles. They tried to nudge us out of the way, using their vehicles as weapons. They constantly flashed their lights at us, maybe because we should have been in a different lane. They honked; they drove straight at us. It was not fun at all to be riding along there, and when the stretch of road suddenly had lights, it was a big relief. But the big relief didn't last long—these things never do.

I watched my fuel gauge carefully as the miles ticked by. All I could do was hope the secondary tank was working and that the careful speed was helping us to maximise our range. We made it to the brow of a hill, and I worked out roughly a distance of twenty miles until I ran out. We could see an ocean of orange lights, and it was a welcome sight, indeed, as out tanks were draining and night had crashed in all around us. We made it to the outskirts of town, slowly limping along at our most economical speed. Marcin wanted to try the banks, hoping that big city banks might work. They didn't. We tried our cards in the ATMs, and they were all rejected immediately.

We were approached every time we stopped. In contrast to the border town, the people who approached us were suddenly very friendly and were only too happy to help. We were advised to go to the biggest central bank, as they should be able to help we were told. We were completely out of money, and our petrol was waning. We followed a lead to a street with some cheap hotels on it and found it, thanks to the navigational skills of Marcin. Mine are virtually non-existent by comparison. Because Marcin's socials skills are virtually non-existent by comparison, I went in to negotiate for a room.

"No, we closed," said an old man, eyeing me suspiciously.

I tried another . . .

An old man said, "There is no shower."

I said it was no problem. He kept shaking his head and then told me to leave, his voice barely more than an angry growl.

I left and tried another . . . and I was told to leave again. By that time, I was getting a bit worried. We were in a strange town, and it was too late to do anything much except sleep, and we didn't even have the money to do that. Moreover, the people were mostly proving to be rude, aggressive, and hostile towards us. All that didn't bode well.

We rode around looking for a hotel that was showing on the GPS. We found it, but it was long gone and had been exchanged for a large crater. I suggested we had two choices at that point. We could either head out of town and find somewhere to camp or try the airport, as they would have free Internet, local hotels, and some advice. We were cold, but by now we were also hungry and thirsty, not having eaten anything since breakfast. We decided to give the airport a try, and if that failed, we would camp somewhere out of town.

The road to the airport was a minor adventure. Dogs were wandering around the motorway, and cars with no lights suddenly drove backwards towards us at high speeds. Three young men met us as we finally parked up, unscathed but more wary of the driving than anything else. They said they could get us into the airport.

To enter the lounge, we had to go through a metal detector. We were in full bike gear, and mine contained a Leatherman multi-tool, pockets full of spares, and other metal stuff. We put our bags on the conveyor and walked through, setting off the alarms. The young security guard just smiled and said it was no problem.

Finally—something was no problem.

There was free Internet, but we couldn't get it to work. I switched on my web-browser and went to search but got an error message straight away. We were told the Internet didn't usually work.

We found a man working on an advice stand for an upmarket hotel, and we were lucky enough to talk him into booking us a reservation at a cheaper place. With directions, we headed miles back the way we came, and again, Marcin found it with no difficulty.

They confiscated our passports as we booked in, but at least now we had a room to be miserable in while we slowly came to terms with our own stupidity. The man in charge was quite unpleasant—he just kept laughing and making snide comments his staff sniggered at, knowing we couldn't understand.

What we did understand was that the place had beds, a shower, a heater, and a fridge with cold water in it. We struggled on a bit with Google but got nowhere. It eventually dawned on us that Facebook, Google, eBay, Hotmail, and even my blog site were censored by the government. It seemed that all attempts to communicate were being deliberately blocked.

So, eventually, we came up with a plan, the only one that was really open to us. We would make an early start, have an early breakfast, and then try to get some money from the central bank as we were told we could. Failing that, we faced a trip back to the border to see what we could arrange. We would empty all the remaining fuel into my bike, since it used half the fuel that Marcin's swallowed. I would take every last coin we had and stretch it out until I could cross back out into Turkey, where I could get as much money out as possible. Marcin could stay put in the hotel until I could find a way back in, less than a week, at worst, we thought.

We slept like logs that night. Stupid, unprepared, and very stressed-out logs . . .

16

Fools and Their Money

Date—November 1st
Location—Tabriz, Iran
Mood—Worried and increasingly so

We woke up to the first light of the morning sun, filled with optimism, but not yet filled with food. We remedied that by cramming ourselves with eggs, bread, and odd little bits of soft cheese by way of a meal. Marcin said he was eating a lot in case we didn't get lunch, but the truth was that he always ate a lot, and a free buffet is a scary place to be standing in front of him. Breakfast was good—the food was simple but decent and tasted fresh. There was more Turkish/Iranian tea and still no coffee.

I needed coffee like never before.

So with no money, we headed out to try our luck at getting some. We made an early start, cursing our alarms that dragged us from some much-needed sleep, but this absolutely had to happen, so we got on with it.

We got to what we were told was the main bank just as it opened. We'd taken our bikes, not realising how close it was to the hotel; just a few metres down the road and really not worth the ride. Once inside, we struggled to find someone who spoke English. Eventually, someone came up and helped us out with directions to halfway across town, where they might be able to help us with some chance of getting a Visa debit transfer. Worrying about fuel, we took the bikes back to the hotel, as we were both showing empty by that point, and neither of us were going to make it. We tried to go down a side street, but it turned out to be an alley, so we had to turn about. That was far easier for me than it was for Marcin.

By the time we got round, the police were waiting for us with frowns and accusing scowls. They just wanted to give us some hassle, nothing more, it seemed. They checked my passport but were only really interested in where we were from; nothing else seemed to be of any interest. They asked silly questions, such as what was in Marcin's cases and what my fuel tank was, and then they left without another word. We left too and headed back, slightly confused about the encounter, which might as well have never happened. It was barely worth mentioning, but we had the feeling that this kind of thing was going to be happening a lot. So far, it seemed like Iran was going to be difficult for us.

We took a moment to contemplate what our next move might be. Whatever it was, it seemed that it would include a considerable amount of walking.

We had until 2PM to sort out our situation, and armed with the knowledge that the central bank could help, we decided to head there first. It was meant to be the largest, most important bank in the city, where dreams were made reality; perhaps even I could get a heart, and Marcin could get a brain.

We were not in the best of moods—optimistic, but slightly gloomy—the road ahead was a difficult one, and we weren't relishing the prospect of walking it. I'd hoped that I'd left behind all the endless bureaucracy, the struggling for visas, the paperwork, and pointless questions. Neither of us wanted a repeat of that part of the trip.

Every one of us on the road has had to endure the ceaseless, endless applications for visas, paperwork, and permissions to be allowed into various countries like a slave adjusting his ownership papers. It felt like we were right back there, dealing with the kind of mentality that was more interested in holding things back than driving them forwards.

We'd avoided doing too much research, as we wanted to see things with fresh, unbiased eyes, and that had come back to bite us on the arse, quite hard and with venomous jaws. What little research we'd done had told us not to trust the touts and ignore everything they said. We had done exactly that, and when they'd told us that we couldn't get money in Iran, we'd turned a deaf ear.

We knew we were in trouble. The setback, if we crossed back into Turkey, could end our trip for good, and we were desperate to avoid that. Getting visas was by no means a certainty. To Iran, it required an invitation which hadn't been easy to arrange. As we were walking along, we came up with as many options as we could, none of which was a good solution to the mess we'd gotten ourselves into.

We trudged along the road, our shoulders hunched and our mood sombre, and we came across a travel agency. It just occurred to us that they may be able to help, or at least offer some advice. Three young ladies in typical Iranian dress and head-scarves greeted us. One spoke reasonable English, and by reasonable I mean it would have been good enough in England, let alone out there in the Middle East. We explained our problem, and then there was a mad scramble between them for a solution to help us. The two who couldn't speak with us were very interested in Marcin. He slouched in the chair they invited us to sit in like he owned the place, and the novelty value of a giant Viking-cowboy-thing sprawling in their sofa reduced the ladies to the approximate level of giggling school girls. I could almost smell the hormones.

The one speaking with me gave me some paper and told me where the bank was. The best they could do was advise us to continue on our mission to the central bank, telling us they couldn't improve on the advice we were already following. She said we had to get a cab and produced a note, a piece of currency. Another girl produced a note, and they came around to hand it over. Marcin and I exchanged slightly confused glances; he even asked me what was going on.

I wasn't sure, but it looked like they were trying to pay for a cab for us. They were indeed—they offered us the money for our ride out to the bank, warning us it was too far to walk. We refused very politely, but were more than a little surprised at this generosity to a pair of complete strangers with no way to pay them back. If nothing else, it brought smiles to our faces.

We left, our mood somewhat lighter. To the shame of my home country, I doubt this would have happened in London. If an Iranian was lost and in need of assistance, I doubt they would have found too many people who would have tried so much to help them if, in fact, at all.

We walked on and stopped at another bank for advice, where we were once again given directions to the central one we were apparently in need of reaching. We still didn't know our way around the town, and every stop was making that even more painfully apparent. Tabriz was much larger than we would have liked.

We were walking slowly along, noticing the amount of Peugeot 405s there were, and there were thousands! Every second car we saw was a Peugeot 405, sometimes called other things, but always the same to look at. Then, another one passed us, honking its horn and pulling over to the curb. We had learnt to ignore being honked at.

Honestly, there is no point in America invading the country with soldiers, tanks, and guns, even though they seem hell-bent on doing so. If they really wanted to do some damage to Iran, then they don't need to use weapons at all. To really cause chaos and break the morale of the country, just take away their car-horns. Then the country would slump into a deep depression, their driving would become joyless and empty, and the place would plunge into apathetic silence.

We looked as this car carried on honking its horn, apparently at us. It was the man we'd seen from the bank where we'd asked directions, and he was offering us a lift. This time, we accepted the generous offer, and on the way up we were glad we did—it was a long way, and he pointed out all the things we should see, like any man proud of his city. In fact, it was good for us too, it showed us a good slice of Tabriz, and it was turning out to be a very beautiful place. So he dropped us off at the bank, wanting nothing more than to shake our hands and wish us luck. This man knew we had no money so couldn't have wanted anything from us. Again, we were impressed; after the previous night when people had been so against us, this was a much warmer welcome.

The "Milli" bank was large, guarded by police, and looked important. For the first time all day, I had a sense that we just might be able to get this sorted out. We went in, and the man at reception stood up and greeted us with the usual big smile and "Welcome to Iran," which was occasionally interchangeable with "Welcome to Tabriz."

We explained our problem and were told the Visa department was upstairs. A strong sense of relief washed over us, and the mood lifted. We had hope!

We headed up and asked our way to the department, to be met only by a man who explained it was not possible. Dejectedly, we sloped outside to revisit our options. We were left with one other suggestion that the touts trying to exchange dollars might be able to help us. In desperation, I went back into the bank and talked with the man on reception. He seemed quite annoyed that my service had been less than I had hoped, and stormed upstairs to shout at the man I had spoken with earlier.

This time, he said it was possible and began doing the paperwork. It seemed like we were finally out of trouble, and it was a nice place not to be. I had my passport copied, I filled in some forms, and I waited for my cash. Finally, the man came back and asked me for the money. I reminded him that I had no money and that I wanted to get some on my card. He repeated that it was not possible—he just thought it might be for a minute and did the paperwork. I had no idea what he thought he was doing, but what he wasn't doing seemed painfully apparent, and depression returned.

So I left, and we met up outside the bank. We were beginning to worry. We went and found one of the black market cash dealers, who said it would be no problem. He took us to a place with a glowing neon sign that said, "Visa Card". We breathed a sigh of relief. If you can't trust the black market, who can you trust? He came back and said that it was not possible.

We tried a few other people in a few other places, and it was always the same thing. We even went back to the Visa place ourselves, but the results were always the same.

Next, we went to find tourist information, as we'd been advised they might be able to help. They were just typical government officials with their hands out looking for a bribe. We told them what was going on, had some free tea, and listened to the man assigned to us explain that this happens a lot and that he could help us.

We had one other hope, a somewhat vague hope, but we were clinging on to anything we could get at that point. We had met some other bikers outside of Istanbul, and they were heading the same way as us. Their bikes were larger and faster than ours (mine,) and they might have already been long gone, for all we knew.

The official let us try to ring them on his phone. They didn't answer, and we didn't know if our texts were getting through either. We hoped that they could pick up some currency for us, and we could send them the money by bank transfer between our home countries. It was the only chance we had left.

The man then tried to charge us for the phone call. Even Marcin looked bewildered at that horrendous display of stupidity. I told him we'd come back and thank him properly later, and he seemed happy enough with that. It wasn't like he had any choice, since we literally had no money to pay him with, which was something we'd explained at length.

In desperation, we rattled together our loose change left over from other countries. We had about £7.6 Euros and fifty Polish Zloti between us. It wasn't going to get us far, and it certainly wouldn't pay our hotel fees. The tourist assistant helped us turn it into the local currency, and it should have been enough to fill both of our bikes and get us back to the Turkish border.

Of course, the hotel had our passports, and we owed them money. What I could do at the border I didn't know. I was hoping I could wing something, bribe an official to let me get some cash at a cash-point. I just knew we were getting nowhere in town. My bike was by far the more economical of the pair, and I knew I could get to the border easily. We hoped that Marcin staying would be enough to convince the hotel to release my passport to me.

Of the few things I was confident of, I was sure I could find a way to get out and back to a Turkish cash-point without a stamp on my passport. If crossing borders had taught me nothing else, I knew that money talked.

Back at the hotel, I borrowed a phone and called the embassy. I spoke to a woman called "Sandra," who asked the obvious question, "Didn't you know about the situation in Iran?"

Well, I would think the answer to that was pretty obvious by then, and she grunted at me when I explained the pointlessness of her question in painfully sarcastic detail. In the end, she had a partial solution. I could transfer money from my account to a company, who would forward it to the embassy in Tehran. It was still a long day of riding to get there, and we didn't have the fuel for it. We also didn't have any passports, but I took the details anyway. It might have been possible for me to make Tehran and return with some money to get Marcin moving. At that point we were exploring every possible option; at least I was. Even Marcin was rattled, and it takes a lot to trouble him more than an empty stomach.

We waited patiently for news from our fellow bikers, and then finally, a miracle happened. A text got through saying they could lend us some money.

I can't explain the sense of relief that message brought to our lives. It was like the first yellow rays of a brilliant sun shyly poked through the parting clouds of the worst storm you ever remembering seeing.

Finally, we were getting somewhere and were facing the very real possibility that we might actually be able to get somewhere. Now we could get to Tehran and collect our money once we arrived. It looked like we wouldn't have to turn back or give up on our journey. We were free to blunder on, once again, and see how much more stupid we could manage to get without dying. That's probably proof that the world is a silly place, but it was our world, and we were going to blunder through it if we wanted to.

We went back out for a walk, this time with a bit more enthusiasm and a far lighter mood. Marcin wanted to buy a bulb, an H3 spotlight bulb to replace a blown one on his motorcycle. Why he wanted to do that was anyone's guess, since his headlight was an LED bulb that was probably out of a low-powered torch. He would have had more visibility riding backwards using his brake-light to see with. We went into one place to be told they didn't have one and couldn't help.

While Marcin was asking what to do and beginning to grumble about things, a young man came round and invited us to follow him. He took us to what he told us would be the best place, a big mini-mall selling nothing but car spares, and then led us to a shop he said would be good—the cheapest and most reliable in town.

We had assumed that they simply couldn't help us and left it at that, but no, in Tabriz at least, if they can't help you, they help you get to someone who can. Another example of generosity and decency you wouldn't easily find in London. We were growing increasingly impressed. We tried at the shop the young man had led us to. The owner came back with the right bulb after a search of only a few seconds. We asked how much and were told, "It's no problem. It's a gift."

Before we could really say anything, they brought us out tea and chocolate cakes, and they asked us very politely if we could spare some time to stay and talk with them. We chatted about the country and left with nothing more than a handshake between us after a very friendly chat. For the next few hours we wandered around, and it was the same everywhere we went. People were friendly, interested, and just wanted to come and meet us. Nobody wanted anything, which was ideal, since we had nothing much to offer.

We stopped to take photos of people's bikes, and in every case they invited us to sit on them, just happy we were interested in them and their city. Even the police wanted to talk with us this time. There was no suspicion, they were just people who happened to be in a uniform who wanted to talk to other people who happened not to be.

We took a bus ride, and a gentleman came up to us and introduced himself. We asked him how we were meant to pay, since it wasn't obviously apparent. He explained that locals used a card, but for foreigners there was no charge, and we were free to use their services at our leisure.

At one point, we went back to "The Bazaar" market in a quest to find a place that might have a secret stash of alcohol, since Marcin had begun to dangerously sober up. He had heard a legend that alcohol could be found at newspaper stands, if you were persuasive enough.

A young man dressed as Mickey Mouse wanted to have his picture taken with us! It was all a lot of fun and very interesting besides. With the prospect of our problems behind us, things seemed brighter, and we were free to enjoy the city and the enormous hospitality of the people. It was like stepping into a Twilight Zone story, where almost everyone was happy and polite, the polar opposite of London, where almost everyone is a miserable arsehole.

As the hours dragged by, we began to worry a bit about our friends, as text messages didn't seem to want to get through. We finally got a message saying where they were, and that they could spare us 250 Euros. We rode down to the hotel, which was only just down the street from ours, and it was nice to ride our bikes without the bulk of the luggage on them.

My little single managed 201.5 miles before we were able to fill up, and still she showed no sign of going onto reserve. I was pleased—that was a return to her normal form and a sign that she was running well. It was also a sign that the local fuel was respectable too.

I hadn't thought that fuel quality could vary so much from country to country when it was all advertised as the same thing, but it clearly did and quite wildly so. My motorcycle had one of the best electronic management systems available at the time and ran with a boring degree of predictability. The variance in her range could only really be accounted for by a stark variation in the octane level of the fuel as we travelled from one region to the next.

At the hotel where they were staying, we were told our benefactors were out getting some food, so we wandered about the town to kill time. We found a bar full of old men smoking those glass pipe things that you see in any movie that features the Middle East. They saw us looking and started waving to us, so we went in to say hello.

We were invited in with lots of hand shaking, and tea was brought out for us. We were invited to sit down and ended up at the back with the younger guys who spoke the best English. We were still not sure how the pipes worked, but the guys didn't seem to be particularly affected by it; we presumed that no drugs were involved.

One of them explained to us, "What else is there to do? There's no drink, no dancing, no girls!" You can't argue with that. The town was devoid of women, as we'd seen before; the young men were banned from socialising in any way that we were used to seeing as normal and healthy. We spoke about that, and there was clear resentment from the young people against the restrictions their government placed on their actions.

Marcin asked pointedly about alcohol to anyone who would listen, but there was none to be had. If there was any, Marcin would have found it.

Finally, we met up with our friends. They were set to be in Tehran in a couple of days, as we were planning to be once the money situation was sorted out properly. We thanked them for their help, took what Euros they could spare, and arranged to meet them at a later time to buy them a drink and thank them properly for their help. I was confident that we would find some alcohol; Marcin was highly motivated, and I was resourceful. If there was a way, we knew we'd find it.

The population of the town was amazing. Everyone was interested in what we were doing, and there was a real sense of pride in the place, the culture, the history, and the people. In a way, I'm glad that this happened. It got us off the bikes and got us mixing with a warm and welcoming town in a great way that we probably wouldn't have experienced otherwise.

If we had to judge the town just from the experiences we had when we'd arrived, we would have reported a very different impression. Hotel owners had been hostile and severe, and we'd assumed that was the norm. Now we'd found out, from meeting a much wider selection of people, that wasn't the case at all.

One of the many people we'd spoken to had told us, "The Iranian people are great; only the government is bad." Where is that not true?

17

Salty Cheese

Date—November 2nd
Location—Still Tabriz, Iran
Status—Relieved to be moving on

We had money in our pockets, enough to get us moving along, and if we were very careful, enough to get us out of the country. With that in mind, it was time to leave Tabriz. It was the first time on the journey that I'd been a bit heavy-hearted about leaving. The road was always beckoning to show us more, but sometimes you just want to see more of where you are first, and this was one of those times.

I had not managed to arrange a bank transfer, because our hotel was not equipped with the latest advanced technology, such as touch-tone phones. Calling my bank was a non-starter, because I had to sit in an automated switchboard, and without the use of touch-phones, there was no possible way to navigate through.

We decided to get an early start and head for Tehran, stopping somewhere for lunch to make a Skype call or perhaps borrow a phone around the time the UK banks opened. That way we could get the money back to our benefactors who had leant us enough Euros to get us moving.

Breakfast was the same as the previous morning, salty cheese, eggs, and bread so chewy it posed a moderate threat to our teeth. I was woken by Marcin's alarm, which played this slightly odd noise that my brain couldn't quite register as an alarm. Then I got hit on the leg, and slowly the fog parted and I was alive . . . and still shattered.

We had settled the bill the previous night. I had a brief conversation with the manager, one of the few people we'd met who wasn't warm and pleasant. I had brought up the issue of his behaviour and how it was at odds with everyone else we'd met, why the police had randomly stopped us, and why no other hotel had accepted us and offered us a room. He shrugged with a sarcastic grin. I asked him if it was because people were assuming we were Americans. He had grinned some more and nodded in agreement.

I hadn't decided if that meant I liked him more or less when we left, but it didn't matter either way.

After loading the bikes, we headed out to the road ahead to listen to some more honking horns and to take our lives in our hands.

We rode past some of the great things we'd seen with a tiny tinge of regret about missing all the many things that the town had that we hadn't yet explored. We rode towards the touts, who were offering to exchange our Euros for local money, with which you can't buy beer, or anything else that might be particularly interesting or fun.

So far, beer had eluded us, what with it being highly illegal. But that hadn't stopped Marcin grabbing strangers at random and demanding they sell it to him. Once the money exchange was dealt with, we got on the road properly and headed onwards so that Marcin had new people to terrify by shaking them and demanding they sell us beer or other random intoxicants.

The way out showed us tantalising glimpses of historical buildings, and waterways we'd never been close to before. We'd missed so much, but had no time to stop, as we were hours late getting onto the road. We still had a very long ride to Tehran ahead of us.

Long rides were pretty much mundane to us by then, and we took all that on the chin, barely registering the hours of nut-crunching agony we were about to endure.

It took us nearly an hour to get out of the city, as it often does. Cities are rarely well-managed, and consequently, traffic is usually heavy. Getting around in cities is the worst part of any long journey, almost without exception. It's not just worse, it's usually the most time-consuming and definitely the most frustrating part of any trip.

We stopped for fuel, and paid suspiciously more than we should have, before getting on our way to the main roads. The fuel quality in Iran, so far, had been really excellent—the bikes were running well, and the mileage we were getting was top notch. We still kept a close eye on mileage and did a set of routine maintenance daily. I knew my bike well and checked everything that might need attention. Marcin kicked his balding tyres and laughed like his skull was full of angry rats. I knew bad things were coming and hoped they weren't coming to me, because Marcin would never, never let me forget it if they did.

Marcin's motorcycle was a KTM and had many horrible problems. But there was also a slightly baffling issue in that, while he was carrying brand new tyres, his rear was so worn out that the canvas was hanging out and slapping against the road like a cat in a washing machine. I insisted on him getting that sorted tomorrow morning, because I objected, in principal, to scraping his massive carcass off the sandy roads.

The first time I pointed out to him that there was no rubber left on his tyre and that his chain was flapping around and dragging on the tarmac, he just grinned at me and said, "Let's drive faster," with a big grin that showed off his fly-splattered teeth.

The difference between us was certainly significant but had pretty much become forgotten by now. We were just Jack and Marcin, motorcycling idiots. We had become known on the various Internet forums as "those two idiots," as we bumbled our way around from one minor disaster to the next. I was actually rather proud of that.

He had recently looked around for someone faster to ride with, and to be honest, I actually did sympathise with him. At one point in Turkey, we had been riding along at a speed I could manage, and our new friends passed us and shot off into the distance at a speed we couldn't get close to, but a speed I would have been far more comfortable riding at myself. The little single was cramping everyone's style somewhat, being ideally suited to rougher terrain. But apart from some potholes, we hadn't actually dealt with anything yet that she was designed, or even very well-suited, to handle. But for now, all this was forgotten—we had bigger problems, and because we were mostly causing them ourselves, we figured it was likely we'd have even bigger ones to come.

So once we were out of town, the scenery started to change. We couldn't get onto the motorway, try as we did, but that didn't bother me unduly. Signs were confusing, and for a while we went in circles trying to find entrances to roads that might well not have existed. For quite some time as we battled our way out, the economic speeds were not just expedient but were vital for our survival. The driving was so bad that even Marcin slowed down. It's worth noting that Marcin never slows down for anything, with the occasional exception of unleashing his inexorable appetite on an unsuspecting population.

It wasn't that they drive fast, so much as that they drive sporadically, changing lanes suddenly, forcing you out of the way, and wandering across the whole roads at speeds they can't seem to deal with. They overtake without warning, just to sit in front of you at the same speed. In other words, they drive just like Marcin, but only if Marcin was wearing blinkers, drunk, and texting a pizza order after having recently suffered an unprofessionally-executed pre-frontal lobotomy.

We went up again today to around 2,200 metres, and the mountains were snow-covered and cold.

They were really very cold.

It was one of the coldest days we'd suffered though, and that was saying something. We were reading six degrees, but the wind was biting through us, especially me with my summer jacket, worn-out gloves, and no heated grips.

My bike's development had traded the usual large electrical generator for a smaller one that allowed for faster acceleration, and consequently, the power output was limited. Heated grips were a luxury I couldn't justify. The electrical system struggled even to power an airhorn.

We stopped for a photo and to do our next stupid thing in Iran—not as stupid as before, but we were trying our best and working with what we had. We found a nice little place in the mountains, and Marcin decided to stop off to take a picture. It was a snow capped mountain with rugged scenery, and grand sweeping jagged peaks stretching away into the distance. It was a fine place to record a few memories, especially since we were inflated with optimism at having full pockets and the promise that we might find a source of alcohol ahead, somehow made even more exciting by being illegal.

We rode straight through the gravel to the dirt, but the dirt wasn't really dirt at all—it was clay of some sort, soft and sticky, and nowhere near as solid as it looked. It filled our treads and turned our tyres into muddy slicks in seconds. After we got the pictures, as quickly as we could, we headed out. There was a step to ride over to get off the clay. I only got grip enough to jump up onto it by standing on the pegs and bouncing for more weight as I spun the wheels. It worked, and I got out with my dignity more or less intact.

Marcin didn't.

His massive extra weight and lack of rubber on his back wheel left him sliding around like a . . . well, a heavy bike on soft clay, I guess. I ran over to help, grabbed the rear rack, and pushed. More sliding. I got a better footing, and he gave it some power. I got sprayed with mud, and we didn't move an inch.

As we looked up, a car stopped—a white Land Rover equipped with lights and bars. At first, I thought it must be police, but it was just some local guys stopping to help. I think we probably would have been OK—the bike was beginning to move—but it was still welcome help indeed.

We got her out in a minute with all of us pulling and pushing, leaving me more than just a little muddy. Marcin looked me up and down and noted solemnly that I was now covered in mud. I told him I was sure he would do the same for me. He shook his head, frowning, as if considering the matter greatly, and finally conceded that he hoped it would never come to that. That made it feel that it was all worthwhile.

We stopped, of course, for handshakes and photographs, and then we were back on the road, filthy, cold, and impressed at the endless hospitality of the people we were meeting.

At first, the roads were amazing; the scenery, even after we joined the motorway, was truly spectacular. The sheer scope and scale of the rugged mountain landscape was awe-inspiring, a truly magnificent view that you have to experience for yourself. Words simply can't do such a thing the proper justice. Soft, rounded green-tinged mounds built into ragged rocky needles scraping bluntly into the cloudless sky all around us. White snowy peaks blended into the horizons at the edge of our vision. At times, there was nothing else, just an endless tapestry of rugged natural beauty as far as could be seen.

Even the bleakness had a sense of austere beauty, and make no mistake, it was as bleak and dangerous as it was interesting. We passed a sign warning that it was dozens of kilometres until there would be mobile phone reception. I hadn't seen anything like that before. It hammered home in no uncertain terms that this place wasn't to be taken lightly, certainly not as lightly as we were taking it.

We really were idiots, I thought to myself. We had blundered into a freezing desert with hardly any water, less than 200 miles of fuel range, and *The Boys are Back in Town* playing through my earphones.

Driving down a hill, I heard a strange, sudden rattle coming from my bike, the last place in the entire universe I wanted a strange, sudden rattle to be coming from at that exact moment. Not wanting to be stranded in the middle of nowhere, I listened intently, looking for where the noise might be coming from, while I reached out for where the noise appeared to have emanated. Suddenly, and without warning, the worst happened.

My bike completely died!

She stopped running; everything went dead, the dash, lights, everything. I had no power, so I coasted to a halt on the shoulder, hoping Marcin would notice I was missing, and come back up the slip-lane to offer sage advice and sound wisdom. Realistically, I'd probably have to settle for a tow.

Thoughts suddenly flashed through my head of recovery trucks, blogging about how bad these BMW single-cylinder motorcycles are, pulling fuses at the side of the road, replacing wires, bodging some kind of workaround fix from my magic bag of spares. It all came at once in a jumbled blur of mad imaginings in a matter of less than a second. I looked down, and something didn't look right—the key was moved.

I tried it, and everything came back on, as if nothing at all had happened. I must have caught it with my sleeve and turned her off while feeling for whatever had come loose. As I turned the key, it became apparent that one of the other keys on the loop had slipped around and was causing the rattle as well. Absolutely nothing was actually wrong, at least nothing that wasn't in my own head.

That speaks of the attitude a place like this instils in a person travelling by such precarious means. With a total motorcycle failure, I would have been in serious trouble, and the thought had clearly been bothering me more than I realised.

I caught Marcin up, and we carried on until we stopped for fuel in the middle of this cold and foreboding wilderness. It was surprisingly less bleak, a stark little pocket of normalcy in the middle of this grimly threatening place that stretched on seemingly without end.

I had done some calculations in my head and put it to Marcin. We weren't going to make Tehran that day—we had too far to go, and it was already cold and would be dark soon too. I also needed a phone and Internet access as early as possible to arrange the wire transfer.

We had hoped to do it in a fuel station at the side of the road, but the fuel stop barely had fuel and seemed genuinely surprised that anyone had stopped to buy something.

Looking around, there was nothing about except the few chilling motorway signs telling you where you could stop to use a mobile phone, since there was no coverage anywhere else. We agreed, with some reluctance on Marcin's part, to head for a large town on the way, only 150 miles ahead. The transfer could take two or three days, so it was vital that we got to arrange it as early as possible. It was not so important that we made it to the city to collect it. After explaining this with the use of simple words, diagrams, and broad hand-gestures he finally, sulkily agreed.

The scenery after that was totally different. It was a real slog that dragged on by, with cold and miserable miles racking slowly up. There was nothing but a flat, dirt-plane to look over, with white mountains framing the horizon for hour after hour. The wind kicked up too, not enough to be dangerous but enough to bring an added nuisance to an already tough ride.

Finally, breaking the monotony, we hit potholes. It was like the road was just breaking up beneath us, leaving behind the boring two-dimensional design of a normal tarmac surface to break into a more interesting three-dimensional version. I enjoy potholes, my bike enjoys potholes, but when they suddenly come at you after a day of riding through a freezing desert, somehow they have a lot less charm than usual.

The roads were among the worst we'd seen; the holes began as a nuisance, and quickly became dangerous. Smaller bikes would have been in trouble—they were harsh enough to snap a cast wheel if you hit a bad one dead on. A smaller or faster bike would crash, and there was no question of that.

A constant thought rattled through my head, since you have time out there on the road to think, and when you ride, thinking becomes a constant companion.

I wondered what might be going through Marcin's head. Possibly it was some kind of near-pornographic display of huge servings of meat racing him along the road on a gigantic, flaming motorcycle. All the while he laughed like a Norse God, flushing down roasted cow-legs with flagons of ale, while smoking cigars the size of baseball bats. The sounds of singing came from a number of naked females on the rear seat of his terrifying machine, all with tiny IQs and long, tousled hair blowing freely in the wind.

I decided that it was probably best not to know, and consequently, I never asked.

My head furnished me with a more single-minded and equally irritating thought. "I wonder if my Millie would make this?" I had once owned an Aprilia RSV1000 Millie. I had a burning need for a litre-class V-twin, and no other bike was going to satisfy me. I settled on a Suzuki SV1000, and the one I found for the right price turned out to have some serious, but not deal-breaking, damage to the front end. The owner was awkward and refused to acknowledge that the damage should reflect in the price. It was the bike I wanted, but as a plan-B, I looked at an Aprilia, just in case. Now I'm a fairly pragmatic person—the Suzuki would be a fun bike but still be practical enough to function as a daily runner. I suspected the RSV would serve me far less well and would prove to be unreliable and uneconomical.

My brother came with me. He and I are also very different people. I enjoy books, whereas he's proud of and will brag about the fact that he's never read one. He was working in security at the time. He's my size, but somehow bigger and more openly aggressive, whereas I keep my temper mostly in check, while not around Marcin. Mostly.

We met the guy selling the bike down an alley. He invited us to a disused warehouse to view it. My brother was hefting a large Maglite as a weapon and was growing increasingly tense, warning me that perhaps this was a mugging. I reminded him that we had nothing worth stealing, and the gentleman in question was literally half his size.

We slipped into this small warehouse, and the lights slowly flickered to life. There she was, beneath the harsh brilliance of the strip-lights, the most beautiful thing I'd ever seen. The place was empty save for this one, black motorcycle. It bore a striking black finish, without a mark; not a single scratch anywhere on the custom-mixed polished black-mirrored surface. My brother huffed that if I didn't buy it, then he would. I just said I'd buy it, and he reminded me that we'd not even discussed a price. I didn't care, it had to be mine from the moment I saw it.

The previous owner had crashed it at low speed. His friend, owning a custom paint shop, had given him a simply beautiful repair job, but he was intimidated by it now and had settled for a 650cc instead. When I rode it, I was at first disappointed but found you could de-restrict it by cutting a blue wire. After that, she came alive, a thing of violent acceleration, and sheer, awe-inspiring silliness that painted a constant smile on my happy face.

I sold it some time later from lack of use, as I was preparing for my trip. That bike, like no other, left a permanent mark on my very soul. A man may have one great love, sometimes without knowing it. He will compare every woman he dates to that one perfect girl who got away. I'm the same way with bikes—I still compared everything I rode to that Millie.

As I rode along the freezing desert with potholes that could swallow up a small truck, I wondered if she would have made it. Soft, lightweight cast alloy wheels battering against solid, uneven rock would have jarred my spine and shaken her around mercilessly. I could have slowed down, negotiated the road with more care, perhaps. The BMW soaked up the abuse with only the occasional jarring crunch as I misjudged the scale of a rut. Nothing deflected her from her path as she ably dealt with what the world served up to her. Still, this bike was capable, but being capable leaves no mark on your soul. It was the Millie I was still comparing her to, and really it was her I still wanted.

For mile after mile, that was the single thought that went through my head.

Eventually, we found the town after around 150 miles of riding with no further break or stops; a new personal best for us and even more impressive since the conditions were not quite on our side.

It was a pretty big town with only a couple of hotels, so we just stopped at the first one we came to. They charged around £35 a night, give or take the exchange rate, and it came with breakfast and free Internet use as well. On the way in, we passed an area full of cars and bikes, although all of them were far smaller than our own machines. We attracted a lot of interest—people stopped what they were doing to stare at the silly-looking strangers.

At one point, we had got ourselves stuck in traffic, so Marcin suggested we ride down an alley to hopefully cut through it and find a shortcut. He had the only working sat-nav and twice my sense of direction, so I agreed, assuming rather more of his navigational skills than he might be able to actually deliver.

He then drove through a market into a narrow alley with a right-angle turn he simply couldn't make. I stopped to help him bump the bike round the corner so he could carry on.

He dropped it, of course. The massive, ponderous bulk of the thing lost the fight with gravity, and it took both of us, and a lot of swearing, to stand the lumbering monstrosity back upright. We just about made it round the corner. I got back on mine and followed to find that he got a few more yards and stopped once more. He looked back and said with a grin, "Shit!"

A local guy came up to laugh at us, telling us that it was a no-through road, and he was now stuck. Some more bumping, and a lot more swearing, and we turned it around. We filtered as hard as we could and found our way to the hotel without doing anything else particularly stupid.

My being covered in mud from head to toe hadn't gone down very well, but we got the room, and it was of a pretty respectable standard, even if we weren't. It was more than good enough for a pair of weary travellers who barely understood the concept of "standards," in any case.

We went out to get some food and found the same problem we

had in Tabriz. No kebabs! In London, a red and blue neon sign means that a kebab shop is nearby, but there everything has the same kind of signs, even if they sold carpets. I suppose that makes perfect sense if you think about it, but I tried my best not to.

We explored the whole town with no luck—no food anywhere, other than a couple of sandwich shops.

People there were different. It was strikingly more lively than Tabriz, and being a university town, the people on the streets were younger and more rebellious maybe. A lot of them showed interest in us one way or another. Most people eyed us up and down, Marcin attracted a lot of attention from them, eyeing him suspiciously as he swaggered about with infinite confidence.

One girl didn't notice him until he was fairly close, and as she saw him, she shrieked and hid behind her boyfriend when she turned to find him standing behind her.

This time, though, a lot of people were less positive about our presence. We heard a lot of shouts and giggles and had a lot of nasty stares aimed towards us. Several times, guys came up to us and asked where we were from, but everything was fine when we told them. They just smiled, shook our hands, and welcomed us. The problem seemed to be that people were taking us for Americans, and there was a very obvious prejudice there—an understandable one at that.

They clearly didn't see a lot of white people, and the resentment ran very deep. Everyone asked us where we were from and were always fine once we explained that to them. There was a definite feeling that things would not have gone so easy if we had been American. We had stopped once at a motorway toll and asked how much. The young man working there asked where we were from, his voice low and cold as his eyes bored fixedly forwards. When we told him, he just smiled, his hostility melted away, and he let us through for free with no further problem.

The resentment might well have come from a different direction, as we noticed something else that was a little disconcerting. It became fairly obvious as we moved along that most of the stares were aimed firmly at the region of our groins. Women smiled coyly, and men frowned, but the stares were firmly gravitating to the area on our bodies that was most likely the source of the funny smell in our room. I don't know what rumours or legends might be behind this behaviour, but something was clearly going on.

We eventually did manage to get some food in the end and were told proudly it was traditional Iranian food. I found some Falafel and ordered that, while Marcin ordered spaghetti—an Iranian delicacy, apparently. We were pretty surprised when both came in a sandwich. Marcin decided that a spaghetti sandwich was fine, but just to be on the safe side, he ordered another sandwich with chicken and some soup.

Washing all that down with a lemon-flavoured alcohol-free beer was very strange. The food was OK but nothing special As it was just a sandwich shop, we weren't hoping for too much from them. We hadn't found much else there—there didn't seem to be any restaurants or other social eating places. We were hoping Tehran might be better in that respect, but had read that in terms of food, it wasn't likely to impress us all that much. The food in Iran had been frustrating—we were keen to try some traditional dishes, eat some local food with local people, but that didn't seem like it was going to happen. Perhaps we already had? Perhaps the breakfast food and simple things we'd eaten really were the traditional local fare.

We were planning on taking an easy ride into Tehran the next day, but we couldn't risk the journey with Marcin's rear tyre in the condition it was. Finally, even he had to admit that having rubber on the back wheel would be a benefit and agreed on getting it sorted out as a priority.

Sadly, my fuel system had given up again. I had no idea why, as everything looked perfectly fine; it just didn't want to cooperate. My only thought was that it could be the cold, somehow, preventing the fuel from feeding. It was a pressure-operated vacuum system, and not a great one at that. My modification used the breather vent as a makeshift suction device. It was only choosing to be difficult when the temperature got very low and had done the same thing before. I was hoping it was nothing more serious than that. Certainly, it was proving only a minor inconvenience at that point, since I carried two litre-sized bottles and we had a five-litre jerry-can with us as well.

I was looking forward to arriving in Tehran. We would be waiting for a money transfer, so we should have enough to comfortably get through the rest of the country. It would be nice to have sufficient cash back in our pockets, and even nicer to be stuck somewhere for a number of days. I was looking forward to leaving the bike parked up and taking a well-earned break from my uncomfortable seat.

18

The Worst Thing that Can Happen Is Nothing

Date—November 3rd
Location—Mash'aldar, Qazvin, Iran
Status—Alert and prepared for anything

We had a fairly easy day, aside from being followed around by the spectre of death everywhere we went; and he appeared to have something to prove. We woke up in some quiet little town that was nestled in a desert, somewhere between Tabriz and Tehran, with only about seventy miles left to travel in order to get us into the city. That meant that, just for once, we had a very easy ride ahead of us, and enough time to explore the city a bit once we got there. For this ride, that seemed to be an unprecedented event.

Breakfast was pretty standard. The only downside was that they fed us western bread instead of the home-spun variety, which we found more interesting. It wasn't that either was particularly better than the other, but it was always nice to do the local thing when we got a chance—how often are you having breakfast in a small town in the middle of an Iranian desert?

Three American women were staying at the hotel, and they were attracting a lot of the wrong kind of attention around the lobby with their loud voices, as they barked at one another and then collapsed into braying, animated laughter. I wondered how well they were going to fare on their travels.

I guessed that perhaps it was easier to blend in for women in Iran. With a scarf covering most of your head, it might be easier to go unnoticed. I'm bald with a shaved head. Marcin is the opposite, and has filthy blonde hair streaming from his scalp in all feasible directions. We tended to stand out like a pork pie at a Jewish wedding or, indeed, an Islamic one.

Our motorcycles too attracted a great deal of interest everywhere we went, Marcin's particularly. The sheer size of the thing made it striking and imposing, and it never failed to get people staring. We'd spoken a lot about our bikes, and even Marcin was starting to accept that it hadn't been the right choice. It had cost him a lot to get the paperwork to allow him to travel, and on top of that, he was burning somewhere between two and three times the fuel I was, even at our moderate pace.

I had looked very seriously into a KTM myself. The "Adventure" was available in 950cc and 990. The slightly smaller one was naturally-aspirated and was known to be much more reliable than the injected version. An owner had told me his had proven to be a solid bike, but I wasn't solidly convinced. Speaking with mechanics who worked on them solidly convinced me otherwise.

Perhaps some years later we'd be sitting in a bar in Cambodia with our families, our first-born children, and some friends while we drank our way through enough beer to drown an adult elephant. He would eat a local dish and then say something like, "This was alright, but now I think it's time to order some food," and we'd tell one another stupid stories and laugh at just how stupid they were. He would then show me a picture of his current ride, a Harley-Davidson that packed only seventy bhp, and I would laugh at him.

Defensively he might say, "That's enough power."

I would agree, of course, but remind him that it was he who had said it. He would then explain that on our next trip to who-knew-where we'd need Honda 650cc singles, they were boringly reliable and much cheaper to set up.

Perhaps, who knows what the future might hold? We were barely smart enough to work out our present situation.

Luckily, it didn't need a lot of working out. We headed back to our room, and in consideration of the relatively light schedule we had for that day, Marcin finally got around to addressing the other elephant in the room: his bike was in urgent need of maintenance, including, but not limited to, putting a tyre on it before the canvas exploded, killing him horribly in the process. While I wasn't entirely averse to that, I didn't see any benefit either. While he went to get that sorted, I stayed behind to do some maintenance of my own.

Although large motorcycles were a distinct rarity, getting it changed would be no problem, since he was carrying a set of spares with him, together with a clutch, major engine components, most of his kitchen, enough electronics to start a reasonably-sized shop, and several complete changes of motorcycle clothing. Marcin doesn't believe in travelling lightly, and after sharing a toilet with him, I had come to believe he didn't believe in doing anything lightly.

I stayed behind to clean up my clothing and remove some of the dried-on clay that had sprayed over me while rescuing Marcin. The previous day the people in the hotel were hesitant to let us stay due to the state of me. It was pretty obvious I needed to do something about it. It actually turned out to be rather a good job I did stay behind, because something I'd eaten finally caught up with me and was keen to make a rapid escape.

We'd both been feeling less than ideal since we had left Europe and were both getting a bit run down. Neither of us were at our best. Our faces were red from the cold and the burning cold wind that was lashing against our skin constantly, our lips were chapped, and our stomachs were just barely holding on as best they could. Well, mine finally stopped holding on—I had to make a mad dash to the little-boys room and exploded in a way that would have offended even the most steadfast of farmyard animals. After a couple of clear-outs that were so ferocious that I felt it might be a good idea to count the bones in my spine, I felt washed out, but actually a little better for it.

We were both somewhat dehydrated, as a general shortage of money and shops was making water difficult to find. They tended to buy in bulk in Iran, since they have a different economy and culture, and we simply couldn't carry large packets of small bottles, so we were stuck searching for big ones. Luckily, the last few hotels we'd stayed at had fridges with water in them, and we'd been surviving on drinking that. As it turned out, it was just kitchen tap water, and we'd been mostly fine on it, give or take the odd morning evacuation. Even so, I didn't entirely trust it, and we made of point of trying to carry as much sealed fresh water as we could squeeze into our luggage.

Marcin finally came back, riding on a shiny new TKC80 tyre, which was the same as mine but had a radically different tread pattern for some odd reason, but it looked like it was ready for anything, even if the rest of the bike wasn't.

He grinned at me, asking to guess how much it cost him to have them fit it. I already had a good idea and was right on my first guess—they did it for free, of course. From the attention we got, especially the giant KTM, I knew they would probably do that. They even cleaned up some of the dirt and stopped to pose for pictures, apparently! In Iran that was totally believable, since the first little hiccups we'd had in the border town, the welcome and hospitality that had been extended to us had been outstanding, and Iran was both of our favourite countries so far.

So, eventually, we got ourselves back on the road. The hotel had been hot and stiflingly unpleasant, and the fresh air of the bright, sunny morning cleaned up my head and guts nicely; the bug was forgotten quickly for the time being.

As we were riding out of town some people in the opposite direction narrowly missed being obliterated by a bus, and the thought occurred that it couldn't be long before we saw our first road death. We both watched as two tiny bikes blasted past at full speed, screaming the engines to snapping point, while the riders wore no helmets and were trying to talk to one another. It was actually more surprising we hadn't seen one yet.

We had taken a brief interval at the hotel to call the embassy on our way out, but there was still no answer, and the message box was full. It wasn't a massive problem, as Tehran was close now and we could afford to relax a bit. We planned to find a hotel and then head straight there once we arrived. We had a hotel in mind, found off the Internet, cheap and highly recommended, and it was already loaded into the GPS. We were looking forward to an easy day on the bikes, and it was, but we suffered from the same slogging conditions as the day before, with nothing to see and an easy straight road lying ahead of us.

This was the kind of slog where your mind wanders, and it's surprisingly hard to stay focused. The blue sky faded to white at the edge of my vision. The yellow sand stretched out to the sides, melting into the beige rocks off in the far distance, framing the horizon. The road was straight and plain, cutting a direct swath through the fixed scenery, and what traffic we saw was extremely sparse. For long stretches of time it seemed that we weren't moving at all. Hot air blew through my helmet, the bike rumbled beneath me, and the sound of the engine was so familiar by then that it barely registered. For a while it seemed we were literally sitting still, the desert a static image around us, as if riding through a sand-filled snow globe.

Doing this for hours on end messes with your head. You actually start to feel like you're standing still, since the only really striking things around you are in the far distance, and they don't appear to be moving. The road is a dead straight line, and the sand at your level is virtually featureless. It wears you out, and your brain slows down. We needed frequent breaks to wake ourselves up so we could stay sharp. Every minor feature was an adventure, and we stopped just to look at a particularly pointy rock or an especially yellow patch of sand.

I got the impression that Tehran was going to be big when we hit the city sprawl twenty miles before the signs said we were due to arrive. Even by the time we reached that distance, the roads were getting busy, and the driving standard had deteriorated badly. We plodded onwards. Attention from other drivers was positive, but not always very welcome. People leant out and waved, honked their horns, and tried to chat with us at sixty-five mph, swerving around and wobbling dangerously close, while other drivers blindly lurched in front of us. We were both exchanging worried glances, as the roads ahead, beside, behind, and all around seemed loaded with the weaponry necessary to brutally rearrange our physical forms.

I had taken to checking statistical data as we rode along to get a better idea of what we'd be facing. As we progressed, the recorded levels of deaths on the road were getting higher, and Iran appeared to be one of the most dangerous places we'd be facing. It wasn't too hard to see that this was probably true. Marcin, who had also travelled in Africa and South America, agreed that this was among the worst road conditions he'd seen so far, and we still had India ahead of us. It was a daunting prospect.

The roads got more and more congested until we ended up stationary, trapped in a solid bunch of vehicles clogging the road completely. In fact, everyone was stationary. We seemed to have reached into town to find that the entire core was blocked lanes and motionless vehicles. We went through a tunnel and fought our way to the front down bus lanes, which seemed to be open to bikes, as far as we could tell. Bikes, in fact, seemed to be ignored by everyone. In fact, at one point, a policeman told us to use a bus route to get out of a jam, pointing and smiling at us. Everyone was as helpful as they could be, but the sheer weight of traffic was just too dense.

We had been told by various sources that the locals paid a different price for fuel than travellers passing through. That seemed fair enough, as they paid their taxes, and in any case, fuel was cheap enough. We stopped to fill our tanks along the way, managing to creep and edge slowly along until we found somewhere to stop. Marcin tried to argue for a better price than was posted on the forecourt. Logic and reason seemed to have escaped him completely, but that wasn't a recent thing.

That was one of several reasons why the negotiations were usually left up to me. Obviously, he just got replied to with odd looks, while people sniggered and pointed at us. The pumps advertised 4,000 rials per litre, but jumped to 7,000 when the gas started to flow. The Internet, shockingly, was quite wrong about how things work. In fact, the locals apparently got a gas card entitling them to only sixty litres at the cheaper price; after that we all paid the higher rate. Bikes got no concessions at all, only car drivers, and presumably they had to apply for the privilege. To me, it seemed like a reversal of the British road tax system. In England you apply for the privilege of paying tax before being allowed to drive to get to work, so you can pay even more tax. It appeared that in Iran you applied for the right to drive on the road and then actually got money back off of your petrol for doing it. This all sounds like it's potentially a great system, except the tax has leapt so high, and so suddenly, that I can't help thinking that the locals, with their captive economy, must have been feeling the pinch.

We sat in still more traffic, seemingly endlessly, where nobody was moving beyond crawling a few inches forwards every couple of minutes. At one point, we were stuck for some time on a hill, where the lights changed every three minutes for about twenty seconds, so we all just crept along, sweating in our cold-weather gear and helmets, too big with our luggage to slip through the tiny gaps between cars. Not that there were any gaps, and if we were slow enough to leave one open for the briefest of moments, then four or five cars tried to jump into it. It was chaos; there was no logic to it at all. We were just trapped in a hot, depressing gridlock of cars, driven by people who had no clue how to drive.

My bike had a lean-burn engine, using minimal fuel in order to improve economy, but this translated into a very hot bike, and she was getting hotter. I turned off the engine as often as I could to help her to cool down, but even so, she was overheating badly. The fan was running constantly, and the frame beneath my legs was getting hotter and hotter, to the point that even sitting on it was getting uncomfortable.

She was never a great city traffic bike—she liked to run free and frolic in the wild green yonder, running wild with her kind, not being stuck in traffic, stared at by the entire population of a town while they crammed themselves into gaps that didn't really exist, all making a horrible problem, far, far worse.

I told Marcin I wanted to pull over and let her cool down, just in case. He didn't seem keen; he was never keen on suggestions that threatened to slow his rampant progress forwards, even when there hadn't been any progress forward for nearly an hour. To say he was single-minded about that would be something of a drastic understatement, like saying the western political system is slightly corrupt, American education was a bit poor, KTMs have some reliability issues, or Marcin was often hungry.

Then his clutch seized on, lurching him forwards without any further control of his engine. It surprised us both; his front wheel lurched a few inches into the air and he plunged forwards. He grabbed on the brakes reflexively and managed to avoid ploughing into the mass of stationary metal that had us boxed in. He suddenly came round to the idea, and we pulled off to sit a while on the curb.

Mine was pinking and growing increasingly bad as she got hotter, and his was playing up too, cutting out and sputtering. Both were pinking slightly under heavy acceleration, so I wondered if the fuel quality was declining again. It seemed likely, since both of our motorcycles seemed to have the same issues in synch with each other.

So we stopped, finally, at the hotel, which the GPS took us to after what felt like hours, and on checking the time, it had actually been hours. It was pretty obvious it wasn't the one we'd found online. This meant the GPS had been lying to us, and we'd spent half a day sitting in traffic being taken to entirely the wrong place. We weren't impressed, and the hotel wasn't really a good fit for us either. We were looking for cheap; they were going for rich.

They offered us a room for a hundred dollars a night. I negotiated it down to seventy, which was still expensive for us, but actually a bargain for that particular hotel, which was made entirely from gold-covered plastic and had staff that actually called us "Sir" as we made a mess on their carpet. It was still early, so Marcin thought it best to find something cheaper, since it was his turn to pay (funny how that works), and so the mad frenzy of riding around looking for a hotel began once again.

First, we got lost, as we often did, so we stopped and asked for directions. That got us nowhere, as asking for advice from someone who speaks a massively different language cannot end well, and consequently, it didn't even start well. In the end, one of the locals got into his car to lead us to a hotel he knew. We followed for around an hour, until we eventually pulled up at a slightly dishevelled place that was far more our style and looked well within our budget, which was ideally half of the least amount possible.

I went in because, as Marcin put it, "I'm better at that sort of thing," and I began the negotiation. That was all entirely true, as Marcin has the social grace of a hungry gorilla with itchy genitals. They wanted even more money than the last place, so we left! My negotiating skills were insulted, but not as insulted as the man behind the desk, who had learned several new English swear words.

Outside, a couple approached us and asked if we spoke English. They were lost, and the irony of them coming and asking us was not lost on anyone there. We asked where they were staying and got a card from them. The driver of our volunteer tour guide insisted he knew it, and we headed off to sit in stationary traffic for another two hours, during which time we moved barely 200 yards. We saw him using his phone and asking drivers for directions; I had a bad feeling about that. In the end, after a painfully long and dangerous ride, we did find the right place, down an alley, between two shops selling car headlights.

For the first time on the trip, I had significant doubts that tomorrow would be a thing I'd actually be seeing from anything other than a hospital bed, or a wooden box as the lid slammed shut. I came as close as we ever came to a lethal accident, and to this day, I don't know how I avoided it happening.

I was stuck between moving cars, one behind pushing me to fifty mph while only a few centimetres from my rear wheel, and another in front, again, almost touching, as I was virtually being pushed into it from the rear. From the side, a slip-road opened up, and a car raced straight into the gap I was occupying, with the metal railings next to me completely caging me into the death trap. I shut my eyes momentarily and just waited for the impact, cursing the damn luck. Somehow, I didn't manage to die. What happened in the next few fractions of a second I literally have no idea. By all rights, nobody should have walked away from that.

Marcin was both more and less lucky. A truck drove straight into him while he was stationary. His huge metal boxes took the impact, and the truck still kept going, even though he must have known he'd impacted another vehicle. With a sickening sheering sound of torn metal, the entire front panel of the cab tore off, and the driver just carried on, as if that was all just perfectly fine, driving off with the pale blue front of his truck flapping freely in the breeze. Marcin suffered no damage at all, luckily. He just peered around bewildered, like a dog on a vets table, wondering why there was something very cold sticking out of his arsehole and why he had a strange urge to clench. He turned to the side and shrugged with a kind of horrified and confused grin on his face. My eyes were just fixed on him, my jaw hanging open as I watched what I thought was something that was going to end much worse.

I negotiated the hotel down to 40,000 rials, which apparently worked out to only about £20. Marcin wanted to find somewhere cheaper, but cheaper meant no breakfast, nowhere to park the bikes, no Internet, and a free-standing Calor gas heater screwed halfway up the wall.

I decided the hotel we were at was fine, and £20 was cheap enough, so I politely invited him to shut up and do as he was told for once. The man who seemed to be in charge was the kind of guy who is so keen to do everything imaginable to help that he flusters himself doing it. Nothing was too much trouble or too complicated for us.

He was unspeakably proud of a positive review he got in a travel magazine and showed us the article at length, many, many times. After unpacking our gear, we went for a walk to find the British Embassy and get things moving. Our long wait in traffic had meant that normal office hours were over, and we were now relying on the twenty-four-hour duty staff, who were probably by then very, very drunk.

We were allowed in, but they were closed for the weekend, which falls a day ahead of ours in the West. That meant nobody was available to process our cash until Sunday morning, a full two days. We left, pretty dejected. We'd lost a day already just getting into the city, and that was after making good time getting this far. Our visas were short, barely enough time to get us through the country, so we had very little spare time to waste.

We discussed other important matters with the man in charge, such as the availability of black market alcohol. We were advised and provided a map to the Armenian Club, which was likely to satisfy our somewhat dubious and quite illegal needs.

With nothing else to do, we went in search of it and found it on foot with little trouble, using Marcin's strangely sharp navigational instincts. It was an oddly anonymous grey building with spikes, barbed wire, and armoured doors, with bored and seemingly redundant guards standing by trying to look as threatening as possible. Anything with that much security can't be good, but we weren't afraid of a few risks. I'd shared a bathroom with Marcin; there was nothing left in the world that could scare me.

While we wandered aimlessly to the club, we discussed our options with heavy hearts, the previous gloom we'd experienced in Tabriz returning to a more reserved degree. Our equipment contained nothing of any value, and most of our organs were only useful by then as novelty paper-weights. With what little cash we had left, the only option seemed to be a dash to the border. We'd forego eating, sleep on the road and hopefully not be noticed by police, travel at the most economic speed, and hope against hope that we'd be able to get some money in Pakistan. According to the Internet, even that wasn't likely.

We would have a long journey to the first place where we could actually withdraw cash. The situation was looking grim, but it didn't seem like we had all that much choice.

19

Turning that Frown Upside-Down

Date—November 4th
Location—Tehran, Iran
Mood—Contemplative

We woke up with the intention of stuffing ourselves full of breakfast, ready for not eating properly for at least a couple of days. Marcin had crashed out early, but I stayed on the net and did some homework in the somewhat unrealistic hope of finding some kind of solution to our problem—something that we'd missed, perhaps. We couldn't get cash from an ATM until we were hundreds of miles into Pakistan, so the idea of the rush to the border was looking a lot less likely than our roadside ramblings made it seem.

The border town was looking like it was very run down, and wouldn't have much there beyond donkeys and machine-guns. We later discovered that it also had sand. Whatever banks there were would be in a major city, by Pakistan standards, and would rely on satellite communication. They wouldn't even work if it was raining.

We could also be facing additional fees at the border and probably a few bribes to get things moving. On top of that, there was a large tract of land on the Iranian side that was controlled by the military, and so camping was out of the question. We would be legally obliged to use hotels, as the ones there would be government mandated. Nothing was ever easy, and it was looking increasingly like nothing ever would be.

Over breakfast, while we were chatting with the Australian couple who had recommended the place, I decided to ask the well-informed manager if he knew any way to transfer cash, more out of desperation than any realistic hope of him having any advice to offer.

Of course he did, but he warned us that it would take several minutes.

On hearing this, we suddenly felt like maybe, just maybe (but probably not), things might not be as bad as they seemed. We finished up and talked to him, more to see if this was actually true or a proud boast that would come to nothing. We hoped for the best, but prepared ourselves for the worst. We'd had a lot of advice that had also come to nothing, so we were slightly more dubious this time, and I wasn't getting too excited.

It seemed he had a friend in London. We would have to transfer the cash to her, and he would simply give it to us out of the till as soon as it went through. She would forward the money to him, which would take months, but he didn't mind, as he was happy to be helping us out. We began the process over the Internet. Relieved that our problems seemed to be behind us, we decided to cancel the transfer at the embassy, which didn't seem to have actually started in any case and probably wouldn't have for several more days.

I didn't have Internet banking, and the phone connection was so poor that a bank transfer was out of the question. Marcin did it from his account, instead, and it took only a few minutes for confirmation to arrive that the transaction had gone through. We waited excitedly, and then, a quick phone call later, we were being handed cash from the till. It was just that easy. After days of hitting walls of every imaginable kind (except actual walls of any imaginable kind), our troubles were finally over. What couldn't be achieved by the embassy, the government offices, the largest banks in the country, or the touts, whose sole income comes from handling and exchanging currency, turned out to be a simple task for a hotel manager who just wanted to help. In fact, he seemed slightly confused as to why exactly we were so happy after doing such a small thing to help.

We walked back out during the day, taking tourist-type pictures as we went, our spirits finally lifted. We were still objects of fascination, but it was a more reserved atmosphere than in the smaller towns; tourism was rare there, but not unusual. We got into the embassy with more difficulty than before and got moaned at by the diplomatic police for taking pictures.

Once we were in, we were told the staff were on full alert for an upcoming riot. It was the anniversary of the Iranian Embassy siege in London, and we were advised to stay well away from the area, in case we got caught up in the carnage. Of course, nothing happened whatsoever, apart from several people offering to clean our shoes.

Do we really need governments? They don't seem to do anything useful for us, don't seem to have any relation to the real, actual world, and when you actually need them they've closed for the weekend to go out and get drunk spending your money.

To our surprise, considering we were just the wrong side of filthy, we were, indeed, admitted directly into the Armenian Club with no blagging involved or negotiation required. I was slightly disappointed that things had suddenly become so easy, as I was so used to fighting for everything, struggling to wrench whatever we needed from the iron grip of a world that seemed to hate us.

There were looks of horror as we went in from the guests eating their lunches, but the staff were friendly to us and ignored my muddied clothes and our wind-damaged faces. We told them we were simply making inquiries about coming back later. We left to go back to the man on the door, and he told us we could drink there but only if we brought our own booze. We asked if he could get us any, and he made a call but "regrettably" could only offer us wine or whiskey. We went for Scotch, which was only about the same price as you might pay at home in an average-sized supermarket.

We now had money, booze, and had earned back a whole day or two on the road. We headed slowly back to the hotel, picking up other bits we needed, and put our illegal Scotch in the fridge, very proud of ourselves and very much looking forward to burning through it later, and then talking nonsense until we argued, and then fighting until we slept.

I checked my emails, and then quite suddenly and out of nowhere Marcin insisted he wanted to see the tower, the fifth largest in the world. I had little interest in it, but he made a sad face, so in the end I agreed to go with him and keep him out of trouble. Escorting Marcin, keeping him mostly out of trouble and cheering him up when he did the sad-face seemed to be my main function in life for the moment.

We rode out through the insane traffic of Tehran, the craziest driving so far on our trip. It wasn't as bad over the weekend, but was still awful, and as we got off our bikes, I made a sad face myself. There was still daylight, and we got a few pictures on the way, but when we got there, I have to confess, the tower was quite impressive, and I ended up being quite glad I'd done it.

We had to get tickets to go to the top, and then we had to wait to be allowed in to go up to the observation deck. While there, we met up with three Asian tourists we'd seen briefly in the hotel earlier during breakfast. Like us, they stood out somewhat, as tourism was relatively rare. We all got chatting and decided to meet up in the hotel lobby later for a discussion about the intricacies of human interaction within a foreign sociological environment or about riding motorbikes too quickly, whichever happened first.

The sightseeing was unremarkable, but they had metal detectors to make sure you're not carrying anything dangerous, like a Leatherman multi-tool with two razor-sharp blades. I was, so I just put it in the metal tray and passed through the detector. Nobody even bothered to check the contents of my pocket that I'd emptied out right in front of them, so that was OK then, our safety was clearly assured.

The view was impressive! The town was actually huge and stretched out before us into the darkness, punctuated by a myriad of winking lights all the way to the edges of the horizon. The top deck was filled with a display of modern art, which translated into Christmas-tree lights stuck to a blue wall.

As we do, we chatted with everyone and made a bit of a nuisance of ourselves, but randomly people came up to us and chatted, asked us about ourselves, and even gave me a handful of assorted nuts, which seemed to be a custom there; or, more likely, an insult. I didn't care, because I like nuts.

In the lobby a security guard was driving a Segway. He wouldn't let me drive it, but he let me stand on it for photographs, and then I did drive it, but not very far, because he looked a bit sad. They're quite cool. I definitely need to have a proper go on one at some point, never having crashed such a thing before. It was very surreal to stand on an electric device that does your balancing for you, almost like driving a BMW R1200gs, which thinks it knows better and grumbles at you if you have the audacity to modify your own motorcycle.

Sadly, this is the future. Motorcycles are no longer ridden by humans. They have electronic controls to take the actual skill out of pretty much everything. It's already pretty self-evident where all this will end, since it's already started. Honda is producing self-balancing motorcycles, and BMW claims to be developing the technology to make it impossible to crash. I mean, where's the fun in that?

The ride back was a bit worse than the ride there. It was completely dark by then, and the traffic was heavier and a little angrier, and it was angry and heavy at the best of times. More annoyingly, my GPS was no longer working at all, and Marcin's didn't help very much, so we had to take the long way back to the hotel. We can make electronic gadgets to do the work of various parts of bodies and minds, but the whole system falls down when none of them actually work. It doesn't bode well that we're removing the skill and experience from people and cramming it into electronic devices that constantly let us down.

Once we had our bearings, we went out to get some food in the part of town we knew from our search for the embassy. The night before we had sandwiches, and the food was quite surprisingly good, but the place was closed, so we went to another. I had a vegetarian pizza, which had no tomato sauce, but it did come with two sachets of ketchup. Marcin had a kebab, which turned out to be mince in a plastic tub with a ton of bread piled all over it. With an economy closed off to the excesses of the West, junk food chains couldn't get their greasy claws into the population's health, so at least the Iranians were largely spared from diabetes, cancer, and morbid obesity. The chains they've created to fill this void did their best, but were a pale copy of the vague approximations of food served by the corporations back home. We were both unimpressed, but no longer hungry. We hadn't managed to find any specifically Iranian traditional food or even restaurants that sold it. We were a bit disappointed in that.

Finally, we went back and had a glass of whiskey and Coke in our hotel, not wanting to risk taking the bottle out of the room and offending anyone's beliefs. After that, we went down to the lobby to write blogs and play online, never really expecting the other tourists to turn up and join us. That didn't last long. An Italian guy joined us nervously, a lone traveller in search of a conversation, and then a New Zealander came and sat with us, far less nervously. We all chatted for a while about motorcycles, life, the universe, and everything.

By the time he left for presumably, better things, our new Asian friends came back to the hotel from their sightseeing. We later discovered they were a couple from Indonesia and a not-very-old Chinese girl, who was actually travelling alone. We had presumed they were all together, but apparently they were not. The young girl had latched onto them and followed them around all day without their permission, and they had been too polite to ask her what she was doing.

In speaking with her later, she seemed to be quite the most insane person I had ever met, and I once dated a paranoid schizophrenic who went on, after we split, to attempted murder when the voices in her head told her to kill someone and were fairly indiscriminate about who.

We all hung out in the Internet café at the side of the lobby, chatting and exchanging experiences. One of the staff caught on that we had access to alcohol, so he asked if he could join us, but refused a drink himself. He offered to officially close the lobby, making it a private party; that way we could bring some whiskey and relax. The gentleman who was manning the reception desk invited himself to join us too and proved to be a seasoned alcoholic, drinking like the drinks were free, which to him, they were. The mood quickly shifted to a very social party atmosphere, with hotel guests and staff all having fun together.

The Indonesian couple were artists as it turned out, going from country to country getting people involved in projects that demonstrate reactions to their creative ideas. We spent hours watching videos of their performance art that involved normal people on the street just having fun. The young Chinese girl was strangely interesting, but very strange in an interesting way, and twenty minutes of talking to her gave me a headache. A few others joined in, and we ended up stuck there until well after 3AM, after which I point I stopped counting.

That night we slept very well for a change.

20

Finding Yourself Lost

Date—November 5th
Location—Tehran, Iran
Mood—Argumentative and increasingly belligerent

This was a day of highs and lows, and not just because we went up into the freezing cold mountains again.

True to form, we woke up pretty early and had ourselves some breakfast. Luckily, as most of our alcohol had been poured into the night staff, we had passed on the hangover to them. Everywhere has a different way of doing things, but this hotel gave us a breakfast menu on the table, listing the various options available. After considering our choices carefully, we decided we'd have it, all of it, and with an egg on top.

None of the others from our previous evening were there, so we ate basically alone. Presumably, it was too early for them. The food was okay, but unimaginative—just standard Iranian bread, cheese, and eggs, served up with coffee. I prefer buffets, especially when I'm hungry, but anything is better than nothing, while nothing is only better than Bulgarian food.

The look on the faces of the staff were something to see. They weren't used to someone like Marcin, which is fair enough, because he is a unique specimen of what happens when nature isn't paying proper attention. He looked up and down the menu options, smiled, and handed back the menu, telling them that was fine. They returned a puzzled stare. He explained in simple terms that the menu was fine. Bring it. In fact, he told them to bring it twice, and whatever I didn't eat, he would. They were smart enough not to protest, food was brought and subsequently inhaled in roughly three seconds.

After a while, it was time to head out, so we left the dining room to begin packing up. Packing up after two days is never fun. You tend to spread out, so everything gets lost, unpacked, and confused with other things. Any pretence at being organised is gone. On that note, packing up after one day is never fun, either, for almost identical reasons.

By the time we took our stuff down to get it strapped onto our bikes, Jojo, the Chinese girl we met the morning, afternoon, and evening before, was having breakfast with a large group of Tibetans she'd never met before but had somehow joined up with in such a way that she had managed to blend into their group, just as she had the day before to a completely different group.

She came out to say goodbye, with her usual exhausting enthusiasm. We loaded up while she followed us with her camera making engine noises and odd comments. Luckily, she was more interested in making them to Marcin, since he had made the mistake of seeming politely interested.

He gave me a worried look and said, in a way that could only come out of Marcin, who basically filters nothing so that every thought he has comes fluttering immediately out of his eating-hole, "Perhaps she wants to have sex with me." I told him that it was best for everyone involved if we didn't know what was going on inside her head. While it might be true that he expresses every thought he has, fortunately he has remarkably few of them, so it basically balances out.

Marcin agreed that we should meet her in a different hotel that evening, as she was going the same way we were, albeit by coach.

We exchanged details while I glared at him angrily, and then we rode back out into the snapping jaws of Tehran's city traffic with some idea of a plan where we were headed. As Marcin had a hand in it, I had little doubt that we'd end up somewhere completely else.

I love travelling, and I was enjoying this trip, but some things are hard. Occasionally, you meet people or see a place and the only thing your bike can do in the morning is take you away from it. Time was always against us, and of course, you burn through money when you waste time, so the road was beckoning us away. We were both carrying tents and sleeping bags in the hope of camping rough, but the opportunity had simply not presented itself so far. We knew it wouldn't be a prospect in Pakistan and imagined the same might be true in India. Hotels were warm/cool and fed us in the morning, so for now, we were making the most of it, but it was eating into our limited budget. The previous night had been great fun and exactly the reason I was on the road. We'd met and chatted with some intelligent, interesting people. We'd met others who were on the road and on their own journey for their own reasons, and we'd finished a bottle of black market Scotch with them.

Everyone who travels has their own personal reasons for doing it, but mine had been to challenge my perceptions with new, fresh, and interesting perspectives; to expand beyond the experiences I've had on my own and hopefully change my life for the better.

Tehran was a big city, and there was always a personal stigma to them for me. They're ugly places, impersonal, and difficult to navigate. Traffic is usually horrible, and the people are never as nice as the ones you meet out of town, since people aren't really meant to live in such close conditions. Tehran, just like any city, suffered from this, as well as having a special place in the world as possibly the home of the worst driving, outside of a hospital for the totally blind and partially bewildered.

I was ready to leave Tehran. It just felt like all the other towns of Iran but on a larger, busier scale, and with somehow less character. I was keen to move on to smaller towns and meet the real people that lived there. Still, there was a momentary pang of regret. The people we'd met and the time we'd spent had been fun, and the evening had left an impression on me. Even Marcin seemed to have a momentary pang of emotion, but perhaps he was just hungry—it was often difficult to tell. It turned out to be a fart.

So, with some difficulty, we made it out of the city, but the sat-nav was not on our side, and obviously nor were the drivers. At least we got out with less difficulty than we got in. Maybe the earlier hour made a difference, but the struggle wasn't as horrendous as we'd braced ourselves for. I won't suggest it was easy, but we made progress for the whole time and at no point were part of a stationary mess of grumbling, impatient drivers.

Iranians drive to kill—there's no taking of prisoners there—and it was a dangerous slog. The women actually seem worse than the men. This isn't a comment implying women can't drive; after all, it's aimed at a country where it seemed nobody could; it's just that the female drivers were incredibly aggressive, which is strikingly the opposite of the usual case. They nudge up behind you, forcing you to speed up or swerve out of their way, and seem intent on getting past you at any cost. The worst drivers are usually young men, pumped up with testosterone and out to prove themselves to the world, but in Iran, the women were worse than any of the men we'd seen behind the wheel.

We got safely out of the city limits and looked for fuel so we could continue to put ourselves through this endless nonsense. One woman blundered into our way, twice, nearly taking us off one by one as she wandered around all of the road until she settled into a bit that she liked. She just aimed her car for us and swerved through both lanes. She hammered her little Citroen to pass us and then cut in front, just to pull back after and force us to slow down. We stopped in for petrol, and she pulled in behind us into the service station. She wound down the window and leant out to talk to me.

At that point I was thinking how, if I wasn't a guest in her country and she were a man, I would be having more than a polite discussion about her skills behind the wheel and taking it all far more personally. For a moment, the thought flashed through my mind that perhaps she had been deliberately attempting to run us off the road and was now going to yell abuse at us for some reason. Instead, though, she asked where I was from with a smile and gave me her number on a business card. I have no idea why. She just kept saying it was in case we ever needed help with anything, and acted like we were all old friends.

I was surprised. Instantly, my anger turned to annoyance and that, in turn, turned to bewilderment as I tried to make sense of why such a friendly person would drive so dangerously and without any consideration of other people's safety. My mind momentarily refused to process the two extremes, and I stood there just trying to make sense of it in confused silence.

We filled our bikes and were just sorting out to leave the station when we heard the unmistakable crunch of two soft metal panels creasing one another up in an accident. A van pulled out into a car, or vice versa, probably without looking. It was the woman whose card I had in my pocket and a grey van that had collided with one another. There were a few pockets of laughter at first, followed by the two drivers shouting at one another, and then some driving off. No details exchanged, and no worries about repairs. Nobody even looked at the damage!

It made me wonder why the country insists you have insurance when it seems a bit pointless, and by the state of the indigenous driving, a bit cheeky too. With no reliable sat-nav, we asked directions and were told we were heading in the right direction, which made a refreshing change and startled us both.

So after about thirty miles we escaped the reach of the city, the traffic got lighter, and the run got far more pleasant without the constant fear for your very life and limb. The towns, and the urban sprawl beyond, melted away into desert, and this time it was a proper desert, like what you might expect to see in fictional TV shows, such as Fox News.

We stopped for photos at the side of a stretch of road where sand and rocks were punctuated by dusty green shrubs, and you could almost imagine a news correspondent telling a camera how terrible things there were, while two locals looked at each other, perhaps a little puzzled about what he was doing, before deciding it might be nice to offer him some tea.

Eventually, we plodded along until I ran out of fuel rather earlier than we expected. The neoprene hose I was using to siphon fuel was not working again, and so we had to find a garage to fill up on "Benzine." We made it twenty-seven miles into my thirty mile reserve and filled up in a small town called Seman, where it all went a bit wrong, just for a change. The greeting we got was typically warm, but this far out of the city we were novelties again, and crowds gathered round to stare at us while we did the most mundane of things.

Checking maps, we discovered that we had taken the wrong direction. We had somehow missed the quicker and easier route and were a fair bit out of our way. After a brief break and a drink, we went off in the somewhat vain hope of making up our time and getting back on track.

We headed off to a junction with a sense of wildly misplaced optimism that we might get ourselves back pointing in the right direction. An old man in a white car was gesturing in the direction we were heading and saying, "No, it is the wrong direction." I couldn't understand what he was saying, but figured we hadn't spoken to him before, so how did he know where we wanted to go?

We checked once again, and sure enough, the map pointed to the road he had told us was wrong, and the road would lead us back to where we wanted to be. By then the old man was gone, and we couldn't quite make sense of the encounter; he had no idea where we were headed, so how did he know which way we should go? The road signs pointed to the town we wanted, and the map agreed with them, for all the use that was.

We carried on along the road, which should have connected us to our destination, according to a map I downloaded from the Internet, or at least the small part of it that worked in Iran. The scenery changed again, and the desert was even more interesting and even more deserted. Even traffic was light, and we were stared at more than usual. This carried on until we finally came to the end of the road. It split into two small tracks, one branching off in either direction. My compass needle pointed right, but Marcin's partially functional GPS said to go straight on, even though there actually was no "straight on" to go.

In the end, we had no choice but to follow along with the GPS. Not more than a few yards along, we were stopped by two workmen who tried to signal us that we couldn't go that way. They didn't speak English but seemed to insist that the town we wanted was there, but we couldn't go to it, for some unknown reason. They told us we had to take the other road. We did, and it led us directly into the blockade of what was apparently a secret army base.

We got more directions while the soldiers laughed at us and were told that both the place we were looking for was on the other road, but that it wasn't as well. So we turned about and left as quickly as we could, and before we got arrested, to meet at the junction and look at an actual paper map and try to puzzle all that out

We argued over how to proceed. Marcin insisted we should ride down the first road, but there was clearly a reason why we weren't allowed to, and I said we had no choice but to head back to the town and take the longer route out to the border. Marcin argued that he wanted to go there, but everyone nodded enthusiastically when I suggested returning to Seman.

I knew there was some reason we couldn't follow the route on the map, and we had to return to the town and get on the proper road to get back on track. By that point, Marcin literally regressed to the age of five and began stamping around in the midst of a temper tantrum. He accused me of being scared to ride, of being scared of sand, of being only half a man, and of being entirely responsible for making a decision that was going to utterly ruin the entire rest of his life.

While we talking loudly and in a highly animated fashion, the army came to arrest us.

A big yellow HumVee pulled up, and two people scurried out nervously. An officer who spoke little English asked for passports with a serious expression, while a young soldier was holding place back at the rear of the car looking terrified, cowering behind a very old-looking AK47. The officer looked mine over and saw us arguing over GPS and maps, and I guess he pretty soon realised we were just lost and started laughing at us. We did the ballet of hand gestures and half-remembered words that people do when they can't speak the same language and reached something like an understanding.

I gathered from our broken conversation that the road was restricted for military use, some kind of supply line that you have to have special clearance to drive on, and that there was a military airfield nearby. After clearing that up, the officer suggested through gesture that we come back to the base for some lunch and tea, such is the hospitality of the people of that country. I actually quite fancied that, but we were late, and now we had to backtrack for thirty miles, the prospect of which was making Marcin vibrate with furious rage.

Checking the time against the maps, it was clear we didn't have any more to waste if we didn't want to end up stranded in the middle of nowhere as the evening temperatures plummeted. We had no choice but to forge on and try our best to get to a reasonable-sized town before nightfall.

Marcin rode angry. I couldn't keep up with his larger bike, but he followed directions that now took us hundreds of miles out of our way. He deliberately pulled away from me, knowing my smaller machine was falling behind. Eventually, we stopped for gas and to find out what was up ahead. There was nothing. We were literally about to ride into the desert, the old fashioned kind, with nothing but sand and camels and warning signs (mostly about camels). There was a town some 150 miles away, and night was closing in, bringing with it dropping temperatures and crushing darkness.

We had little choice really, so we headed off. Our fuel range should have been just enough to get us there, and we had around forty-five minutes of light left, so the chances of it actually working were somewhere between slim to none. Still, we were adventurers, after all, and more importantly, we were idiots.

After a blast through the desert, we saw the light of the town on the horizon, a mess of tiny orange pinpricks of light that made up a larger haze on the way ahead. A big town you can see from twenty miles, but we were on top of this one before we saw the lights. Trucks were gathered around the few shops at the front, and there was petrol. We filled up first, and a local man with surprisingly good English skills came over to speak with us.

I asked if we would be allowed to camp at the side of the petrol station, being that it was safer to be close to some kind of civilisation. He told us we should be able to stay at the government office, instead, and he would help to arrange it. We were resolved to the idea of camping by then in any case and were actually quite looking forward to it, even though to camp properly you need booze and lots of it.

While we waited to see what he might come up with, we got some food. It was simple enough, but it was also some of the best food we'd had in the country. We sat in the cool wind of the desert night at the side of a small road, trucks to the side of us in a cluster of three roadside buildings that seemed to us to be the entire town. The scene was lit by a few economy lightbulbs that sent shadows dancing around us as the breeze gently blew them about on the end of their cables.

We sat, eating some grilled bread and fried vegetables as the austere beauty of the evening desert stretched out before us, and we listened to the sounds of crickets chirping as we spoke of how desperately we wanted beer and lots of it.

We chatted to one another, now that the mood had settled. Marcin is a tense knot of emotional gristle, but once he settles into the inevitable, all is forgotten, and he was now perfectly happy with the situation. I was working through the map to see how long it would take us to fix our errors and get back to the world.

Unlike Marcin, I liked being lost, it meant we would be doing and seeing things that we otherwise might have missed. In any case, we were now in the real Iran with real, normal Iranians. They were still some of the most helpful, friendly people we'd met and still couldn't drive a vehicle much better than a chimpanzee wearing boxing-gloves.

The man from the petrol station arrived at the shop, and we were led to the rear of the building, where we were shown an empty room with carpets laid across the floor. They gestured "moto" outside, meaning we should park there, and we hoped they were offering us a place to stay. We arranged a price which came to less than £3 for the night to rent the room, and it was more than good enough for us. With things now settled, we took a quick ride around the town to get a feel for it, and it was awesome.

It was much more than it looked from the road, and we found a tiny little desert village with no traffic, other than a few CG125 bikes that followed us, cheering and waving enthusiastically. There was a highstreet with an Internet café and, very strangely, a vinyl record shop that was decorated in '70s-style retro posters. It was startlingly clean and organised, like nothing was out of its place. Small trees and plants had been lined up at the side of the roads, all perfectly arranged. It was a place that might have been fun to spend more than a night in.

When we got back and parked up for the night, the crowds gathered around us again, and Marcin was passed a phone. We were invited for a barbecue the next morning for breakfast, and then the man with the phone wanted us to follow him, but we had no idea why; it was all communicated with hand gestures.

We jumped on our bikes after unpacking our gear and followed along. No helmets were required in the town, or probably in any town where the police station is an old caravan parked or dumped in the middle of a road. Again, the locals greeted us warmly on the road. I'm not sure where or how we found this out, but I'd picked up that this man had restored a house and wanted to show us, but we still had no idea what was going on.

It was fun, though, and as it turned out, it wasn't a house as we understood the idea, it was a small castle type of building, and we were allowed to ride around inside it. We got off our bikes, assuming that just showing us was the point, and we would have been happy with that, as it was a fantastic thing to see. The building itself was very impressive and something you just wouldn't see anywhere else. It was carved or cast from sandstone, a mixture of simple sand and tree-sap, mixed together and baked in the sun, sometimes in bricks and sometimes in larger parts. The walls had been smoothed over, so the entire thing seemed like it had been made whole just right there in place. Sadly, the nature of the construction made it weaker than traditional brickwork, and the buildings aged poorly. This one was being rebuilt, restored to its former glory, and now had two motorcycles parked inside of it with two confused, but impressed, riders.

He invited us inside, so we followed along, still with no idea what was happening. Inside were a dozen people welcoming us to Iran in perfect English and offering us food and hospitality. It was an amazing greeting. Even after the other warm welcomes we've had in this country, this one caught us way off-guard. The whole family welcomed us into their midst.

We were happy to join them and were asked to remove our shoes and wash up, which we did. They had food and drinks to offer and wouldn't take no for an answer. Luckily, "no" wasn't our answer and would never have been.

It was all quite a surprise at first—the women were all free of scarves, since they were no longer in public and were free to take off their covers. Still, it was the first time we'd seen such a thing in days, and it did seem oddly unfamiliar to see female hair once again.

Most of them spoke English to an exceptional standard but still apologised for not speaking it even better. Sadly, I'm hopeless with languages and have nothing but respect for anyone who can master a foreign one, and these people had.

They were all friendly and warm, and we stayed for hours, chatting about where we were from, where we were going, and our thoughts on Iran. They were especially interested in the last of those. They were intelligent, passionate young people, and it was a pleasure to meet them like that.

Marcin insisted, as he does, in asking for illegal beer, but that was no problem, and several different brands appeared—a bottle of Scotch and some home brew was offered to us. Again, I was surprised. The home brew was great—it tasted like a cider but was made from lemons. It was a fair bit stronger too, but how could we refuse that kind of hospitality?

Eventually, we had to leave, but frankly, I would have stayed all night if I could have. I learned a lot about what it is to live in that country from the people who really understood it best. I felt that I had grasped a little more of their culture and their belief, and that was exactly why I was making this trip. I had heard Iranians were warm and friendly, but saying so does not do them justice.

In the end, time was catching us up, Marcin was tired, I was getting there, and the man who owned the house wanted to take us back to our cupboard. We arranged to meet in the morning, around nine, for breakfast and pictures of the house. All they asked in return was that we would take them out for a spin on our bikes. To us, that was like asking if they could give us beer!

21

The Road To, From, and Around Nowhere

Date—November 6th
Location—Jamdaq, Iran
Status—Awesome

We slept in a room that was sparsely furnished with only several carpets dotted around and a heater that didn't work. We didn't need it—the desert actually surprised us by being warm and comfortable, and the temperature in the room was perfectly fine. The floor, being a floor, was pretty solid, but we were tired enough that we could have slept anywhere. Motorcycles will have that effect on the human body, I find.

I dozed into the morning, half asleep in my sleeping-bag, and vaguely remember it being dark and then suddenly light in the space of around three to four seconds. Maybe that is possible in the desert around the mountains, or maybe the lemon cider/beer was even stronger than I had thought. We'd seen it before, darkness coming in like a curtain being draw across a window, the light suddenly vanishing as we rode around the brow of a mountain. My exhaustion was the more likely explanation.

We got up before the alarm to a hectic morning schedule, but I was growing used to that. We had arranged to meet the family at 9AM and had to be on the road shortly after if we were going to have a chance of getting to Zahedan for a crossing into Pakistan the next day, or even the same day if we made good enough time. Usually, we looked to spend a whole day on border crossings, since they were unpredictable and beset with a multitude of possible things that could go wrong, but wouldn't, and couldn't go wrong, but would. In terms of making problems for ourselves we were becoming experts.

We went around the town and took a few pictures. Having come in at night meant we really had no idea what it actually looked like—we'd not seen the scenery, the building, or anything else properly. The town was small but impressive, new buildings mixed with ancient, traditional structures, but just like human nature, it was basically the same as we knew things to be, albeit on a different scale.

The high-street sat at the heart as the community centre, with the suburbs arranged outside where everyone actually lives. The industry was arranged on the outskirts, spreading out into the sand.

People seemed pleased to see us, even though it was early and we were generally noisy and imposing on our big western bikes. We found the house, which was far more impressive by daylight. We parked up and knocked on the door, but there was no answer. We knocked again, but didn't want to impose on their already impressive hospitality, so after a while we left them to it and began to head back.

The man who owned the house seemed to have arranged a tour of the building, so we went around inside a different part to see just what it was they were doing. It was impressive, but the tour did seem to drag on a bit. The man doing the tour spoke not one word of English, and we understood nothing at all of what he was saying. Still, there was no sign of the family, and we waited as long as we could. Eventually, we had to break it off. We shook his hand and thanked him, but it was well past time to leave.

We went back to our little alcove and packed up and went to get some breakfast. We had eggs and bread with yogurt and juice. Once we'd finished that, Marcin had a kebab, just to be safe, he told me.

We hit the road later than we wanted, but optimistic that reaching our goal was still quite possible. It wasn't. It wasn't even close. Hoping for the best wasn't always the best way of dealing with things, but we'd never found anything that worked any better. Maybe we never would.

I maintain that, technically, we could have done it if the map we had was even close to accurate. The roads, which should have been straight, curved miles out of their way around the mountain ranges, and we lost hours winding our way through the admittedly awesome scenery. The desert there had many faces. That day the canopy was grey and hostile, whereas the day before we rode through a crystal blue and cloudless day.

We had a few spots of rain early on, which was a worry, because a storm there is unlikely to be a friendly thing. I noticed that the few cars there were coming towards us were dry, and the mountains ahead were likely to contain the rain. In fact, we headed into a brighter sky, and the weather was never bad enough to cause us any problems.

At first, the landscape was baron and yellow, but it went to darker shades of brown, and then through rugged rocky passes. The rocks were softer there, not jagged and pointed like the European peaks, shaped like the cutting teeth of a predator, but more rounded and smoothed off by the hot and sandy desert winds.

Still, it had the look of a place man simply doesn't belong and isn't at all welcome. What survives there is just surviving and will never thrive. It's not a place to be taken lightly, even for a day. My lungs burnt from the dust, my nostrils burned from the salted air, and my eyes ached, burning into my skull. During the morning, we rode through our exhaustion.

The scenery was so repetitive and so empty that there was just nothing interesting to see, so your mind had nothing to deal with. You're faced with a long, empty road, with sand both sides stretching into the horizon, punctuated by the foggy white threats of mountain peaks somewhere just away from your perception. It seemed to shut down your brain, and we slumped into a kind of weary depression, the ride sapping our energy and leaving us feeling empty and drained.

My fuel system still needed sorting out with a proper rubber hose, because it was the only thing on that day that wasn't drained. It was getting quite unreliable, and annoyingly so. The heat seemed to be expanding the neoprene so it no longer formed a tight seal, and when that happened, it no longer fed fuel. That meant I had to top up in the desert from a can. Marcin usually grumbled about every stop we ever had to make, but even he welcomed the break from the road this time.

That morning, my bike pinked horrendously and delivered nothing more than the lacklustre power of an XT660 that had been tuned for performance. The fuel quality was declining; it didn't smell right, and the bikes were suffering right along with us. Marcin's machine showed fewer problems, since he had more power on top, but we were both struggling with loss of performance, sputtering, and difficulty starting.

We carried on, but there was nothing to see, just desert, sand, and rocks. Eventually, we came to a fork in the road, and both GPSs had different suggestions, as we both had different maps loaded. While the touch-screen on my unit had failed, we still had it loaded with a map so that it would follow us and tell us where we were. It had seemed like an obvious precaution that we should install different maps so we could cross-confirm our decisions. With both maps telling us to head in opposite directions, and with mine was still playing up and badly, we followed the other, which did seem to be pointing in the more correct direction and more or less followed the paper maps, even though it wasn't following it as close as I would have liked. We were then stopped at our first police checkpoint of the day and our first ever in Iran. It was a mark of things changing and not for the better.

They checked my passport, but stopped at the first page, and we were quickly allowed on our way. Three younger officers, barely more than teenagers, tried to make a fuss, but an older man in a uniform barked at them, and they backed off sheepishly. We tried to get them to pose for a picture, but they became quite agitated and angry. Marcin tried to pose for one away from them, but they grabbed for the camera, so we gave up and moved ourselves along.

There was no being friendly with them; they made it very clear that they didn't want us there. The young ones were particularly hostile.

Things were definitely changing. Faces were getting darker; moods were more sombre. The people were different, and I got the feeling that it wasn't going to turn out to be in a positive way.

We plodded and plodded on from one petrol station to another and had four more police checks as we ran down towards the Pakistan border, but we had no more trouble. It was all just routine, except that first one.

Eventually, we stopped in a small town for fuel. It was a typical desert roadside town, and the main road had roadworks that we had to ride through to get anywhere. We went over piles of gravel and sand and through ditches. That was fun and a very welcome break in our routine. Even though it was barely a hundred metres, it perked both of us right up. Finally, I was getting something close to hard terrain to ride on, and my little bike was useful.

After four more hours in the desert, I insisted we stop for a drink so I could adjust my rattling chain and check the map to see how well we were progressing. There was no argument from Marcin, and that was strangely disquieting. It was clear we were both struggling.

The map showed us that we weren't making any progress, and I took it hard. After a day slogging through the desert until my throat was dry, my lips were split, and my face was burning red, we were still not even a third of the way to our goal. That was a difficult thing to take, and for once, it was me that was angry about our lack of progress.

Marcin wanted to blast on through the night, pointing to towns hundreds of miles away. I said we could make a town called Birjand, still 190 miles and more than three hours ride ahead of us. On my map it was big enough to offer at least something to eat and somewhere to camp, but the maps were not to be trusted, that much we knew by then.

He grumbled, but the fact was he was suffering every bit as much as I was, and he knew we weren't going to make it through the night. Luckily, his arguments dwindled away to nothing very quickly. We had already both had enough for one day, and finding out that we'd achieved so little at so high a price had demoralised us both. But that wasn't going to stop us, we were determined to get a little further.

We slogged on into the distance and then slogged on some more as night closed in all around us. Other towns came and went, and I seriously thought about stopping short and just giving up for the day. But I really wanted to get there, or else the day would feel like a complete failure, and we'd end up just having to do it all again the next day to make up the difference. That thought alone kept me just motivated enough to continue.

Marcin later told me he had been thinking the same thing.

Finally, we saw the signs as it grew closer, and it was a huge relief to us both that we would soon be able to stop. To our surprise, the towns were growing bigger and closer together, street signs were offering more than just warnings of impending camels, and the roads were becoming dual-carriageways. When we finally arrived at the outskirts, the city was, in fact, huge. To me, this meant the possibility of a shower, food, Internet, and bed. I was past caring about anything else.

After some creative navigation, we made it to the town centre and started asking around for a hotel.

It didn't go particularly well, but finally we found a guy who spoke some English. By then, we were teetering on the edge of exhaustion, and he offered, kindly, to lead us to a hotel, perhaps taking pity on us.

I explained that we wanted a cheap one but had no idea how much he was understanding. He drove and drove until the city was a blurred mass of streetlights in the distance behind us. Eventually, we arrived up a mountain pass at a huge, sprawling hotel complex, which didn't look cheap at all and, in fact, couldn't have been much more of the opposite.

The police and army were camped outside and ran at us, but backed away as we entered the hotel grounds.

It was too expensive. After haggling the price down to only £22 for a double room with breakfast, Wi-Fi, and parking, they suddenly decided to charge that for each of us and began adding taxes. We decided to leave, and the guy who had led us there offered to take us to a cheaper place in town. It was no better, another huge and expensive looking place, and they were asking the same price as before. I negotiated it down to £25 for the pair of us, which was actually a bargain, and we finally agreed, settled in, dumped our stuff, and flopped down on a bed.

A quick shower filled the bathroom with sand and mud—the desert had found every crease and fold of my clothing and had managed to get into every unprotected hole in my body. Every breath I took brought the smell of the desert rushing back to my senses with such potency that I could taste it at the back of my throat.

We might have left it, but it hadn't yet left us.

While Marcin was doing whatever horrors it was that Marcin does in the bathroom, I checked the map against the Internet. We were facing a solid eight-hour ride again to the border in the morning. Somehow, we had managed to lose a complete day and were back in precisely the same situation as we had been the morning when we had left. After what the day's ride had taken out of us, that was a depressing thought indeed.

22

Iran Turns Nasty

Date—November 7th
Location—Iran, but not for much longer
Status—Increasingly difficult

In Iran there appears to be a rule that all things abide by. If it's easy, then something will happen to make it difficult; if it can go wrong, it will go more wrong than you can possibly imagine and in ways you couldn't possibly believe.

We woke up in our top-class hotel, for which we paid bottom dollar, thanks to some negotiating skills that essentially involved me saying no very grumpily and then them offering it cheaper and cheaper until I finally said yes. We ended up paying about £25 a night, with free breakfast and Internet.

Breakfast was a buffet, quite simple, but we stuffed ourselves full to the bemusement of the other guests; who stared in abject horror at the filthy bikers who had invaded their otherwise civilised discourse. At one point, we were followed by staff trying to clean up after us, and that became a sort of challenge for us to make even more mess.

It's safe to say, we made a lot of mess.

Having only a handful of euros to settle the bill and no local currency left, we headed out to the banks, as the staff at the hotel reception had told us they opened at 7:30. We went as soon as we could, hoping to hit the road and make an early start to make up for the disaster we had endured the day before.

We knew we were in trouble when the banks weren't open as they were meant to be. We found a gentleman who spoke some English, and he told us it was like Christmas, and there would be no banks today. The clocks were ticking, and we had no way to settle the bill. We drove on to find someone to ask some advice on where to get local money. We stopped at a store to ask, and nobody spoke anything like English.

We got the usual crowds around the bike, but it was different this time. This wasn't friendly interest at all. There was a certain negative vibe, and we weren't made to feel welcome. Several people shouted, "Go home," and gestured off down the street angrily; crowds were beginning to form, and they seemed angry.

Nobody was trying to help us out with changing currency, and with the situation threatening to turn nasty, we rode away to find some other place to get advice. We stopped some way down the road and explained the situation to a cab driver who spoke some English. He didn't speak much, but we got an understanding between us, and he told us to follow him. He drove us back a few metres to a bank and then got out of his cab gesturing to the bank, telling us it was shut. We agreed.

I'm still not quite sure what his point was.

So then he took us to a jeweller. I chatted with the owner in broken English, and in the end he agreed to change some currency. The problem was that they had no concept of euros. They thought that dollars and euros were the same thing when euros were worth quite a bit more, but we finally thrashed out a deal that would get us to the border, if not much further beyond.

Once we were back at the hotel, I laid my bike down in back of the hotel and oiled the chain. When the chain had been sold with a mileage guarantee, they obviously hadn't factored in a ride through the Iranian desert. The sand and heat was giving the bike a pounding, and the chain was wearing out fast. Even after cleaning and oiling it, it still clattered afterwards, but it did seem to be no more serious than a dry link or two. It needed attention later, when I might have more time to give it to it. Replacing it was going to be difficult, if that became necessary anywhere along the way. Perhaps I should have packed a spare.

We finally headed out, leaving nothing more than greasy puddles on the hotel car park floor, and began our ride towards Zahaden, a town close to the Pakistan border. We got out of town fairly easily and were on the road by 9:30, a good start by any standard, especially with the problems we had already dealt with.

We made it two hours into the desert before we needed to stop for fuel. The scenery was more industrialised than before. Everywhere you looked for the first fifty miles of our ride someone had dug a quarry or built some ugly, grey skeletal metal structure.

After that, the mountains came in, and we were once again riding through the middle of nowhere. There was a strange passive-aggressive wind blowing us at first. It seemed gentle enough, but it made riding in a straight line more challenging than it would have been after drinking a bottle of absinthe. Then the wind stopped being passive and moved up to fully aggressive. Within a few minutes, we were lucky enough to experience our first sandstorm.

There was some rain, and then the winds blew sand all over us, a yellow mist that blotted out the sky. It was as tough as hell to ride through, and it slowed us down a lot, but we powered through it, not really having any choice in the matter. At one point, I could only manage fifty mph and had to hold my breath as we dragged ourselves along.

And then suddenly, it was gone, and we could ride normally. At one point, the wind blew a circular tunnel of sand into the sky, like a finger reaching out from the desert sand to swat the unwary bikers. The first missed. The second caught us square on, blasting hot sand against us painfully.

That went on for hours, until we stopped for gas at around 130 miles into our day's ride. Marcin kept wanting to ride faster and longer, and frankly, I was bored with his constant bitching about the distance we were covering, and I was tuning him out; his grumbling barely registered.

My bike was not always feeding from the auxiliary tank, certainly not with any degree of reliability. Petrol stations were rare, dotted around every sixty miles or so, and with the desert conditions, it was ideal to stop for a bottle of water and a five-minute break. I insulted him, he insulted me, and we got back on our bikes and headed off without another word said between us.

Once back on the road, we made good time for a refreshing change. By the first stop we had averaged sixty mph, and fifty-five mph on the second through pretty rough conditions. The second petrol station put the worst fuel so far into my poor little bike.

The quality had been so bad that I could literally not use top gear—she simply had no power to give me and tried to stall if I changed up to fifth. I had to keep her in fourth to perform the fairly modest task of climbing a hill at more than fifty mph. We were eventually stopped at a police checkpoint, where I warned Marcin of my difficulty with the bad fuel. His was suffering, but his engine made twice the power mine did, so he was having no difficulty with the performance, as he was only matching my speed. However, his bike was running lumpy, trying to stall, and was sputtering.

The police that time were a complete joke. They had no idea what they were doing, were rude, and tried to bully us. The officer, an older guy, just kept laughing, while the younger toy-soldiers tried to examine Marcin's bike, giggling the whole time like children. In the end, they waved us on, but it was beginning to leave a nasty taste with us.

Iran had changed; the warmth and hospitality was far behind us, there was no doubt left in my mind about that. This was our last day in Iran, and I didn't want our experience to undo all the positive feelings I had about the country, but it was beginning to happen.

After stopping, the bike did run better—there was not so much pinking, and she managed to give more power, if not quite up to her usual form. It was strange, as nothing really had changed. I presumed stopping and starting her had reset the computer. Bikes can be fussy things, BMWs especially so.

We made good time into Zahedan, arriving around 2:30PM, and joined the ring road to the border. Suddenly, the temperature dropped. It had been up to thirty-five degrees that day by my slightly inaccurate gauge, a constant heat that was tiring to ride through. It was still cold to ride in the desert air, but the sun cooked me inside my gear, and I had to take off my fleece at a fuel stop.

Now I had to put it back on. After that, we headed off to the border, and then I saw something that made me slam on the brakes.

Camels, dozens of them, a whole wild herd stretching way out to the horizon before us. I stopped for a quick picture and dashed up the road, where Marcin was waiting. He was grumbling about having to stop, as usual. "Camels!" I exclaimed excitedly, pointing off to the side of the road.

We rode out onto a sandy outcropping of rock so we could see further into the distance to take some pictures. We watched as the herd made its way off, freely roaming in this barren arid landscape.

The next bit is where it all went a bit more wrong again, and even more so than it usually does when it all goes wrong again.

We were stopped at a military checkpoint, as I thought we would be. Sure enough, they wanted to give us an escort, purely for our safety. So they chose a kid in uniform with no weapon who was dancing to imaginary rap music. He came out to high-five us, but we both just stared at him until he just shook hands like a normal person. Precisely how much protection he would be and against what was debatable.

Marcin was dubious about taking him, but it would have taken longer to have him follow us. Around that point we were told the border closed at 2PM. There was a town close to the border, where we could stay, or we could head back and cross in the morning. I didn't really mind, but leant towards staying at the border. Marcin wanted access to the Internet.

They told us the border town had it, so the decision was made. When we got there, it was certainly cheap, but there was no Internet at the only hotel. That didn't bother me, but then the owner began messing with us about with the price. It suddenly doubled, and he kept coming up with lists of extra charges.

We decided to give up on him and head back into town to try our luck there. By then, it was getting dark, and we had to wait for a police escort. He turned up eventually on the smallest bike I've ever seen and took the young soldier with him on the back. He begged me to let him ride on mine, but my entire back seat was covered in luggage. We were led out at around thirty mph as the tiny machine wobbled all over the road. I was getting the feeling, about then, that we should have stayed where we were.

The police bike stopped suddenly, weaving across the road in panic, before nearly dumping them both onto the floor. He somehow managed to hold it up and clambered off, kicking the rear wheel angrily.

He had a flat tyre, so I held the torch while he pumped it up and made a bodged repair. He seemed quite embarrassed as he slowly tried to repair his bike. The soldier begged to go on my bike once more, as Marcin had now got himself a better one—his new soldier was armed with an AK47 and was on the right side of puberty, but only just.

I had no space for a passenger, so I just ignored his begging. The flat tyre was more of a problem than it first appeared to be, so the police just waved us on to continue without them. We stopped at the next junction and were met by a van-load of guys, also armed with AK47s. They were dressed in desert headgear and no uniforms, so who they were was a mystery to us. It turned out they were border control, and we did a relay right to the first checkpoint, where we stopped. We chatted and waited until Marcin and I started bickering at one another—you drive too fast, you drive too slow, you do this wrong, etc. Pretty much the usual thing for us, but it was getting annoying now.

After waiting with the car-load of kids with guns, eventually a fat police officer came out, walking deliberately slowly, and did nothing but look at our papers. He was quite rude and was clearly on a bit of a power trip. It was like dealing with the UK police force, except he was even fatter, ruder, and more irritating. The country was trying quite hard to leave us with a negative impression of it, and it was definitely starting to work.

Eventually, he let us go, and we followed our police escort back to the town. By then, we'd figured it out. They were trying to wind us up, and frankly, it was working. When we finally arrived at the hotel, they recommended, it was too big, too nice, and too modern for us to afford. We only had a few notes left, and the place looked way out of our league. I went inside to ask, and although it was actually cheap, it was still too expensive.

And so began an escorted ride around town for a hotel in our price range that accepted euros and had some kind of Internet access. Being escorted meant following the chief of police, who was carrying his baton and riding on a tiny 125cc motorcycle with a teenager on the back carrying an AK47.

We ended up wearily resigned to the fact that nothing in this town had what we wanted, and in fact, the first place came closest. We annoyed the escort further by saying we were going back there. By the time we got there it was a full six and a half hours after we arrived at the first military checkpoint. We were pretty fed up with that town by then. It was nothing but children pretending to be soldiers and throwing their weight around, endless checkpoints, endless rules, and constant rude comments that made the soldiers giggle like a pack of teenage girls; teenage girls with AK47s.

One of them was a particularly annoying prick. He wasn't even allowed a gun—he had a stick and kept coming up to our faces and banging the floor with it, threateningly. I finally lost my temper with him and stepped forward to confront him, but he backed up and ran away, and we didn't see much from him again. One soldier, either through a misunderstanding in the translation or to annoy us, said he loved me, so I gave him a special hug, and we didn't see him again either.

Finally, we got into the hotel. It was okay, and breakfast was included. Internet access was typically rubbish, but I had expected no less. In fact, I'd pretty much given up on the Internet while in Iran, quicker than I gave up on the dreams of alcohol.

So we booked our escort back to the border for 7AM, kicking ourselves for not just staying in the hotel at the border, where we could have left with the friendly local policeman on his tiny bike first thing in the morning, instead of spending nearly seven hours trying to travel less than fifty miles while dealing with the absolute dregs of the Iranian population.

23

How the Other Half Lives

Date—November 8th
Location—Zahaden, Iran
Status—Painful

We woke up expecting our escort at 7AM. Well, not really expecting it, more kind of hoping he would arrive at any time before noon. We optimistically, and somewhat unrealistically, brought down our gear and ate some breakfast in no kind of rush. Then, at around 7:45AM, he actually did turn up. A police officer in a car more battered than a dead fish swaggered in, demanding our passports at the very top of his voice. Another arsehole.

We left our food and began packing up. He kept shouting about our passports. I told him, pointing to the hotel office, that they had them, in accordance with their local customs and laws. He knew that—he was just being awkward for the sake of it. I told him that after making us wait all night, they could manage to wait five minutes while we loaded up, especially since *he* was late.

So we went to pay, and the price went up, as expected. They charged us for Internet access, despite the fact they never mentioned the charges before and it didn't even work. In my hour of access, I managed to send only three emails.

We argued and even refused to pay, but the police officer started to leave, so in the end, I stopped him, and we had to pay the extra or be stuck there. I told the staff exactly what I thought of them, and they sheepishly apologised, but they didn't mean it—they were just embarrassed at being called so many horrible things so loudly by a so very angry Englishman.

We followed the police car to a compound. They drove through the gates, and a pre-pubescent soldier waved us in. We rode in, and then they told us to wait outside for some unfathomable reason. We had to wait for a man on a motorcycle to relay us to the next station. At the next station, we had to wait even longer.

That time they offered us breakfast and made us tea—that was far more like what we'd seen in Iran. These were just guys doing their job and trying to help, not like the snide comments and arrogance we'd seen all morning and most of the previous day. I still wanted to like the country, but it was getting harder all the time. By then we were fed up with it.

Eventually, we got a young man in a uniform, which was basically different shades of brown printed on pyjamas, and we had to take him along with us while he held the passports. I was told it was a dangerous ride. I asked if he was going to protect us and was told he would. I looked at the poor little unarmed, hopelessly lost kid, and laughed at him.

Marcin rides even faster when there's someone on the back, and the poor kid's uniform blew up like a balloon. We experienced the usual shocking standard of driving all the way to the edge of the country, swapping our soldier for another one, until eventually we arrived at the Pakistan border with yet another different kid on the back, making six in total.

The first office was a small box with two guys outside smoking cigarettes. The next was customs control for the exit side of Iran. They wanted to know if we enjoyed the country. I exploded into my usual social observations to blank faces who didn't understand a word I was talking about, but to be fair, people who speak my language usually react the same way.

Finally, they found us another place to wait at the border while they did still more paperwork.

The border was a wire fence that had been left open. People from both sides casually wandered in and out, and nobody seemed to mind. This was our first glimpse of Taftan, the town that had built up on the other side, and the country that lay beyond.

Pakistan was strangely horizontal; buildings were exclusively single story, the roads were made of dust, and the view was bleak. I couldn't wait to move on into something new, as I was by then, quite happily finished with Iran. In my head we'd left now, and a whole new country was right there ahead of us, waiting to give us chronic cases of food poisoning and more problems than anyone should ever have to face.

Eventually we could—the door to Pakistan was finally open to us, with much less trouble from the officials at passport-control than we got from the military and police.

The entry was very easy but very time consuming. It was a chaotic ballet of endless offices with men writing details in books that had oddly inappropriate cartoon characters printed on the front of them. They relied almost exclusively on paper records, and computers were nowhere to be seen.

They kept asking if we were tourists as they stamped our books with happy smiles set on their rugged, sun-damaged faces. We spoke about that later and at length—if we weren't tourists, then what did they think we were? Spies? Spying on either country would be easier than riding too fast on an Aprilia Mille. The whole region was less organised than a cheap sandwich. Marcin set his video camera up on the handlebars and wore a pair of novelty glasses with yet another camera built in. I just took pictures until my battery ran out. They asked us not to, but we said we still would, and they seemed fine with that, just shrugging, saying that they didn't really care and posing happily for pictures.

Generally, I couldn't see any actual real reason not to take pictures. There's nothing special or impressive about a border crossing. In Pakistan the border control was just the right side of hilarious, and perhaps that's the reason they didn't want it captured for posterity. We were met by two touts who wanted to swap our money for us, and they invited us into a hut. In the hut we got our entry visas and saw the only computer for the next hundred miles, but it didn't seem to be plugged into anything, and it certainly wasn't working.

After that, we went to customs-control, an office that also sold sweets. Then we went to various offices having various things stamped and inspected by people who clearly didn't have a clue what they were doing or why they were doing it. We drove around twice looking for the office in which to have out carnets checked, and we got directions which were, "The small white building over there with the cars on the roof." That didn't narrow things down!

It was never less than completely friendly and courteous, and usually, totally hilarious as well. The people there were strikingly friendly, and we weren't asked for any bribes whatsoever, nor did they seem to be expected. This was a stark contrast with Iran and probably the friendliest, most laid-back border crossing I'd ever seen.

The rather sombre mood that had settled over us both on the final leg of our ride through Iran started to break up. Being treated all day like old friends by people who asked for nothing but to be allowed to help can't fail to lift your spirits. Even Marcin, on his savage crusade to ride a little faster, made no impatient comment all day. It might not have been quick, but everyone we dealt with gave us the impression they were doing their absolute best for us.

We chatted as we waited between filling in cartoon-animal-covered books with our details. We had been left with the feeling about Iran that mostly the people were very friendly, but it was disorganised to a horrendous degree and trying to pretend it wasn't. Those in charge shouldn't be allowed to run a tap, and the military, and almost everyone choosing to be in it, should be recycled into something useful. My vote was for a really big curry.

On the other side of the border it was incredibly disorganised, far beyond anything you could possibly imagine; it was like an epileptic seizure with people living in it, but they were some of the most humble and decent officials we'd ever come across. But what impressed us most was nobody tried to pretend they were anything else. Nobody had anything to prove.

We were, however, escorted. I thought we would be, and we were told it would be all the way to Quetta, and probably beyond. Not that anyone really knew for sure, because nobody knew anything for sure. Questions were usually answered with a friendly shrug, and serious questions were answered with an even friendlier shrug and perhaps a little smile.

At the final office we had to visit the escort, who arrived after yet another lengthy wait. We had enough money to get to Quetta, barely, but had done nothing all day but paperwork. Marcin was eager to make some progress on the road, and I was eager to see some of this new country, so we aimed to head out just as soon as that was possible. I made sure that Marcin understood that we would have to ride with the escort and match their speed. We weren't at liberty to ride as fast as we wanted to or even to ride at the times that suited us. Pakistan was a dangerous place, and we were to be watched the whole time, as frustrating as that was for everyone. He understood well enough and even seemed to care.

While we were waiting at one of the many offices, which was really just a building with a broken car in it and people reading books upside-down, a man came to chat with us. He spoke pretty good English and was confused when we told him that we weren't married. He kept saying that at our age we should be. I took him to be late in his fifties, or perhaps early sixties, and he guessed we were in our early twenties. He had completely white hair and a bushy beard that was peppered with the occasional black hair amidst a sea of white. His dark skin was sun-beaten and was beset with heavy, deep wrinkles. In the end I asked, and he replied that he was only forty-two, just a few years older than me! Marcin and I exchanged worried glances and went very quiet. Life must be hard there, we assumed.

The escorts didn't appear to take their jobs too seriously. As they got into their car, the passenger sat with his AK47 in the footwell, arranged so that the muzzle was pressed into his abdomen, pointing up directly into his heart. I was guessing that these guys were trained to keep the chamber empty until they rack the bolt. If not, then a live round was pointing directly up through him and would easily blow him apart like a hammer hitting a banana if anything went wrong, and with Chinese-made AKs that might well happen. He was fiddling around absently while waiting, playing with the controls on his assault-rifle. I felt safer already!

The car itself was a red Toyota Hilux with a blue light stuck to the top with gaffer tape; the lights were smashed off, and most of the panels were slightly different colours, imprinted with a visual history of a long life of abuse. Just exactly who they thought they were protecting us from was anyone's guess. They wore no uniforms and had no badges, we simply had their word that they were who they said they were. The distinction between the police and the people they were there to protect us from was, apparently, that these ones weren't shooting at us. Beyond that, who knew?

They impatiently honked their horn while we went to a shop and bought enough food to keep us going and then enough gas to get us most of the way there. The shop was a wardrobe turned over on its side to function as a counter, with a peg-board behind to hold up an array of home-made shelves. Supplies were limited to a range of dusty cans of food.

Petrol was served out of a plastic bottle and filtered through a filthy rag as it was poured straight into our machines. We weren't filled with confidence so far.

Once on the road, they swerved around semi-aimlessly for a few miles. There had been many online discussions about the road quality, and I'd done some reading into it myself. The research I had done had actually prompted me to take such a small and light motorcycle. She was built to be ready for any extreme, and so far, had just been used on largely tarmac roads, the only place she really wasn't in her element.

I had heard it was appalling, but so far, seventy miles along, while it was certainly bad, it was far from terrible. In fact, at that point, Turkey had been quite a bit worse. The wind had blown sand across the road, and if it was deep, it was certainly hard to ride on. There were massive potholes and areas where the tarmac had sunk, but in all honesty, the roads were no worse than in most London suburbs. The main difference was that most London suburbs didn't have deep sand and people with machine-guns wanting to kill you.

We managed to average around fifty mph, and there were areas we made a comfortable seventy. The roads were disappointingly passable, and we thought it might be possible to make Quetta by the evening. Certainly, we had to keep our wits about us as we rode along, but we were more than used to that by then.

After riding to the first checkpoint, the escort let us go to ride off on our own for a while. The checkpoint was an old sand-stone castle with a few soldiers inside. The boss came out with a big smile to shake our hands and welcome us to his country. I asked if I could look around inside, and to my surprise, that was fine—I was invited to help myself.

I wandered in, leaving Marcin to do the paperwork. (I'm a great friend!) Inside, the building looked fairly recently built, painted white, with a few offices off to the sides. I rounded the entrance to find a turret with a general purpose machine gun and a Heckler and Koch G3 rifle, both armed and left unattended so bikers could nose at them, even take them if they were so inclined. A guy met me and showed me into the barracks, where some other soldiers were sleeping, and then the office, where he told me nothing ever really happened.

Nothing was too much trouble, and it was a strikingly different experience than that of dealing with Iranians in uniform. These people, so far, were really lovely, hopelessly disorganised, but really lovely. The man in charge even let us take pictures, which was not really allowed, but I said please, and suddenly it was perfectly fine. He even posed for a few snaps with us.

The desert looked very different from the ones we'd dealt with before. It was somehow more of a desert, more in line with what we'd expected and the idea that comes to mind when you hear the word. The sand was finer and rolled on further over the tattered tarmac. There was none of the desert-depression we'd seen before. Perhaps it would come later, but the heat and exhaustion didn't catch up with us that day, although later on, the heat did start getting really noticeable. We were very aware by then that we had crossed into a new country. Borders tended to be on natural divides, with a mountain range or a river breaking them up. Conditions on either side were often strikingly different. This was an example of that. Pakistan was strikingly different and the terrain wasn't the same as anything we'd seen before.

We arrived at a second checkpoint, where the guard clearly lived with his entire family. The barrier blocking the road was a piece of rope held on with a hook made from a wire coat-hanger.

A swarm of happy children came out to look at the bikes. Again, it was very informal, friendly, and welcoming. They were just happy to see us and treated us very well. Marcin invited the children to play on the bikes, while I took my turn to fill in the paperwork. We had bought some sweets and handed them out to the kids as we made our way. We left behind bright smiling faces and happy officials waving goodbye. If Pakistan continued to be like that, it was set to be my favourite country so far.

It was to be our last checkpoint that day, and reaching Quetta was nowhere near likely to happen. The sun was setting, and we had about an hour of light left, plenty of time to make the first town on the map, we thought. We made a good pace while the light was still good, until we were asked to stop at the side of the road by a group of soldiers. They did some brief paperwork, and then a policeman came out and met us.

He told us we had to rest there—no more travelling at night, as it wasn't safe any longer. We were reconciled to that anyway; we knew the situation and what it was like in that part of the world. His concern for us was genuine, and when he told us that, we took the advice seriously. Even Marcin showed no disappointment and seemed happily resigned to his fate.

We asked where we had to go, and he told us he was taking us to the police station, where we could stay. That suited us nicely, so we followed along with him. We picked our way through a ramshackle town made of tarpaulin stretched over metal frames and little sandy domes made from local materials. When we arrived, the sun was setting, and a slightly cooler wind blew across the town. It felt fresher, but we weren't exhausted this time. The upbeat attitude we'd been met with had lifted our spirits, and we were in a good mood. We were also enjoying our time experiencing something so alien to us, something so refreshingly different.

We arrived in the compound, a disused yard made from sandstone with softly rounded walls, eroded, we assumed, by the dusty winds. Our motorcycles joined a pair of vans that might only run out of sheer obstinacy, if at all. Such was the disrepair that they might have been wrecks or police-vehicles, we had no way to tell which.

We asked where we could pitch our tent but were told that wasn't good enough and that the chief of police would clear out his office and let us sleep there. They made it clear we were guests and free to go anywhere in the town that we pleased; they arranged water and anything else we might have wanted. We discussed their treatment of us, which was among the warmest and friendliest we'd seen so far, and the officer replied modestly that it was just their duty and that we were honoured guests. Still, he smiled very proudly and seemed very pleased to hear it.

After we settled in, the police brought us tea and offered us sweets. We weren't able to speak with them, but our body-language and gestures conveyed our intents. Nothing was too much trouble, and they all introduced themselves and shook our hands.

In England police seldom behaved the way we were seeing there. Certainly, there are good ones, and I've had positive experiences, but I've had just as many bad ones and have grown wary of any dealings with people in uniform.

The standard of living may be lower there in material terms, but the way of life seemed quite good. People were supportive of one another; connected in a way that seemed more natural. That more basic way of life has a lot to remind us about the right way to treat one another.

That night I wrote my diary in the local police station office under the stars in a desert, a cool wind blowing through the building, and myself full of excellent local food and beans eaten from a tin pulled open with a pair of pliers. The next day we were making an early start on the road, and we expected to be in Quetta by nightfall; we should have had no trouble making it, if the maps could be trusted. Certainly, it wasn't too far a distance, but with the escorts and routine stops, it wasn't possible to say for sure what we were likely to find.

There were no petrol stations between where we were and the town, and too many miles for us to travel on what we could carry in our tanks. People all along the way sold bottles of fuel by the side of the road, so we were confident we wouldn't have any issues; so far, we'd managed to get by with the local fuel, and our bikes were running better than they had in Iran. We aimed to stock up whenever the opportunity arose, and we were carrying plenty of spare gas in cans, enough to fill my bike up if necessary, so I could go for help or get more fuel. Even with my paltry ten-litre tank, I was sure we'd have no trouble.

I should have learned my lesson by now: optimism rarely translated into reality, and this was sadly no exception. The bike had started worrying me again. She'd been pinking badly on the local fuel, which we were still carrying, burning, buying, and running on. The quality must have been lower than I'd assumed. On my routine checks I noticed oil on the frame. It was clearly coming from something high up on the engine, but the oil was clean and yellow, and the marks were too high to have blown from the head gasket. I had a slight concern that she might have over-heated badly enough to have damaged the engine, but I could find no evidence of that. The level was still fine, and it was the right colour, but I would be checking her more often to make sure things stayed that way. So long as the problem got no worse, she'd keep going with no more trouble than keeping her topped up and wiping off the oil.

I much later discovered that it was a known issue with the Rotax engine, although it was a known issue that's rarely spoken of. It was a blockage in the oil-filter, which is a very sensitive part of those machines. If blocked, the bike tends to eject oil through a breather hose. Many years later, I took the head off and inspected the damage, expecting this journey to relegate the bike to the scrap-yard or at least down-grade her to a commuter bike. The engine looked like new and continues to this day to run perfectly well.

She was running very hot too, and the radiator overflow tank appeared to be empty. It certainly wasn't leaking, and there's no emulsification, so again, it didn't seem like it was anything too serious. I would fill her up in the morning and hope for the best until we reached Quetta. We were taking a break there, probably spending a whole day. I was aiming to change the plugs and give her a little attention. Marcin said he intended to do the same to his, and we would enjoy being able to draw out money from a cash-point, use the Internet, and drink beer again before tackling the next step of our mad dash through the Middle East.

While sitting under the stars, and with the stress of a border crossing behind me, my thoughts turned back to Iran.

Iran is difficult. It's difficult to get in, and it's difficult to stay there, even for a few days. All the money you need you have to take in with you, although this is hardly their fault. The Internet is heavily censored, and the quality of communication is poor. Mobiles don't often work, fuel is so weak that modern engines don't like to run on it, the people are different from town to town, and there's a huge desert in the middle of it, where maps, logic, and even the laws of physics break down completely.

The driving in Iran is so bad and so dangerous that even Marcin slowed down. He was clipped more than once and even run off the road at one point by an idiot who tried to nudge him out of the way with his car. The driving is such a negative point that it makes you wonder about the people. Who would drive in a way that is not just dangerous to themselves but potentially deadly to others? It left a bad feeling in me about the country in general. If a person gets behind the wheel of a car in any country and then drives straight at you, you're not going to think of them as a good and decent person, and yet the whole country was doing precisely that with no regard for what we might take away from that.

On the border we were ripped off by a government official, and both of us had trouble getting our visas while still in England, mine taking most of a day. There was no reason for it; they just seemed set on making it difficult for us. Other government officials gave us problems, always wanting to get paid for doing something, usually less than their actual jobs.

In the hotels there were always hidden charges, there was always a different price to pay at the end to what we agreed at the beginning. The first question people asked was where we were from and then how much our bikes were worth. Everything had to have a price; people and machines. Everything had to be assigned a label, and the label was usually a measurement of its value to them.

On the other hand, there were many, many people who just wanted to help. The greetings we had were always very friendly (until we got closer to the border). People were often quick to offer us whatever we wanted or needed without hesitation. There were some people whose generosity and warmth took us utterly by surprise, especially in Tabriz, as well as out in the desert.

We were told early on that there were different people in Iran—the Turks and the true Persians. I'm not sure who was meant to be better by the measurement of the person who told us, but certainly the people were strikingly different. The first towns did, indeed, have people that looked Turkish. Later on their skin darkened until, by the border, it was difficult to discern Iranians from Pakistanis. Ironically, the darker Iranians who looked most like the Pakistanis were the ones who gave us the most trouble, but the people in Pakistan were far and away the friendliest we'd met so far.

I think that Iran is a country that's very divided. There are different peoples and different attitudes alive and intermingling, and the country has achieved a kind of uneven balance, a balance that's tipped very much against the interests of the average person. The general feeling is that there is something wrong—the people have had a smell of freedom, and the changing international environment could well prompt a revolution there. Certainly, we were told often that was what the young people wanted. I hoped that they understand that there's a difference between being truly free and having a say in deciding who tells you what you're not allowed to do every few years.

I worried for their country that the revolution they wanted was coming, a change that would wash away the unique identity of that place and replace it with an open door and red carpet for the profit-machine of the capitalist West to roll in and rape it of its resources—a quiet occupation from the banks and corporations. Once that happens, Iran might be invited into the world banking system at gunpoint, the quite little, internal financial infrastructure will collapse; the debts held by the banks for houses and cars will be swallowed by the new regime, massively impacting the value of the loans, breaking the economy into a system where the people will belong to the same banks that hold the West in virtual slavery.

This will be painted as opportunity, a chance for the people to own new cars, new iPhones, new products that they've not needed in decades, but the sweeping broom of consumerism is a powerful and equally destructive tool.

The people there are varied and diverse, but the best of Iran seemed to be found in the first parts, as well as in little pockets of rural or desert life. There are some truly amazing, friendly, and welcoming people in that beautiful country, and I recommend everyone to see it while it's still there without a McDonalds on every corner.

But feelings of oppression run deep. Booze is outlawed, women are treated as second-class things instead of people, information is censored, and teenagers are pressed into military service.

The teenage years are a buffer between the time as a child, when you're looked after and taught, to the adult years, where you take full responsibility for your own life. Those few years are a time to do the stupid stuff and get it out of your system, the time to make your mistakes and learn from them. It's a time to be out experimenting with life and society, but in Iran it's a time of wearing a uniform you don't believe in, of being indoctrinated into a system and having the responsibility of an assault rifle thrust onto your narrow shoulders with the real possibility of life and death that all that entails.

In the West those guys would be playing video games, chasing the opposite sex, and drinking beer. Neither is exactly right, and the truth is probably somewhere in between, but then neither one is a truly balanced system. It's a dangerous time in the life of a young man, and the time when this country demands a great deal of them. And from what I had seen, more than most are capable of delivering.

It's a poor thing too, to divide the population by superficial means, such as race or age, but they find it acceptable to do it over sex. Women are treated poorly, forced to cover their heads, and not taken seriously in society. In a modern world I don't think this will be allowed to continue for much longer. I hope that if there is a change, it will be a positive one.

The people there are often warm and generous, but the cracks were showing all too well. The government officials, the people who are in a position to profit, seem to take any opportunity to do so.

I had loved my trip through Iran, we both did, but it had been a place of highs and lows. There are enough experiences there for a traveller to come through and not like the place, but we were lucky enough to meet some really good people too, and they made up for so much. The people who change your tyres for free, the free bulbs, the lifts, the offers of money for cab rides, and entire communities that welcome you with open arms, right through to families that invite you into their homes for dinner. All of Iran is not like this, but mostly it is, and it's more than enough to make this country something special, which it most definitely had been to us.

I have said before I wanted to see it before it's gone, and I have. I feel a change is coming—a girl will refuse to wear a scarf one day, or a guy will refuse military service because he believes it's not right. This is a dangerous time for Iran, because it only takes one person to create that spark, and a fire is ready to burn. There are a lot of people who are ready to follow, and they're waiting for someone to lead them. I just hope the next system doesn't hand the banks this great country in exchange for a taste of democratic freedom that will just be a different kind of shackle. Really, the place deserves better than that. But above all, it does need to change.

24

A Good Day

Date—November 9th
Location—Pakistan border
Mood—Surprisingly upbeat

I didn't expect the day to be particularly remarkable, and I certainly didn't expect it to be any fun. Far from it, in fact! I expected it to be a boring slog of waiting for escorts and signing forms between short hops along the highway. I expected Marcin to bitch and moan about every wasted moment until I prayed for my brains to leak out of my nose so I had something to block my ears up with.

We were planning and hoping for it to be a relatively easy ride to the first city, Quetta, along the main, and only, road that even qualified to be described as a road. We had heard that it was meant to be very bad and not really possible to cover it in a day. We were confident we could do it, powered by my curious need to see what would happen if I did stupid things and Marcin's constant moaning about pretty much everything. We had the power of our own stupidity driving us and not enough common sense to know what couldn't be done. We could do amazing things, and as we'd already proven, we could do amazingly stupid ones; I figured that this should be even easier.

We woke up in the police station office as the sun rose and lit up the sleepy little town all around us, blowing in a cool and sandy breeze through the building. The staff had slept on the floor of the ledge outside. They had insisted that we were their guests and that we must take the office. We didn't want to offend them or refuse their generosity, so we decided that we would leave the door open and more or less join them.

There was a weird vibe there that I wasn't particularly liking. We saw it in Turkey and Iran, but it was far more obvious in Pakistan. There seemed to be an attitude that we were somehow quite different than they were, and they were accordingly treating us like we were somehow special purely on face value.

Whenever we turned up anywhere we got an adoring audience, and everyone we talked to said how wonderful we were and how great England is compared to their own country, despite never having been there, or ever leaving their own village. The previous night the policeman offered us the sheets from his own bed, which meant he would have slept on bare concrete—obviously we declined.

They brought us tea and did everything like they were just staff in a hotel. It became quite unsettling after a while. We were not there to be wrapped in cotton wool, we were there to see it like it really was and only wanted to be treated as equals.

We packed up and were on the road around 8AM when the sun had firmly established itself and the place had really woken up to the promise of a new day. The sun didn't rise until later than we thought, and we were ready for it. Marcin was always ready to get moving along. I was too, albeit with some reservations about the drudge we were about to experience. It was going to be a long day.

It wasn't long until we encountered our first stop-check in town, the same place as the night before, when we made our way out of town back to the main road. We argued that they'd already taken our details, but that didn't stop them from taking them again. It only took a few minutes, so it was better all round just to get it done. In that part of the world they loved their pointless records and endless bureaucracy, and it was quicker, easier, and less hassle to just follow along with it.

We were sent on our way without an escort, which seemed good to us—we might make some better time than we had thought. That was encouraging, since my mind was made up that we were going to make it to Quetta, especially since people said we couldn't.

I love a challenge.

The roads were pretty good as we started out; they were flat and smooth and maintained a decent quality, with relatively few broken-up areas of serious potholes. As we made our way along, the weather seemed to be on our side for the first twenty miles, but then the wind kicked up hard, and things began to change. For a while, the conditions were pretty bad—we had to ride at an angle to head straight, but we could hold an even sixty mph that meant, according to quick mental arithmetic I did along the way to keep my head clear, that we should be able to make Quetta after all. Of course, we had no way of knowing what was up ahead. The roads could collapse into nothing for all we knew, we could only hope for the best and never forget that I was on a well set-up adventure motorcycle, so I was prepared for the worst. Marcin, however, was on a KTM. I might have been able to prepare myself and my bike, but there was no way to anticipate Marcin, who doesn't follow any of the societal norms of human behaviour, to such a degree than in online-testing the results came back that he was probably some kind of horse.

We picked up our first escort at the next border; they seemed like nice people, introducing themselves with warm handshakes, like they were actually pleased to see us, rather than annoyed at our presence. We did the usual paperwork, and we all rode off together. The guy with the biggest gun had to sit on the back of Marcin's bike. I gestured Marcin to overtake, so I could get some pictures of the scene. The police were driving a battered Toyota Hilux and driving it hard, as everyone seemed to do out there. It was a terrible mess of a thing and was only held together by some automotive miracle. Still, for all its horrible wear and patchwork of bodged repairs over the wrinkled and creased metal bodywork, it was still running well and being used harder than any other machine of its type being driven in the West. The Hilux continues to impress me to this day; it's a clear miracle of engineering.

The roads were starting to break up, potholes were everywhere, and sand was belching onto the tarmac from both sides. Neither of us were used to riding on sand, and it was hard to adapt. The top surface was alive, slipping and sliding all over the place as we made our way over. Marcin's heavier bike might have had a slight advantage in digging in, but neither of us were finding it easy. Worse still, the really large potholes were often filled with sand and smoothed over, so we could be diving into one without knowing it. When that happened the bike slid around helplessly, and I could only keep on the power and hope the momentum would help the bike to recover itself. So far, it had, and we'd had no serious problems.

The wind was so high that it had even blown rocks over, some as big as my fist. That meant that the surface was even more uneven and was getting more hazardous as we went along. Not only did we have to contend with holes that might buckle our wheels and a slippery surface, we now had sharp rocks jutting up out of the tarmac. We swerved to avoid patches of loose sand, wary that the larger potholes could be filled with it, and if we hit those, we could lose control easily. We were in a place with no proper medical services and were both grimly aware that we were on our own there.

All too soon we had to stop at yet another checkpoint, and the guard with the gun was replaced once more. We were invited to sit while we did the paperwork at the side of the sandstone office, to which someone had fixed a wooden frame that served as a sun-screen. Some children stopped to watch while the police brought out some really quite decent tea for us, and we all sat around drinking it together.

Again, they brought us chairs, but we chose to sit on the floor with them, on wicker mats made from local materials. After that, we filled the bikes with the deadly-looking roadside petrol, served from a plastic bottle that was so old that it had turned orange, and then we made our way forwards yet again.

There were officially no fuel stations between the Taftan border and Quetta, but actually there were dozens of people selling it from bottles and cans. It was probably rubbish, more water than petrol, but it would get you where you're going if you can't afford to be fussy. Unless you've got a forty-litre tank and excellent fuel economy, then you can't, but then Pakistan is not a country where the fussy will be very comfortable.

While we were there, I bought some more cakes and water—the water to keep us hydrated and the cakes to give away along the road to the local children who frequently came forward to see the weird, filthy, and increasingly smelly bikers. We were quite the novelty and attracted little gangs of amused and curious children at every stop. We both liked children, which came in handy years later when we accidentally got our respective partners pregnant, and we liked being able to hand out sweets; it felt like we were giving something back, even just in some tiny sense.

Once we got back on the road, we made pretty good time. The roads were still quite good and much better than expected, but there was then a weird new twist to the desert-depression. In addition to there being nothing to see, there was no way to see it. The sky above us was clear and blue, but all around us the distant scenery was veiled behind a white dusty mist that made it impossible to see the horizon. It wasn't dangerous, because it was far enough out to allow us to ride carefully, but it meant we had no distant markers to judge our position. Our brains recoiled in horror, and the same old crushing sense of apathy washed over us. Desert-depression returned with a vengeance, and the lack of stimulation while riding meant that I began to feel exhausted, weak, and tired. Marcin was feeling it too and complained that it was worse than before. I had to agree.

We plodded on until we had to change car and driver, again. This went on and on until we lost count. Sometimes that van would lead us, sometimes it would follow. Sometimes it would drive along with us for a few miles and then wave us off, other times it would stick with us all the way to the next checkpoint. There was no set formula; they were clearly just making it all up as they went along.

This next time we got a guy with something to prove. I didn't know what his issue was with us, but he was just plain dangerous. He drove flat out as fast as he could over potholes and through sand so that the dust he kicked up made it hard work trying to follow him.

By the time we had made it about half way to our destination, the roads finally collapsed into complete chaos. Tarmac, and in fact any kind of surface, vanished altogether. First, the potholes took over, growing larger and larger until they became the norm and the concrete and tarmac surface only existed in little patches. Then as we went further, the road was simply gone, leaving us with thirty miles of gravel, rocks, sand, mud, and water to contend with.

The Hilux ploughed on at full power, never dropping below fifty mph, and at some points going through mud at just over sixty-five, kicking up showers of spray as he blasted on. He was trying to show off, to get away from us and humiliate us, but I kept with him. I was struggling with my crappy fuel problem, but I managed (somehow) to keep pace with him over the really crappy terrain. I love a challenge, and very quickly I began to really enjoy myself as we blazed along way too fast and for way too long.

For once, Marcin couldn't keep up with me. The weight of his KTM made the going harder for him, but the Toyota couldn't pull away from either of us, and if Marcin trailed behind for a short way, he always made the speed and caught up on a better section.

There were a few very dodgy moments that made me realise just how stupid all that was, but by then the adrenaline had taken over and I was lost in the moment. I caught a nasty step in the road, a verge or rock hidden from view. I hit it too fast, around fifty mph—I caught some mud that sent the back spinning out, and I slithered around like a snake that just had its first encounter with a lawn mower. Luckily, I caught her, and she corrected herself just fine, snapping back on track as the momentum kept me heading forwards, true and straight.

I just remembered the enduro code . . . "Look up, stand up, speed up; and in mud, expect to fall down." I did all three until the Hilux was fishtailing all over the road trying to pull away, trying to show us up and to better us with his skill and experience. It all ended badly when he spun out and ended up nose-first in a ditch.

It wasn't too serious, and he was able to reverse up and back out of a shallow hole filled with muddy water. He revved his engine hard, sending a curling wisp of blue smoke puffing from the exhaust, and the tyres spun as he roared off, even more determined than before. He managed to carry on with nothing but wounded pride, and we took off after him.

He couldn't get away from us no matter how hard he tried, and the harder he tried, the more fun it actually made it for me. I hadn't realised how much I needed that. The days on long, straight roads had taken their toll, it had been a constant reminder that Marcin's bike was bigger, faster, and more impressive than mine. It had left me always feeling like I was holding him back and constantly thinking I had made the wrong choice about my motorcycle. Now, I was riding my bike in her element, and she delivered admirably, bringing a smile to my face and chasing away all the doubts and the grumpiness of our many problems along the way. This was an adventure in just the way I was looking to find one.

When he stopped, the driver came over with his head hung and offered his outstretched palm to shake our hands—a broken man. I told Marcin to behave as if nothing out of the ordinary had happened, just another day on the road to us. That seemed to annoy him even more, exactly as I had intended. Actually, my heart was pounding and my head was light, we had both enjoyed it immensely, big children that we were.

When he left we split into ear-to-ear grins and babbled about how much fun that was to one another like excited kids. We were happy to have finally got some enduro riding in and even happier to have done something to really break us out of the routine.

We'd both gone for a form of adventure motorcycle, thinking that those kind of conditions were something we were going to be seeing far more than we had. I had done some off-road riding before back in England, but generally a lot slower and not over such difficult terrain while following an armed escort across Pakistan. Certainly never at speeds that would have gotten me a speeding-ticket in England on a decent main road.

We got something to eat at the checkpoint, cracking open a tin of pineapple to go with some biscuits. It was time for a break, to take a chance to rest and to check over our bikes. The roads were never as bad again that day, but were still poor for another hundred miles or so from that point. To be honest, I had expected much worse. Although the bike took a pounding, shaking across the rocky surface, she had hung on perfectly well, and at the end of the day, there had been no damage that wouldn't polish out.

Even better, after that experience, Marcin never questioned my riding again. I never heard another comment about me being scared to ride off road from him, but he still did frequently question my sexuality and parentage. I hadn't expected such narrow-minded prejudice, but what else can you expect from a Polish person?

After having something to eat and swapping out drivers yet again, we carried on. The swaps and checkpoints were getting closer and closer, and time was not on our side, as it never really was. We wanted to make Quetta before nightfall, but the constant waiting for paperwork and worse, waiting for escorts, was holding us up. We had known it would; even Marcin accepted this and never grumbled unduly.

We held on to our patience as we kept on doing this, changing drivers, cars, and stopping for endless checkpoints all day. I lost count of how many hands I shook and how many villages we passed through with tiny little offices, where people wanted a slight variation of the same information. I did notice while signing the books that there were other foreigners up ahead. At first, we were a whole day behind, but during the course of the day we were catching them up, and I hoped we might meet them on the road, share a meal and swap stories.

In a small town, some way up the road, we were led off the main highway and into a large compound by our escorts. The whole area was walled off and sealed up with a very heavy steel gate. We were taken into a little office to do the routine paperwork. At that point I had everything memorised, and we could do the entire thing in under a minute.

The man in charge was much younger than usual and was lounging in his chair with a cocky grin on his face, a beaten chequered scarf wrapped round his head, and a long set of off-white robes draping down past his knees. He sat like a rapper, in a pose you might find on the cover of an album. He waved dismissively at the paperwork and asked questions about where we were from with a likeable waft of measured arrogance.

He began gabbling excitedly in broken English, and Marcin and I were left staring at one another, wondering what was going on. He jumped up from his chair and began rattling away on an old computer, a sorry, beaten-up old thing that we hadn't noticed before but suddenly looked out of place in this sandy little hut with carpets hung on the walls. It wasn't on his desk, more off to the side, and wasn't a part of his work, such as his work was. He told us we had to watch.

A video, made by himself as he held a phone-camera in front of his face, appeared with the man staring angrily forwards with all the attitude he could mutter. With an excited grin, like a child about to bite into an ice-cream, he told us to watch this, it would be the best thing we'd ever seen.

It wasn't.

He began to rap for us on his video, and then he followed up with a live version, singing to us over the tinny music playing behind. It was terrible, and we didn't know quite what to make of it. It was like a lasagne made by someone who didn't know what pasta, tomatoes, and cheese were. None of it fitted together, and the clashing noises would have made a dog cry in pain. Music from an '80s video game had hard-core, but home-written, lyrics growled over it by a voice that wasn't really cut out for growling. His face had the severe look of a man laying down the cold, hard truth, but the lyrics were about the importance of sweeping the floor so the boss doesn't shout at him again. He began to dance. We bit into our bottom lips until they bled, trying not to laugh.

It finished, and he sat back down, immensely proud of himself and telling us that this time next year his life would be different and he'd be the most important musician in the world.

He wasn't.

He sat with his arms kind of crossed over him, but not quite over him, while the other officers gazed at him with maybe hero worship, or perhaps solemn hatred at the shame he'd visited on them. It was tough to say, and an air of quiet awkwardness descended on the base. We applauded politely and assured him of his undeniable talent, while he swelled with pride.

Then Marcin found a way to break the spell. He spotted something and asked if he could play with an AK47 that was lying causally against the wall. We were all friends now, and apparently that was no problem at all. So he posed for pictures, playing with it like the clueless lump of gristle he was. He looked down the barrel, scratched his nuts with it, and waved it around triumphantly. He insisted I hold it, and he threw it over, drawing his camera to record everything.

When I checked, the gun was loaded with a full magazine, and cocked with a round loaded in the chamber, a weapon with sufficient fire-power to have killed every person in the room in a matter of seconds. It was more than slightly troubling that this was offered as a toy to a stranger they had never met and who had no idea how it worked, and who had no of an idea how anything worked, in fact.

Their disregard of the dangerousness of weapons was disconcerting, especially since they had access to so many of them.

Pakistan was a strange place, and we were starting to realise just how very strange it was.

We survived all that and headed out back to the road, ready to face whatever was ahead and hoping it would be as bad as what was behind. My bike had suddenly decided that only ninety-three miles would put her on reserve with the bad local fuel, so we had to stock up once again. She normally made a hundred, so this was hardly a complaint; she was doing sterling work.

Gassing up was never easy to do when you had to buy it in old tins and feed it to your tank through a funnel with a cloth tied to it to filter out the lumps. It was even more tricky since my fuel tank was under my seat, which seemed to blow their minds completely. Several times that day I had to explain that sometimes fuel tanks are under the seat now to people who had absolutely no idea what I was saying but seemed very impressed by the voodoo magic of BMW and their fuel system placement. Marcin's, of course was much simpler, just a gigantic hungry thing on top, and because it was Marcin, there were two holes to fill.

Our escorts varied from civilian-clothed people in blue Toyota Hilux vans with no number plates or brake-lights to properly marked police vans with the guards in some kind of uniform. At one point the escort was an unarmed fat-bloke wearing nothing but a towel round his waist and riding a 70cc Chinese moped, wobbling across the road on tiny, skinny little tyres. I felt sorry for him and got the impression of the poor man being dragged from a morning shower he badly needed to clear his head from a night of heavy drinking.

It was all quite funny really. Nobody had the vaguest clue what they were doing, and if you asked them why they were doing it then they didn't really seem to know, and if they did know then they certainly weren't telling us. All questions were answered with, "It's our duty."

So on one side of the border we had the Iranians protecting us from the Pakistanis, and on the other we had the Pakistanis guarding us from the Iranians, and on both sides we never encountered any problem we couldn't fix by ignoring it. We still hadn't really understood what exactly that was all about, but we would come to see it for ourselves before long.

At one point, we stopped along the road beside a little ramshackle village while we waited for the escort to arrive. A camel meandered by, so we were able to get some close up pictures. Now this country felt really quite alien and strikingly outside of everything we'd been used to back home. Now camels were wandering the street. I'd personally never been so close to one before and can assure you that they smell every bit as bad as you might imagine. Having said that, it might have been that the camel came up to us to complain about Marcin. Who can tell the mind of a dumb beast? But I asked him anyway, and he said it was definitely the camel.

We both sat down, watching it for a time, Marcin saying it was almost as ugly as my mother, and me asking if he would try to date it. Marcin wasn't cautious at all and went straight up to it, hopefully not to ask what it was doing later that evening, and the animal reared away, letting him know that touching wasn't invited. So for a time we just watched as it slurped up water from a dark, steaming puddle of cloudy, sandy, and suspicious liquid. Presumably, it didn't have taste buds, because the stream seemed to be running directly from the office toilets.

By then the paperwork had been prepared, and so we went back to join the three members of the local police force, who were sitting down outside wearing what looked like pyjamas. They asked where we were from and seemed impressed; one even said it was the best country in the world to be from. Marcin laughed, plunging the audience into an awkward and confused silence.

They carried on, slapping us on the backs and telling us how wonderful we were, how great our county was, and how fantastic everything we did had been up to that point. It was all getting a bit much, so I decided to show them our more human side and to remind them that we all use the toilet the same way. (I later discovered that we all use the toilet in massively different ways.) The timing couldn't have been more perfect, as the germ-infested tea was sloshing around in my rotting innards, turning me into a gigantic human bag-pipe.

I couldn't hold it in any longer, and so, regrettably, I farted as loud as possible, while a white bearded elder was talking about our bikes like they had sailed down from the sky on a chariot from heaven. There was a brief, but poignant, moment of silence, and then a young guy had to walk away laughing, with tears running down his face, and then ran inside to tell others. The old man stared at me, mystified, He blinked twice, chuckled, and then also broke into laughter.

It wasn't even a huge fart, nothing like the appalling explosions of devastating faecal gas that Marcin exhausts every few minutes, the kind that could strip tiles off of walls or inflate a bin-liner from ten metres away. They sound like he's been torn, from the navel round to the top of his spine, by an industrial wood-saw, and afterwards he tends to ask politely if you heard it. It's not like there could possibly ever be any tiny shred of doubt. After an average one there will generally be no glass left in the window frames, car alarms will be going off all down the street, and there would be a lingering smell that made your eyelids roll back in terror, while your teeth melted and ran out of your face. Still, it made a worthwhile point about the dignity of Englishmen and the hygiene standards of whoever made the tea, and it gave them all something to talk about later.

The further we went, the better the roads got, until eventually it was back to the same standard we'd found just outside of Taftan. Eventually, we could see Quetta, but we still couldn't get to it. The mountain roads took us miles around it, and even though it had now grown dark, they still changed cars every few miles.

By then, I was hungry and tired, and Marcin needed a dose of Internet-porn and was asking everyone about Wi-Fi—even the donkeys at the side of the road. To be fair, they did seem equally qualified to answer.

We crawled slowly along, around and about as the weaving road taunted us frustratingly by flashing glimpses of the town up ahead but then veering off so we lost it again behind a hill. Finally, we made it to the edge of town; the escorts said they were handing us over to the police now, and that was that. We were then in their hands.

This meant, of course, that we'd made it. We'd got the whole distance covered in a day, and that realisation kicked the cobwebs out of our minds, the stains and the stresses of the day melted away, and smiles began to form on our faces. It wasn't possible, but we'd done it. We'd proved once more that all you really need to be able to achieve the impossible is suicidal-depression, several serious emotional disorders, rejections of your sexual advances by a camel, appalling home-spun rap videos, crappy fuel, the appetite of a hungry elephant, and a near total lack of common-sense. We had it all!

The police agreed to take us to the best hotel in town only a mile away, but we still changed escorts another three times along the way.

They eventually delivered us to a hotel—not the worst one I've ever seen, but if it really was the best, then it hardly said much about the city. But at least we found somewhere to stay. By then, neither of us cared, we just wanted to end our day, put our feet up, and enjoy the evening. We had made it. We'd earned it!

We'd done what the Internet told us couldn't be done. We'd managed to cover the whole distance in a single day, the advice we'd read online telling us it was more like three. We'd put conventional wisdom and good judgement on hold and claimed a victory for being too obstinate to know any better.

Luckily for us, they had a restaurant, so while we booked in, we ordered some food. Menus were brought out, wiped clean of whatever was splattered all over them, and recommendations were made. We listened and took advice about the local dishes, interested to see what was going to happen. A member of staff took the order and then walked off outside, got on a bike, and went off to collect it. This was an interesting approach to hotel management and something I'd certainly never seen happen before.

Marcin wanted access to the Internet, but apparently it no longer worked, due to recent rain. "Nothing works in Pakistan!" the manager told us proudly with a happy grin. He was really rather oddly very proud of it. Marcin grumbled about that, and I could see a flash of darkness in his eyes. Someone was going to pay for that outrage; probably me.

But much, much, much more importantly, we got beer. We managed to get something in tins that tasted a bit, but not very much, like beer. In came in three flavours, as was explained to us; green, red, and blue. What the distinction was, or even if there was one, seemed to have no bearing. We just went ahead and drank it. It was something like beer, although it didn't exactly make you drunk—just tired, and an interesting variation on nauseous.

After driving from 8AM for thirteen hours, I was pretty-much exhausted, but it was a good kind of exhausted, where we felt like we'd actually achieved something a little bit special. We didn't know what Pakistan had in store for us, but we were ready to face it. Pakistan was a tough country to get into. The visa requirements were so harsh that not many people even bothered to apply. This was an important part of the trip for both of us and something that we'd never forget, especially since I had already lost twenty percent of the use of my colon.

All day we had seen the signature of a Hungarian couple as they logged into checkpoint-books ahead of us. They had taken two full days to do the same trip we managed in one, so that was a boost to our confidence and enough to keep Marcin from moaning for almost an entire hour.

We later found out why. They were staying in the same hotel and apparently driving a three-wheeled car that appeared to be made out of a series of bent tubes and a dead cow. The hotel owner proudly showed us their vehicle, describing it alternatively as a "jalopy" and a "tuk-tuk." To be fair, as I stood gawking at it, I had no better idea than he had about what it actually was. It was like a brown leather umbrella had been stretched over a go-cart.

We were expecting to meet the pair of them further up the road and hoped to find them and have a conversation over a coffee.

I was now desperate for coffee.

25

A River Runs through It

Date—November 10th
Location—Quetta, Pakistan
Mood—Lazy, for once

We actually did approximately nothing all day for once, but it was still interesting, at least to me. We woke up to the streets of Quetta, Pakistan. Actually, I woke up several times in the night to the drumming sound of heavy rain pounding on a plastic roof outside. This made me think that the next day was going to be fairly unpleasant to ride in. We had no intention of riding, in any case, as we all needed a day off the road—me to rest, my bike needing a little attention, and Marcin to do whatever it was that Marcin did when he wasn't trying to ride faster. Presumably, that was thinking about riding faster, or whatever it was that Marcin did when he looked like he was thinking; presumably, farting.

We had been following two Hungarians all day the day before. We kept seeing their names after signing into the checkpoint books, and they were staying in our hotel in a strange three-wheeled car. We had hoped to meet them, but unfortunately, they had left before we got up from our beds.

While we weren't planning on riding anywhere, we still had plenty of things to sort out, which should keep us quite busy. Firstly, we had the issue of having no money to address, which should have been as straightforward as finding a cash-point and simply withdrawing it, although this actually turned out not to be anything like straightforward at all, shockingly enough.

Marcin still insisted on finding somewhere with Internet access, but I cared about nothing more than getting the issues sorted before we worried about creating new problems, which weren't really problems at all. Marcin has his logical side, probably somewhere, but I'm more practical and insisted that we do it my way. Some days, I felt like a parent with a gigantic potato-headed child to look after.

We got dressed and woke up slowly before setting out into Quetta to see where the day would lead us. It led us straight to a flooded street, where the combined smell of shit and piss threatened to choke the life out of us both. The streets were running with water, water that had flooded out from the exposed sewers and was creeping through the town several inches deep, but much deeper in parts. It was black and frothing, with yellow foam on top, and the smell was making the locals gag as they trudged carefully over the roads beside it along the little pathways of higher ground that had been spared the worst of it.

I had been concerned the previous night by the lack of soap in what, we were assured, was the best hotel in town. From the sight of the streets in the morning, basic cleanliness was not very high on the list of priorities in that place.

At the end of the road was a petrol station with a concrete machine-gun bunker on top, the black steel barrel of a weapon poking out over the top of a pile of sand-bags. The only traffic on the road to be seen was a donkey towing a wooden cart, piled high with bricks. But somewhere in the distance was the unmistakable sound of life, the bustle of activity when large numbers of people get together. We headed towards that.

We carefully wound our way through the filthy urban swamp that had claimed the roads towards the town centre, trying to gather some information about how everything worked there and what our options were, if we had any at all. I wanted to stay where we were long enough to use the Internet café later to get everything up to date and contact the people who were probably by now wondering if we were still alive. Marcin wanted to pack the bikes and move to anywhere with Internet access in the rooms. I tried to explain that we didn't have the cash to settle the bill yet and had to check out by twelve noon, so his option just wasn't going to happen for a very large number of reasons.

So we checked out the availability of local Internet cafés, and around that time Pakistan, or at least Quetta, had not yet come fully to life. The first bank we went into was guarded by a man who was so old that the angel of death itself must have got bored waiting. He was packing a rusty Remington pump-action shotgun over his shoulder, the barrel of which was his chosen tool to scratch the side of his head. We went in through the metal-detector and set off the alarms, which didn't appear to cause any concern, but clearly Quetta was not quite as safe as we were led to believe it was. They had incredibly old security guards who were reckless with pump-action shotguns, but the one thing they didn't have was any money.

We were sent to another bank further along, and Marcin had news of a hotel with unlimited access to the Internet, which sent him off on a frothing frenzy of excitement. We tried in every hotel we passed—most didn't have computers themselves, let alone Wi-Fi, and those that did told us that the rain had been so bad that the Internet no longer worked anywhere. To be fair, the rain had been quite bad, but how it managed to cut out the Internet was an interesting question. One man told us with a happy shrug, "It's Pakistan; nothing works."

As we made our way along the highstreet we stopped a number of times, anywhere we might get a working ATM. We made our way inside one, and the security guard stood up sharply, standing to excited attention. He told us to please go through the metal-detector. I asked why, since it wasn't plugged in. We were told again, please pass through the metal detector, the guard adding that it was for our safety.

I asked how it was for our safety, since if we had any weapons then we'd be safer keeping them. Also, and more importantly, the metal detector wasn't plugged in. The cable flex was lying on the floor, trailing along beside it with the plug just resting peacefully on a floor that had never been cleaned.

With no hint of sarcasm, he told us that there was no point plugging it in, since it wasn't working. Please pass through the metal-detector; we did, and shockingly, it didn't go off. After all that we discovered the bank didn't have a working ATM either, although they had still taken the time to actually plug that in.

We wandered on, semi-aimlessly and feeling increasingly despondent, since we hadn't managed to get any money out and it was looking increasingly likely that we wouldn't find any. Bank after bank seemed to have no working ATMs, as if the rain had managed to knock out the whole town.

We finally came to a bank that had a working cash-point, using a satellite uplink that connected to our banks at home. I went first, and sure enough, money came out. Marcin went next and had no problems, either, and we both enjoyed having some money in our pockets, a feeling that lightened our moods, made everything easier, and fixed a lot of our problems. Sadly, no amount of money was going to fix Marcin. With that, the troubles that our stupidity and lack of planning had caused us entering Iran were over. We would have to find new all new troubles for our stupidity to cause us. I suspected it wouldn't take long.

We quite accidentally found the fabled hotel with Internet access, although it was actually a very small town, and it would have been more difficult not to find it. It was advertised as a fort with bedrooms, and was guarded by dozens of men with automatic weapons. There was a sign on the door asking you to check your guns in at reception, but inside it was very nice. It was very expensive too, way out of our league, but we got some breakfast and chatted about it over some pretty good food while we ate our way through an endless buffet. Even Marcin was full by the time we left, which is more than I can say for the buffet.

I watched an enormous man sat in a chair in the hotel. He was a local but conspicuously well-dressed. He ordered food to be brought to him, because the effort of doing something for himself was clearly beneath him. He had an omelette made for him, for which the man who seemed to be in charge of the dining room came and made it at his table. Not once did he make eye-contact or show any sign that he regarded him as a fellow human being.

The only people he even showed irritation towards was us, since we were clearly contemptible bikers, filthy and ragged, and yet we could easily afford to dine to the same standard as him.

I hate people like that and find that you can usually judge the character of a person by the way they treat the people they don't have to be polite to. I treat everyone as an equal and show respect to everyone I meet, unless they show me they're not worth it.

We finally agreed to stay put in our hotel and use an Internet café later in the day, if we could find one that worked. We would then head back to the nice hotel for an early breakfast the next morning before we left, because the food was just that good. We had found the one place with decent food in Quetta, a place where they fill you up, instead of emptying you out, and we knew enough to work out how rare a treat that was going to be.

We headed back through the town and stopped in a few gun shops, mostly to browse around and annoy people. People let us play with everything, which was cool, but they wouldn't let us buy anything, which was not. The salesman huffed indignantly, rolling his eyes at us when I asked if they were allowed to sell us guns. He then quoted the rules as if bored and made a gesture with his index finger rubbing against his opposite palm, indicating we could have whatever we wanted for a small bribe. We didn't want anything more than to answer that very question, except to annoy people, and we seemed to have done that, so we were happy.

We were told that the Internet cafés worked fine, so we simply headed back to the room to prepare the stuff we wanted to upload. After ten days with no access, that could take hours, especially for Marcin, who insisted on putting all of his videos online. People needed to see blurred and shaky videos of the sky with the background noise of bikes being revved to their limits. I didn't have a video-camera, but we'd ended up with an arrangement where he would edit the video and I would put forward the appropriate piece of music for it, usually based on some pun with the title.

We went to the Internet café, which actually wasn't very far. I was done in an hour, not wanting to spend the entire afternoon stuck in a little booth, but Marcin stayed put as long as it took. We uploaded our data, and I went back to the hotel to wait, as Marcin would be some time, since he was trying to post videos on an Internet connection that was running so slowly that it would have been quicker to tie the information to the leg of a pigeon and hope for the best.

I put on some music, played solitaire on my laptop, and just did nothing. It was the first time I had just done nothing in weeks, and it was just fantastic. I hadn't realised just how tired I was. The tension and stress had kept me going, and finally I could just stop and take stock.

As I reflected on the day, I remembered an interesting thing that had happened to us earlier that day. In the morning the roads had been so flooded that we couldn't find a way across to the opposite side without getting knee-deep in human waste, so a tuk-tuk driver offered us a lift. He took us in the back, and two other passengers were holding onto the outside. It was only over the road, but I tried to give him something for his trouble. He refused it to the point of being almost insulted. He kept doing that for some time, just riding people back and forth across the road. Another case of the people with the least giving the most. He seemed to spend his morning just ferrying people over the road through the river of raw sewage that smelled so bad that it made you question if you really wanted to be alive in this world.

Later, a group of young people piled out of a car excitedly to take pictures with us. They spoke perfect English, and I did struggle to see the point of their enthusiasm, as they were unbelievably excited to see us in their town.

I talked with a security guard while it was Marcin's turn to withdraw money. He was old, pushing sixty at least, but it was difficult to tell out there, where life was hard and people were so very different. He said it was his dream to one day save up enough money to take a trip to England to stay with his cousin. It puts things in perspective somewhat how a minor inconvenience to one person might be a lifelong dream of another.

We saw the police arresting someone and beating him mercilessly with sticks. What he'd done to deserve it we had no idea. This was, like Iran, a county where the people have one face they showed to us and quite another that they wore beneath. The friendly welcome we got as we travelled was a facade, and we'd seen it crack many times. None of that was real, and the ugliness and brutality was right there, if you just cared to look a little deeper.

I spoke with Gunter, the hotel manager, who told us, rather belatedly, that it was illegal for people from other countries to walk around the town. In fact, there was a curfew—anyone out after 8PM would be shot on sight. He then shrugged and said that they probably wouldn't shoot us. He certainly couldn't remember that happening to anyone he knew. He pointed to a sign on the wall that said as much to make his point. It was hidden by a poster for Coca-Cola, but it was there, technically. That did explain a few things.

With that in mind, I went back looking for Marcin, but he was already just finishing up and was already on his way back. We were both happier, now that we had got things up to date online and the people who cared about such things knew we were still alive.

I grabbed some food to eat back at the hotel and agreed to settle the bill then, so we could leave early in the morning. We had bought eight cans of really lousy beer that really wasn't beer at all and then found that we had paid the price of the hotel rooms twice over for them. The manager looked away awkwardly when we questioned him about it. We got excuse after excuse, but the simple fact remained, he was ripping us off, and we all knew it. It soured the experience, but nobody was shocked by it.

We paid in any case, but the Bloom Star Hotel was clearly run by a man with contacts in the police, and they were very obviously not to be trusted. The police escort took us there, telling us it was great. They had done the same to the Hungarian couple with the three-wheeled Velorex car. It was not great at all, and we were disappointed, not with the standards but with being cheated.

So we drank the remaining beer and made the best of our last night in Quetta. It was not a place I would be sorry to leave.

26

The Lucky Pen

Date—November 11th
Location—Still in Quetta
Status—Rested

So today, we went from Quetta, a toilet, to Sukkur, a dustbowl, which was also a little bit of a toilet. Along the way a lot of things changed, and among them was my opinion.

We got ripped off at the hotel—hardly a new experience, and we took it on the chin like the seasoned travellers that, by then, we were. For the morning, we had arranged for security to meet us at 8AM and went to a better hotel for breakfast at 7AM. Technically, we weren't allowed to leave the hotel, especially by bike, but we did anyway because, well, why not? That morning we were blessed by the lucky pen. I'm not normally a superstitious person, but in the pen we can trust.

It was a long story, and I explained it at length to Marcin, who listened in rapt silence. I call it my lucky pen, because it got me out of trouble while in Europe once. My GPS didn't work even slightly, so I had to write directions every morning and stick them to my bike screen with tape. It worked nicely, but I had to be very careful not to lose my pen, or else I would be in trouble—I'd need to buy another one.

I came by it just outside of Mulhouse in a petrol station. I needed a pen and asked to borrow one. The young guy working there took one out of a pot of pens on his desk, all advertising his brand of petrol, and gave it to me. He then charged me four euros for it. So in fact, it's not lucky at all, and the interesting story by which I came to own it is that I simply paid many times more than it was worth for something that was probably intended to be given away for free.

But the pen brings me good luck on my travels, I believe. I don't really believe it, but we joked about it so often that the idea ended up becoming a superstition between us, and we actually started to take it seriously. I wonder how many religions started in just the same way? Probably most of them, I would think.

That morning I heard the familiar tapping of rain, but when I threw back the door to face the world in only my underpants, I was relieved that there was, in fact, no rain. Instead, there was a blue, cloudless sky for us to ride under. Of course, this was around 6:30 in the morning, so there was quite a considerable amount of staggering around, swearing, bad breath, and comments I wouldn't want my mother to hear being made.

We woke up the man who was responsible for the hotel reception, who slept on the floor of hotel reception, which seemed slightly weird but did make him easy to find. He made no objection to us performing an act which was punishable by death, so we rode out into the streets on our happy motorcycles, which hadn't had any of the attention I'd promised to lovingly administer. The roads were unpleasant and so was the smell, but there was no flooding, no open sewers spilling into the streets, and curiously enough, no people either. Those were more or less the ideal ingredients for a town in Pakistan, or at least the best you could hope for.

The hotel was close, and security let us in with no problems, rather exactly what we expected would happen. We went through the metal detector, which went off, but that seemed to be no problem, and they apologised, and that explained that apparently nobody knew how it actually worked, so it was probably just their fault in some way. That was quite an admission for a security team to make to a pair of strangers wandering into a heavily armed and armoured hotel in a country where firearms could be had on every street corner for a bribe of less than a hundred dollars.

Breakfast was the same as the day before but spicier and with more coffee. I had to wake up, and the only proper substitute for sleep is good coffee, at least when I don't have access to any class-A narcotics.

Actually, I don't respond well to drugs and once took an over-the-counter cold remedy that rendered me unconscious for nearly forty-eight hours. Coffee and beer is about as adventurous as I actually get, but that's still fairly adventurous when the coffee comes served in a rusty bucket, and the beer comes with a warning that consuming it is punishable by a slow and torturous death.

Breakfast was excellent, and we charged it to the room of the gigantic fat man that we saw the previous day. It's surprisingly easy to do that in Pakistan, and we were sure he'd appreciate the joke.

So we headed back to the hotel half an hour late, and the police still hadn't arrived, but we were hardly surprised at that. I adjusted my chain quickly and did my routine inspections. Then I loaded my gear, and by the time I'd finished, they had arrived to lead us out of town.

It wasn"t far, but then it wasn't much of a town, barely more than a high street with a few extra roads crossing through it. The septic backlog had cleared, but the buildings were of the worst possible kind. People lived in conditions the RSPCA would prosecute you for if you exposed a dog to them.

Donkeys walked through the streets dragging decaying wooden carts, ramshackle sheds were collapsing all around, and concrete slabs were arranged into squares to form makeshift houses with no plumbing or heating of any kind. In the place of such humble conveniences were machine-gun emplacements on every roof. More worryingly, the people seemed oblivious to the abject poverty; the appalling conditions in which they were forced to eke out a subsistence lifestyle. There was a sense of hopelessness between the army checkpoints; no education and no hope of escape until they were eventually freed by the icy touch of death. Some people we had spoken to were desperate to get to England in the vague hope of a new life, but with the additional cost of living there, there's not much hope for them making it. Most people didn't even seem to have a dream, they just wandered around in meek acceptance of the grim finality of their fate. It was really quite a depressing place to be, even for a visit, and I felt quite sorry for the people.

We were relayed out from the town, and the cars swapped a number of times. Somewhere along the line, it had all become routine, and we barely noticed any longer. We rode on through winding roads into a tiny village, where people waved and the buildings looked cleaner. The poverty was still blindingly apparent—we passed a place where small children were standing by the road side holding out an egg in the hope, I assume, of selling it to us. We had to stop for paperwork and to change our escort at one point, and children were sitting cramped into a hole in the rock for the day with a few eggs to sell and a bottle of something to drink. They didn't seem to have anything to eat, unless the eggs doubled as lunch.

Marcin seemed to have lost his money, meaning I had to stretch out what I had until we could get to a town and draw out some more cash. Hotels were relatively expensive, but a necessary evil in towns where people will steal the paint off of your car if you turn your back for a second. Camping wasn't just advised against, it was patently insane.

Our driver, and the person who carried the AK47, left the safety of the most battered Toyota van I have ever seen to come and introduce himself to us. I was more interested in the van; how those things hold together was anyone's guess, but they seemed to be near indestructible and could handle more abuse than a teenage girl whose step-father had boundary-issues.

Without any hint of a joke, I have come to respect the mighty Toyota Hilux. The abuse that was visited upon those machines was incredible, and they clearly seemed to absorb and deal with it without consequence. I only wish that Toyota made a Hilux adventure motorcycle—I would buy one!

Our two escorts then got onto a 70cc Chinese motorcycle. At first I assumed they were heading back, but sadly not. They beckoned us to follow. We did, through some very impressive winding roads that I enjoyed riding immensely. In fact, the little bike made a good pace, but the rider's skills were on the wrong side of dangerous. The road had a sheer drop to the side, not high really, but at around a hundred metres, it was still a lethal fall. He rode where he liked, snaking around the road into the path of oncoming trucks, which swerved around trying to get out of his path.

At one point, we came to a puddle that had to be two or three feet deep that had pooled under a bridge in a single lane. Lorries and cars were fighting to get into it, and nobody seemed to know what the actual rule was, so it was a chaotic struggle to get through. After that, we were waved on and free to go on our own and at our own pace.

The roads were lousy—gravel and rocks, potholed, unsurfaced and uneven, winding through mountains, deserts, and half-finished archways.

We loved it!

We kicked up the speeds to a decent, safe but quick pace, and I led the way. Our bikes ripped up the roads like they were paper, and we had a real blast being allowed to run at our own speed for a change. There were only two stop-checks along the way, and I was riding so fast by then that I overshot one of them. It was the best riding we'd seen so far; magnificent scenery and roads that felt truly adventurous. We were in our element.

We were stopped at a checkpoint occupied by a young policeman who had been stationed under a beating sun with nothing to occupy him on the outside of his skull. He came out of his booth, scratching his head and straightened up stiffly as he saw us, struggling to look all respectable and efficient. I was in an elated mood from the sheer fun of riding the terrain and walked up to him and hugged him warmly.

Marcin burst into laughter, and then the confused young officer followed along, and we all just shook hands and had some fun by the side of the road, playing with the bikes while we filled in the obligatory papers.

Sadly, after that, it all went a bit wrong. Twice. For once, it really wasn't our fault.

I was still riding high from the awesome ride we were having as I led us into a mountain pass with holes cut into rocks for the road to run through and a drop to the side down to a lake. The weather was brilliant by then, and people had gathered to swim and enjoy the sun. We snaked around, and Marcin flashed me to stop.

I didn't notice—the sun had glinted off his boxes a lot that morning, and often all I could see was a glare in my mirrors. Then

I saw he wasn't there, so I went back. He had stopped for pictures, and I also took out my camera to record a few sacred memories. A couple of men came over and started inviting us for tea. I was up for a break, and I needed some water in any case. Then a truck stopped and a dozen or so younger men came out, all wanting to shake hands and say hello.

I took pictures, they posed, it was all very friendly at first. The van left, and then the two young men started trying to steal our gear. They grabbed my camera and said it was a gift to them. Then they started opening Marcin's luggage and rooting through. It was the kind of behaviour I expect of animals or, at worst, children. There was no respect, no boundaries. At first, we thought it was a joke, and we firmly played it down, but it started to become apparent that it wasn't, and they really were trying to take our stuff.

One of them said he would shoot us. Marcin was the picture of restraint, but I was losing my temper. We firmly told them to back away, we put Marcin's stuff back and left with no harm done, but after that I was left with a feeling I couldn't shake. It put a gloom over the rest of the ride for both of us. No longer was making speed and heading onwards a thrill. Now, it was just about putting miles on the gauge before the clock counted us out for the day and to just get as far as possible towards India.

Of course, it got worse, as these things frequently do.

We passed the scene of an accident and stopped for a look. There were two policemen sitting in the road, so we assumed, wrongly, that it was a checkpoint—we pulled over to present our documents. We were told we could just ride off, so we asked what had happened while we packed away our papers. They told us that a car had hit a bus, and it had overturned in a ditch. The police greeted our curiosity warmly, as they always did.

I asked if anyone was hurt, and it turned out that everyone had been. More specifically, it transpired that they had all died when the bus caught fire. It was still there, with no emergency services to clear up the mess. The bus was on the way to a school and had many children on board. But nobody seemed concerned, and they acted like it was nothing at all. The driving there was so bad that it came as no surprise; in fact, it was more of a surprise that we hadn't seen a lot more of that kind of thing. We moved on again, packing up in silence.

I couldn't shift my bad mood, and Marcin was also rattled by that.

We had to stop for petrol later on. In the morning, I had filled up with "Super," and the pinking was massively reduced. There was none where we stopped, so we were back to the usual junk fuel, and my problems came back. I was a bit snappy with Marcin, I think, but not sure he even noticed, as he seemed to be in a foul mood too.

Mostly, we just carried on in silence. We had a checkpoint to stop at, and I tried using my sat-nav, but the screen was completely frozen, and it was utterly useless. There were forks in the road up ahead, so I told Marcin he would have to lead again, since I had no maps. He rode a bit too fast, and I had trouble keeping up. In fact, I didn't even feel like trying, and when we stopped for fuel, I told him to slow it down, and he did without further comment. No problem. I still couldn't shake the bad mood—Pakistan was definitely beginning to get to me, and Marcin besides.

I started to let my mind wander. Eventually, we picked up a police escort and had to follow them at silly speeds. Before we had been making sixty-five mph on average, even a little higher, but suddenly we were restrained to only nineteen. The heat was rising, and it was getting very hot. With no mountain winds to cool us, the temperature was getting decidedly uncomfortable. In the mountains twenty-five degrees was cold, but there twenty was feeling hot, and it rose to thirty-five degrees while we were still wearing full bike gear—the same gear we had worn through the Turkish and Iranian mountains. Marcin was still wearing two jackets, in fact, one over the other.

I noticed the colour of people changing, the looks of the faces, the clothes, and the buildings. People were getting darker as we rode along, and things were increasingly undeveloped. Then I saw a few small pockets of much lighter people wearing tatty but brightly coloured clothes. They stood out vividly against the background, and then I realised—these were refugees. I checked the map, and we had entered the edge of a part of Pakistan that had recently flooded. I looked around, and it all fell into place. My dull mood had left my mind working over how things fitted together as well as dealing with the matters of riding, and I had blindly forgotten where we were.

Lakes replaced fields; endless pools of completely stagnant, motionless water stretched out on both sides of the damaged roads with the brilliant sun flickering across the suspiciously even surface. Buildings lay around the edges of the new waterlogged scenery, wrecked by the flooding. We weren't just being escorted, we were being slowed down as the roads got increasingly bad.

I saw a shelter, a community made from white metal boxes, like the backs of cheap trucks, with military green tents pitched between them, spread around unevenly, people sitting at the edge of the roads, broken and lost. We passed a field with a proud banner that said the aid was supplied by UK Relief. There were less than thirty white tents, each maybe large enough for a few people.

In fact, the area seemed to have recovered well. People were mostly smiling, and looked like they meant it. Those people had so little in their lives to begin with that even the loss of their homes couldn't take very much away from them. The poverty there was so grim, so overwhelming, that it colours every facet of your perception. People seemed utterly desperate, huddled together in dusty and broken little communities, trying to claw an existence from the land, a land that had treated them all so badly. It was a humbling thing to personally witness that, a place that I had only seen on the news.

Relief of sorts had not managed to find its way there yet—these people were not rebuilding, not creating new lives, they were barely getting on with it, living in home-built tents or shacks and trying to survive, as though they aspired to nothing more than just spending the rest of their lives only muddling through.

As we moved on, things got worse. We left our escort finally and were into the last leg of our journey before we reached the city of Sukkur. The roads just got worse and worse and then got busier and busier. People drove like they lived, with no thought, no hope. People wandered across the road, aiming their cars and bikes at whatever they pleased. The roads were made of sand, and then mud, rubble, rock, and pitted tarmac. Buses, trucks, cars, and bikes clambered together to drive faster and more dangerously. Even Marcin held back—I'd never seen him so cautious before.

At one point we were stuck behind a slow-moving truck with no gap to pass, so he waited, and then a car overtook us, followed by two van-loads of people with more people hanging on to the outside. How they made it I don't know, we couldn't even see through the dust. It was crazy! Life meant nothing to them, even their own.

Villages were turning into horrible blurs of yellow and grey concrete hovels at the side of the roads, filled to the point of teeming with people and carts planted at the sides of the road selling rotting fruit and other spoiled wares. If we stopped for a moment, we were swamped by them, clawing at us greedily. Bikes came up to ride with us, and although they seemed to have good intentions, they were too close to be anything but dangerous as they wobbled uneasily along.

The sides of the roads were littered with the carcasses of broken trucks smashed in accidents, and I wondered how many bikes lay beneath the water beside the road.

People came from all around to stand gaping at us in silence. If we stopped to check a map, we had the usual mob of people grouping around and staring blankly or begging for anything we might have to give. Nobody spoke or interacted with us, or even with each other.

In the end, you just learn to ignore them, but it makes you feel uneasy at first. It's unnerving to be surrounded by a silent wall of cold, dead eyes just staring blankly forwards while you do the most mundane things. We waved, we pointed cameras, and there was never any response. They just stared like frozen statues as we tried to communicate by some means. Waving and smiling meant nothing, and there was no sign that anything we did registered with them.

That leg of the ride was pretty awful, and then I heard a noise that made it even worse. A grinding noise every time I went over one of the sizeable potholes—holes deep enough to swallow a small bike. Finally, I stopped, fearing the worst. Luckily, it wasn't as bad as I had feared, only the spare fuel can had been lost. A bungie had snapped, and it had fallen into the wheel or chain and had been cut wide enough to have shed five litres of spare fuel, cutting my range down to 120 miles if my auxiliary tank failed, which it would probably do in the heat.

I was annoyed at the loss but caught up to Marcin, and we carried on again. We battled through to the highway. We tried to talk, but in the village we'd stopped in the noise became deafening as people started crowding us, so I went back to a petrol station to fill up my tank. Actually, my secondary tank had worked, increasing my range instantly, so we headed straight into Sukkur, which was now easily reached without a further stop.

The town itself was not as bad as Quetta—cleaner and more vibrant, with a hint of character. Again, people crowded us on the road, trying to say hello or just get a look, but it made riding almost impossible. We got directions back to the only hotel in town, where they locked the gates and had frequent patrols by a man with a pump-action Remington shotgun.

After that day I could see why.

Quetta was a militarised town. It was essentially an army base with shops in it, but the truth is they're not worried about terrorism or Iranians. The threat is internal—its own people are the threat. Pakistan is at its best when there are no large groups of Pakistani people about. The scenery is impressive, and to ride it on an adventure bike had been a real treat, but to deal with the people was endlessly stressful. A lot of them were just trying to be friendly, but there was an undeniable undercurrent there of malice. It really wasn't nice, and we just didn't want to be there any longer.

There was no beauty created by the people there; no art, no contribution to the world as a whole beyond the manufacture of weapons and people willing to use them. We saw only one building that was nice to look at, and it was literally square and featureless, apart from square windows and a door. Pakistan seemed to be a country afflicted by its people, over-run without any harmony between them and nature, no harmony even between the fact of the people and their own natural needs.

Gone were the warm welcomes we got on the road from places such as Tabriz, but even then, we only met professionals and civil servants, educated people who wanted to help. Since that time, we'd mixed with normal people, and it had been increasingly difficult.

Certainly, the place had its challenges, but it didn't, and can't, excuse everything. The villages and small towns were filled with donkeys dragging carts and buildings that were an amalgam of mud and sticks. If it wasn't for the input from the western world, I wonder if that country would have socially evolved at all in the last few thousand years. There were places where you could point a camera and travel back in time to a forgotten age that still lives on there. Iran and India are very careful not to let the borders remain open to those people, and I was starting to see why we had heard so many negative things.

In the hotel we saw the unmistakable Velorex that we had only glimpsed in the hotel back in Quetta. The Hungarians waved at us from the balcony, and we arranged to meet them later for something to eat in the hotel restaurant.

Like us, they were trying to go as fast as they could to get away from the place, but we had caught them up, making up a whole day. We all wanted to make the border town by the next evening, but it seemed very unlikely, as it was still too far off for a single day's ride. As I looked over the maps, I thought that two days might be possible, but the next day we were resigned to an early start and a long ride until the light started to fail. At that point, we were ready to do anything to get out of there and move along with our journey.

I was optimistic about India. Looking back, that seemed incredibly naïve.

27

MORE OF THE SAME

Date—November 12th
Location—Sukkur, Pakistan
Mood—Bored

Not every day on the road can be exciting and this one certainly wasn't. Once we were used to the escorts, the mad driving, and the wrecked roads; it all became routine, and none of it was particularly interesting anymore. It was just the same old thing, over and over again. The driving was appalling, the scenery was repetitive, and the conditions were poor. This never changed and clearly wasn't going to.

As I was riding my mind wandered, and I began to wonder what I was actually going to write about, since all we actually did was follow a police van all day, sometimes flat out, which was still fairly slow and sometimes so slow we never even got out of first gear. The scenery was nothing special, since we were stuck on a main road, and the weather played nice—not hot enough to be uncomfortable but certainly not cold. After sandstorms, snow-capped mountains, suicidal driving, and our own stupidity, it was all oddly anti-climatic that nothing went even a little bit wrong.

We got up and had some breakfast at our hotel. We asked for traditional Pakistani food and got a small omelette with a cheese slice, some toast, and coffee. Well, we got a jug of tepid water and a jar of Nescafé, which was nearly the same thing and close enough to get me started in the morning.

Coffee had been near impossible to find in Iran, and it was a relief that it had returned to our menu, albeit in a slightly disappointing form. I have a bit of an addiction to caffeine that has only gotten worse. It's sometimes so bad that in the toilet you can actually smell coffee when I pee.

We packed up and headed out to meet the security van we had hoped not to see, but sure enough, it was there, and we were stuck with it.

We'd made it there on our own the previous day and were hoping they might let us continue on our own, for part of the day at least. We would make better time and certainly have more fun if we did things at our own pace. But sadly, they were waiting and told us we had to be escorted; we had no choice in the matter.

Even worse for Marcin, the Hungarians in their customised Velorex three-wheeled car had to join us, and they weren't even up yet. He turned red, he paced like a wild animal trapped in a cage, and his teeth wore down to blunt little nubs as he angrily ground his jaw.

We talked the security escort into taking us into town for a visit to a cash-point and to fill up with petrol while we were waiting. Using some of our spare time in some constructive way helped to stop Marcin's head from exploding.

The usual crowds gathered but with the unpleasant addition of young (seemingly around ten years old) pregnant girls pulling at our clothes and begging for change. The police pushed the crowds back far more forcefully than the situation called for, smacking very young people in the heads and kicking at the older and larger ones. The crowds broke up, and we just watched in horror. As we left, even a street cleaner tried to beg from us as we rode past. He got the universal symbol of disapproval, and we moved it along, ignoring him as we did.

Once we got back, the others were ready in their Velorex for the road ahead, much to Marcin's relief—and mine, since I was the designated primary recipient of his moaning. We all rode out together from the hotel and got back underway, heading out to who knew what. Well, more of the same, as it turned out.

We then had to stop for the Velorex to be filled up with fuel. Even through my helmet and the background noise I could almost hear the sound of grinding as Marcin chewed angrily on his own teeth once again.

The day was hot, and as we rode along it got hotter and hotter still. We took a break and stopped for some water, and by then the temperature was over thirty degrees and climbing fast.

I tried to talk with a police officer as we waited for the others to pay. He was an older man who seemed quite professional and concerned about our safety. I tried to chat with him about that, but all I could get was that it was dangerous to stand about; he wouldn't go into any detail or elaborate on that in any way. Despite stating the dangers, he also claimed that wherever we were was perfectly safe, and he seemed immune to the two oddly opposed extremes of his points of view.

I offered to get the escorts a bottle of water, but he declined. I offered to get them something else, if they preferred. He said it was no problem, we were their guests, and it wouldn't be right to accept a gift from us.

So we plodded on, following a variety of slow and quick police, some barely moving, others driving as hard as they possibly could, sending plumes of acrid black soot from their exhausts.

The Velorex attracted a lot of interest wherever it went—crowds were flocking around it and leaving us alone, which was nice at first, but Marcin and I actually started to miss the attention a little bit. Marcin grumbled that his bike was nicer than their car and stamped around a bit in annoyance. His bike being by far the larger of the two, I had always got less of a crowd than him, so I was used to it.

The Velorex was an odd contraption, a bullet-nosed three-wheeled car with a single wheel at the back driven by a bike engine. It had a steel frame with a brown fabric bodywork stretched over it. It was designed to have only a small amount of power, but the engine had been swapped out for a Honda 650cc V-twin and the front modified with uprated suspension. He had done all of the work himself, and it was certainly an impressive and unique travel machine.

That carried on all day, more or less. For a while, we had a decent crew who meant business—they cleared the way, sirens blazing and guns pointing out of every hole in the van. Just as often, we had a team of apathetic morons driving at twenty mph and laughing at things which were inexplicably amusing to them while pointing at us.

Things changed that day while we were riding, and quite noticeably so. We entered the Punjab region and almost expected a difference to become obvious straight away, but it was slow to come, catching up as we drifted deeper along. It came eventually as people noticeably changed once again; their skin got lighter, the colours of clothes got brighter and more vibrant, and the buildings looked more solid, often held up with brickwork and concrete, instead of luck and very poorly misplaced faith in local workmanship. Civilisation started to take hold, and behaviour changed accordingly. There was less begging, more smiles. Children were flocking out of schools in uniforms, instead of selling their meagre wares to people at the side of the road. All that was quite a welcome thing to see, and all of us were relieved that we seemed to have left behind the worst of it.

We saw three different crashed trucks on our ride, all capsized onto the edges of the vaguely surfaced highways, shedding their loads and clearly shredding their inhabitants along with them.

All that just carried on and on; bad roads, bad driving, and following the police constantly on the one and only road in this region—one that inexplicably opened at the narrowest part of the country and led to the exit at the other end, after riding the full length of Pakistan.

Eventually the boredom subsided, and we reached the outskirts of Multan. It was a big town with signs of civilisation, but was heavily militarised, and unashamedly so. We had to go through half a dozen checkpoints, secured with heavy machine guns, to get to the high-street. Why they were there was anyone's guess, since the soldiers were mostly asleep, and those that weren't would probably have been more useful if they had been.

Barracks dominated the way into town, while the grass verges outside were filled with simple people taking their livestock to graze, unnoticed or ignored by the soldiers. The police took us through them all and into the heart of the town. They took us to a hotel we clearly could not afford and then to one we could.

The manager told us we had gotten a very special price, but I pointed out that we turned up with a truckload of people with machine-guns, and that did make negotiations a little easier for us.

We weren't allowed to go out, but we did anyway—the rules only appeared to be of a number of options there and weren't taken seriously at all, especially by us. We took a young man who worked there as a guide and were allowed to go to a restaurant for something to eat. We had some traditional Pakistan food, which was delicious, really good stuff, and after a few days of eating second-rate food and being violently ill, it really hit the spot.

We took our escort in with us and paid for him to eat, which seemed to confuse and delight him in equal measures. He seemed to enjoy the novelty of it all immensely. We spoke with the Hungarian couple at length, sharing our stories and enjoying a welcome break from the drudgery of the Pakistani roads, which had become quite a monotonous effort to deal with.

Driving under those conditions is hard, we all agreed. You have to be constantly alert, always watching ahead, and that means you're always tense. You watch the vehicles ahead, you keep an eye on your mirror, and you're aware of everything around you. You don't, because you can't, relax for a moment, because even the act of glancing away could literally be fatal. There were potholes large enough that hitting them would take you clean off your bike, and cars were coming at us constantly on the wrong side of the roads. It was utter chaos and was totally exhausting.

After dinner, we headed back, since going out to a restaurant was one thing, but going out to explore the town was quite another. We happily bent the rules but knew where the line was drawn and didn't want to push our luck or get our guide into any more trouble than we might already have done. The escort arranged to get us a few beers, and he hung around with us a while in order to help us drink them.

He seemed pretty smart and knew where to get anything we wanted, and he bragged about such things quite proudly. I jokingly asked him if he could get us a gun. He frowned thoughtfully and said it would cost around $100; he hoped that was not too expensive for us. We had been laughing and joking together all evening, and I was a bit surprised he had taken that seriously. It was also quite scary how easy it would have been to get a weapon there.

A little online research told us that in Pakistan handguns aren't even considered weapons, so the police don't actually bother with them. It was a stark reminder that we were in a very different culture, where life had less actual value and was as uncertain as online currency.

Our room adopted an open door policy, and with beers on the way, we expected a happy, cheerful night with the Hungarians and staff coming in to help us make lifelong memories or horrible, horrible mistakes. It's often interesting how narrow the line is between the two.

Our guide had a glass of beer and got instantly incredibly morbid. He started telling us about how he had moved to the town to avoid his family after they disowned him for dating a girl from a lower caste. He showed us pictures on his phone, and said he stares at them every evening for at least half an hour, occasionally kissing the screen while quietly sobbing himself to sleep.

We made polite comments, but by then he had started getting a bit odd, and whatever was happening was clearly going to play itself out whether we liked it or not. It takes me a few more drinks than half a glass to get quite that weird, even if I was drinking paint-thinner.

So then he told us all about how she'd left him for another man, presumably one who had a higher tolerance for alcohol, and how he'd consequently attempted suicide many times. His family never accepted him back, so he had been stranded alone in a strange town with no family, no girlfriend and no hope for the future.

Clearly this wasn't going to be a great night, so I went back to my writing, and Marcin made videos of us riding until the guy left and we could speak without fear of pushing him over the edge in some way with a careless comment. After he left, all we could think of to say to one another was, "she wasn't very pretty, was she?"

At least we had beer.

28

Always Wear Your Helmet

Date—November 13th
Location—Multan, Pakistan
Status—Ill

Breakfast was served in our room, which was a surprise but quite a welcome surprise after being lumbered with a guide who was happy to tell strangers about his latent desire to blow his brains out through the back of his skull. Breakfast was tiny, and Marcin had to order some food to go with it. I had enough to eat and thought that what there was was pretty good.

I had a slightly upset belly and had to visit the little boys room twice before we left. That was actually a good start to the day for me in Pakistan, a less pleasant start for the cleaners who had their work cut out for them later.

We knew that we were going to suffer in that part of the world and, in that respect, we certainly weren't disappointed. We had been given some tablets in Quetta by a pharmacist who demanded we buy some off of her or enjoy the experience of the entire contents of our digestive tracts exploding out of our anuses at speeds that NASA would struggle to track. We thought it best to do exactly that. It wasn't possible to say if they helped beyond admitting that at least some of what we ate was being digested.

Hygiene was a joke, and consequently we were suffering. We'd stocked up on tinned-goods, but that had long since run out, and we were now surviving on what we could find along the way. What we were finding along the way was having a similar effect as constantly ingesting filthy razor-blades served with rusty barbed-wire and washed down with a blend of battery acid and fresh camel dung.

That morning, I thought that it was a good idea to lube the chains on our bikes before we left; we didn't have many good ideas, so I thought it was best to make the most of the ones we had. Since it was quite possible that Marcin couldn't identify a motorcycle chain if he was trying to eat one, I pointed to the sorry, dragging brown clump of corrosion and offered to share my lube with him.

Mine was, indeed, in a sorry state, but Marcin's was far worse. I dropped my motorcycle on her side and tried to clean it with soapy water and a toothbrush, but the dirt stuck to it like glue, and the filth resisted any attempts to weaken its grasp. In the end, I scrubbed it with petrol and got some of the worst of the grime out from between the links. Really, it needed soaking in alcohol overnight, much like myself. In fact, it needed replacing and, ideally, as soon as possible. It was going to get me all the way there, I was confident of that, but Pakistan had really poured on the abuse, especially after the Iranian desert had done its worst too. Even worse, Marcin's was so slack that it was coming away from the sprocket, but he thought it was fine—he just kicked it and shrugged.

Marcin and I were by then friends, maybe even more than that. We'd gotten over the differences we had, and the journey had created a bond between us that felt very much like family.

Years later, we had gotten together, and he had come round my house for dinner. He wanted to show me pictures, and then I caught sight of his laptop. It was a bit of a surprise that, of all the different makes and models available, and with us both living in different countries with different budgets and needs, we'd both ended up with exactly the same make and model. We just laughed off the coincidence and carried on. Then I noticed his operating-system wasn't Windows and asked what he was using. Like me, he was using Linux Mint, a very unusual OS that is rarely seen. Even more strange, we had chosen both the machines and the software for exactly the same reasons. The only differences were that his had been fitted with a bulky larger battery for extended power, while mine had an SSD hard-drive for additional durability and reliability. So we weren't really very different after all, and the minor disparities in our motorcycling philosophy seemed to extend to everything else in our lives for many years to follow.

He was always fun to be around and an interesting travel partner, but he remained deeply unsophisticated, very much like a lump of rusty iron smashed into a skull. Every question was answered with a grin and the words, *"It's fine, let's ride longer/faster/more stupidly."* Even vaguely sophisticated arguments failed to impact on the surface of his brain. Subtleties like stopping for fuel before we ran out and having to wait while we filled up spare bottles, costing us hours instead of minutes, simply didn't register. Stopping for fuel brought on a tirade of moaning about how long everything was taking. His moaning, of course, took longer than anything else. I almost admired his single-mindedness, but in much the same way I admired the single-mindedness of a resourceful serial killer.

To be fair, while in Pakistan we had been stuck behind escorts for most of the trip, and he'd behaved very well. I had prepared myself to listen to him argue and moan with the police, but he had been pretty responsible and stayed in formation like a perfectly imperfect gentleman. You have no choice there—the driving is so bad that it borders on lethal. You can't take your eyes off the road for a second, unless you've decided already that it is the place you want to die.

So with very slightly cleaner and very slightly oily chains, we headed out for the roads with a security escort leading the way. They were certainly frustrating, but they were mostly just reasonable people doing their jobs, so it was hard to feel anything negative about them.

It would have been far nicer still if anyone could have told us what their job actually was. We argued with them occasionally, just trying to get a solid answer as to what exactly it was they were protecting us from. The guards just repeated the same old rhetoric that it was safe, but we needed protection anyway. The subtleties of the English language escaped them, but my general perception was that it is far from safe, and the government fears its own people will behave extremely poorly. It seemed an entirely valid point from what we were seeing all around us!

We made reasonable time at first on what was an easy run, for once. We expected to be in Lahore by around 2PM. We were invited to stay with a friend of Shandor, the Hungarian driver of the Velorex, so it should have been a free night too, and there may even have been beer, we hoped. We had water already and fuel, so we got out to follow the escort to the main road. It was hot again—it reached forty-two at the height of the afternoon, but in the morning it was only thirty-two. Even the relatively modest morning heat felt brutally hot through our motorcycle gear. My arse was not interfacing well very with the gel-seat saddle, presumably because it was by then as hot as hell, and my arse was sweating like a teenager who had just found out his mother had cleaned up his bedroom while he was out.

I had other problems with that particular bodily region in the morning. I often had issues, but that time was the most violent it had been so far. I clenched and held it back, but there was something in my guts that was dead set on getting out and escaping into the cold light of day. It made it clear that it cared nothing that the way was blocked by a wall of tense muscle backed up by Kevlar-lined trousers that smelled better without my stomach acid etching itself into the fabric.

I passed Marcin with the intention of waving to the police to stop at the next petrol station, but then Shandor pulled over the Velorex by the side of the road ahead of us. I was going to suggest that whatever the problem was, we should go somewhere with a toilet, and go there pretty damn fast. Then he got out with a toilet roll and ran off into the bushes with a sense of urgency that I found quite impressive. I wasn't going to last long myself—I had a matter of seconds left before I had a childish accident, so I grabbed a roll myself and found a quiet spot, running into the bushes with my toilet roll help aloft and shouting out my best war cry as I ran, clenching my cheeks together for all I was worth.

With a blast of unspeakably awful power, my problems were all behind me, quite literally, and quite horribly too. The explosive evacuation left everything my arse was pointing at dripping with yellow slime. I instantly felt a hell of a lot better, but my stomach was still churning like a frightened cat was trying to escape from it. The two weary travellers trudged back to the road amidst curious stares from our guards and sarcastic laughter from Marcin. Shandor's partner put some wood chips into my bottle of water—it tasted foul but did help to settle my churning guts. The taste grew on me after a while too, but I don't think we'll ever see anyone ordering it in a bar.

We headed back to the road. It was kind of a relief that other people were having problems as well. Marcin seemed to be made of solid gristle and immune to such minor things as illness, variations in temperature, exhaustion, emotions, and any vaguely intelligent argument. He had also never seen *Futurama*, which I found honestly unsettling.

It's certainly true that misery loves company, and it was nice to be riding with a fellow human who suffered from explosive diarrhoea when he eats or drinks anything from Pakistan. I felt more normal somehow, even if normal for me now was running into a field to violently shit myself all over a bush.

After our first swap, we got a hardcore team—they made ridiculously good speeds, and the sirens blazed, keeping traffic out of our way, but it didn't last, and the next team took a leisurely ride at their own convenience. There was never any real continuity that day or any other day, come to that. Again, they all drove horribly battered but completely functional Toyota HiAce vans.

When they originally made the old TV series, *Knight Rider*, they should have used one of those things instead of the TransAm. They wouldn't have had to bother with any stupid made-up sci-fi explanation for why it was so tough—they could have just said, it's indestructible because it's a Toyota HiAce, and that would have been fine. Everyone would have completely understood, and it all would have made perfect sense.

So we plodded on, and my guts were wrenching away at me, and my head was spinning from lack of sleep, heat, and from the gourmet delights of that fair country, delicately seasoned with monkey faeces, razor blades, powdered glass, or whatever the hell else was causing my insides to try to be outsides. I was wondering again what the hell I might write about in my blog—endlessly following the police is hardly entertaining stuff, but I had my lucky pen, so I knew something would come up. It slightly misfired this time, as is often the case since it's really not very lucky at all.

After a while, it became my turn to have an accident.

We were honoured guests, and trivial things like toll booths were of no consequence to us, apparently. The police raced ahead and arranged for the toll gate to come up and allow us through. It raised well enough, a white painted wooden beam with red stripes to warn motorists that it was a solid object and not to drive through it.

As we came up to pass through, a mistake in the booth meant it came down too soon on me, riding at the end of the convoy, since I was having the least trouble keeping up over the rutted roads. I slammed on my brakes and pulled up just as the gate closed on me. The wooden beam just touched my windscreen, just literally barely touched it. The plastic flexed very slightly without much more than a slight sigh, and no harm was done.

Well, nearly no harm.

The wooden beam simply fell off, clattered down into the road and kept rolling off into the distance. The booth operator came running out, covering his face in abject horror. The police came back, and someone was shouting from their van, "Are you alright, are you alright?" I just sat there without a single scratch on the plastic screen and told them that my chances of surviving that incident were pretty good.

Later on, the Velorex had to stop in at a town/village/hole in the dirt, with half a dozen garages dotted around it that now had been turned into a bustling metropolis of sorts. Shandor said there were problems with his spark plugs and set out to replace them. I tagged along to find some rubber hose to refresh my ailing fuel system, which had never really quite managed to work properly, except in England, where it didn't matter at all if it worked or not. Neither of us managed to get anything. We rode on for a few miles, and then the Velorex began chugging, hunting, and losing speed.

I headed in front and flagged the police down. We stopped at another town that didn't have any of exactly the right plugs, but we managed to find something similar that should have done the job. By then, the usual crowd had gathered, and a Highway-Patrol car had stopped to assist us by interfering and getting in the way. Our guards and the other police tried to disperse the crowds, but it was getting too dense, and we could tell that the police were worried.

In the end, we decided that the best thing to do was to get away, so we said we'd chug along to the next petrol station and swap the plugs out there. We limped on, hoping to get a few more miles, but very quickly it just gave up and stopped at the side of the road, the Velorex deciding that it was going to decide where and when we were going to stop, not us.

Changing the plugs didn't fix the problem. The bike engine still wouldn't stay running. I suggested upping the fuel mixture and limping the last hundred miles towards Lahore to make a more detailed fix. By then, Shandor had already begun stripping out the carbs, airbox, and everything else even vaguely removable from the engine bay and didn't seem totally sure what he was doing or even what the problem might be.

We all wandered around a bit and gave fairly useless suggestions. It slowly became obvious that there were a number of things wrong, so we gradually ended up fixing them one by one until the engine wanted to run.

It was around then that we heard a crash on the opposite side of the road, as the lucky pen worked its dubious magic and gave me something interesting to write about. A motorcycle had crashed into a donkey-cart carrying bricks, and not just crashed, but crashed really, really hard.

The police wanted to do nothing but stand around being useless, whereas Marcin and I wanted to help, if we could. I went over to see if there was anything we could do. A young lad, only around thirteen years old, had been riding with no helmet—probably had been watching us instead of the road—and had hit a wooden cart head on, landing face-first into the back of the cargo. He had hit it hard enough to knock the cart into the ditch and upturn the bricks and had managed that using the awesome power of his upper jaw. They dragged the lad onto the grass and just let him roll around in agony. He was stunned and in shock, and his head now had a number of new and interesting dents that I assumed didn't come as standard.

We put him in the recovery position, as there was no longer any point in keeping him still after he had been dragged along a grass verge by his arms and thrown to the side by a growing mob of angry Pakistanis. He had abrasions to his neck, and his clothes were torn at his elbows and knees, and he seemed completely unable to stand or even make sense of what was happening around him. As he rolled about, it was pretty obvious he had hurt himself quite badly. His head had a nasty cut, and his jaw was obviously broken. He was missing a few teeth, his lips had already swelled up massively, and he was spitting out lumps of thick red blood as he coughed. The police brought him a bottle of our water, and Marcin had come over with our first aid kits after freeing them from our luggage, but there was nothing we had that was going to do him any good. I kept the crowd back, as they were forcing their way forwards with insane grins painted on their faces and not much going on behind them.

One old man had begun shouting at him by then, and then, as he was clearly incapable of intelligently responding, he communicated through the international language of kicking him in the face.

It was fair enough and would have been hard to argue that what he'd done was stupid, but even so, this was all a bit redundant, since he had clearly learned his lesson, if enough of his brain was still functioning well enough to allow him to do so.

I made him back up, and he did as he was told but seemed oddly curious as to why I should object to this broken young man being kicked in the head. Another man was taking pictures on his phone and laughing. I made him put that away too, and he blinked in wonder at me. Perhaps I was merely a guest in their country and had no right to intervene, but I'm not someone who could stand by and do nothing, and nor was Marcin, it seemed.

Realising that there really wasn't much we could do for him, we spoke with our escort to see what could be arranged. All that could be done was to load him into a passing tuk-tuk and send him to a local clinic. We paid for that to happen and stood around feeling rather impotent. The police escort, at least, managed to understand that he needed help, and some kind of help was actually sorted out. In the end, they dragged him onto a tuk-tuk and wheeled him away to a hospital, they told us. I don't know where he really went, but I doubted he'd be getting the very best of possible care.

We saw two other accidents as well that day, since the lucky pen just didn't know when to stop. A truck had run off the road, and a bike had hit a barrier. Both accidents had wrought carnage on the machines, and if anyone survived, then they'd be walking funny for the rest of their lives. The people living there were clearly not competent to operate heavy machinery. They drove like maniacs, there didn't appear to be any strict rules on the highways, and I had never seen a people who needed rules more strictly applied before.

After we got the Velorex going, we told the police we needed petrol. No problem, they told us, and they turned and drove the wrong way down the dual-carriageway to go to a station on the opposite side. It had no fuel—well, the pump was smashed, in any case. I explained we had a reserve and if they could just take us back to the right side of the road, we would top up at the next one that came up. That seemed to translate into, "Please find a way to cause the maximum problems possible and risk all of our lives to get to the nearest petrol station in the shortest possible time!"

Finally, we did manage to fill up, and while we were doing it, we called the friend of a friend where we should be staying. After a lengthy explanation of who we were, we were told they were 200 miles away and wouldn't be in Lahore that evening.

So we limped on towards Lahore in any case, the Velorex running seemingly well, another change of police later, and then the new ones pulled to the side of the road. Normally, we picked one up on the road, but this time there was nothing. A truck flashed from behind. We assumed it was them and allowed it through, but it was just another half-witted person driving like a total moron, and we were lucky nobody was hurt as he ploughed straight through us, narrowly missing us by scant inches. We wound our way into the town on our own, in what was now heavy traffic, as the afternoon rush-hour had built up on the roads. The one time we could have actually done with some help—when you go into a strange town and don't know your way around—the police buggered off and left us to our own devices. Our devices were broken or badly malfunctioning in each and every case.

We battled our way in, and Marcin picked up a hotel on his sat-nav called "The Internet Inn." He was increasingly obsessed with web access, so he could upload videos and blog entries, he said. It was down a backstreet and had no parking, but it was cheap and had space for all four of us. There was no parking, and against Marcin's protests, we absolutely had to have somewhere to store our vehicles safely. In the end, we left it and headed off to find somewhere else. We found a proper hotel, which was cheap, but again, there was no available parking.

It was getting dark by then, but Marcin, with the only working sat-nav began a mindless crusade to visit every single hotel in Lahore and then find fault with every one of them that we could actually afford, while wanting to stay in all of the ones we couldn't. In the end, I decided angrily that I'd had enough, and we planned on going back to the first, cheapest one and try to sort out some kind of parking.

The last place we visited, thanks to Marcin's GPS, was someone's house. The previous was a college, and the one before that was a bush. Our patience was wearing thin. The man in the house pointed us to a guest house, who pointed us to another. They wanted more than I was going to pay, but as we walked out, they suddenly dropped the price to something we would pay, and so a deal was struck, and our quest was finally over. The next day, we were heading for the border. Marcin was already grinning and ready to drive faster, but I had a feeling that it was going to be a tough crossing. India does not like Pakistan, and it was unlikely that they were going to make it any easier for us. In fact, the only way we might get through quicker was to say how much we hated the place.

At least we wouldn't have to completely lie!

29

My Love Affair with India Begins

Date—November 14th
Location—Lahore, Pakistan
Mood—Deeply unimpressed

All we managed to do for the entire day was cross into India. I didn't think we'd get much further beyond the crossing, and I was right about that.

We woke up to what was a free breakfast, because nobody remembered to pay for it, and the hotel forgot to charge. The previous evening's dinner was not quite as good as the night before, but it had the added benefit of not making my arse explode in a bush at the side of the road, which is always the preferred choice.

Sadly, we didn't get hold of any beer, which was disappointing, but we were too tired and too fed up to go to the trouble of sorting it out. It was our last night with Shandor and his wife, but we didn't know that quite yet—we had no set plans in that department, but we were heading in the same direction, so anything was possible. We were enjoying travelling with them; in Pakistan we had no choice—we were simply part of a convoy and we had to ride together, but we had all enjoyed doing that. They were good people. Shandor's wife had taken on the role of group "Mum" and busied herself with looking after us all. That did keep her quite busy.

So we headed to the border. Now that would, on the surface, seem to be a fairly simple task, but nothing is simple in Pakistan! Many times we'd asked why something wasn't working, and the stock answer the whole length of the country was, "Nothing works; this is Pakistan." So we packed our gear up to an audience at the hotel. There was some animosity from the man on the reception desk, who had wanted to charge us more for the rooms, and he glared at us accusingly. However, once we paid in advance and were chatty and decent, he warmed up to us fine and came out to wave us off in the morning as we took to our saddles and made off for the unknown horrors of the highways.

We headed out to follow Marcin, who had the only working GPS unit, which led us more or less straight to the border. We had to battle our way through traffic, which seemed to be consisting entirely of grinning idiots, who wanted to be nice but actually just nearly rode straight into you, idiots in cars who just swerved around honking their horns, donkeys, and occasionally any of the above driving straight at you in your lane. It was totally crazy—it's what you'd expect to see if you put eleven year old children in charge of running a country—eleven-year-olds with an attention deficit disorder and a drinking problem.

A quick flick through Google revealed the average IQ in that part of the world was at least twenty points lower than in the West. Now, twenty points is a lot. It's the difference between a guy working in a shop and a guy working on a cure for cancer. Those twenty points are just an average score, meaning that the ruling class is way higher, and the workers are probably a fair bit lower, since nobody is likely to test the man who cleans your toilet for anything much beyond the ability to have extraordinarily low expectations.

The cultural divide in Pakistan was horribly apparent—the darker skinned people are condemned to a subsistence living under home-made grass tents at the sides of roads, while the cities are full of a different, higher caste of people.

Even the cities are of a poor standard compared to the West and are filled with the darker skinned, forgotten people milling about like hopelessly lost souls, begging for change and getting their children pregnant. Was the problem a lack of education, was it that they were separated out for reasons of bigotry, or were there biological reasons why they were treated differently? Without being able to mix with them, we would never find out for ourselves, and they were dead set on us not mixing with anyone.

My guess is that there was a very good reason for it and one that outsiders wouldn't necessarily understand. The people we did mix with certainly didn't want to talk about it; they wouldn't discuss the matters of their culture with foreigners. Whatever the way the country was run, or wasn't, I got the impression that it ran (or didn't) that way because it had to.

There is a term in politics: *useless eaters*, referring to the poor, who consume and give nothing back to society as a whole. They're just considered a burden on the economy by the ruling elite, who are, ironically, the real burden on humanity, not that humanity has been quick to wake up to that fact.

In Pakistan these people are just shut out entirely. They have no choice but to huddle in little makeshift villages made from rubble or camps made from cut down trees. Nobody cares. They're invisible as they walk the streets scratching for a few coins or sweeping the clogged gutters to earn their family something to eat that day. Along the sides of the road you can see young girls sewing animal excrement into the soil to grow crops with their bare hands, because they're literally cheaper than tools. They are treated no better than animals; they're ignored until bricks have to be dragged along the highway or something clogged has to be unclogged. They're largely self-sustaining, but Pakistan doesn't even see them as a workforce—they're looked upon as a parasitic infestation clogging up their economy, with no education and no future to look forward to. The government is berated freely by the people. Whoever you speak to has little time for them, but they only see their own points of view, their own needs or wants. Nobody seems to realise that their community is a place that needs to serve the needs of all the people that live there.

Like in Iran, where we were told the government restricted the actions that affect the young, Pakistan had rules which inhibit the behaviour of its inhabitants, and they're frustrated and want less restrictions. What humanity means to me is an ability to empathise with others, to connect with the whole, with something greater than yourself, and I saw no evidence of that there, even though I was really looking for it.

Many people made considerable efforts to make us feel welcome, but they were clearly putting on a show just for us. Down alleys or back-streets, when they thought nobody was looking, we saw a very different story.

I heard no consideration of the forgotten poor, who overwhelmingly dominated the population. The people there weren't gifted or educated, and with propaganda and indoctrination, they have forgotten that the vast majority of their own people are living in abject poverty right in front of their faces. While I have nothing but sympathy for the plight of the people in that country, I have to say that I feel that they bring their problems largely on themselves. By by the time I left, most of my sympathy had gone as well.

Nobody we met seemed to want to connect with other people. You're either a job or a source of funds, that was all we were treated as on our journey through. If people showed interest in the bike, it was purely material, asking how much it was worth. Nobody was interested in what we were doing, or any other of the myriad details that made up the trip, they were only interested in the surface value of the things and never looked any deeper.

Marcin's KTM cost twice what mine was worth, but my bike was worth far more to me than what I paid for it. His is a bike, nothing more. I built mine, I loved it, and it was proving to be a brilliant machine. A simple thing like that is beyond the grasp of the people we met in Pakistan.

Of course, there needs to be better education to help these people reach whatever their potential is and take some control over their own lives. They need to be shown the world to know that it exists. They stood in rapt awe at our bikes, these things from a world they've never heard of and never expected to see. To us, it was fun and then quickly annoying, but in the end it was just sad. It was a reflection of the poverty and the emptiness there.

Life just carried on as it has for millennia, things passed down from one to another, but now we live in a modern world that is passing those people by, rendering them nothing more than manual workers, essentially nothing more than tools and certainly much less than people. Maybe that's what they want, but those who spoke to us seemed to dream desperately about leaving. The silent, emotionless crowds didn't ever seem happy to us. It was a country of few smiles.

We passed it by too, led by police who made sure that the crowds were moved away. We weren't allowed to speak with them, to interact, to even get too close. They told us it was their job to protect us, but they also told us there was no danger. Were we just a virus threatening to infect the simple folks with an idea that there might be a bigger world outside of life in the village? I doubt that much thought had been put into anything. The reality was that people who have nothing are dangerous, and in that respect, the country had turned its population into a threat.

Pakistan, finally, was not much more than a nuisance along the way, a long diversion to get from Iran to India. Geographically, we should have crossed the country in a matter of hours, but the borders demanded we ride the entire length of the country, and it was a difficult country to pass through. It had difficult roads, people we struggled to relate to, armed escorts everywhere, and towns so run down and primitive that, by our standards, they were barely even towns at all.

The people need help, but that help has to first come from themselves. They're like a man who's dropped himself down a well and just sits there waiting for someone else to sort it out for him, and if they don't, he'll just put up with it. Even if someone reached down, would these people reach back up, or just do what they had to do to settle into whatever routine was being set for them? Without talking to them, meeting them, and finding out for ourselves, I just couldn't say.

I did give some children a little money when we first arrived. It wasn't much, but they seemed like friendly kids, begging and playing, so we gave them a little cash. It can't have been very much, just a few pennies probably, since we weren't used to the currency and it was difficult to tell for certain. They seemed happy with what they got, but after that you very soon have to stop doing it. Giving a little money to a few children brings a lot more children, and with those come adults.

There are never-ending people begging for money, and you just can't give it to all of them, so eventually you just have to look away. We got used to having conversations about those people while they were crowding around us in silence, their oddly yellow eyes peering forwards emptily. You have to—they're everywhere you are, always gathering about like moths to a flame. At first we tried—we tried English, we picked up a few local greetings and spoke in their own language, we waved and we smiled, but nothing worked. We were just stared at us blankly.

You eventually just learn to ignore them like they're not human, just like their own government and their own people had done. Because of all that, I found Pakistan to be a sad experience. I was doing this to meet people, and this had been an example of people at their very lowest, as if their humanity itself was barely managing to hold on.

I don't know who was really at fault for allowing it to get so bad, but there is one thing I believe and that's that the responsibility for your life is ultimately your own. That's what it means to be human. Those in power might try to take that away from you, to dictate your life, to wrest control from you, but it's never theirs to take, only yours to give. I have little respect for someone who blames others for where his life has led him, and with that in mind, the people of Pakistan are the architects of their own disaster.

We weren't sorry to leave.

So eventually we went down a dirt road that brought us out to the final path that led to the border. The exit was far different than the entrance. It had a structure; guards armed with assault rifles who were wearing uniforms. It even had doors!

We entered and headed into a customs building. Once inside, we were told that the rest of us were there already. Obviously, we didn't know who the official was talking about and stared back at them rather blankly. We tried to get someone to explain what exactly they meant. We were still travelling with the Velorex, and the four of us were right there, crossing together.

Eventually, we were shown to a window where, outside, were parked several more motorcycles. It turned out that four other adventure bikers were there being processed as well, two on BMW

F800gs Adventures, and two on Yamaha XT660z Teneres, both of which were bikes I had considered for my trip.

We met them while having our exit stamps sorted and got chatting, as bikers the world over tend to do. The man doing our exit stamps was rude to the point of being irritating, so I made sure he found me far more irritating than I found him. That speeded up the process quite considerably.

After our papers were pointlessly molested for hours, we were allowed to go to the Indian side to be further molested. We filled in dozens of forms and were pushed from office to office, place to place, while getting things stamped and stamped again. In the end, it was time for our inspection, and all they did was check our frame numbers, and that was it. We were finished and free to go about our business.

The four other bikes were clean, gleaming things, with expensive Touratech bolt-on parts. Ours were filthy, caked in mud and grease, and by comparison, looked like they might fall apart at any moment. I asked, "How did you manage to keep them so clean?" One of them frowned at me and shrugged, "We washed them."

Marcin looked at me in horror. I slapped his arm and said, "Why didn't we think of that?"

It all sounds easy when you say it quickly, but the paperwork took most of the day. We were mired in mind-numbing bureaucracy, which seemed to exist purely for the sake of it. Several times I asked what the forms were for, since we had already given them that same information several times, and even the people dealing with us didn't know, or at least said to us that they didn't.

The staff were of the worst possible kind; self-important, rude, and just plain incompetent. We never got the feeling that anyone had a clear idea of what they were doing or cared enough to do it properly. They were arrogant and condescending, much like we had come to expect from government officers on borders, but even though we'd all encountered that before, it was by far the worst example we'd ever seen.

We all headed off through the deadly traffic of India to the first town, only twenty miles away; us, the Velorex, and the other adventure bikers all riding in convoy. It was really fun to be riding with a number of other bikers, two with less powerful bikes than my own, for once.

The traffic was brutal, the worst we'd ever seen. It was chaos taken to a whole different level, and the convoy was difficult to hold as they weaved around the road haphazardly, often straight at us or trying to cut though, forcing us to weave around them.

Shandor stopped us and said that he had decided he was going to head off alone, perhaps because of the difficulty he had staying with us through the insanity of the Indian roads. We knew we weren't going to ride together for much longer, but still, it was a bit sad. I had drawn a picture of the Velorex, since souvenirs were hard to find, and Marcin and myself had signed it. We gave them that, took some photographs, and they split off. We shared our details with one another and hoped to meet up in Thailand at some point, as they were heading in that direction as well. They were nice people, and I hoped we would manage to stay in touch.

Sadly, we never did manage to meet up again, but we always exchanged emails for years to come. Such are the strength of the bonds you form on the roads.

We then battled our way to a hotel through utterly mad roads, with utterly mad people doing utterly mad things. We weren't ready to give up just yet, but we stopped to join them for some belated lunch and to swap stories. We got something to eat, which was neither good nor bad, and then tried to decide what to do. The others were going to stay for the night, and I wanted to stay too. There was no point heading off into who knows what when we could stay there, settle down, and get some rest. Even Marcin seemed fine with that, so we looked for somewhere to stay that could accommodate all six of us.

As we left the café, a strange Indian man began barking and shouting, waving his arms around like his armpit hair was on fire. We all looked at one another in surprise and shrugged, having no idea what his problem might be. As we strapped on our gear, he began shouting and pointing at our bikes, which were nowhere near him or his place of business and were parked neatly on the opposite side of the area. He then, even more oddly, began kicking over other peoples scooters, and there was considerably more waving of arms and extremely high-pitched squealing.

We all stood for a moment in surprise, just staring at him. We'd never seen anything like it before on our travels. People were either genuinely decent, or had a genuine interest in appearing that way, so we'd give them money, but in any case, this kind of display of aggressive, abject stupidity was new to all of us.

One of our new friends threw his leg over his 660 Tenere, and the bike wobbled over and crashed straight down to the ground. I was just about to go and help him, but he hoisted it back up with no problems. I was a little surprised—I'd never seen an experienced biker drop his machine in such a silly way, but he didn't seem fazed by it at all.

The other European with a Tenere also told me he'd had a crash on his. Everyone I know who has owned a Tenere has dropped or crashed it, without exception. Even my brother, who had never dropped a bike before, managed to lose control twice while slowly manoeuvring. It was just that issue that put me off from owning one—there seemed to be some kind of balance issue, and they did seem to pack most of their weight up high, exactly where it didn't belong. I had spoken with a touring company at a bike show who used the same machines. He had told me they retired them after 20,000 miles, as they developed a whole host of problems after that. That also didn't fill me with very much confidence.

A Yamaha dealer also warned me that they rot away just out on display in his forecourt. That was a shame—they looked like a near perfect bike. If Yamaha had thought to put the TDM900 engine into the same frame, it would have been close to the ideal adventure bike for me.

The GPS led us through a market—not *near* one, *through* one. It was like riding a bike through Camden market back in London, only it was bigger, and with more people and with traffic coming in every conceivable direction all at once while everything smelled like a toilet had exploded nearby.

In the end, we gave up and tried asking for directions to a hotel. We found one that was not too bad for not too much cash. That only left beer to find . . .

30

Anything that Makes Pakistan Look Okay Can't Be Good

Date—November 15th
Location—Amritsar, India
Mood—Hung over

We paid the price for a great night in every sense that you can pay for a thing. We ended up staying in the same hotel as the other adventure bikers that we met crossing the border. There was a strong vibe that something needed to happen, so it happened, and it happened hard.

We all decided to hit the downstairs bar for a few well-deserved beers in the evening. After a few beers, we had a few more, and then the night descended into one of those nights on the town that made up for the fact that we had just spent a week stuck in Pakistan with no beer, and even less dignity.

The four guys were great, and we all had a fun time doing the kind of stupid stuff that we were all still laughing about the next morning. We went out first for a few warm-up beers, to follow the pre-warm-up beers we'd had before in rather large quantities. The single guys in the group wanted to find some girls to try their luck with, which was misguided, but perfectly reasonable.

The psychologist in me thought it would be interesting to watch, so I supported the idea wholeheartedly. At the very least it would be funny to watch. That would seem like a simple enough thing, but we only managed to find one bar, inside a shopping mall, after a whole hour of hunting around for one A security guard tried to search us, so I gave him a hug, and suddenly the rest of us didn't need searching, and he waved us on with a slightly awkward smile.

The bar was okay, but it was deserted, apart from us. The shopping mall itself seemed very much like the ones back home, albeit a little more basic and with styling that might have fitted in better during the 1980s. The bar looked like every single bar or café that you might find in any mall anywhere in the world. It had the look and feel of a low-budget chain, with generic fittings and an impersonal vibe that told us nothing about the country, people, or culture.

We stayed for a few drinks and for Marcin to fill up his always empty guts with complimentary peanuts. They were almost guaranteed to be just below a level of infection that would be considered lethal with a host of devastating viruses. But he didn't care, he just grinned and ate them faster while I tried to point out that nothing in the world actually works that way.

Just drunk enough to not really care what happened next, which was our normal level but more so, we then went on in search of somewhere that normal people go to get drunk. We assumed that from what we'd seen so far of the driving, chaos, and general behaviour, that rampant alcoholism was the norm in this town. It slowly became painfully apparent that normal people didn't actually get drunk in the normal social sense of the word, and in this town, women never went to bars either, so our desire to mix with the locals was not off to a flying start.

We found a couple more bars after a late night ride around town in a tuk-tuk, all six of us fitting where we could inside, outside, and on the roof of a two-seated vehicle. We offered locals cigarettes as they passed, and one crashed his bike into the central reservation which, as nobody was hurt, was pretty funny, even to the young man who crashed. He laughed at himself in awkward good humour. I don't think it was his first time.

We went all around town drinking until we somehow got split up from one another, Marcin and I ended up with one of the adventure bikers and got ourselves lost in some random backstreet. We grabbed a tuk-tuk, but even he was lost, although he claimed, with a strongly held conviction, that he wasn't.

It was somewhere around then (or maybe not) that I decided it was time that I fell in love with Royal Enfield motorcycles. I found a really nice dark grey one and asked if I could sit on it. I was assured it was no problem and sat down to play with it for a moment, imagining the wind rushing through what very little was left of my hair as I sped along slowly at full power. A man came rushing out at me, waving his arms, bulging his eyes, and screaming like a girl trying to swallow a water-melon at me to get off his bike. I pointed to the man who said I could sit on it, and he just shrugged and said, "Oh, it's not mine."

The next morning, we woke up pretty late with sore heads, a burning need for coffee, and a desire for the previous night to have never happened. We had somehow acquired a bottle of brandy along the way and had drunk it after we'd got back. One of the Europeans was lying on our floor, face down in a slightly brown liquid that his snoring was blowing bubbles out of. The room had a not entirely fresh aroma, but that also seemed to be the norm in India in any case.

We had a really top notch breakfast in the hotel, which was also pretty cheap, while we assured the others that their friend was still alive. They seemed mostly pleased to hear it.

It was around twelve noon when we left with about 350 miles to cover in order to reach Delhi, but we thought we could make it as the hangovers were pretty light, except for the adventure biker who came back to our room and drank half a bottle of brandy. It was fair to say we had broken him, and he wasn't going to be quickly fixed.

Compliments were thrown around—we were described as "animals," and that it was "a pleasure to see us in action." It was a real pleasure to be in action, and a good time was had by all. It was a night that recharged our batteries and gave our morale a real shot in the arm.

We said our goodbyes and headed off into the worst example of driving ever seen in the modern world. The people there had no rules on the road; cars, tractors, donkeys, bikes, and everything else just spilt into one another all over the roads in every imaginable direction, and all at once, and as quickly as possible.

The main road didn't even exist. It was nothing more than a building site that stretched on for the entire distance we managed to travel. The metalwork was already rusting away, implying the construction had been going on for a very long while. The GPS map we were using was five years old and showed the road quite plainly, but it was still not quite there in the really-real world. We rode for around a mile or two on half decent stretches, and then it would always break off into a diversion through a town or village, clogged rotten with some of the most appalling drivers I'd ever seen, honking their horns and bashing into one another. The driving was so bad, so aggressive, and so outright stupid, that we couldn't help but begin to hate them for it.

Once we finally stopped, we chatted about it over a drink of water. It was all utterly exhausting. In Iran, you can relax when you're riding out of town, take time to think about the world, but in India you're quite literally in mortal danger the entire time. You're watching the mirrors, the sides, and the front constantly, going for gaps with hands on the brakes, waiting for the cars to swerve into you. It's a hateful place to be on two wheels, or in any kind of vehicle that doesn't have armour thick enough to drive through a wall unscathed. This place would even test a Toyota Hilux!

We had more near misses than I could count. Young men on bikes whizzing around, swerving into us to shout "Hello, Sir" while laughing and seemingly deliberately trying to run us off the road. It made me wonder how it had gotten so bad. People surely wouldn't accept this for themselves; they couldn't be happy with the horrible dangers the roads posed to them, unless their brains literally weren't capable of processing such things.

So we spent the day dodging the insane driving, stopping briefly for fuel, water, and to take a few pictures. When we stopped, the crowds gathered, and it was far worse than Pakistan. The exhausting ride was getting to us, and frankly, my patience began to fray, since I just wanted to move along, hoping against reason that this might be a local issue, and we might outrun it and find a better standard up ahead.

To them, we seemed to be this amazingly weird thing that is brilliant to laugh at, to point at, and make snide comments about, but to us, they were just another one of a thousand people who had come up to ask us the same old questions, time after time, since we'd begun—"Where are you from? How much is your bike worth? Where are you going?" It was getting harder and harder to smile while we answered these with a friendly attitude, when we'd spent the day tense and angry from having to deal with the pressure of staying alive on the insane Indian roads.

We didn't find the crowds quite as isolating as Pakistan—they seemed to try to engage, they made eye-contact, but still not in a healthy or reassuring way. There was a horribly dark mood coming from the locals. Few spoke to us, and the others either glared angrily, or made rude comments, and we were having to get used to ignoring them. It was an oddly dark place—the people were exactly the opposite of welcoming, and we felt wave after wave of bitter resentment. It was like no other country we'd seen in that respect.

These people loved to touch. They were all over our stuff as soon as we stepped away, which quickly became pretty annoying, pretty quickly and meant that we couldn't venture far from our bikes. At one point, we attracted a particularly large crowd, mostly silent gazing, but a few people tried to speak with us in broken English. It was nice that they wanted to talk with us, but it was always the same, only interested in the value of our belongings. They were touching the bike as I was riding off, one even grabbed the exhaust while it was running, a mistake he'll never make on a lean-burn engined motorcycle again, as he left most of his fingerprints on my machine.

In the end, we just always wanted to get away from them. The crowds swarmed from everywhere, blocking the road, so it was difficult even to get moving. As soon as we parked, they were pressed up against us, so even getting off the bikes was next to impossible.

To be fair, the driving in Pakistan had been worse—they were even more thoughtless, illogical, and outright stupid, but there weren't so many of them, and they weren't driving so quickly. They were everywhere, all the time in India, with no apparent idea of what they were doing.

We left the city in the morning. Normally, a city thins out, but that one never did—it just kept on going. The buildings and the town just seemed to stretch on and on indefinitely, merging and blending into one giant city sprawl filled with endless, hopeless, and ultimately, mindless people.

Sometimes, the buildings gave way to ugly little camps, tents made of filthy fabric, where people lived huddled together in appalling conditions with their children. It's disgusting that this is allowed to happen in the modern world. The standards there were incredibly poor—the worst we'd seen, even compared to the slums of Thailand.

Like Pakistan, there was a caste system—the darker you are, the lower down the food-chain you seem to go. The really dark-skinned people appeared to do the most menial work, riding the push-bikes lashed to carts, or digging dirt in the middle of the road. It was rare to see them even riding a motorcycle.

Again, like Pakistan, stupidity wasn't just apparent but seemed to be revelled in. You could be riding down a single carriageway, and a tractor would come in the opposite direction in your own lane directly at you, the driver utterly oblivious of the danger he was causing; or a car would look through you and pull out from a side road directly across your path, no care as to whether or not you had time to stop. There was no organisation there, nothing at all; and no sign of planning. It was like the cogged wheels of a gearbox, all suited to mesh perfectly with each other, but it was lying smashed in the bottom of a box with a dog-turd on top of it. People just milled about aimlessly with no structure, no form, and the situation didn't seem to change as we moved along.

While I don't disapprove of chaos in theory, there needs to be an organisational structure of government in place to keep things running smoothly. Instead, that place had a post-apocalyptic look—buildings were crumbling, rubbish was piled everywhere, and everything was incredibly makeshift, done to the lowest possible standard. With over a billion people living there, the country is massively over-populated, and the net result was total chaos and people that were just painfully difficult to deal with.

Marcin is fearless. He seems incapable of anticipating the future to a degree bordering on mental illness. This day when the sun set and it got dark, he stopped at a hotel complex and said it was just too dangerous to carry on. That's right—he pulled over and said that to me. He was right, of course, but it was a little surprising to hear him say it. It was dangerous there. Pakistan has an AK47 for every nine people, but you're far more likely to end your days on Indian roads than at the business end of a Chinese-made assault rifle that would more likely explode in the hands of the operator than actually send a bullet towards the thing it was pointing at.

So we packed it in and set up in a small hotel place at the side of the road. Not cheap by local standards, but only around the price of an F1 hotel in Europe and with breakfast included. Inside it was actually very decent, for the money, and we were pleasantly surprised.

Unfortunately, the lack of organisation and basic intelligence caught us out again. When I booked into the hotel, I showed them my Visa card and asked if it was OK to pay on it. Of course, I was told it was, but later when I paid for dinner, it turned out that it wasn't OK at all and, in fact, not even close. They asked if it was an Indian card, which struck me as a fairly ridiculous question, especially from someone I had spoken with at length and discussed the fact that we had just arrived in the country while the same member of staff examined the card closely.

So the next day, we faced having no money and a bill to pay before a short ride to Delhi. We were hoping to arrive around noon, but our bikes didn't run on hope, and I had little faith that things were going to go our way.

31

Insanity, and Plenty of It

Date—November 16th
Location—Karnal, India
Mood—Starting to get a bit fed up with it now

So we had a pretty easy ride into Delhi planned for ourselves, in theory, but of course, nothing is easy in India, and if they find something that is then they'll change it, either by burying it under a mountain of rubbish or simply hiring local contractors to repair it, rendering it dangerous to the point that it would only be at home as a gag in a cartoon.

An Indian friend of mine I used to work with back in London messaged me to say that he was in Delhi, and so we decided to meet up. Getting to Delhi was one thing, getting across from one side to the other was quite another. There were no ring-roads (of course, that would make good logical sense, and besides, it would make it all too easy), and so the only way was to ride straight through the middle of the teeming mess of insanity that makes up the capital city.

We set off from a slightly surreal hotel in the middle of nowhere, quite early in the morning. It was like an oasis of civilisation in the midst of a chaotic shambles of dirt and craziness. They messed us about though, of course, since doing any less would be making life just a little too easy and maybe even fun.

While the clerk was aimlessly scratching his head and poking the buttons on his Visa machine, I wondered just what the hell it was they were teaching in the local schools, as that one seemed to have an advanced degree in incompetence, but little else. Perhaps he hadn't shown up on the second day.

When we had first found the place, I made a point of explaining that I had no cash money—only a debit card. I showed them my card and was told it was no problem at all and would be accepted without issue; a sign on the desk also said much the same thing. When we had dinner it turned out it was, indeed, a big problem, because my card didn't work, or rather it did, but nothing else would. So in the morning we tried again, and on the second attempt, it worked. Probably . . . you can never really tell.

So we had breakfast, which was radically different to what was described, but it was food, nonetheless, and we didn't have to scrape off an inch of dirt or fight the cockroaches for it. We headed onto the road with full stomachs, ready for the ninety-mile ride into Delhi—on the map a veritable walk in the park for a pair of seasoned motorcycle riders like us. But the reality of the journey we were facing stretched out before us looking more like a run through a minefield than following a main road to a capital city.

The post code was set in the sat-nav, and we were ready to face the horrors of Indian traffic, although *prepared* or *reconciled* might be the more appropriate terms.

The roads were just terrible. We had a five-year-old map showing the main road into Delhi, but it still wasn't finished—in fact, it still wasn't even *close* to being finished. We dragged on for a few miles with constant diversions through little dust-bowl towns with the maddest driving we'd ever seen—even in India—with everything getting increasingly worse. Progress was ploddingly slow, hot, and uncomfortable, while all around us were screeching sirens or blaring horns as they blazed past one another without looking. Nerves frayed quickly as we made our way along, wincing as they cut in front of us, cut us off, drove directly at us on the wrong side of the road, and generally did an array of creatively stupid things to threaten our lives.

We stopped for water after a while; hot, tired, and feeling the stress of all that. Straight away, the usual crowds gathered to stare at us from behind their fixed expressions and dead, yellow eyes, much like we'd become accustomed to in Pakistan, only this time the crowds were huge and far grimmer. Everyone frowned; everyone glared emptily. There was a muttering, like a distant chatter that filled the air as those crowds just watched us hungrily. Rarely did we feel anything except unwelcome. Did we remind them of what they'd never have, did our superior bikes or larger sizes offend them in some way? We certainly felt that something like that was at work.

A gentleman from the shop we stopped at came to ask where we were from and how much the bikes were worth, just for a refreshing change. Although hearing that was like having claws dragged down a blackboard, we tried to keep the atmosphere upbeat and give polite replies as much as we could. After all, a polite and friendly question deserves a similar answer. I hoped it might encourage the conversation to divert to a more interesting avenue and perhaps allow me to find out a little more about the culture of the place.

It didn't.

I hadn't drank any of the offered coffee that morning through fear of the water causing still more stomach problems, but I had a can of coffee later on that hit the spot nicely, chasing out the ghosts from my achingly tired brain. We had taken a wrong turn and gotten off a section of road into a town. I was following behind and didn't see any turn-offs either, so how that had managed to happen was something of a mystery. But it was less of a mystery when you considered that there were no signs anywhere, and the roads were essentially bricks dropped onto a dusty building site, with maniacs giggling like mental patients as they blasted through at full throttle, narrowly avoiding the blood-soaked carcasses of crushed, twisted wreckage lying sprawled around everywhere.

That diversion cost us about half an hour of being stuck in stationary traffic while people stared, wide-eyed and nudged one another, before dropping their trousers and crapping on the floor, while laughing, inexplicably, at us.

Marcin and I looked at each other and just carried on. What was there to say; what could we say? We had to be in Delhi, and we focused all our efforts on that and tried to ignore everything else. Certainly, while we were moving that wasn't a problem; we had to concentrate fully just to not end up as a bloody, twisted wreck ourselves.

After what felt like hours, because it was hours, we finally saw the first signs for Delhi and, in fact, the first sign to anywhere. We had battled on for a measly few miles, but it was just taking so long to move through the solid traffic that ninety miles was an all day long business, and a miserably demoralising business at that.

Once we finally made it into the actual city, we were transferred to the second level of hell itself. The city was stationary, with people honking horns constantly, without relenting, and forcing their way into whatever gap you left. Even moving your foot seemed to be an invitation for a truck to edge forward. We had to turn the bikes off in the traffic jams—the heat from the engines built up alarmingly! Mine was a lean-burn engine and tended to get extremely hot, and it was already thirty degrees in the shade. The situation was grim.

We had to take off our helmets and drink water to keep us going, but it wasn't a problem, as nothing was moving anywhere as far as the eye could see. At one point, three small children came up begging—they were tiny and stared at us with old eyes that had no innocence left behind them. They already knew all too well that the world was not a friendly place, and never would be to them. We couldn't give them any money, but we played with them—they felt the hot gas from the exhaust and liked it when we blipped the throttle, sending a little rush of warm air at them. Marcin even let them twist the throttle and make his engine roar. He never normally lets people touch, but those were just tiny kids, and I guess he had a soft heart in there somewhere after all, to go along with his soft brain.

They were filthy and hopeless, two young boys and a girl; none could have been more than eight, but we knew that if we gave them money, someone would take it off of them. We knew how it worked in those places, having been warned constantly. If they managed to hold onto the money, then they'd likely spend it on glue or whatever cheap drug they could get their tiny hands on. And why not? Those poor, forgotten children had nothing to lose. These kids needed someone to just take them off the streets and give them a home, but the streets there were littered with camps and slums where families and entire communities lived rough.

Child prostitution is reportedly in India way worse than Thailand, or anywhere in Southeast Asia, I had heard, and poverty was out of control. It was yet another depressing thing to see, the futures of these street kids going nowhere at all, rather like the Delhi traffic.

Due to an error on the GPS, we ended up on a building site in the middle of nowhere. Most of India was a building site in the middle of nowhere, and most of the building sites had no signs of progress, or anyone working on them. It was like the entire economy simply collapsed at some point, decay set in, and started eating everything alive. The building site showed as a main road on our maps, but was nothing more than sand and mud, like many of the roads there, and far too much of the roadside food.

Eventually, we checked the address and got a lock on where we were meant to be—fifteen miles away, so how that big of an error had happened was anyone's guess, Marcin's navigation was usually excellent. That all added up to a hell of a long ride through the bottlenecked torture of Delhi, but finally, through more luck than judgement, we managed to find the place where my friend was staying. We texted him and then settled down for something to eat in a Chinese place that looked clean while we waited.

The food somehow magically doubled in price, and people kept coming in to introduce themselves and say how much they liked our bikes. While we appreciated the enthusiasm, it got a little annoying that it kept happening while we were having lunch, and we had even struggled to find a quiet little corner to eat and try to laugh off the stress of the day.

During the ride one guy rode up to us on a tiny scooter, looked straight at us with a deadpan expression, and simply said, "Awesome!" before he rode off. At least that made us smile.

So by the time we finished my friend, Anuj, had turned up. He was in a hurry to get somewhere, but Marcin was busy arguing over the bill, the fact that food had turned up he never ordered, and conversely, that the food he had ordered was nowhere to be seen. In the end, we had to go, so we resolved the matter using logic and tact, which just frustrated them more. It was clear they were trying to simply rip us off, so we simply paid the price of what we'd actually ordered as it was printed on the menu, and then we left them to sort out their stupidity between them.

We dropped our bikes back at the flat, jumped into my friend's car, and dashed off, still wondering just exactly what the hell was going on. Anuj was Indian himself and, therefore, genetically incapable of operating a vehicle safely, or anything like it. He was talking on the phone and got caught by a traffic police officer, which seemed very oddly out of place, as he was among the safest drivers on the road at that time. In fact, he could have been on the phone, watching a DVD, eating a live chicken, taking a dump, writing a diary entry, and being punched in the face and still would have been one of the safest drivers on the road at that time.

He went very sulky after that, like a naughty child that had been scolded. He respected authority absolutely, which we also found quite odd as he hadn't struck me as that sort of person at all back in London.

We chatted and caught up about things back home during the drive, and it was very strange to be talking about things so mundane during something like this trip, where we've broken down so many of our own barriers and done so much that was new to us, like exploring new cultures and shitting in a bush. It was great to see him, but it felt very surreal to be discussing my old life in the middle of my new one. On the way back to his flat, we got a box of beers, and a few cold ones for the ride.

When we arrived, my friend was horrified to discover we had no clothes to change into for a night on the town. We tried to explain we weren't really into nightclubs—a bar would be ideal, but he had a plan which required nicer clothes than we'd packed. The plan led us to a club that was pretty awful. Beer was the price of solid gold, and nobody seemed to want to talk to us—fairly typical of India so far. There was none of the warmth and sociability of other countries, in fact, *all* other countries.

We did strike up a conversation with one group, who wanted to know where we'd come from. We explained our trip, and they began an insane rant about how appalling Pakistan and its people were. We politely declined to discuss things with them further and suggested they seek medical help for their psychotic delusions.

32

The End of My Rope

Date—November 17th
Location—Delhi, India
Mood—Hung over (again)

We woke up in Delhi with slight hangovers and a long, arduous ride ahead of us, knowing it would be longer and more arduous than we could possibly imagine it would be.

My friend asked us to stay another few days for a bachelor party, and honestly it was tempting, but the road was beckoning, and we were both keen to get the hell out of India sooner rather than later. Marcin and I were not liking our time there, and that was putting it mildly.

I considered the fact that the reality was not meeting my expectations and thought about what a shame that was. I went on that trip expecting India to be a highlight, but it had proved to be the opposite, so far. I had even toyed with the idea of staying on a few extra weeks to explore on my own, leaving Marcin to continue his mad quest alone. That had been a lifetime ago when we weren't enjoying riding together as much as we now were, and before I'd seen just how bad India actually was. Now I was even keener than Marcin to make progress forwards.

The people were rude and frequently offensive towards us, insulting us openly and then laughing, with us left wondering what exactly it was that they were laughing at in the first place. The country was horribly disorganised—a total mess—and the driving was shocking. We were constantly sick from the food, as hygiene appeared to be non-existent. We had been told in all seriousness that after crapping they wiped their arse with one hand and cooked with the other. Consequently, life expectancies were short, and the food was more dangerous than the roads.

We were told that it was part of their culture to be rude to people, they thought they were better than everyone else, and such ideas were even rolled into their religion. Anuj explained to us that you can't be polite to Indians; they believe that manners are a weakness and rudeness is a show of strength. I routinely treat every individual I meet as an equal and found the advice somewhat jarring. I had occasionally lost my temper in India, and suddenly, the rudeness and problems had gone away, so there might well have been something to that advice. Still, it didn't leave me feeling very comfortable.

To put it frankly, they struck us as stupid. They were so painfully stupid as to have utterly destroyed their own country. Those people were not the ones I had known from London—I had Indian friends and many of them were engaging, interesting, and seemed perfectly normal. The people here were completely different. If it was just stupidity, it would almost be acceptable, but it was also their attitude that left us wanting to move it along. They were rude—offensively rude, and constantly so. England is an unusually polite country, and we don't accept bad manners readily, but it felt like more than just a clash of cultures to me.

I had put this question to my Indian friend in England, asking him why they behaved this way. He too had told me it was their culture—they were better than everyone else and were proud to be Indian. He wasn't able to tell me exactly what it was they had to be proud of. He also didn't have an answer when I asked him if he realised that if they were rude to everyone, then people wouldn't like them. He just shrugged and said that they didn't care.

They certainly didn't appear to care about anything to us.

After we left, we made barely 200 miles all day due to the horrific conditions on the road, and we only stopped for water and fuel. We didn't even want to chance the food. We rode solidly for nearly eight hours. Along the way, we had seen every possible act demonstrating a near total lack of intelligence and basic tenets of civilisation.

I can't even begin to describe the immensity of the scope of the idiocy we witnessed on the roads of that country. When we crossed the border, we met with four other European bikers. We had stopped to have lunch together and had been shouted at by people outside as we checked the menu in a café. We were all taken back—after our experiences in Iran and Pakistan where, for all its failings, people are generally pretty decent; while in Iran you have to work hard to find someone who isn't extremely nice to you.

We had all been left a bit surprised by the appalling displays of behaviour all around us, but honestly, it got no better. People seemed totally self-absorbed, locked away behind their immediate wants. We were instantly made to feel that we weren't welcome there at all. We were objects of fun, people mimicked the sounds of our bikes and laughed, they rarely wanted to say hello or to meet us, although it was nice when they did (so long as we were not having lunch). The culture just didn't really explain or excuse it. It didn't excuse the constant rip-offs either or the low standards, or the children begging by the side of the roads in conditions you shouldn't leave an animal.

And in terms of animals, the way they were treated, again, displayed a lack of human empathy. Carts were everywhere, and the animals pulling them were beaten mercilessly. Corpses were left rotting in the roads, and livestock tended to be nothing more than malnourished sacks of bones.

That was by far the worst place we'd visited. The driving was the worst I'd ever seen, and Marcin, who has travelled extensively around Africa and South America, said the same. I asked him how it compared to what he'd seen before. He cut right through bullshit like a laser cannon and replied, "Africa was nice. This is sickness."

I left England and embarked on the trip with no prejudices and with an open mind, ready to learn new things about new cultures, and hopefully expand my horizons. Sadly, I'm going home with a whole set of new prejudices and wide open eyes. On the other hand, England is too polite, bowing down to people's feelings and being way too careful not to offend anyone, but people need to be offended. People need to hear honest opinions and decide if there's something about themselves that they could do better. Offence is a driving force for positive change, questioning ourselves is important.

Some years later I was working in an Asian school. In that particular country there were few manners, ugly people were called ugly, and racism was the norm. I was teaching a middle-school grade and trying to explain to them what it meant to be a vegetarian. One of my, admittedly less gifted, students asked me with a quizzical expression, "If you don't eat any meat then why are you so fat?"

I had been sick, I'd suffered a horrible bout of flu and hadn't been able to exercise, and I had put on a bit of weight. Should I have been offended by her opinion? I laughed and realised it was time to watch my diet a little more and hit the gym a bit harder. That's the mature thing to do, not to wave your hands in the air and scream about your delicate feelings.

But it remained that I could see no real culture there in India. It was just endless mess, buildings crumbling, streets in tatters, people dishevelled and drugged out of their minds at the side of the road, or in one case that day, lying in the road with his legs out while cars were driving straight at him. The place was a sad shadow of the India I had expected to find. It felt like a grim joke. It was like civilisation just pulled out and the country lost its foundation, collapsing to the state of a typical third world country, only with delusions of grandeur.

The most jarring thing about the place was the attitude towards Pakistan. The subject came up a lot, and we'd often been told that they were crazy, dumb, or evil. Invariably, the people telling you that had never been, of course. Now I'm not defending the place—Pakistan needs a lot of help. It's a crumbling mess itself, and with a government bent on keeping the people under control, but the people are far nicer to deal with—they're welcoming hosts, and the educated ones are quite respectful. Certainly, we'd not been ripped off very often.

Conditions were worse there in a lot of ways, but India has no right to look down on them. Indians are essentially the same people, only with an attitude of superiority and a culture of uneducated rudeness.

Anuj had made a comment about how ridiculous it was that Muslims won't eat pigs and mocked Pakistan because of it. I asked how that reflected on him, since he wouldn't eat cows because of them being regarded a "sacred animal," despite seeing them dragged along by their nose and routinely beaten with sticks. He just said that was different, because cows really were sacred and pigs really weren't. I asked him if he could explain his religion and tell me how it actually worked. He thought about it briefly and then just said, "I don't know. I just do what my dad did."

As we made our way further along the road, we saw an increasingly horrendous mixture of the stupidest driving it's possible to imagine. Several times we were literally run off the road, driven off the edge into a verge. We would be occupying our own lane, and a truck or a bus would come directly at us, so we had to ride off the road into the dirt or die. Time after time, the traffic ground to a halt due to there being a junction where they were all fighting to get round, so they all ended up totally stopping and just honking horns at one another, as if that might be some kind of solution. The noise added to the sense of chaos on top of the burning heat and the terrible smell. Even the air had a distinct yellow hue, as if the world was being viewed through a mild sepia lens.

We'd already had too many near misses that day to be comfortable. Marcin had to slam on the brakes when a woman led her kids out in front of him, and we'd had to swerve dozens of times as cars poured around corners on both sides of the roads without looking up. Tractors suddenly come towards you down a motorway in any of the lanes they choose; pedestrians stop and chat on dual carriageways. It was just insane—it was like the entire place had been chemically lobotomised.

We drove past two trucks that had collided. They'd shed their load and come off the road into a ditch. As we passed, the entire cab of one was collapsed—nobody could have survived. In Pakistan we saw the aftermath of a crash and stopped to chat with the police. This time, we just drove by; we had seen so many by then, so much bloodshed that we barely noticed. I was no longer surprised by it, and frankly, I had no sympathy left for any of them.

We plodded on and only managed a scant 200 miles. The miles just wouldn't tick away like they normally did, since we were constantly stuck behind things. The roads were nowhere near able to support the level of traffic using them, and we just had no way to go any faster.

Eventually, the sun began to set, and we started looking for a hotel, having no real choice, since the night was even worse than the daytime. The first one wouldn't accept us for some reason, and the man running it just started screaming and waving his arms around. We decided that it was best to head into town before it got dark.

The GPS took us to a newspaper office, but we got directions and moved along, although by then it had gotten quite dark. Next, we ended up in an alley. A couple of young girls came out from a local house and gave us directions in near-perfect English. Then a man appeared from the same house and offered to lead us to a hotel he knew. They were visiting family in the country and lived predominantly in England. We were very grateful for the help, especially as a large group had started to appear and was literally blocking every available exit in every conceivable direction.

And then it finally happened. We all knew it would. It was unavoidable. The clock had been ticking down to this moment since the beginning.

The KTM broke down.

I was just glad it was him and not me—I would never have lived it down. Marcin would simply never have let me forget it. There would have been insults, mocking, and ceaseless reminders, just as there would be now for Marcin.

It wouldn't start—the relay just clicked, so it was a dead battery, we surmised. That seemed odd, since it had been the one thing that hadn't played up before, but KTMs are creative in their ability to fail on you. I went off to find the hotel in this terrible little town which was nothing more than a shambles of crumbling brick boxes with grandiose titles like "Fashion Centre" and "World of Beauty," when actually all it was was a filthy lock-up selling generic hats and lipsticks. The hotel was actually strikingly good, with a great looking restaurant attached to it.

There are two things I loved about India, and both are double-edged swords. The first is the food. It's awesome, it's delicious, and it caters for vegetarians, so I wasn't having to survive on side-orders of chips any more. Every day I just grabbed some new thing off a menu, and it was always amazing. It gave me the shits, often violently, but the food was a great experience on the way down, if not on the way out. My only regret is that the markets offer things that looked far more impressive, and I wanted to stop and try everything, but the conditions were so poor that I knew it would make me crap my spine out. Several stalls had actually refused to serve us, telling us the food would probably kill us.

The other thing I was loving was the Enfield Bullet. I'm having one at some point, it was as simple as that. They're awesome bikes, and I aimed to own one. I found myself dreaming of an "Enfield adventure" as I rode along. The bike should be equipped with a new and updated set of forks, headlights and clocks. Better rear shocks, and a few other improvements would build to a solid, durable and cheap adventure tourer. Further research did not bear out my optimistic appraisal, and the dream didn't survive long enough to leave India with me.

I had found the hotel and booked us in. Now that I had my bearings, I returned for Marcin with the hope that the KTM had realised her mistake and was now purring like a kitten. As expected, it still wouldn't start, but Marcin had a solution. Sadly for me, the solution was that I tow him through the streets on the end of a rope.

As I tied the rope on, we were, of course, surrounded by a huge crowd of dead-eyed locals staring at us in virtual silence. I had to ask one to move back—I politely asked him to excuse me. He parroted me, trying to mimic my words, and then laughed, braying like he had made some hilarious joke. I stared back, wondering if I'd actually heard that right. My tolerance was at an all-time low, and he clearly caught that vibe and ran off into the depths of the crowd, just moments before I knocked his teeth out for him.

Then things descended into the bizarre situation of my little single-cylinder bike, which Marcin derided daily for being too small, pulling this mammoth pudding of a motorcycle, with a mammoth pudding of a man on it, through the streets of this crazy market street, with everyone trying to overtake us while laughing hysterically like lobotomised baboons. All the while my front wheel was bouncing into the air, and my mind was ready to snap inside my skull.

We made it to the hotel, but my bike was not happy with the extra weight, which was more than double her own weight, being dragged along behind her.

We stripped out the battery, which by then was completely dead flat. Marcin had a charger among the endless supplies of rubbish he was carrying along, but my fear was that the battery was really dead, and we were now going to have to source another one before we moved on. I didn't think that getting a KTM battery there was going to be easy in a country populated by generic 125cc bikes with names that outclassed them by a mile.

We were led to our room and discovered the ultimate horror, and that we might be sinking to an all new low. The room was a double, and even though we'd strictly stipulated that it had two separate beds, it only had one that we would have to share.

I wasn't thrilled about that, since I'd never shared a bed with someone I'd not had sex with, and Marcin was chuckling, perhaps for the same reason. I liked Marcin a lot, but very strictly, as a friend.

No problem, they assured us, and a dozen workers flocked into the room. They told us they'd simply unscrew the two halves of the double bed and make it into a pair of singles for us. It took twelve of them to do it, and we simply stood in horrified silence just watching as they flapped around, shouting, kicking, and screaming at one another, trying to make it happen for over ten minutes.

Eventually, the designated leader came up to us and told us, very apologetically, "Sorry, it isn't that kind of bed."

What *is* easy in India? Dying in a road accident is pretty easy. It was actually harder not to.

33

The Day from Hell, Part One

Date—November 18th
Location—Sitapur, India
Mood—Pissed off

Today we had a bad day, so we made it stretch into two days, so we could enjoy suffering even more and even longer. We punished ourselves mercilessly and took insane chances that should have killed us but luckily didn't. Here's the how and why of what happened.

We woke up in a nice hotel in a crappy little town in the middle of nowhere. Well, India, but I'd stopped thinking of that as somewhere by then and just resigned myself to the fact that I'd feel better once we'd escaped it.

Breakfast was a lacklustre serving of spicy soup, with some kind of bread with potato in it. It didn't matter what it was—the fact was that whatever we ate was going to explode out of my arse almost as soon as I ate it, another thing I had also become resigned to.

And that is precisely what happened, even before I'd finished eating. After several mad dashes to the toilet, I gave up on food, or maybe it had given up on me. We didn't drink the coffee either, as it was made from local water and was definitely contributing to the problems, maybe even causing them, for all I knew. All I knew for sure was that the pain in my gut wasn't going away until we got away from India and into a country that had discovered soap.

So we left the restaurant more hungry than when we went in, and by then, I was feeling weak, my stomach was hurting constantly, and no food was sticking in my system long enough to be digested. We packed up ready to go and dragged our crap downstairs. Marcin's battery had taken half a charge only, so I suggested strongly that we should go out to town and look for a new battery that would fit the hole. He insisted it would be fine.

Guess what happened?

I have joked before about my lack of preparation, but really I prepared my bike pretty carefully. I bought a bike that had an engine with decades of proven history, and a reputation for reliability; a fuel-efficient, lightweight machine. I had modified it to improve suspension, I'd minimised the weight, I'd maximised range and power, and added protection to make sure she could handle even the roughest terrain—even survive an accident or two, if it came to that.

Then I rode with someone who had bought a KTM.

So after the half-charged battery was put back, there only remained the important mission of leaving the hotel, which became a circus in itself. In typical Indian fashion, everything was a total shambles of absolute chaos with a spicy dash of added danger and a twist of total insanity.

We had parked in an alley that led to a larger car park at the rear. It took the bikes off the road and meant they were locked away and guarded by security. Someone had parked a car there, and we asked if they could move it. Well they did, but it took eight of them to do it, all shouting at one another and doing everything in the stupidest way imaginable, while we could only watch, wondering what exactly was going on, or even what on Earth they thought was going on. I'd be overstating how complicated moving a car is if I said that all you had to do was find the keys, start the engine, and roll it back in a straight line for four metres, but they managed to turn this into an epic disaster that seemed to take all morning.

We took the bikes out to load our gear and got an audience, our worst one yet. People blocked the entire road, laughing, taking pictures, and making clearly derisory comments to one another about us. Such seemed to be the attitude there, and we had just stopped taking any interest.

Eventually, the security guard grabbed a broom handle and started hitting people with it to make them leave—it worked on some of them, enough to make a gap we could ride through so we were finally able to escape. We were troubled by the fact that a grown man was beating young children with a stick, but we knew we had to make a dash for it—the whole situation was threatening to turn into a riot right in front of us.

Riding through town was not fun, but we'd come to accept that we'd left fun a long way down the road behind us. Tight little lanes with idiots spilling out in every direction were the order of the day. The road surface was smashed to pieces; concrete, rocks, mud, and people ran into the roads shouting at us. The constant laughing as complete morons pass you on their tiny 125cc bikes, usually three-up as they revved the nuts off them to overtake the bigger bikes, is really pathetic and was grating on our nerves.

It was stressful being there, and every second was more of the same grinding punishment. India has a massive inferiority complex, which is fair, because it really is quite inferior when compared to just about every other place on Earth, but it had to desperately over-compensate with constant irritating dick-swinging behaviour that was increasingly dangerous and wildly stupid.

We finally got out of the clutches of the nasty little town into the country lanes and stopped off to fill up with petrol. Once we had done that, the problems started once more with the KTM. The problems may have started, but the KTM certainly wouldn't.

The battery was dead again, as predicted. Marcin got a piece of wire and connected them to two points on the engine for some reason. We tried jumping it from my bike, but nothing happened, so we asked the owner of a tractor to come and give us a jump. He came over and deliberately came within an inch of crashing into Marcin's bike at full speed and then just sat there glaring at us with a sort of angry grin.

By then, of course, the audience had gathered—stupid people making stupid noises and touching everything while we were trying to work; pushing to be within a few centimetres of us, tripping over themselves to see something as mundane as two people trying to fix a motorcycle. We were spending as much time keeping them out of our gear as we were working on the bike.

In the end Marcin thought it would be best to try a better cable. We asked for some and got a roll of proper copper wire, which they tried to charge him more than the bike was worth in exchange for. We made a better set of cables, but it still wouldn't work. After I complained, he swapped the connection to the battery terminals, which he should have done in the beginning, but being that he's a professional electrician, I stupidly thought he knew what he was doing. I don't know why I ever thought that!

Suddenly it worked, against all the odds. We left the jump wires connected, so I could jump-start him conveniently from my own bike from then on, and we headed out. Of course, they wanted to charge even more for the wire by then, around seven times what we'd paid for our hotel room, but we refused, and the price slowly came down to something Marcin was willing to pay. This was a very stark contrast to the generosity we'd encountered before in other countries—in fact every other country.

We didn't get far. The bike kept cutting out badly. We only made it a few metres at a time, and every time we stopped we got crowds of people grabbing at everything we owned. Eventually, we had to accept that this problem wasn't going to go away and we'd have to do something about it. We stopped in a field that gave us some shelter from the road, provided by bushes and trees. We were hoping that people would just leave us alone so we could try to fix this bike and get it moving reliably. We were already talking about finding a truck to load it onto by then. We knew it was not going to be an easy fix, and the situation we had to fix it in couldn't have been much worse.

Marcin thought it could be a blockage in the fuel system, so he wanted to take it all off and check. Nothing is an easy job on a KTM, and we spent four hours finding nothing obviously wrong with anything, still fighting back crowds of total morons as they flooded in through the bushes. The man who owned the field kept fighting them off with us, but they still gathered to stare with their dead yellow eyes while laughing, or making more cackling and noises clearly meant to be insulting, while trying to steal tools as we put them down.

In the end, nothing we did made any real difference, but the bike seemed to work a bit better after tinkering with it, probably only because it had cooled down. The battery was working for some unknown reason, but it still cut out fairly often. We figured it only cut out when hot, and if we gave it five minutes, it usually ran OK again for a short while afterwards. We hoped we could make some progress like that while we figured out a better solution and found a place where we could work on it and get some proper advice from an expert. Even more annoyingly, this problem was a new one and couldn't be related to the breaking down of the previous evening.

We pressed on. There was a town, Lucknow, only sixty miles away, and we thought we could make it—even like that, if fortune favoured us. The sun was low, it was well into the afternoon, and we had barely travelled eleven miles. We pressed on and did make up some time, but darkness was chasing us, and things could only get worse.

Again, the roads were insanely chaotic, with absolute disregard for personal safety explored on every corner and every stretch of the pitifully inadequate roads. We were barely making twenty mph at most points—we couldn't overtake, because the traffic was solid in all directions.

We made it to yet another small town about fifteen miles outside of our goal as night fell and the country was shrouded in darkness. Most drivers didn't even bother to put their lights on. Those that did used full-beams, so there was a constant glare through the dust that blinded us, and half the other vehicles became invisible through the haze until we found them driving straight at us. It was nothing less than a horrendous death trap.

So far, we'd already seen several accidents that day, including a tuk-tuk rolled over in the road, crushed lorries, and various twisted lumps of metal that used to be poorly ridden motorcycles, and we were in no particular rush to join them.

Marcin had decided to find a ring road around the town, so I stopped him to ask what he was doing, since he had the lead and his choice didn't make any immediate sense. He wanted to ride on into the night—his bike ran better at night, as it was cooler. I wanted to go into town, stop, and try to fix it before carrying on. So we argued, and came as close as we'd ever come to falling out. He insisted on riding through the night, but I knew he'd never make it. I tried to compromise with him, but he refused to budge. In the end, I took back my papers he was carrying, and we finally, angrily, agreed to go our separate ways.

Then, as we angrily shouted at one another, something was said—I don't remember what, but we had suddenly reached a compromise. The truth was, I guess, that we wanted to ride on together, and I wanted to get out of the country just as much as he did. We had agreed that we were going to leave the first thing in the morning when the traffic was lighter, the only way I could think of to make some kind of safe progress. Marcin was happy to do that, but wanted to leave even earlier than me (of course). In the end, we agreed and carried on into Lucknow.

We made it into town, but Lucknow wasn't just another little town, it was a massive place, and we struggled to find a hotel with a car park or anywhere to safely store the bikes. We couldn't leave them on the street—they would have been wrecked or gone by the morning, most likely stolen by one of the many sticky fingers that were constantly clawing at them every time we pulled over. We got into town, and after trying for an hour to find somewhere, we stopped at a petrol station amidst the usually chaotic driving, by then at night and in total darkness.

We both had the same new suggestion, but I spoke the words first. I wanted to get something to eat and head out of town towards the border and camp on the road—we were both desperate to escape. So a plan was formed between us, and we headed out into the night once more. We saw our first motorcycle accident first-hand that we weren't involved in, but Marcin missed it—a car hit a bike, the bike went flying, but the rider managed to catch his footing and stay standing up somehow. I don't know whose fault it was, but I'd suggest it was both of them to some degree, and by then I hardly cared one way or another. It was hard enough just making sure it didn't happen to us.

We ate at Pizza Hut, hoping against hope that the hygiene would be better. It must have been, as we had no problems with our stomachs later on through the night. The people working there were actually pretty decent—they came out to chat with us and were a little sharper than most of the people we'd met before. They still asked the usual questions, but we got some new ones too. They asked if the bikes were foreign or if they were made in India. That was my favourite question!

In was a huge relief to speak with people who were just a little more switched on. We ate outside with our bikes, and several of the staff came out to join us, sitting on the floor and just chatting away about life in India. That actually lifted our spirits somewhat, and by the time we left, we left with smiles.

We headed out onto the main road to the border. It was hardly a main road as we know them, just a single lane, and progress was slow. After forty miles, a fog bank rolled in, and our vision was almost completely lost. I couldn't close my visor any longer—people had been playing with it every time we stopped, and it was so greasy I couldn't see through it. Of course, there was no soap in any toilets that I could use to clean it.

We didn't want to stop—we wanted to get as far away as possible and as quickly as we could. I was even considering riding through the night, just to get out of the situation. The fog changed everything—it was wet and thick, and I had to stop every few minutes to clean the fog from my glasses. Finally, we made another fifty miles before we had to make camp. The border was only 150 miles ahead of us, so close we could feel it. We fantasised about breakfast in Nepal, and desperately hoped that the border would cut the two countries apart; that life would be different on the other side, like it had been in Pakistan before.

We got our torches and explored the verge of the road. There were places where we felt we could safely camp, but we found a concrete bunker that was clean and flat, so we parked on it and pitched one of our tents. Marcin's didn't need ropes or pegs, so it was the ideal choice. Someone walked past a few metres from us and didn't see us, so we were happy to camp there for a few hours of desperately needed sleep. We planned on getting up at around 3AM and riding when the roads would be at their most quiet. With a little luck, we could be at the border before the roads were occupied.

We certainly had no problems sleeping.

34

The Day From Hell, Part 2

Date—November 19th
Location—Bast, Uttar Pradesh, India
Mood—Exhausted

We slept for four hours and got up at 3AM as planned. There was a strange smell—stranger than usual. India has an aroma all of its very own, which can be so strong as to make you pray for the sweet release of death in order to escape it. While Marcin packed up, I took my torch and climbed down the verge to explore. The area was littered with bones and torn up carcasses of large animals. They hadn't been slaughtered—they'd been ripped to shreds by something large and hungry. Remembering that India had tigers, I climbed back up and told Marcin that packing up faster might be better for everyone.

The fog was still heavy, and there was still traffic, but it was much lighter than before. Although we both knew that driving through it was a stupid thing to do, we felt that we had no choice. Conditions were really so bad that we felt that riding exhausted through heavy fog was the safer option all round.

We headed out into the dark, hazy grimness that stretched out before us. Visibility was poor, down to about ten metres, and the roads were still dangerous, even allowing for the horrors of the weather and the wet road surface that it had left behind. We found trucks loitering on both lanes, either running slow or stopped with no lights. Cars were still overtaking flat out, and there were even people driving straight at us, but the traffic was lighter, and we felt it was markedly safer than driving during the day.

We made poor progress, but still better than if the roads were clogged with a solid mass of drivers that couldn't actually drive. At one point we passed three motorcycles. Minutes later, they passed us, shouting and laughing, until they exited off a slip road. Twice I had to slam on the brakes as we encountered trucks that were just abandoned in the middle of the road. I had to do an emergency stop to avoid hitting two guys literally squatting in the middle of the road taking a crap. They ran off, leaving a trail of excrement flying out of them as they trotted off into the mist, but at least they avoided getting the arses wiped by a fast-moving TKC80 enduro tyre.

Put simply, that was an idiotic thing to do, but to understand why we did it you would have to drive on these roads yourself. It's an act of pure desperation to ride into the night in fog, and when that is preferable, it really speaks volumes about what the conditions were like.

As I was riding I was wondering how they lived like that every day. How did they deal with that being their world? How can they happily jump into their vehicles and just head off, knowing how awful their roads were, how disgusting the conditions were all around them. They faced a real danger of being killed every time they stepped out of their homes, but that just didn't seem to register with them at all. They seemed blind to the children in such poverty, they seemed utterly ignorant of how their behaviour made them appear to us. They laughed at us, as if our being in their country was some ridiculous joke. From the back of my motorcycle it seemed they were right about that part, at least.

Suddenly, grey light began piercing the darkness, although the fog was still heavy. Marcin pulled to the side, and we had some food—biscuits and nuts, energy food, since we were both pushing through exhaustion and needed any help we could get.

We headed along the road for a while, then Marcin stopped again. We pulled off the road, and he slept under a tree for ten minutes. The drain was hitting us both hard, but I managed to stay awake somehow. Within half an hour the sun started to make some headway into the sky and the temperature rose. We watched as dawn opened all around us, and the fog began to melt away into a mist, and then finally, was gone altogether.

I had to stop next. I was literally falling asleep on the bike and found myself waking up while still riding along. A quick shot of water and a stretch and we carried on—neither of us wanted to waste that quiet time that we had earned ourselves. Traffic was still light, and we made a good pace on our way to the border. Eventually, we hit a town. and that all changed—the usual story of nightmare traffic was told all around us once more.

The GPS took us on a very roundabout route that dragged us, kicking and screaming, through the city slums of broken-down houses and people living rough on the sides of the streets. We saw people running out to crap at the side of the road, men and women, adults and children, hovels made from rags with families surviving in them. The only problem, I thought to myself, was that this might not be a slum at all. For all we knew, and in all likelihood, this was just a normal neighbourhood. We saw no nice buildings, no houses other than these crumbling shacks.

So we finally made it out, and the temperamental KTM behaved itself fine—it overheated and cut out a few times, but it always started again straight after with no trouble. I was still wearing a fleece under my jacket and was getting hot, but I didn't want to stop and lose precious minutes out of fear of attracting the same kind of audience as before—a crowd of foul-smelling mindless things pushing so close to you that you can't physically move, while they claw at your belongings to see what they could steal. We battled on, and by then the traffic was normal in the usually Indian abnormal way, but with only fifty miles to go to the border, we carried on with steadfast resolve. We made it out of town, and I saw my second motorcycle accident in India.

This time, Marcin was in it.

A young man, a typical Indian moron with something to prove, rode up to us, giggling and making comments, and then tried to show off by buzzing past Marcin flat-out. Perhaps he was trying to impress us with the awesome power of his 125cc bike and his sub-par ability to judge simple situations. He misjudged it badly and went straight into Marcin's metal side box.

Marcin wobbled, but held his balance and stayed upright, against all the odds, although he swerved badly, lurching violently into the other lane. The Indian wobbled from peg to peg and then lost control and planted it in the dirt, crashing roughly with the usual sickening noise of metal being dragged across the road. Luckily for all of us, there was nothing coming from the other direction, or it would have been a far uglier story—Marcin would have been killed, without question. They both ended up on the opposite verge. Marcin seemed fine but still had no idea what had happened—the others were picking themselves up, the rider and the pillion, who was clearly injured.

Marcin said he was okay and asked if he had hit something. I told him what had happened and then went to shout at them, and perhaps if they weren't hurt correct that issue. The rider was sheepishly apologising, his head bowed over and his hands up, begging for me not to hurt him. Anger had washed away all fatigue, and I was ready to release all my pent up frustration that this country had caused in us both.

Seeing this pathetic creature grovelling just made me realise how sad these people really were, and I calmed down and managed to swallow my temper. The passenger was clearly damaged and was howling in pain. They couldn't lift their bike up. I did it with one arm and calmed the passenger down. He had probably broken a few fingers in the landing. It certainly looked like it, since they were now bent in exciting new angles, a painful injury indeed.

There was no damage to the mighty KTM, apart from a black rubber scratch, so I had to assume his bars caught the box as he deliberately cut it too close. Honestly, I was shocked that something like that hadn't happened before, and we considered ourselves lucky.

A hugely fat man stopped to ask what had happened. I told him, and he laughed and told us to just leave them. I turned back to the broken men and told them in agreement that this was their fault and I had no sympathy. We set back off and left them to pick up the pieces.

Finally, we made the border, which was nothing of any consequence. It was a tiny town, and the border control was hidden inside some shops, somewhere amidst the sprawling chaos of a dishevelled high-street. I was leading and rode straight through into Nepal without realising it and had to go back and find Marcin and to get my visa properly stamped.

At last, we had reached our goal and were facing the last obstacle to getting out of this country. But now we had the worst kind of people to deal with—bureaucrats.

At first, we had to get our passports dealt with. We had more forms to fill in to do this, for some reason, but the people were basically friendly, so we were basically friendly back. In fact, it was nice to meet some Indian people who were cordial and decent and didn't expect money to change hands. We made the most of it and chatted with them a while. Several other tourists walked straight past the offices, and Indian officials were chasing after them to come back too, so my initial mistake seemed easy to understand and wasn't just a result of my lack of sleep or horrendous stupidity. After filling in the forms and getting our exit stamps, we then had to fill in more details in their books. We did it as quickly as we could and left the same way.

We then had to head over to another office and have our carnets processed. In that office were typically Indian people, as we'd come to see them—rude, condescending, and utterly dense. The first one just pointed and grunted to the other end of the building—we went there and were told to take a seat. Great. He seemed polite, but then he took the paperwork and just walked off. We asked him what was happening and how long it would take, and he just waved a hand at us and told us to sit and wait.

The other officials were glaring at us, and the audience started, people just staring straight at us, wandering in to just stand staring for no apparent reason. I waved at them sarcastically, and they all looked behind them in unison. Then the officials found a large book for us to fill in our details, having to blow dust from the cover. I asked what it was for; they said it was a formality, and everyone had to do it. I asked a bit more pointedly why I had to do it—I told them to explain why they wanted my details.

They sat in silence, angrily glaring at me. That's what I thought—they had no idea what they were doing. I then pointed out that the last entry was over a week before. I asked why nobody else had crossed the border in that time, when the border was teeming with people. Again, nothing but arrogant silence. I lost my temper and told them I was going to fill it in—I wrote down some utter nonsense, and told them what I was doing, daring them to stop me. They sat in silence, just watching.

We got our carnets back and left in silence. I can't thank people for this level of rudeness and incompetence, so I didn't. Instead, I told them how disgusting their behaviour was and asked what they imagined I must be thinking of them. They seemed quite embarrassed and were certainly flustered as they looked away, hanging their heads in apparent shame.

We got on our bikes, changed the Indian money for Nepal rupees, and we left. Crossing the border was a joy—even though it was just a few metres, it was the best few metre ride I've ever ridden.

We parked up in the Nepalese visa office and applied for our entry visas. It only cost twenty-eight dollars. It would have been twenty-five if we'd had US cash, but we paid in their own currency. The people were different straight away.

Everything was different.

There was a heavy mood in the visa office, and the man being served ahead of us queried what kind of visa he wanted, since he wasn't sure on the duration of his stay. The man serving him just laughed loudly, but it was a friendly well-meaning laugh. He put his hand on the man's shoulder and said simply, "This isn't India any more. Don't worry." We all looked at one another, and the whole office full of strangers just started laughing. These people were just trying to help, and we all felt the weight lifting.

The official who was working on our passports made jokes with us, and even though we were shattered by then, it was such a relief to be dealing with decent people once again. The Nepal side was dealt with quickly and easily, and we were on our way, formally welcomed to their country by people who really sounded like they meant it.

At that point, it was still a little worrying—the town didn't look massively different, but we headed out for something to eat, and the whole thing suddenly changed, and quite radically too. The driving was still bad, but not in the same league as before—there was less of it too, not so much traffic on the road and none of the blistering arrogance. Buildings were nice, we saw proper structures, and there was far less dirt and chaos.

We stopped at a place and ordered some food, choosing that over the alternative option of collapsing from exhaustion. The staff came to chat with us in a friendly way, and a lot of the mood lightened still more. Nobody was playing with our bikes—people were interested, but there was none of the frantic touching, fingering, and pushing that there had been in India. People were more laid back, friendly, and a bit reserved.

I'm not saying Nepal seemed perfect—it was far from it, but it was such a relief after where we'd been that we felt better immediately. In India things looked yellow; even the water and air has a dirty yellow haze to it. It was like viewing the world through a cataract. In Nepal the air was clean and fresh, the sky was blue again, and the roadsides were green with rolling hills, mountains, and rivers. Nepal was not a choked toilet with massive congestions and a failed economy, it was just a place where people lived, and a beautiful place at that, from what little we'd seen so far.

I finally had time to collect my thoughts. India had been a truly horrible experience to someone who really wants to believe the best of people.

When we broke down, we had to hide the bike away to work on it, to stop them shoving in to have a look and grab at everything. If that had happened in Iran we would have been offered endless help; in Pakistan someone would have come to try and lend a hand. Indeed, when the Velorex broke down, the local police chief came out in his own car to try to offer assistance, asking only "What can I do to help?" The Pakistani people were failed by their government, and the most impoverished were so poorly educated that they were hopeless, with no impression that a larger world even exists. We're too different for them to relate to, and it made problems for us.

In India people don't want to relate. We were never made to feel welcome anywhere we went—even hotel staff were abrupt and difficult. When we did get a good one, we tipped and never got left alone again, so we even learned that it was dangerous to even do that!

Nepal seemed to have more than a few idiots, but you don't judge a country by the actions of a few, but by the actions of the general population. In India the general population is not likeable. They have a massive inferiority complex, and they over-compensate with a rudeness and arrogance that often gets them into trouble. Like Pakistan, their government has completely failed them. The country is a total shambles, massively over-populated, filthy to the point of being dangerous, and the economy has been used against the people like a weapon, turning it into a giant factory, much like China, producing second-rate items for export. It's all a total mess, but the people were so appallingly unpleasant you just stopped caring, and we quickly decided that they were welcome to their lot. I was genuinely excited to go to India—I had met and worked with so many Indian people that I believed they were an example of what to expect from the population, but they really were not.

In Pakistan I had sympathy for the people living in appalling conditions, but not in India. That is one of the principal problems with England at the moment. It's trying so hard to make multiculturalism work, and of course, it can't. Countries need their own identity—they're not airports, places where different cultures need to be catered to—they're meant to be different, unique, and interesting. Certainly, Pakistan and India were interesting, and I certainly didn't regret my visit. The impression they left me with, though, was not entirely, or even largely, positive. I felt that I had seen the bottom. I had seen how far humans can sink, and it had made me wonder how far they had to sink before we stopped thinking of them as human at all.

I had been asked many times what I thought of the country, but they didn't want to hear that you didn't like it, all they wanted is cheap compliments. They didn't really want to know what you really thought at all. It's childish in the extreme to be offended by people's opinions, but that's what England teaches now. A child hearing something it doesn't like will have a tantrum. A mature adult should compare it to what they know and take appropriate action. If someone is overweight, as I have been, that's their problem, and they should be doing something about it, instead of pretending that it's excusable and nobody else should draw attention to it. If a country is a mess and the population is unpleasant, then it needs to know that so it can decide if it's happy being unpleasant or if it's time to deal with the issue. I can only leave that up to the Indian people to decide for themselves, if they are willing to address their own many horrible social problems.

India is an incredibly awful place, with absolutely terribly behaved people. Now, I wish it wasn't, but if the rest of the world doesn't say it, then why would India ever need to change? India should be ashamed of itself. Pakistan is already ashamed of itself and wants to change—we were told that many times.

In India my feelings were that the problems are too deeply rooted in the people themselves—they want the world to blindly ignore the shortcomings of their country and just quietly pretend that their ethnic heritage means something of great value.

Mine, of course, means nothing to me. I'm just me. I'm not proud of being white or English. These are accidents of birth, not things I've achieved, and I have no right to be proud of them. No sane and intelligent person should be. I wonder how failed the lives of people are that need to be proud of wherever they came from; how little they have managed to do with their lives, that they're nothing more than where they were born or the colour of their skin.

India desperately needs to wake up to itself. It's a third world country deluding itself that it's something special. It needs a massive drop in population and a good wash. The people need proper education, and hygiene needs to radically improve. Children need to stop begging on the streets for money, which apparently they then spend on super-glue to get high on. People need to learn to drive or ride properly, and the road needs to be regulated (and I guess built properly first). Behaviour needs to be brought up to standard—it's not okay for men and women to shit on the pavement in a modern world. I'm pretty sure it's not the rest of us that are out of step on that one. Rubbish was piled everywhere, animals lay dead on the sides of the road, flies swarmed onto everything. When I put my helmet on, the visor was smeared with thick yellow grease after someone had handled it. In India we stopped shaking hands fairly early on.

It wasn't even intelligence that was causing the damage. India and Pakistan were level, pegging at only an average IQ of 81; Nepal was even lower at 78, yet it was a different world, clean and friendly and welcoming. You have to expect some issues, but you know that, and you tolerate it. IQ is a useful way to measure some aspects of a person's intelligence, but it isn't the only thing that matters. We can easily excuse someone who isn't as smart as other people, but it's much harder to excuse a less gifted person who tells you he's much smarter than you, shits on the floor, and then kills someone in a head-on collision.

As we travelled on it was like the rest of the trip, only with added exhaustion. The few towns we passed through were cleaner and tidier, but the long day got the better of us fairly quickly, and we stopped in a small town around two hours ride from Katmandu. The town was fairly frantic, but we found a place with the criteria we were looking for—two separate beds, Internet, somewhere to park, and a supply of beer to help us round off the day.

The guest house was cheap—the money there was worth approximately two thirds of what it was in India but bought you far more than the face value. The food we were offered was a mixture of curry and Chinese food, it appeared to us, but everything we ate was very nice. We experienced no stomach problems, either, as an added bonus. The guest house was actually very pleasant. The room was good, and it had a bar, so we went down to play on the Internet and have a few quiet drinks.

We walked about the town, and within ten minutes, were offered drugs and girls, which is unpleasant, but a fact of life in the third world. It took us a few minutes to get rid of the tout who singled us out. He seemed to want to hang out with the foreigners and see the bikes. I wasn't going to tell him where we were staying or show him where they were. Whatever he was smoking was working—he could hardly speak and was clearly a danger to himself as he staggered around, stepping in and out of the road.

So we went back to the bar and chatted with the owner. He had a drink with us, and he introduced us to the rest of the staff. They were all really nice people, and we had a great night chatting and sorting out our ride for the next day, which would be us heading up to the city, and then sorting paperwork for our flight to Thailand. It should have been a very easy ride, although I had some minor trepidations.

It was nice to be back with smiles on our faces.

35

The Last Leg Up

Date—November 20st
Location—Bharatpur, Nepal
Mood—Relieved

Today, all we had to do was ride a hundred miles. That's nothing after what we'd done so far, but of course, nothing is ever that .straightforward, and if it was, what would be the point, I guess.

We woke up in the guest house in the middle of the little town, actually feeling that we'd had a good night's sleep for the first time in a long time. Marcin woke up before me and was playing on the computer, doing whatever it was that Marcin did on a computer. I always felt it was better not to know.

I slept until I couldn't sleep any more, which still felt too early. I woke up to a fairly grim, dark day, but luckily, it was the insect screens making it seem gloomy outside and not the weather that made it dark. Spirits were consequently raised considerably. Once the screens were back the day looked perfect, and that brought a smile to my face.

We were heading for Kathmandu, and I wasn't really looking forward to it. I don't like heights. In fact, I like heights less than I like pretty much anything else, and I was anxious about what might be ahead. We had very little choice in the matter though; there was only one road all the way into the city, so we had to follow it while it snaked upwards around a kilometre and a half from where we were currently situated. I had previously ridden the Pyrenees, and that had taunted me with many sheer drops and terrible roads. At first, it had been a horribly nerve-jarring experience, but it quickly subsided and I got over it.

I expected more of the same; that after a while I'd get accustomed to the conditions and my fears would subside. Even though I knew that, I was fairly certain that what we would have to deal with in Nepal was going to be much more challenging than Europe.

We got up and had some breakfast. I ordered a typical Nepal thing of local bread, jam, and curry soup. It came quite quickly, and it was interesting. There were three small breads and a spun sugar thing that appeared to have been fried. It was all delicious, and hopefully wouldn't try to burst out of my belly on the road somewhere. Marcin had ordered the same. When it came he ordered another order of the same, and with a side order of anything dead.

There was a young girl working there who wasn't able to talk. The young man who ran the counter told us she couldn't speak, but he didn't seem to know why, and we didn't want to press him too much. She was dressing her son and was unspeakably proud of him. She gestured to us that he was hers and that he was off to school to read and write; all the time her face held a bright, beaming smile. She could hear us and make noises, so I wondered why she wasn't able to talk herself. I imagined her story would have been an interesting one, but she didn't even know sign language, so maybe it would never be told. I liked to think that whatever demons might have haunted her past, she'd managed to outrun them. She certainly, in that moment, seemed to be the proudest and happiest person I had ever met.

The young guy running the place was a bit flustered and seemed upset and very awkward. He had charged us too little for the beers the previous night, and obviously, the boss had been shouting at him about his mistake. By the time I came to pay it, there was a shortfall of about 600 rupees to cover. That came to around £4, so it was no problem for us, but seemed to have been a big deal to him.

He was relieved when we paid it, to say the very least. We assured him it was no problem, but he seemed very embarrassed, especially as the few beers he'd missed were probably the ones we'd bought for him. It actually took some reassuring from us that everything was alright. He was bright red, trembling, and looked at us from under a bowed head. We laughed it off and told him we all make mistakes; we were getting rather good at making them ourselves. I felt sure it wasn't an attempt to rip us off; it was an honest mistake. If it had been a scam, it certainly wasn't a very good one, since the amount it earned was very small and his acting to get it deserved an Oscar.

We packed up the bikes, and the staff came out to chat with us and just see us off. We left to a great deal of hero worship, which was getting a bit awkward by the end. We took some pictures with them all, which made everyone smile, and then we were back on the road where we felt like we really belonged. We left the small, friendly backstreets and crossed a bridge out of town that led us to the mountain road up to the capitol.

That part of the country was quite beautiful but was nothing compared to what was coming. Someone shouted, and I looked over. It was a western guy on a black Enfield Bullet. He waved, but we were stuck in traffic and couldn't get to him. I would have loved to have a quick chat—I was still loving the Enfields, and we would always stop to meet fellow bikers on the road if we got the chance.

So we headed on, and the traffic thinned out a bit. The driving was still bad, bordering on horrendous, but to us it seemed fine by then—our standards had been forcefully reset by our previous experiences, and things looked different now to our more seasoned eyes.

It's funny how the human brain adapts so quickly and easily to new routines, except Marcin's, of course.

The roads out of town were very rural; villages melted away into tiny communities of people living by the roadside, with no shops or signs of civilisation. It grew stark, but the starker it got, the more beautiful it became.

The country was strikingly wonderful. It wasn't as austere and foreboding as Switzerland and didn't perhaps have the depth of vibrant colours of the Pyrenees, but it was still quite spectacular, and every turn of the wheel rolled us further into a canvas upon which was painted craggy hillsides with shades of pastel green sprawled on top in the broadest of strokes.

On the other side towards China that would probably change, and drastically so, I imagined, with colder climbs, more rugged mountains still, and harsher conditions all round.

We were still on the low side of the country, and the road climbed as high as 300 metres while a burbling river flowed heartily along beside us. There was nothing that could be called a safety barrier, and it was a single lane track with several lanes of traffic fighting for possession of the bit in front of them. The road surface was good so far, but there were places where it broke up, frequently in corners, and some were quite bad. The surfaces had been ground away, since they weren't up to the job in the first place, and beneath the tired concrete the sand had turned to oily mud that was slippery and treacherous.

Traffic pooled in these patches, as trucks and buses had to slow down to cope with them. We stopped a few times to take pictures, but to be honest, anywhere you might point a camera in that country was a perfect picture for a postcard. The country was green and beautiful, and we were lucky to be riding under a clear blue sky in perfectly comfortable temperatures. It was quite literally the perfect day on the road, the kind you dream of when you're stuck in a city centre in an office while you watch the hands of the clock count down your time, or anywhere in India.

It wasn't fast—a hundred miles took us close to five hours, but we had spectacular scenery to look at, fresh, clean air to breathe, favourable weather, and no engine troubles to keep us happy. We made good time—good enough, at least. We were able to overtake most things and kept a good speed up for most of the day.

But all the while I kept my eye on the altitude, and we climbed to 600 metres with only around thirty miles left to go. With Kathmandu sitting at 1,400 metres, I knew the last bit was going to be rough on me, and it didn't disappoint.

By then the road surfaces had degraded to the point where they were quite bad. They were very pitted with gigantic wide and deep potholes, but apart from a few hairy moments, it wasn't scary at all. Several times we'd lean into a tight corner where the lane would reverse itself suddenly and the back wheel would step out, sliding on loose gravel that had been doused with leaking oil from the many buses that took the same route. Those moments weren't too frequent and we were used to it all by then. We knew our bikes and had taken them to the extremes of what they could do, day in and day out for weeks, riding all day and almost every day. Not much could phase us.

The climb was pretty steady, and the mountains were fairly shallow in the region, and blind terror never managed to grip me. It wasn't something to take lightly, by any means—the roads were difficult by any standards, but they weren't terrible and were well within my comfort zone.

In fact, it was one of our best days, even for me. Marcin, of course, had no issue with heights, and because bikes aren't dangerous enough for him, he also had a license to fly microlight aircraft. In various crashes he had broken just about everything—arms and legs, hand and feet, and most of the solid things in-between. He'd also broken his neck once, but that, in his defence, was while diving into water to impress some girls without first checking that there was actually any water to dive into.

So we arrived in Kathmandu after a relaxed and very enjoyable ride. It was a big city, and like all big cities, it was congested and choked with traffic and too many people. We had a pretty easy task to navigate to the Kathmandu guest house, but both GPS units crapped out on us, and we had to ask directions for the final leg of our journey. That bothered neither of us unduly; it was pleasant to be arriving in the middle of the afternoon with the sun shining above us and knowing that we had time to waste. It allowed us to explore a few streets and pick up a little of the tone of the city. It wasn't like any we'd seen before and seemed more planned and structured, with narrow roads bearing buildings with quite striking architecture, often beset with decorative red castings.

Something remained unspoken between us. For me, this was essentially the final leg of our journey. My trip went from London to Thailand, and we were now about to arrange the short hop across to Bangkok. My ride was essentially over. We were going to relax in Thailand together for a time, and I'd ride with Marcin to the border, but for me, it was really now over. I had gotten to where I was going. Marcin knew that just as well but had never mentioned it. We'd often justified keeping up the pace to earn ourselves the time to let our hair down and enjoy some relaxing time together in Thailand before he carried on. We knew that from now on I was just a tourist.

We made it through the growingly dense traffic and found the office of Eagle Exports without any real trouble. We obviously looked stressed and tired, because we most certainly were. The month on the road had taken a toll that was impossible to hide or erase with a single night of sleep. We went directly to their office and began working out the next and final leg, to plan our flight over to Thailand.

At the time, Myanmar was still closed to outsiders, since it was the victim of a very long civil war. Those with more local knowledge than we had said the problem was that there was likely huge open graves that hadn't yet been covered over, and so foreigner visitors were heavily restricted.

They told us there was no way the bikes could fly before Wednesday, and we couldn't fly cheaply until Friday. The difference in flying earlier was over £100, so I refused to do it for the sake of saving two days. Marcin was already arguing every point and was desperate to fly as early as possible—all he was achieving was annoying everyone in the office, so I had to take him away and calm him down with a belly-full of burned animal. We ended up deciding to park the bikes, and get some food while we discussed it.

We found a hotel close nearby, and with a bit of negotiating, got a great price—less than £5 a night for the only room left, which was a triple suite. It was larger than we needed, but we had a tendency to fill whatever space we occupied. We filled Marcin with enough food to make him smile, which was a lot of food, and we dropped off anything of value at the hotel. With less baggage we were both a lot more relaxed.

We went back to talk with the guys at Eagle Exports and see what could be worked out, now that Marcin was a little calmer. We asked what the cheapest flight was on Wednesday and they looked it up quickly. We got a good price on the Internet, but with connections in India, which would cost us five hours in the air. So they called around and came back with a flight costing the same as the cheapest flight on Friday, which suited us perfectly well and made Marcin a very happy man. A deal was struck, and Marcin stopped moaning very briefly.

We planned to hire a pair of Enfields on Tuesday to go sightseeing, as sadly, our bikes had to be crated the very next day and cleared through customs. I had hoped for a day off from them, but it wasn't possible. The next day we had to pack up the bikes and deal with the paperwork of getting ready to ship them out. It wouldn't take all day, but it was likely to swallow up a very stressful part of one.

That evening the mood lightened. Everything had been dealt with, we had only to follow along as the technicalities were sorted out, and we had a few days of leisure time to spend in a new town. We headed out to check out a bit of the night-life. The room at the hotel had a balcony that overlooked everything—bars were everywhere, loud and lively, with bands playing live rock music. Tourists were common, so we were not crowded everywhere we went, as we were just not that special anymore.

I can't tell you how sorry I feel for anyone who becomes famous and has to live that way for any length of time. It's no fun being flocked to every time you stop moving, and I really, really didn't miss it.

We went to an Irish bar, where Marcin hoped to get some Guinness, but they only served Nepalese beer. I asked about that, and they couldn't explain it, but that was pretty much what I'd expected.

We went up to the rooftop bar to take in the view and met a guy up there who was drinking alone. He came up to offer us food—Marcin took some, but it was meat, so I couldn't join him. He then shared cigarettes with Marcin and even offered us some of his home-grown hash. I don't smoke, but he wouldn't take no for an answer, rolled a joint, and physically stuffed it into Marcin's mouth. He saw double of everything after smoking a bit of that and then complained loudly that he'd literally gone blind.

We chatted a bit for a while, all of us a little worse for wear after swallowing a bit too much of the local beer. It was thin, weak, and a little too sweet for my taste. He said he loved his country more than his life, which was something I thought was utterly ridiculous, but interesting besides.

We shared our thoughts on Nepal, which were entirely positive—the place was really lovely, as were the people. We got into a conversation about their thoughts of other countries, but he claimed that the Nepalese people loved everyone. There's always a country everyone hates. Iran hates America, Iraq hates America,

Pakistan hates America, etc. We asked who it was in Nepal; who did he hate? He thought about it for a moment and then said quite earnestly, "I hate my wife!"

After that, he proudly showed us pictures of his family, before we eventually shuffled off to another bar after he had collapsed in a drunken heap and we had helped to prop him up in a chair to sleep it off. The next bar was full of tourists talking about trekking. It was a bit too English, but as everything else was closed, we hung about there for a while before finally calling it a night and heading off home.

Nepal was certainly amazing. It was the most welcoming, vibrant, and outright friendly place we'd been. Part of Iran had been very positive, but the experienced had soured as we approached the border. Nepal had only brought smiles to our faces.

We met another adventure motorcyclist, Keith, in the Eagle office. He had done the same trip as us, but solo and only a day or two ahead of us, he told us. How we'd missed him on the Pakistan paperwork escaped us; we presumed he must have been some way ahead but travelling at a slower, more reasonable pace than we had.

We chatted at length and agreed on almost everything as we compared notes with one another. There were other guys in the office, and our experiences all matched pretty closely. India was so stressful that we had all hated our time there to varying degrees. One backpacker said he was snapping at people the whole time from the stress, Keith said he found someone sitting on his bike, trying to steal it, and ended up physically beating him up.

That was a bit strong, maybe, but I totally understood how he felt. We all agreed that coming to Nepal was a breath of fresh air and more than made up for any downsides we'd encountered on our way. I had loved Iran, but I think Nepal was the highlight of our trip. The scenery, the people, everything was just right. I'm not saying that country is perfect, it's not and far from it, but it's got just enough of everything to excuse its faults. It's also very cheap, which is as close to perfect as it's possible to get!

36

Nepalese Boxing

Date—November 21st
Location—Kathmandu, Nepal
Mood—Oddly anti-climatic

I woke up today, after a fashion. I stubbornly refused to allow the fact that my brain had started working, in a certain kind of way, to force my body to function in any kind of way, and laid there trying to get back to sleep, which is where I truly felt I really belonged until lunchtime.

I couldn't get back to sleep and eventually had to get up, which was kind of annoying but just something I knew I was going to have to live with. We had to go to Eagle Exports around 10AM to confirm the flights, so we played around online, wasting time, before taking a leisurely walk to their office, just five doors away. Everything was getting sorted already, and probably more efficiently without our input, so we left them to it and headed off to find some breakfast.

We decided to try somewhere new—there were quite literally hundreds of great little places stuffed into every nook and cranny, so finding one wasn't hard. We went to one that appealed to us in some unfathomable way and checked out their breakfast menu and just ordered pretty much everything on it. Marcin ordered the same but with extra eggs.

It took ages, just ages. We waited and asked and asked and waited before waiting some more. In the end, just as we were about to leave and go somewhere else, they served up a small plate of chips and two omelettes, which was nothing like what we had ordered. They apologised and tried to make us more. We just paid and left, both of us still hungry. We got a cheese croissant from a street seller that was actually excellent, and I planned to get more tomorrow. By then, we had confirmation of everything we needed to fly our bikes to Thailand.

Sadly, Myanmar wasn't open to the general public. It had settled down a great deal in the last year or so, but they had been the self-victim of a long-running civil war, leaving most of the country as one huge mass grave. Consequently, we wouldn't be allowed in until whoever was in charge this week had managed to cover over the bodies, plant a few trees, get everyone smiling by force of law, and figure out all the various ways to fleece the odd drunk traveller who might want to pass through. I had heard of one man who had managed it, but he had only made a few miles and had to be air-lifted by helicopter over the rest, costing him thousands of dollars not to actually do what he set out to do.

We had to meet at 1 PM to crate the bikes, but the flights for ourselves were all sorted out and dealt with. Marcin absolutely insisted on going out for a ride to take pictures, but I refused. It just added a level of stress and trouble on top of the stress and trouble that Marcin naturally caused just by being Marcin. The traffic was a nightmare there, and I knew he wouldn't make it back in time, missing our slot and screwing up everything as, all too often, these things did.

In the end, there was no talking him out of it, so I had to go with him to make sure he made it back. I grumbled, told him he looked fat, and questioned his parentage. He just grinned and rode off. I got him to set the hotel into the GPS, so we could find it if we got lost, and we headed out, with me gnashing my teeth and keeping a firm eye on him. It was largely what I thought it would be—a complete waste of time.

We saw very little other than congested roads that were so small that they should only really be open to pedestrians, certainly not tons of traffic all squeezing into gaps that didn't really exist. We did find the Royal Palace, which was cool—they let us into the security area to take pictures, although they shouldn't have. The guards who let us in got into trouble, moaned at by someone in a smarter uniform than they were wearing.

We left and tried to head back, but the traffic by then was a nightmare. We got lost too—the GPS took us only so far and then it gave up. After trial and error, we made it back, grabbed the gear we were shipping with the bikes, and headed to the meeting.

We were twenty minutes late, so I shouted at Marcin angrily while he just grinned back, looking really rather oddly proud of himself. We found the gentleman who was going to lead us back to the airport, and we got under way, hoping we still had time to get our bikes into customs. They wanted us to go even earlier, as there are usually problems and it can take all day, they explained to us, looking a little worried. On top of that, our Carnets weren't properly stamped at the entry point, but they assured us that it would be no problem to fix that.

So then it happened again.

The heat of the day and the constant sitting in a queue caused the KTM to start stalling badly. Whenever it was stuck in traffic, it died. On top of that, the clutch gave in, so when he *could* restart it he had to slam it into gear to get it moving along, which caused the back wheel to spin and slide all over the smooth concrete roads like a fish on a metal tray. I ran interference at the rear, covering his arse when the bike stopped and clearing a path so he could start it and make another short run until it gave up once more.

We eventually made it to the airport like that through the busy traffic, making short little hops, stalling, shouting at the bike angrily, and then hurtling off as the clutch snatched, launching him headlong into a solid row of scooters that simply weren't ready for him. In the end, we got to the gate, and then it crapped out entirely, leaving us pushing it to the packing area.

Either way, we made it, albeit only just barely.

The previous evening we had a long and detailed (and extraordinarily drunken) conversation about bikes. I brought mine for many reasons that went beyond the immediate journey. When I would get to Thailand, it would be an ideal lightweight commuter I could use on any terrain. I still naïvely believed in that at that point.

Actually, the constant targeting by corrupt police looking for bribes meant I eventually had to stop using her altogether. I even shopped for a scooter but never bought one, as time ran out and I was facing a prison sentence for allowing my motorcycle to stay there longer than was legal, even though nobody had made me aware of that during the very many times I checked.

The BMW was frugal, light, and cheap to get parts for. It was also ideal on difficult roads, and I thought we'd see much more of them than we did, but in any case, it was ready for essentially anything the world could throw at it. During my trip in Europe, I had wished for more power and a bigger, more comfortable seat. I had always fancied an R1150gs, and one of those might have been ideal for this trip too, as the roads would have been quite manageable on a heavier bike than I had.

But with a clear view in hindsight, I had now decided that the best bike for any trip is the one that gives you the least hassle. I'd had a few problems along the way, such as my full-beam HID blowing out early on so that I ended up running on a single light. But I can't blame the bike for that, since they were cheap Chinese units I bought on the last day of preparation as a workaround fix for the better ones, which also died. One of my indicators also broke; it was an Oxford unit I bought, as it looked like decent quality, but it rattled into pieces over the uneven roads quite early on. The word, *Oxford* on the side of something fixed to an adventure bike is about as much use as anything with *KTM* written on it—even Marcin was beginning to agree with that!

We had talked at length about older bikes, the '90s era Africa Twins and such, and came to agree that something larger, less so than the KTM but with more power than I had, would be best. We would now both prefer something older and less sophisticated than our modern machines, since technology wasn't our friend and had constantly let us down. In fact, I probably wouldn't aim for an "adventure bike" next time, more likely some kind of ultra-reliable scrambler, home-made from the ground up.

I have a friend who is a motorcycle tour-guide who insists that there are no more adventures left. I hope he's wrong, but on this trip we'd seldom been really stretched by the terrain, and only the effort of riding for hours on end had really pushed us. But I didn't want to believe that we lived in a world where there was nothing left to discover, and so I chose not to believe that. I think the greatest adventure is in finding out more about yourself, and travel does exactly that.

The packing area of the airport wasn't too bad—not too busy and with plenty of space—so we grabbed ourselves a quiet corner. We were stared at on our way in, with large and seldom-seen motorcycles, one of which only made it by being pushed across the car-park.

The cargo area was a little-used place, and we were allowed to set up inside a large metal caged-off section to do the work. The work we had to do was to strip the bikes down into a package that was as small as humanly possible.

I had to take off the screen, beak, and handlebars. The handlebars were a pain to work on, and I had to strip off all the electronics to get them to fold away. It seemed they had built us a pair of wooden boxes, even though we'd asked for one that was large enough to take both bikes, believing it would be cheaper. They assured us that it wouldn't have saved us any money to do it that way, and with them speaking from a position of experience, we had to accept that this was the truth.

In any case, the price wasn't too bad, considering. It wasn't cheap, by any means, but it was tolerable. I had to check my bank balance, and that wasn't in too bad of shape either—this trip had not been as expensive as I had feared; not much more than a flight really, and far, far more interesting.

So the carpenters came in and started making the boxes around the bikes after we had done our jobs and loaded the parts onto a base. Two guys held her up while I took off the front wheel, and slowly she was packed away in bits. Mine was easy compared to the lardy bulk of the KTM, and Marcin struggled.

We then had to be inspected by a customs official, who tried very hard to look important and went about tapping on things with a cheap plastic pen. He asked me to open the tank and take off the seat, and that was the end of their detailed inspection; what they might have been looking for was a mystery to me. We had heard something about needing to remove the batteries in case of fires, but nobody looked at them or mentioned anything about that to us. My bike was cleared into customs, and the boxes vanished into a cage on the arms of a forklift truck.

We stared for a moment as our bikes were taken away; being separated from them left us feeling like our legs had been cut off. Even Marcin's troublesome KTM had found a place in his heart, and there was something unsettling about watching our beloved machines vanish into a metal cage to be left in the hands of others. Still, there was nothing we could do. We just had to accept that we had just gone from motorcycle-adventure riders to tourists and paid handsomely for the privilege.

We had to hang around for paperwork, but once that came, and quickly went, we were free to head back.

The car ride was awful—really congested traffic had settled in by then, and we sat around not moving for most of the time. The roads were mostly tiny, and the flow of traffic mostly wasn't—it was far too heavy for the small lanes to accommodate. Marcin wanted to walk, but our driver found a way through, mostly by bullying and battering his way between other cars, forcing anything with less dents than his out of the way. He did a good job, made us laugh, and earned a decent tip for his trouble.

We headed back to the Eagle office to sort out last minute stuff and because the boss had promised to help us hire a couple of Enfields to ride around the next day.

I needed an additional favour. I had found the keys from the hotel we stayed at before in my pocket. They were nice enough to call the hotel and explain I had the keys and arranged to post them back for us. Nothing was a problem, as usual, and the young guy at the hotel told us that he knew we'd call to sort it out. Of course we would! The company paid the postage for us, just happy to help out. We paid them back in beer.

We headed out to find a pair of Enfields for the morning, but after a few places we soon realised that it was too short notice and that it wasn't going to happen. Well, I realised it, but Marcin was arguing the whole time, but by then I had come to realise that was just his natural state, and nothing was going to change that.

In the end, all that was just too much trouble, so I went back to the first place and decided to just pick something out of whatever they had. They had a VR180 and a Chinese-made chopper. I liked the VR, and Marcin liked the Chopper, so we told them that we'd likely take those and abuse them like we stole them, which for a daily rental of around £3 we pretty much would have done.

We fancied a night out but were frankly too tired and stressed, having not really had sufficient time to unwind yet—even more so since Marcin was proving to be a considerable source of unrelenting annoyance. There were a couple of other guys at the office, so we arranged to meet them the next day and hit the bar opposite that had daily live rock music, and we planned to see what would happen from there. The owner of Eagle was going to join us too. for some beer at least.

We were officially pedestrians. It was a scary thing after growing to accept that my bike had become a large piece of my life. Packing her up was not fun at all, and I quietly had told her I'd miss her, and Marcin mocked me, telling me I should marry it. He'd always found it hilarious that I frequently spoke to my bike, encouraging her to keep running in traffic and telling her she was doing a good job.

Once I had caught him stroking his and calling it "Katie," so I reminded him of this as often as I could.

It was fair to say that we both missed our bikes.

37

Bullet Time

Date—November 22nd
Location—Kathmandu, Nepal
Status—Nothing to do

We woke up ready to face the world with the misguided belief that we'd still manage to rent a couple of Enfields to go for a joy-ride around the town. We hoped that, perhaps, we could explore a bit further. Riding an Enfield was an itch that needed scratching, the silly little old-fashioned, lumpy pig-iron machines had found a place in my heart. The quirky outdated design matched to the raspy, thumping growl of a single-cylinder engine had made the bike stand out as an idiosyncratic symbol of all that was right in the world. I knew that riding one would cement my love of these machines in my soul or cure this passing bug entirely, like venting my stomach in Pakistan or India.

Eagle Exports had agreed to help us to find them, saying it would be no problem, and that it should cost about 400 rupees.

Of course, nothing could have been further from the truth, but we were at our leisure, and the sense of urgency we'd been under the whole way had lifted, and in fact, I didn't much mind one way or the other. The only thing I was determined to do was explore a little of the town, certainly using an Enfield to do it would be a bonus.

We had breakfast at our hotel that morning, after the place the previous morning let us down. After the previous day's frequent fiascos, we imagined that no matter what we ordered, we'd probably be served an octopus and a candle, and the former would be more likely to be on fire.

That was not so at all, and we were pleasantly surprised when they brought us food. I ordered the Mexican Breakfast, and Marcin ordered the Fruit Lovers Choice, which seemed rather odd and a little scary to a man sharing a confined space with him. In fact, it didn't seem particularly fruity; it was just a pile of fried food with a glass of juice served on the side. When mine came it was bigger and more impressive than his, and Marcin eyed it jealously and grumbled angry noises. It was very cheap, and it tasted good too. I rather enjoyed Marcin's grumbles and described the superiority of my food choice in graphic detail between every single mouthful.

Eagle Exports called us to deliver the bad news, they had been unable to source Enfields. I don't know if it was a busy season for them, although it didn't seem to be, or if there was some other reason. I heard a rumour on the wind that the Enfields were notoriously unreliable and nothing was available in running condition. Considering the rental companies were comparing them to Chinese bikes with tiny engines, that wasn't very reassuring.

We had certainly had no luck the previous night looking for those fabled machines, so I came to the conclusion that it wasn't going to happen. As a man who's dated a paranoid schizophrenic, an amphetamine addict, a cocaine addict, and a Turkish girl, I was used to the world not being very fair and wasn't really bothered.

Somehow Marcin had tapped into my passion for these crude Indian motorcycles and went on a determined rampage to find one, probably just to annoy me by riding one. He found a place online and mailed them, ordering himself a rental. That morning as he checked, he had got a reply saying that there was only one left, and they would bring it to us. He had tried to get a pair, but that simply wasn't possible. With no great interest in them himself, he decided that the decent thing to do was to ride it and laugh at me all day for not managing to find one myself.

Yes, that's actually what happened.

I just went to a small local place to arrange to rent a Chinese bike, knowing that it just wasn't worth the trouble of playing the game of hunting for something better and wasting the day doing it. Suddenly, the price had jumped to 2,000 rupees, a significant leap up from the price we'd been quoted previously. I haggled it down to 1,000 (only around £8), and with an agreement made, we did the paperwork so I could get out and enjoy the day.

Then, he found a problem. The chain was knackered and needed replacing, he told me as I finished signing the papers. He offered me other bikes, but they were all tiny, and I'm not. He had only one motorcycle that looked like it could actually tow my weight along with it. With a grumble, I went elsewhere looking for something while he tried to repair the bike.

Friendly the people might be, but they weren't organised. Kathmandu had a lazy, laid-back feel that was a very welcome and refreshing vibe after the chaos of our journey so far. However, when you were trying to actually do anything, the easy nature of the place was a little frustrating.

One man at a rental place dealt with our enquiry in typically optimistic Nepalese style with a typically Nepalese failure to deliver. He told us he had many Enfields waiting to rent. We asked him to show us them, as he only had two broken Hondas in the showroom, with oily puddles beneath them and fire damage on the sides of one. He then phoned someone and returned to us with the news that he didn't have them after all. We were genuinely shocked to our very cores, I explained to him sarcastically.

The first rental place that we had tried told us that they would have the bike fixed within half-an-hour. Marcin moaned and moaned, and moaned some more, as I trudged back to the first place without sufficient patience to deal with any more empty promises.

Then someone pulled up on an Enfield, and Marcin somehow arranged to rent it from him. I watched in surprise, bordering on shock, that he'd managed to achieve that feat and that the feat he'd achieved actually managed to actually happen.

The VR, by then, was ready, and it was just quicker and easier to take that, so I decided that was exactly what I was going to do. I paid an additional fee for five litres of petrol, and we left together on our mighty steeds, which very quickly made it apparent that they were very far from mighty.

Marcin stopped to fill up with petrol. I checked, and sure enough, there was no petrol in my bike either. I put some in, and we headed out. After a few false starts, where we ended up down roads that went nowhere, we were on our way into the mountains. The roads climbed through a village to a wooded canopy overlooking threadbare and unrepaired roads made of sand and gravel, with threads of tarmac running along the middle in little patches. There was no side protection, just sheer drops into the deadly scenery below. The scenery might have been deadly, but it was also spectacular, although the bikes were not.

Mine had no speedo, and the brakes were just barely functional. That didn't matter, as the 150cc engine generated less power than a lawn mower, and thirty mph was pushing our luck. The Enfield was heavy and seemed difficult to manage, like Marcin himself, but it sounded very nice and looked the part. It could only manage around thirty mph as well, so we weren't in danger of breaking any speed limits.

We didn't care—it was actually a welcome change, after the mad dash across country, to ride something that moved slower than a refund cheque from the Inland Revenue, and we giggled to one another as we blasted along at full throttle, barely overtaking goats that were walking along the winding mountain passes.

We climbed into the countryside, and the scenery just got better and better. The mountains were softer there, green and inviting, and a canvas of pastel shades was painted all the way to the horizon. The people had cut grooves into the sides—I wasn't sure why, but I guessed it was something to do with being able to farm it more easily, as it had been turned into a series of stepped horizontal surfaces. In any case, it looked amazing, and it embodied a unique character that I'd not seen anywhere else. It was an even more impressive achievement because there was no heavy machinery there—it was done by hand with light tools.

There was none of the stark barrenness of Switzerland, where the mountains are foreboding and life is permitted to exist on certain conditions. Here the people had become a function of the environment. They lived off the land and were in closer harmony with it.

It was certainly a simpler way of life. There was nothing much there to buy, and consequently, nothing much to want. There were small pockets of communities as we went along, tiny villages where a few hundred people lived in tune with their surroundings. No pollution, no destruction, just mutual harmony. Little huts had been turned into makeshift cafés serving cans of drinks on home-made wooden tables and seating on upturned barrels. There was little else to see.

The roads got worse as we moved along, and surfaces broke up into shattered concrete, dirt, and mud, and still buses and trucks came towards us with nowhere to pass—the path was always too narrow for two lanes. People were mostly driving carefully. They honked as they approached a bend and generally waited for somewhere to pass. The roads up there dropped hundreds of metres straight down, and everyone seemed to respect the obvious dangers.

We rounded a corner and saw what Marcin had been itching to find. A view of the mountain ranges swam into view, setting a dark and jagged foreground against the seamless blue backdrop. There they were, grey and murky, with unmistakable snow-covered peaks pointing sharply into the cloudless sky like the teeth of an angry predator. It was a striking sight, and the temperature dropped sharply as we stopped to take pictures. It was a humbling sight; the path that led there was enough to kill a person if they failed to prepare, and yet people did; people made it to the top. For a while we just stood and stared, wondering why people overcame such odds to do things that didn't need to be done. Why would someone fight so hard to make their lives so difficult? I didn't have an answer to that, even though I'm a frequent and prolific offender.

We left to carry on for more of the tantalising little glimpses into the world beyond, as the hills and mountains broke to tease us with another little snapshot.

A truck was coming the other way, being driven carelessly. The driver wasn't watching and was barrelling straight at us at too fast a speed. Marcin had no choice but to try and pass on the opposite side, as ours was cut off, and the Enfield skidded towards the precipice. The spinning wheel caught only a few inches from the edge, kicking up a flurry of dried red dirt and a wispy cloud of sand. Marcin sat on the motionless bike, his fists gripping hard enough to the bars to send his knuckles white. He breathed heavily, forced a smile on his face, and just looked at me, blinking in silence.

Neither of us said a word; neither of us needed to. No harm was done, but I wouldn't like to be the person who had to wash his pants the next day.

We carried on, and the cold got worse, until the shadow of the mountains lifted, and then it was warm again as we rounded an edge. We stopped a few times, and everywhere we looked was still more of this incredible green mountain scene. At one point, a huge bird of prey drifted majestically through the air, barely moving its wings, just gliding on the warm breeze.

It was a place that was, in many ways, very special indeed.

Before we left home, we had met a group of adventure touring motorcyclists with stories to tell of their recent adventures. One had asked me to show him my bike, and we stood over it, talking about the modifications I had made. I could tell he was a man who wouldn't take me seriously until he had judged my determination by seeing that I had a bike that was really capable of what I was planning. Once he saw it, he rested his hand on the tank and said to me that at some point we would have a moment where we'd realise that all the stresses, the sacrifices, and the pain would be meaningless, and we'd realise just how lucky we were to be doing this.

We had found that moment.

It was a great day, and it was well-spent. We ran around over the tattered roads, snapping pictures and acting like the overgrown children we really were. It was a truly beautiful place to see, but unfortunately, the roads there were so poor that we had to see it twice. We turned round and came back the same way, since we really had no other choice.

There was a small dotted line on the map indicating a road, but it was little more than a path through the trees, and our bikes wouldn't have managed fifty miles of the kind of terrain that it seemed to be made of. If we had stayed in the country longer, then it would have been a great camping trip, but my little Chinese enduro would have shaken itself apart and forced my spine up through my skull on every bump. The Enfield would have just laughed and spluttered to a halt, much like the KTM.

The ride back was still great—we stopped for more pictures along the way, until eventually we made it back to the little town at the edge of the city. From there, we battled our way against the traffic until we managed to find our way back to the hotel. After a day spent riding, we had our bearings, and we had no trouble finding our way.

Once we returned, we dropped the bikes back. I told the dealer about the fuel, and he laughed and turned away. I told him I would keep the keys until he could find the money to buy them back from me for the price of five litres of fuel.

I chose to believe that it was a genuine oversight, but I wasn't going to be letting him get away with it if it wasn't. He paid me back the money for the fuel he didn't give me and grumbled about doing it. Considering that he doubled the price and gave me plenty of problems, he probably wasn't to be trusted in any case.

That kind of thing was, however, an exception in Nepal and not the rule.

That night we were going to be hitting a few bars and saying goodbye to the country. For me, this was the end of the trip. Thailand was my final destination, and tomorrow I would be there with my bike. I would ride with Marcin to the border, but it was no longer my journey, and I was just going to wave him off. I felt a bit sad, but I didn't think that the realisation had hit Marcin yet.

I have to say, Nepal had been the best country of the trip for me. Iran was nice, and the people were mostly great. It was brilliant to see Pakistan, such as it was. Serbia had been a highlight for me, and it was fun to spend some time in Poland. I had no regrets about India either—I would never go back, but I'm glad I had the opportunity to survive it.

Nepal had just trumped them all with its incredible scenery, warm people, and sheer character. I was going to miss it but was determined that I would return one day, hopefully with my bike, and I would explore further and find more of what the country had to offer. But for now, the road carried on, taking us to the next destination.

38

Flying Is No Way to Travel

Date—November 23rd
Location—Kathmandu, Nepal
Status—A little sad to be leaving

We woke up just in time to catch our flight, which was more luck than judgement, since nobody had remembered to set an alarm. We packed up quickly, but most of our gear had flown out with the bike, so it was really just a case of stuffing things into our hand luggage as we made our way out of the door. Still, we had managed to thoroughly trash the room in the three short days we had occupied it. We apologised to the cleaner for what she was about to discover upstairs and left a very large tip to cover it.

We were slightly hung over after the previous evening, which is a bit like saying water is slightly wet. We had gone for a few quiet beers with the fine gentlemen over at Eagle Export, and the owner got a bit dunk, and the guys who were staying with him joined in. It had been a fun night, so we just stayed there listening to the band upstairs and getting more and more silly and more and more drunk, until everything after that point was a complete blur. I feel certain that whatever we did, it was purely in the interests of science, and if we did anything wrong, then I'm sure we learned our lessons.

By morning, the silliness had turned to headaches, but we fought our way through the fog behind our eyes and battled our way down to breakfast. I ordered the same as the day before. I never do that—I like to try new things, but it was so good that I broke my own rules! Marcin ordered the same with bacon, as a meal without meat is no meal at all for him, he reasoned.

I had come to suspect that he deliberately ate more meat just to annoy me, although it didn't. Much of the reason for becoming a vegetarian was to improve my health. My father had serious heart problems and had endured a quadruple heart-bypass. They estimated that his arteries were ninety-eight percent blocked, and if two red blood-cells had gone through at the same time, he would have dropped dead on the spot.

Hoping to avoid that happening to me, I gave up meat altogether, cutting my risk of heart-disease and cancer down by a huge margin. It's a minor inconvenience for a huge personal gain to anyone that doesn't want their rib-cage pulled open.

On this occasion he became quite belligerent at the very notion that I didn't eat meat and tried to mock me for it. Since I wasn't the one who was overweight and was healthy enough to exercise daily, I didn't bother to argue the point, since I would have had to use long words, and he wouldn't have understood them. I'm not quite sure how, but he found my dietary choices offensive, and in our bleary, half-human hungover state, he got angry about it and demanded I eat a dead thing right there and then. Perhaps I could start with something small, maybe a rat, and work my way up from there?

While we were eating breakfast and were actually managing to find something stupid to argue about while we did that incredibly simple thing, a guy came in to talk with us. He'd been following us around the whole time, saying he needed to talk with us, but we'd been trying to avoid him, since we thought he was just one of the many people trying to sell us something that no human being could possibly have any use for. This morning we were too tired to fight him off, so we listened to what he had to say, while paying only half-hearted attention. He told us that he ran a tour company, and they were planning to expand and run a trip identical to what we've just done, running twenty tourists on Enfield 500s. He then offered us jobs.

So, to get this straight, he wanted to pay us to do what we just did and give us bikes to do it on. He wanted to buy our visas, give us beer, and let us run amok again. Not only that, he wanted to give us money for doing it! We stopped laughing for a moment and then started laughing even harder, before pretty much agreeing to do it, if he could give us some proper details of his offer. He said he was going to be sending us a breakdown of his business plan. I told him I would go over it and explain the long words to Marcin.

So we had to dash off to catch our flight while still chewing the last of our breakfast. Finding a cab took about three seconds, and then we were on our way to the airport. Traffic was light, but the driver was sticking mostly to back alleys that cars simply should not have been driving down. This seemed to help even further, and the trip was short, if terrifying.

We were told we were leaving at 11:20, so we made it to the airport in good time. It wasn't entirely organised, but everything seemed to mostly work OK in a Nepalese way. The airport was a simple place, none of the cavernous entry halls of more popular destinations and only a few counters to queue at. Each had a cardboard thing standing on the top to inform passengers where to go, and the order changed frequently. Clearly, it wasn't a busy place; it had the same laid-back vibe as the overland border. That was fine until you had something to achieve, and then it quickly became frustrating. We hoped everything would go smoothly.

We had a coffee and killed some time waiting for the dynamic squad of security guards to fondle us lovingly and then look suspiciously at mundane objects, completely ignoring the fact that Marcin was a dangerous and highly offensive weapon of mass-consumption himself.

Our gear was X-rayed and then searched manually. There was no screen to monitor the X-ray on, so my guess was that it didn't actually work. The security search showed up a slight problem—Marcin had brought a spork along, a camping kit with a knife, fork, and spoon, and he wasn't allowed to take it on board. How this actually became a problem was anyone's guess.

He grumbled and moaned and got louder and more annoying, demanding he should be allowed to take it on board. Perhaps the pilot could carry it for him was his best and most hilarious suggestion that he offered up. I pointed out that it was a spork, worth less than a decent can of beer, so he should just chuck it in a dustbin and move on with his life. He began looking sad and demanded they fix it for him and find a way to make him happy. As he hadn't checked anything into luggage yet, I suggested he could run back and put it into the hold. Marcin was confused and too large for moving swiftly.

So, obviously, I had to take his spork back to the front desk, past all the security checkpoints, and put it in my gear to be loaded aboard. I had to leave my passport upstairs and head down and then go back up through a passport check without a passport.

I just told the people working there what I was doing—they didn't really understand (neither did I, to be fair), but they let me go through anyway without a problem. *Security* was just a word on a badge in Nepal, and it wasn't taken very seriously. I walked right through unchecked, back to the boarding gate, and all the way back without a single raised eyebrow.

We were finally allowed through with only twenty minutes to spare and got to the departure lounge, breathing heavily but utterly relieved that Marcin was still the proud owner of a spork that he'd never used and that had come free with a sleeping bag (that he'd also never used). We checked the screens, and it turned out that our flight wasn't at 11:20 anymore; it was now at 13:00, so we suddenly had a couple hours to kill with no Internet access and nothing to entertain us—except for the pungent smell of our filthy motorcycle gear and the hilarious way Marcin pronounces *mountain*, which comes out as "Moon-tin" and just made me laugh every time he said it.

So we waited until 13:00, with me still laughing at his pronunciation of simple words and Marcin earnestly urging me to try eating rats until I was comfortable moving up to a chicken. All the while nothing happened until we were finally told that the flight had been delayed again, this time until 14:30. By then it was getting a bit irritating.

So we grumbled, ground our teeth, and just waited, because there was nothing else we could actually do about it. Even Marcin took it on the chin, but frankly, if he'd moaned much more "on the chin" was where I would have punched him. I wonder if he'd have even noticed? I imagined he would just grin back at me and tell me to hit harder next time before making a joke about me punching like a vegetarian.

Eventually, the gate was opened, and we were allowed from one small waiting room into a smaller room to do some more waiting. We were, after a good long spell of waiting, taken by bus for a hundred yards to a reasonably dilapidated Chinese-owned plane that was literally held together with tape.

We taxied out onto the runway, the plane shaking about like we were riding over the typical roads out there on a clapped-out motorcycle.

We were sat next to a young Indian man who had the IQ of a dishcloth, and his friends opposite were similarly intellectually challenged. They had to watch us putting our belts on and then try to do it themselves. They failed, and in the end, the crew had to come out and fix their belts for them. How they functioned in the real world escaped us, but I hadn't even figured out how Marcin did yet, since I didn't function particularly well either.

So we took off, spun around, and headed out to the mountain ranges. It was impressive! We flew right over the Himalayas and saw Mount Everest from the comfort of a heated cabin, which is probably the ideal way to see a snow-covered lump of rock, in my humble opinion. Finally, the crew brought round lunch, which was only just passable, but we were hungry, and I was worried Marcin might start eating the chairs if he was forced to wait much longer, and after all, I was sitting in one of them.

They asked if we wanted the chicken or vegetarian option, and he just shouted, "Meat," over and over again while flapping his arms around angrily. We then had a long and loud discussion about terrorism, where I explained to him that it wasn't actually hilarious.

Then I farted, actually quite proud that the effort hadn't made me soil myself. We were not terribly popular passengers.

The young man opposite needed help feeding himself—the staff had to show him how to eat, so I honestly wasn't sure how he had reached the age that he had. The crew were shouting at the whole group at that point, while we took time out to just laugh and enjoy the show. Marcin said sarcastically that even he could manage to feed himself and then spilled gravy on his lap. If only he'd had a spork!

The flight stretched on and on, but finally we felt the sure signs of a descent. At that point, I was in the toilet, and the sure signs of descent caught me slightly off-guard, the end result being that the cleaner would have some walls to wash after we had landed.

We went down until we saw the lights peppering the horizon, twinkling little pinpoints of light in the sea of blackness that stretched out infinitely around us. And that was it; we were over Thailand. We sunk further to the ground until we hit it with a bone-wrenching crash that was something like a landing. The captain came out to see us off, a man I normally wouldn't accept a coffee from, with eyes that pointed off in different directions and a face full of missing teeth. On reflection, I'm glad we hadn't seen that before; it would have terrified everyone on the plane. He was clearly not someone that could have been trusted with the combined eating power of a free spork.

We were finally in Thailand, my final destination, for now at least. We entered the airport, and then still more problems hit us, just for a nice change. Marcin needed the toilet, and so I split off to head for the baggage claim area to collect our bags. Between me and the place where bags arrive was a queue from hell, as there often was in Bangkok Airport.

Isn't it funny how the explanations for almost every problem we had begins with the word *Marcin*?

It did get better after the invention of orderly queues, but still, it was never less than a terrible place with only the vaguest facade of organised civility. Officials glared angrily, spending as long as possible examining every details of papers and passports, as if everyone except them was a problem.

Once I was accused of trying to cheat them because I had an entry visa in my passport, instead of the thirty-day "Visa on Demand" that you are freely issued on arrival. The accuser was unable to explain what possible benefit I might gain from getting a shorter visa than I had paid for. That kind of thing was common in Thailand, where the people are heavily indoctrinated into believing that they and their country are very special. I have seen people argue over a map that Thailand must be bigger than it really is because it's so important. I have also seen a Thai girl wearing a T-shirt that sported the legend "I ♥ bathroom rape."

It took over an hour to get through, and Marcin never came back from the toilet. I even went to find him, worrying that he'd accidentally flushed while drinking from it, or something else terrible had happened. Nothing. There was no sign of him at all.

I finally got through and found my bags. My helmet, though, was missing a chunk of internal padding and wouldn't fit on my head anymore. It had needed to be taken on as luggage, where it patently hadn't belonged. From then on I had to wear it with a rolled up sock stuck in the left side.

Finally, I gave up looking for Marcin and asked at the information desk. They said I could put out a tannoy call outside, but if I went outside, I wouldn't be allowed back in. In the end I had no choice, so I went outside. They refused to put out a tannoy announcement for some reason that only makes sense if you're brimming with utterly misplaced arrogance, but said there was another information booth further down. I went there, and Marcin was in a shop in the process of buying a phone card to call me with. He had been queuing, and somehow we'd missed each other. I still hadn't worked out how we managed to do things like that with almost supernatural skill.

With stress levels at their highest, we finally got a hotel with free Wi-Fi, free breakfast, and a free shuttle service to and from the airport. We were too tired to sort the bikes out that night, and it was too late, besides, even though Marcin had some idea that we were going to. We had a plan for the morning, once we knew the timing of the shuttle bus and had found out how everything worked.

One of the many things that didn't work was my Visa card, so I no longer had access to any of my own money. That was far from an ideal situation, but I guessed it might have been blocked after putting the shipping on my card in a strange country. I could call them in the morning and get it unlocked, or at least get something resolved, I hoped.

We arrived at the hotel after a short ride in an air-conditioned van. At first glance, it was nice, way better than we thought it would be and one of the nicest we'd stayed at on our trip. It was no small stretch to say it was far too good for us. Still, we would have no problems in finding our rooms, since we left a trail of muddy footprints all the way to the door that we could later follow. They are probably still there to this day.

We went out to a restaurant next door and had a simple meal, which was really excellent, or perhaps we were just really hungry. In any case, it worked very nicely. One thing the Thais do well is food—they have a real flair for it. The food tasted clean and delicious. I just had vegetables and rice, Marcin had meat, and we both agreed that our respective menu choices were of a higher standard than we had either expected or grown accustomed to.

We ordered beer and got an awesome three-litre pipe with ice in it, which was a mobile draught. Even better, the staff filled our glasses from it every time we took a sip, and the staff was composed of ridiculously attractive girls who smiled flirtatiously and asked leading questions about where we were staying and if we were married.

The whole bill still only came to around £12. A visit to the 7-11 bought us two more beers and some water and cost just over £1 each. I loved being back in Thailand, a place I had visited several times before with my girlfriend. With ridiculously attractive staff trying to flirt with me, I didn't love having a girlfriend. I would probably have to do something about that at some point.

But all joking aside, there was only one thing missing for my life to be complete, and I missed her terribly. Marcin and I discussed how we were going to get her in the morning. I am, of course, talking about my bike. Marcin and I got rather drunk and chatted about all that, as we often did. He had named his, but oddly, I had not. I decided it was time I found a proper name for my bike—she'd earned that much at least. His, a KTM, had been named "Katie." Just exactly how I had not come to name mine suddenly seemed rather inexplicable, and I resolved to fix that straight away.

I checked email and got a confirmation of our job offer. It seemed that we were being formally invited to travel for a living. I didn't know if I could do this trip again without killing Marcin, and the offer looked a little suspect. I decided to look into it more thoroughly and do some serious thinking before deciding anything.

39

Predictable Stress, Stress, and More Stress

Date—November 24th
Location—Bangkok, Thailand
Mood—Stressed enough to kill Marcin

It turned out to be an incredibly stressful day, and I actually started hating Thailand a little bit. Eventually, all was forgiven, in the short term at least, since Thailand still had much to teach me in terms of how things really were in that country. In hindsight, it was Marcin I should really hate, but somehow I just can't bring myself to do that, try as I might. Getting very drunk with Marcin made everything insanely complicated, even simple things like getting into the hotel in the evening.

We woke up that morning to a decent, if slightly confusing, breakfast of toast and hot water. We had some toast and some of the hot water with teabags containing coffee, and then the staff brought us plates of more food, eggs, hotdogs, and fruit. Marcin ate my hotdogs and then ordered another breakfast and ate that too and still moaned about being hungry afterwards.

The day was never going to be fun and we both knew that. We had to get our bikes out of customs, and that would mean we would spend a day pitched against bureaucrats in a country where the average IQ was in the low to mid-eighties. At least at the end of it we'd have our bikes, even if Marcin's probably wouldn't run. At the very least, we had arrived in the first country along our way where that might be an issue we could resolve. We tried to remain as positive as possible, hoping that a change in climate and a rest might shake a little of Marcin's mechanical problems loose and he might have better luck going forwards.

We were used to border crossings—they tended to actually be pretty straightforward—but getting a shipped bike out of a warehouse was a totally different thing, and we had no idea what to expect. We even had trouble finding the warehouse, quite considerable difficulty actually.

We got a complimentary car to the airport and then a shuttle bus to the warehouse where we were told our bikes were being kept. Everyone sent us somewhere different, each totally sure they were right or, at least, less wrong than everyone else.

In the end, we caught a bus as directed, with the hope that we were heading in the right direction. The driver told us he was going to the right place, and we ended up in a bus station, where the driver just got out and walked off. We had to get another bus back to the airport, and then that seemed to be going out to international cargo. A fellow traveller on the bus seemed to know where we needed to go and showed us the office. Then he put on an ID badge and told us that he worked there.

That did seem rather odd.

He arranged for yet another man to help us, and we spent the next two hours going from one office to another and then back to other offices, talking to various people and making little to no actual progress. It was a nightmare of bureaucracy. We saw the crates at one point, and they looked undamaged, which was a relief, but we still had loads more to do for reasons nobody could manage to explain to us.

Eventually, we ended up in the customs office. They told us to come back at one, and by two we should be with our bikes. We had to pay a storage fee for them, around £20, and we arranged with a customs official to allow us to go back to the warehouse and work on the bikes while we waited, since they were in pieces and it's usually harder to put them together than to get them apart.

The guy sorting everything took us back to the first office, which was a table in the corner of a restaurant. He then told us customs was around £90 each to release the bikes. We argued, and he got another guy involved who spoke better English. He told us it was the release fee. I said I was going over to customs to discuss it directly with them, and then the fee went down to half. I argued more, and he asked how much I wanted to pay. I told him I wasn't giving them anything, and we left.

It later turned out that they were simply scammers, local mafia out to rip off passing tourists. I was very disappointed to see something like that happening to us—I knew it went on and was actually commonplace in Thailand, but it was still a bit of a shame that our first experience of the country was so negative after all we'd gone through to get there. Marcin was always asking about the conditions in Thailand, and I'd always defended the place, telling him how nice it actually was.

It actually wasn't.

So we left the scammers behind and went back to start assembling the bikes. We discussed the fact that the whole morning would have probably been much easier without their special brand of help. They had most likely been making things difficult to justify the price of their help, or maybe just because they had no idea what they were actually doing. That fact alone had made them seem like proper Thai officials.

Working on the bikes wasn't easy. Marcin had to have the front of his lifted by a forklift truck to get the wheel on; mine was simply laid down on the side, and it was all pretty straightforward from there. Everything went back together okay, and nobody was surprised when she started and ran absolutely fine.

It took hours, so eventually we were late back to customs. We were called in, and an officer who spoke good English chatted with us. He warned us of the fees if we didn't import the bikes permanently, but we knew about those already. In fact, it was impossible to import them permanently in any case. We asked how much it would cost to clear them, and it was free,. There were no charges at all, and then he warned us about the scammers.

It was the officials who invited them in, in exchange for a cut of the illegal additional fees. There were plenty of scams about, and we were told that it was best not to trust anyone and don't give money to anyone who offers to do things for you.

So we eventually got back to our bikes after a long, hot, and exhausting day. We got on them to ride them out, and disaster struck! This time it was mine that didn't work.

As soon as it went into gear the clutch shook and dragged so that it wouldn't disengage properly. Marcin tried to interfere, and I got pretty angry with him for once, as my patience was literally at the very end.

He just kept trying to tighten the cable, but I knew my bike—I built it up, I'd changed this cable and taken it off several times and knew that it couldn't be the cause of the problem, even though I didn't know what the cause actually was.

The intense vibration that shuddered right through the bike was something horribly new. In the end, I managed to set it to a level where I could just about ride it. In fact, the clutch, when engaged, was stronger than ever—there was no slip, and actually she made a little more power, but the vibrations shook the front end as I moved along, making it a battle to hold her straight. She still crept forward with the clutch fully open too, so there was clearly a serious problem in there somewhere. As we went along I tried to work out how an internal mechanical problem could have been caused by taking the wheels off. My brain struggled with the question as I mentally flicked through the schematics of the engine.

Marcin's clutch had also been giving difficulties as well, but we managed to fix it more easily—we simply put oil in it. His reservoir had gone dry, and with a bit more fluid in it worked much better. Still, it wasn't quite right, and the engine still cut out occasionally.

We were glad that at it ran at least. All it had to do was get itself to a KTM dealer.

We had one more thing to do before we were free to leave. We had to have an inspection, and that was just a matter of waiting for an official to come out and see that our chassis numbers matched. They used our carnets for reference but did not stamp and remove parts, just like in Nepal. The carnet was not required there, but having it made life a lot easier. It was still a nightmare border crossing, but I can only imagine how bad it would have been without a CDP. In fact, we met a couple collecting baggage. They took just as long as us to get their stuff back, so most of the bureaucracy was simply the airport. I imagined that an overland crossing would be far, far easier, and later on discovered many times that it was.

So finally, we left for Sukhumvit, where I'd been before. The sat-nav took us most of the way, and then I saw things I recognised and rode the rest from memory. It was great—it was like coming home at last. I hadn't heard from my girlfriend's friends, so I simply headed back to the hotel I had stayed at last time, and there were no problems with getting ourselves booked in. When I finally got to check emails, that was what she had said to do, in any case.

We were both pretty stressed out from the day, and Marcin found himself a KTM service centre nearby. They weren't strictly KTM—they did a lot of other bikes too, but were authorised to work on them. Even though mine was running badly, I went along with him to discuss my problems or at least find a BMW expert from whom I could get advice. I posted questions on various forums, hoping someone might have had a similar issue, and then we left for the cold, dark mess of early evening Bangkok traffic.

Unfortunately, this short, four-mile ride turned into a nightmare as we plunged deeper into solid rush-hour traffic. For the first time we felt like we were in a real city. Bangkok is ridiculously vast, and the traffic problems are in scale with its dimensions. We arrived at the GPS coordinates, but there was no shop anywhere to be seen. We rode around and looked for it, but due to my clutch problem the bike kept stalling, and I lost Marcin at a busy junction as his glowing red tail-light was swallowed by a seething mass of red dots some way off in the distance.

He waited at a junction for me, he later said, but never saw me behind him. I looked everywhere for him, but we must have missed each other in the solid sea of glaring headlights that flowed constantly towards us in the cluttered, busy streets. In the end, I gave up and decided to backtrack to the hotel.

It was dark, and backtracking wasn't as easy as I thought. I got turned around and eventually had to admit to myself that I had no idea where I was. At one point, I saw the overhead motorways and knew that I was totally lost. That was the moment my fuel warning light came on, which meant I had around thirty miles, if I was lucky, before my bike died completely. I still had no money, since my card didn't work in any ATM, and I had very little fuel and no idea where I was.

I pulled up at some lights and asked for directions, but nobody spoke any English that far out from the centre of town. A girl on a scooter-taxi pointed when I said, "Sukhumvit," so I headed that way, hoping for a bit of luck. I saw signs to the airport, and it made sense from what I knew of how that part of the city was laid out, so I carried on. Eventually, I saw a mall I had been to before, so I turned off and headed to where I thought the hotel was. Using guesswork I found the overhead railway line that led directly back to where we were staying. I followed it a few hundred metres and got back to the hotel with only a few miles left in my tank. I was hot, dehydrated, and thoroughly miserable. The stress was really getting to me—I had a roaring headache and was severely angry with the world.

Marcin was already back by then. He hadn't managed to find the place at all. He was sorry to have lost me, but it was nobody's fault that time, just bad luck all round. I just silently fumed to myself until I calmed down, and Marcin respectfully gave me the space I needed.

I refused to do anything else until I had resolved the money issue. I used his laptop to Skype-call the UK and sort out my banking problems. My account had been locked after putting the bike shipping on my card—it was an unusual transaction, certainly, and in an odd place, but a call would have been more useful than just locking my account. In the end, because of their actions, I had arrived in a foreign country with no money. I couldn't even buy a mobile top-up to phone home, so if Marcin hadn't been there it could have been a pretty difficult situation. They said they'd put a holiday flag on my account to stop that happening again.

We had arranged to meet people, but time was not on our side. I was feeling increasingly bad—a cold was settling in, and I was beginning to feel awful in every part of my body. Everyone in Nepal had seemed to be ill, and our immune systems were shot through after being in India, so now I had something infecting my chest and nothing much left to fight it with. I knew it was nothing major, just a cold or something, but it was just another thing adding to all our other problems.

I calmed myself down still more, now that I had access to my money, and I unwound.

Marcin was a stranger there, and so I took him to a little local market for food and a few quiet beers. Food was always a challenge there—they don't cater very well for vegetarians at all, but I managed to get something, while Marcin ate more than several somethings all to himself. We had a couple of beers and felt a lot better about our place in the world, as the many stresses of a fairly miserable day came into perspective.

A live band started up playing. I'm no musician, but I know enough to say that they were just awful, missing cues, playing out of time, and each member largely doing their own thing as they all struggled against one another to be the most important. The singer had a shrill little voice and was always a little off key, but he yelled enthusiastically into his mic, often swallowing most of the head. It was more amusing than good, but it was fun in any case.

Still, Marcin decided we needed more beer and got a tower for us to share. It was like a giant fire-extinguisher filled with an ice tube that kept three litres of beer cold for long enough to enjoy it. We drank that, and I had to tell him I was finally done.

I headed back to the hotel and fell asleep. At 6:30 in the morning the phone rang and it was Marcin, asking to be let in. It seemed he had got so drunk that he'd just wandered around getting even more drunk until he was too drunk to even keep wandering!

Of course, all of this was made even more difficult, as Marcin had lost the hotel key. All in all, it had been a very long day, and it seemed that I was just about to have another one.

40

Guinness Is a Poor Substitute for a Working Clutch

Date—November 25th
Location—Bangkok, Thailand
Mood—Stressed enough to kill myself

We woke up late in the morning and headed over to a local Tesco for lunch/breakfast. Now things were a bit easier, I started noticing the little differences since my last visit. Also, my perspective had shifted a great deal from carrying out this journey—I hadn't actually realised how much until I started seeing familiar things with new eyes.

The small shops along the streets of Thailand are cluttered and dishevelled, and now I was able to see that style in context. They were not dissimilar to the ones in Pakistan and India, albeit cleaner there in Bangkok. I could see how the local cultures had evolved across the wider geography, and it all started slotting into place.

Tesco had a large food hall upstairs where I'd eaten before, but it had a facelift and looked more modern and sophisticated. I liked it better before. We had some food; I had a vegetarian thing with plain rice and omelette—nothing exciting, but it was food, and I was looking to be filled, not excited. Marcin had a Thai soup and wasn't impressed. He commented that the food there didn't work, and went off to get another meal. Something with more meat in it. I imagined he'd come back with someone's pet dog with a little sprig of herbs on top as a garnish and start ripping into it raw, perhaps not even bothering to kill it first.

I got us some tea and coffee, which both came cold and were served with ice. Sadly, my favourite coffee was from the 7-11, and they didn't seem to be serving it any more. Later on, my taste in coffee changed quite radically, but then I liked it with milk and ice.

After lunch, I checked on the bike, not expecting to find anything that would cheer me up. I pulled off the cover to inspect the clutch, and it looked clean and tidy, but things had a bit more free play than I had expected. Not being able to find an obvious fault suggested that the entire unit might need replacing.

I still couldn't work out how that had happened. I am a logical person, and I like to understand and know the reasons for things. I didn't see how I could put a bike with a perfectly workable clutch into a wooden box, and then take it out again with a major mechanical fault that wasn't there before. It was such a serious failure that it had rendered the bike basically un-rideable over any distance.

My first guess was that the trip had killed the clutch, and relaxing the cable had allowed the fault to manifest, perhaps the plates had cracked and then caved in entirely once the pressure was off. Otherwise, the conditions of the flight might have contributed. I didn't know what the cause was, but the fact remained, my clutch was a problem that needed fixing before I was going anywhere.

Marcin took his bike to the KTM dealer. His clutch was worse than ever, but it made it there, more or less. He called and explained that he hadn't been able to find them, so they sent a young guy on a Super-Duke to lead him there through the solid traffic of Bangkok city, and he got a cab back, which took forever, he grumbled.

While he was gone, Shine-Rider turned up. He was a friend of mine from Facebook—a mutual friend of my girlfriend, although we'd never met before face to face. He came with two Malaysian riders, and they all seemed to be motorcycle fans and took an interest in what I was doing. They found me in a situation that they all found hilarious, my bike lying on her side, with me tinkering around inside the clutch-basket, muttering swear-words like a crazy person; although with three diagnoses of suicidal depression and a host of other loose screws, I do actually qualify as an actual crazy person.

They helped me out with advice on where to take my bike, but in the end, the easiest thing was just to get a cab to the BMW Motorrad office to order the parts. The bike was running horribly, and I decided not to risk causing more damage by using it to commute backwards and forwards. Cabs in Bangkok were cheap, the trip to BMW costing only around £2.

It was not quite the BMW service I was used to at home—the showroom was cluttered and disorganised, but the bikes were familiar, and the service was mostly good. I talked to the girl at the parts counter and got an estimate for a new clutch. The price came in at £650 and a three week wait for it to arrive. I was horrified to the point of feeling literally sick! I took a printout of the parts and we left, wondering how best to proceed. The trip back in the cab stretched on forever. Traffic was terrible, and we barely seemed to be moving. Bangkok is just too big. It's a huge, busy city, and it's congested and cramped. I prefer smaller towns these days. I used to love the big city life, but lately I find myself just finding it annoying and difficult.

When we got back, I spent some time on the Internet exploring my options. I emailed my brother about the situation, and he got a quote from BMW about the cost of the parts, and it cut the bill in half. Still, it was a horrible amount to spend, with no guarantee that it would fix the problem, which I still hadn't managed to identify. So I discovered that my bike had a known fault, and there might be a recall on the casing. This suggested that the actuator arm was the problem. It was dark by then, but by the morning I intended to have it apart to look more closely, now that I had an idea what I was looking for.

I emailed a BMW dealer back in the UK—I had a friend who worked there, and she was sympathetic to my cause. By then we were hungry, so we ate at the hotel. The food was good, but the concept of not eating meat is pretty alien, and I was having to pick out little bits of shrimp from everything I ordered.

We headed out and found a bar that served Guinness and just hung about waiting for the morning so I could sort out my bike. We sluggishly rolled from one bar to another, drinking, drinking, and then drinking some more. We talked utter nonsense, which sounded like the golden wisdom of sage experts at the time, but in hindsight, was dumber than an Indian sitcom. Eventually, we ended up back at the little market near our hotel.

We ordered a tower and marvelled at the economy of a country where absolutely stunning women came to pour us drinks from a plastic tube that we bought purely for our own, personal use. These were women who wouldn't piss on us if we were on fire back in England, and yet in Bangkok they were acting like they were the lucky ones in being allowed to speak with us.

Marcin noticed one and said he thought he remembered her from a previous night, back when he had been so drunk that he wandered around getting even more drunk until the morning. He said he thought he had been rude to her, asking her to sell him food when she was only selling beer. He might have been a little short and didn't want to offend her, so he thought he had better apologise.

I watched as he approached her. I don't describe myself as an expert of body-language, but I've read some books and have been through a few classes. I usually have a good idea what's happening around me. He went over and tried to explain what he'd done, but her face was open and her posture relaxed. This shifted rapidly to a blank stare of confusion.

Marcin carried on, beating this dead-horse with a very large stick. I went over and told him that this woman had absolutely no idea what he was talking about or who he was.

He nodded in agreement. He finally told her that he just didn't want to offend her in case he'd been rude to her the previous night. In any case, maybe she wasn't actually her because "You all look alike to me." Marcin went off for more beer, leaving me wondering just exactly how on Earth I would explain that to her if she asked.

Thankfully, she didn't, and we were free to leisurely drink until we leisurely collapsed from drinking.

41

Hitting Things with a Large Spanner

Date—November 26th
Location—Bangkok, Thailand
Status—Moving on

As soon as I could, I headed to the bike with my box of cheap tools from Halfords. By then only a manual screwdriver was left, as the rest of the gear had all broken. I did have a really excellent little set of tools before, but a bungie had let me down, and it had launched itself into a car's windscreen somewhere in Italy.

Anyhow, I laid the bike on the ground, which is always a disconcerting thing to do for a man who grew up on sports-bikes, as if the concepts of sports-bikes and growing up weren't mutually exclusive. Those kinds of machines are flimsy and surrounded by extremely expensive plastic that doesn't enjoy contact with the ground; enduro and well-built adventure motorcycles fare rather better against the unforgiving embrace of solid tarmac.

I stripped off the clutch housing and had a look inside. To my surprise, everything was in perfect working order. The actuator arm was absolutely exactly as it should be—it had no missing teeth and no signs of wear. It was like I was looking inside a brand new machine, which was actually incredibly annoying. There were no signs of anything that shouldn't be working absolutely perfectly and no hint at a cause for why the thing was trying to rattle itself apart like a petrol-driven sex-toy set on full-power.

I cleaned away the oil and looked pretty closely but just couldn't find anything wrong with anything. Eventually, I checked out the bearing the actuator runs in, and sure enough, it was twisted and pushed back away from the edge by around five millimetres, maybe six. So I hammered it back into place with the large spanner I used for removing the wheel nuts and tried putting it back together. The teeth didn't line up, and the bearing got pushed back out when I twisted the lever the wrong way.

Suddenly it all made sense. I'd had to strip off the clutch cable to load the bike, and the lever was left hanging on the side, sticking out. Someone doing the crating, maybe even I, must have pushed or leant on the lever and forced the bearing out of line. Once it was dropped back into the proper place the vibrations vanished, and the clutch felt smooth and crisp, better than before, in fact.

My bike had come with a thirty-three bhp conversion kit on it when I first bought her, so I was assuming that at some point a previous owner had been a learner. They are notorious for abusing the clutch, so maybe it had always been slightly out of line. It wasn't now and seemed absolutely fine once again. If only my other problems could be fixed by beating them with a really large spanner. I had considered it for Marcin on more than one occasion.

While exploring what few options I had, I had contacted my favourite BMW dealer. I was on good terms with the staff, even though I was me and most people find that horribly offensive. My brother even bought bikes from them professionally, or at least not totally unprofessionally. One of the staff there was on the case and was making progress investigating the clutch recall issue.

She now reported that apparently there wasn't a recall at all, but the work was done on bikes brought in with clutch issues. By all accounts, if my bike had the problems as they were described, then the actuator would have fallen to bits by now, and for all I knew at that point, the casing could have been the new version. I was keeping on with my research in case there was a possibility of getting the upgrade, if it could be done out there in Thailand, but now I knew of the issue and had fixed it, it might be safer to just leave it as it was.

So we had the problem covered pretty quickly, and then my friend, Rat, arrived to join us. She was my girlfriend's best friend, and we'd met a few times before. We went out for lunch at the local MK so that we could catch up while Marcin sulked and grumbled about missing his bike.

MK is a strange, distinctly Thai place, where there's a big bubbling pot of oily water you drop raw ingredients into. The Thais love it; westerners tend to not love it so much. Marcin was incredulous and ate everything that was put in front of him, even appalling looking animal parts with tentacles and eyeballs sticking out everywhere. Nothing phased him.

That evening she kindly went with us and helped us with picking up the KTM. Everything was so much easier with the help of someone who knew their way around, and we went directly there. The place was very large, with a huge car-park out front. Behind the glass fascia were an array of stunningly beautiful, but horribly flawed, machinery designed predominantly to separate people from their bank-balance.

We had seen nothing like this when we had gone looking for it ourselves, so clearly, we had been very lost the entire time.

They'd fixed a shopping list of issues but had found nothing that could explain the cutting out. Marcin placed a lot of trust in the repairs, but I was less enthusiastic and felt he had put a lot of misplaced faith in KTM engineers. After all, some of them had put his bike together in the first place!

That evening Marcin decided for us that we should see a more lively place than before. Up to that point, we'd been concerned primarily with dealing with our own stupidity, which had been a full-time job. Now we had a little free time, and I had no excuse not to go out and enjoy myself. I agreed that so long as he could navigate us to whatever it was that he had in mind, then I was happy to tag along.

We made our way to some grim backstreet in the seedy underbelly of Bangkok; and parts of Bangkok are seedier than a McDonald's burger-bun. The street was poorly lit, with red neon-signs adding to the low-quality impression it painted unmistakably on our psyche. That place was about grabbing money at any cost. Girls with nowhere left to fall sold the last things they had left, and men used people as pieces of meat. It was all very much more grim than the Internet had suggested when Marcin had googled "fun things to do in Bangkok." Certainly, having the last lingering shreds of your faith in humanity ripped out of you didn't seem like fun to me.

We were approached pretty quickly by a gentleman who clearly wasn't a gentleman at all. He introduced himself as "Mister Heng," presumably because the name *Satan* was already taken. He asked what exactly it was we were looking for, since all tastes could be catered for. He gave me a very funny look when I asked about doubling the power-output of a Rotax single without adding any extra weight. Marcin normally asked for something dead to be brought to him, but he said nothing along those lines, since this was a place where that could very easily be made to happen, and human meat probably wasn't out of the question. We opted to tell him that we were just looking for a drink, perhaps he knew of a good bar where a couple of weary travellers could get a few beers and not have to plumb the depths of depravity to get there.

Of course, he knew the very place.

He led us through the crumbling brick streets below the flickering neon signs that painted the place with an unnatural palette of clashing colours. The screams of girls trying to get us to screw them for money was washed away in a tide of cat-calls with offers of every single male bodily part fitting into every possible female cavity. It was not a classy place. Eventually we were taken to the perfect bar where we could just get a beer and leave all that behind.

Of course, it was no such thing.

A row of very attractive young girls were led out, each with a number on their dresses. Beside us was a table of Asian businessmen, plump and aged, wearing perfect dark suits that didn't fit any of them properly. The girls stood before the men as they greedily chose the ones they wanted.

Mister Heng explained they were Japanese, and the girls loved that. He told us, "Japs have small dicks and big money. Perfect for whores."

Marcin and I just repeated the fact that we just wanted a beer and never wanted anything to do with any of that. Did fat Japanese businessmen have big money and small dicks? Did whores love that? Now I had that thought in my mind where there was barely enough room for Rotax singles.

Several of the girls were begging, at that point, for us to call their number. They just seemed to want to sit with us and be spared an evening of being mauled by little men who may or may not have money that was inversely proportional to the size of their genitals. It seemed surreal to be telling very attractive girls who were desperate to sit with us that we just didn't want their company. Marcin was uncomfortable, just as I was, and we finished up quickly and wished Mr. Heng a good evening. He grunted and walked away, presumably angry at misjudging us and wasting time without earning a commission. We were happy to be misjudged.

Misjudging things was the order of the evening. From there, we blundered into an upstairs bar. We should have just packed up and gone and found a whole different part of town, but we didn't. We were invited to the "Ping-pong" bar and wandered in for another beer.

What we now knew was that *ping-pong* didn't mean anyone would be knocking little plastic balls about with paddles. It meant that a very talented young lady would be using her super-human gifts to fire things into the crowd, using only the power of her vagina.

Marcin and I discussed this philosophically over a surprisingly cheap set of beers. What would it be like to have intercourse with someone who had, at that point, moved on to firing little pointed darts that were bursting large blue balloons? I imagined it would be an interesting experience but a quite depressing thing to have to explain to an expert in venereal diseases when your penis began to drop off. Marcin, quite rightly, posed the question of how someone even discovers they have that kind of talent. Presumably, there's a situation where a very bored young lady is sitting around naked in a room with a lot of balloons and has a pathological hatred of them.

It was time to leave, but that wasn't as easy as we thought it was going to be. Suddenly, the cheap beer situation explained itself. As we made our way to the exit, the female manager, a frightening blob of sheer hatred began screaming at us in a voice so shrill that it seemed like she must have been a cat and someone, unseen behind her, had run over her tail.

She squealed angrily that we hadn't spent enough money and demanded hundreds of dollars before we would be allowed to go. I was put on negotiating duties and explained that we were, in fact, leaving, and she wasn't getting anything more from us than the price of the beers we'd already drunk. Marcin was happy that I was entirely representing his feelings in the matter.

She barked that she would call security and have us beaten up. I guess that after this night of seeing just how low that place could sink that actually sounded like a terrific idea, and I told we'd love for that to happen. She looked a little bit surprised at our life choices, as many people did, and followed through on her threat.

Two burly men came up and blocked the exit, but while they were solidly built, they were only around five feet tall. Marcin and I glowered down on them and looked perfectly happy with fighting our way out. The manager screamed that she wanted more money. We shook our heads firmly and told them no.

The two guards looked at one another, looked back at her, and said, "Let them go."

We left with a fun story to tell our kids one day, and we went back to the hotel, stopping in the little market first to finish the job we'd started.

42

The Monster

Date—November 27th
Location—Bangkok, Thailand
Status—PARTY!

The next day we went to Pattaya. This town was famous for its red light district, but there was so much more to it than that. There were shotguns too! And dysentery.

Part of the justification for riding so quickly was to earn additional time to spend having fun in Thailand before splitting off at the border. We had made up enough time to justify a few days to let our hair down, even though I literally had none to keep up. I had suggested Pattaya, as I'd been there a few times before—a seaside town that thought it was the Asian version of the French Riviera, but was far, far from it in every possible sense. It was more like a real-world version of a priest's worst nightmare, in fact.

But, perhaps, not a Catholic priest.

Marcin had Googled it and came to me with a deep frown. It said that the town was the capital of filth and depravity for the entire world. Yes, that was it, I told him. He nodded solemnly and agreed it would be ideal for us, before breaking into a wide and happy smile.

We got up pretty late. The chest infection was taking hold by then; my breathing was getting painful, and there was a tickle in my lungs that I didn't like at all. Still, we packed up and headed out of the hotel. We dragged ourselves round to Rat's house, and she had made us breakfast. I don't mean a bowl of cornflakes either—this was proper Thai food, and mountains of it. Everything was delicious, and I didn't even know she could cook. Even Marcin was impressed, and nothing much impresses him.

Rat lived where my girlfriend soon would, in a house that had a salon downstairs in what looked like it had once been a car dealership. When we got there, there were customers there having their hair messed around with. I was introduced around, since I didn't really know any of the people, all of whom were friends of my partner.

A ladyboy was having his/herself repaired. She was very overweight, with dark skin and a white painted face, which had a ton of makeup plastered inexpertly all over it. This person was having something unspeakable done to his/her long, dyed hair that caused him/her to wince in pain.

Marcin leaned over and gaped in confusion while this poor victim of beauty treatment peered up at him from the sink in horror, pressing back from Marcin's fixed stare. "Jack," he said, while only inches from her face and pointing directly at her. "What is this monster?"

Rat had kindly offered to let us leave some of our stuff behind with her so we could travel light. I have been to Pattaya before—it was a party town and had a lot of interesting things to see and do, so long as you're not stupid. We were, but we were not *that* stupid! Well I'm not . . . except when I am.

Both of us by then believed our mechanical troubles were behind us, and so it was nice to jump back on the bikes. It was the first time I had ridden mine since the clutch had caused my difficulties, and she now ran perfectly well. There were no problems with the clutch at all, but the chain had many, many dry links and was way, way past its useful life. I was unreasonably hoping a good soak in petrol would give it a new lease of life, once the dirt and grime has been coaxed out properly. Of course, all that would have to wait.

We packed light. Marcin just took his top box, and I just took my pannier bags, all of which were detachable. We headed out with plenty of enthusiasm and not much else really. It was great to be back on the bikes after a few days off of them. The sun was hot—too hot! Sweat poured off me under the weight of my gear, as it reached forty-two degrees, and it felt like it was even hotter than that. The road was familiar, and apart from the stationary traffic in Bangkok, we made good time. We soon hit the toll roads and, with them, the first of our problems.

It seemed that motorbikes weren't allowed on motorways. I had no idea about that, since I'd never been in Thailand with a motorcycle to try it before. We were stopped by the police, who told us that in broken English. We tried to argue that a law intended to stop scooters shouldn't apply to full-sized machines, but we got nowhere, so it obviously wasn't just a single officer being difficult. It was the law, and we would have to abide by it.

So we turned off onto the secondary roads, but that was a three-lane carriageway in better condition than we'd seen in weeks of riding, so we were still very happy boys. The road went on, and the scenery got more familiar. Once we finally got into Pattaya town, I recognised everything straight away.

I spotted a dingy little cabin that served food. I'd eaten there on my first trip to Thailand, and it had been some of the best food I'd had in the whole two weeks I was there. We didn't stop, but it was still interesting to see it again. It was nice that everything was familiar yet new again, since I was now seeing it from my own motorcycle. Within a few more minutes we were right in the heart of the town.

I took the lead from Marcin, who still had the only working sat-nav, and tried to find the place I had stayed in last time. It was cheap and really quite good, but the one-way system down the back-streets meant that I couldn't get to it. In the end, we found a street covered with hotels and rooms and a row of larger motorcycles for rent. I liked the idea of ours being among them and not attracting so much attention. I wandered into the first place we saw, and it was cheap—a room was only £10 with free breakfast, Wi-Fi, and even free laundry. We saw the rooms, and they were fine—we even had a balcony stretching out the front.

It was getting later in the day than I thought, but that was a good thing with the ferocious sun belting down on us. We decided to have a look around straight away while it was still relatively tame and then go out to a bar later and have some beers. We wandered around and got something to eat before heading back to stock up on water.

We ate some Thai food at a nice place that, while catering for tourists, still seemed essentially honest. I was served first and spoke a little of the language from my other visits—enough to explain with some Thai and broken English that I was a vegetarian. The waitress offered me some noodles and a stuffed omelette. She turned to Marcin and asked if he was a vegetarian too. He reddened suddenly, slammed his fist angrily into the table, and demanded, "No, kill something and bring it to me."

That night we headed out for a few quiet beers. Obviously, what happens in Pattaya stays in Pattaya, so the worst of it must forever remain untold. In any case, here's what happened: We [censored] and [censored] and ping-pong balls were shooting everywhere propelled only by [censored] and [censored] giant black rubber [censored] and [censored] until everything went dark and he just stood there with his mouth open and his eyes were locked open in stunned amazement that they can [censored] and [censored] and I knew at that moment that I would never eat a banana again.

Eventually we found a rock bar, where an Asian band was belting out rock tunes backed by a couple of musicians, and they were doing a sterling job. We hung out there and listened to some slightly wrong renditions of famous rock tunes. We got them to play *Born to be Wild*, which had jammed on my MP3 player while riding through Pakistan and had since become our favourite tune. In all, I think the night was basically successful, since nobody died and nothing else [censored] and [censored].

But how we survived that is anyone's guess.

43

No Kind of Fruit Is Safe from Marcin's Huge Weapon

Date—November 28th
Location—Pattaya, Thailand
Status—Had enough now. Need bed

By the morning even the idea of beer was starting to make me sad. The chest infection had firmly taken hold and wasn't planning on going anywhere without me. We were still in a mood to celebrate, but we were also weakened from the same experience that was fuelling our emotional high. We'd suffered weeks of constant stress, harsh physical conditions, and poor hygiene, and it had taken its toll on us both.

We met up as arranged, since Thailand was so cheap we were finally enjoying separate rooms, and we headed down for breakfast, which turned out to just be toast and coffee, and the coffee was cold. None of that mattered, of course, for the same reason as the rooms. Food was so cheap we could just wander around all day eating, and it wouldn't put a dent in our budget. Marcin would probably do exactly that, in fact.

After eating poorly but feeling strangely well-fed, I went next door and went about trying to get some kind of medicine that would take the edge off the nagging feeling that I might die soon. I was lucky enough to find a woman working in the pharmacy that spoke better English than Marcin, not that that's saying much, and she just took one look at me, made a sad face, and got something that she swore would make me feel better.

I got something for the cough and something to fight the infection, all issued over the counter by someone who gave a passable impression of knowing exactly what she was doing. Considering she was coughing more than me, I wasn't too optimistic but was ready to try anything.

So with breakfast done, we slowly—very slowly—headed back out into town. We had decided to go over to the island, a little place off the coast where you can hire scooters and guns. It remained to be seen which was going to be more dangerous with us in control of them. Marcin had never actually shot anything before, and after being surrounded by weapons throughout much of our trip, he wanted something to go bang in his hand. Normally, Thailand was able to accommodate that need, one way or another. I had grown up in a shooting family, so I knew the basics. My parents were county "small bore" champions and had taught me how to kill at a very young age, and I'd shot "practical combat pistols" competitively, without shooting off any of my or anyone else's toes.

We had a wait for the ferry, so we went and got some food while the lumbering craft docked for the crowds to step aboard. I was still hungry, since my guts had taken every opportunity to empty out their entire contents.

We were still very much not right in that department. I didn't suspect the Thai food, since I'd never had any problems before and believed it was still a lingering problem with our recent ride through the open sewers of the Middle East. I ordered a cheese omelette—I love cheese, and it was hard to find there, for some reason, so it was something of a luxury. Marcin claimed he wasn't hungry but found room for something, and then something else besides.

We caught the ferry, and it plodded its way over, taking roughly forty-five minutes. It was a bargain—only thirty bhats to get over, about seventy-five pence, but the trip back cost 150. That was typical of the tourist industry in that part of the world, and everything else in that part of the world, truth be told.

We finally got there and within minutes were offered a ride to the shooting range. It was actually really difficult—much more so than it had to be. We had to hire scooters, and the staff made everything very awkward. I negotiated, as I was by then used to doing, and bartered the price down to around half what they were originally asking. I then realised I'd saved next to nothing, since they were incredibly cheap to start with, and felt a bit silly about the whole thing.

Finally, we got under way. My little scooter was okay, but Marcin's seemed to be less powerful. The maintenance on the island must have been fairly poor, since only a handful of people even lived on it. The difference could also easily be accounted for by his sheer size, which was offset by an engine that had less power than his motorcycle's starter motor. We finally made it to the range, and it was not what I was used to and not exactly what I'd expected.

Safety standards were non-existent, and the few guns on offer were as poorly maintained as the bikes. Marcin went first and chose a rifle—a Sig Sauer 552. He didn't realise it was just a sporting conversion with a 22lr sleeve and was about as exciting as throwing pebbles at a lake. To give him credit, he hit most of the little metal targets he aimed at, and most people don't even get close on their first time.

The prices were insane, so I settled for a clip in a Glock 19 9mm pistol. There was a choice of two, but the one I chose was apparently broken, so I got left with the other one. It jammed on the second shot and grouped at around eight inches at only twenty yards. Again, not quite what I was used to. We were both disappointed and ended up going for a ride on the scooters to forget all about it. We found a viewing point and snapped a few pics, but clearly Marcin couldn't get the lacklustre experience out of his head, and he began dwelling on it, as he often did.

We went for a ride around and found a viewing tower somewhere near the middle of the island that offered excellent views all around.

We parked up and climbed the steps to the top, gasping at the heat with every step. When we reached the pinnacle the views were certainly interesting, since a young Thai girl was naked and being photographed for some soft-core Internet pornography. We laughed like young boys until she looked close to crying like a little girl. The photographer milled about nervously, while she huddled beneath a towel. We weren't embarrassed and invited them to carry on, but they just smiled awkwardly and waited for us to leave. We weren't in a hurry.

He wanted to shoot something with a bit more power. The dwelling on it had got the better of Marcin, as we both knew it would. I suggested the Franchi SPAS 12 shotgun would deliver the thrill he was expecting. We headed back to the ATM and got the cash for him to have another go. He got seven rounds for about £15, which was a bit steep for my taste, even for a tourist trap like that. He asked for advice on how not to die, so I showed him how to stand and how to hold the butt in close to his shoulder. He refused the ear-protection, and I laughed at him and backed away, so he thought better of it and wore them after all.

He racked the pump and fired at a melon they'd set up for a target. The gun was in poor order, and the shot exploded out with a plume of acrid black smoke blasting out of every orifice. Marcin was jolted backwards and was grinning wildly like a kid with a new toy. Somehow, even the pump-action combat shotgun managed to jam up, but he seemed to have fun with it and enthused excitedly that he liked that one better.

After that, he was hungry, but then pretty much everything makes him hungry, even eating. We stopped on the way back to the beach for him to eat some deep fried dead things on sticks before we headed back to the ferry.

Along the way we were offered a ride on a smaller passenger speed-boat for only 200 bahts each, only £1 more than the slow, boring, plodding ferry was going to cost. We took that, and it was far more fun. It crunched and jumped over the waves, crashing down hard until doors on cupboards fell off inside and the female passengers screamed in horrified terror. It was cool, and we were back to shore in around ten minutes and delivered right to where we were staying.

We were told that we'd been left a message at the hotel. The previous evening a girl had strongly insisted that I take her number. I explained that I had a girlfriend and politely declined. I simply assumed she'd not taken no for an answer but was told by the woman at reception that it wasn't her. We called it up, and it was actually from a fellow biker that had previously lived in the UK. He had moved to Pattaya some six years before and had seen our UK plates and wanted to meet the riders of those horribly filthy motorcycles. We arranged to head out to eat and meet him later at our hotel for a drink.

I guess the omelette had whetted my appetite, and I fancied something that had a taste of home. We found a kebab shop run by an actual Turk, so we decided to give that a try. I had falafel, and Marcin had something with meat in it. It was spicy, but far and away the best Turkish food I had eaten outside of Germany. The food in Turkey had actually been quite poor. That hadn't surprised me—the pizza in Italy was rubbish, I couldn't find a good Cornish pasty in Cornwall, and nowhere anywhere in the Black Forest sold Black Forest Gateaux.

The world is a silly place.

We had a quick chat about food with the owner, who seemed happy to be appreciated, and then we set off to meet the guy who had left the message. We grabbed some beers and sat in the lobby, waiting for a few minutes until he turned up on a huge, noisy Harley-Davidson. His name was Phil, and after polite introductions, we wandered down to the beach and chatted for hours about life in that part of the world. He had an interesting perspective on the red-light district and things in general. He had the sort of firm beliefs that can only come from years of hard experience and spoke with authority about how things were there.

The previous night we had walked through it, and I had begun to find the whole thing a bit on the offensive side. You couldn't walk a few metres without being offered a show or a good time, and it all grated on my nerves quite quickly.

Phil was older and wiser than we were and told us that Pattaya is "Reject City." He explained that all the girls are damaged goods; they've got kids they can't support, husbands who ran off, and families that just don't want them and will no longer accept them—although they'll happily accept their money, of course. Females in that country have little earning power—they make less than £100 a month in honest jobs and, obviously, can't live on that, even more so when they have to send money home to support their children.

The ex-pat men are damaged too; mostly they're fed up with their home countries, they're old or fat, or just not attractive to women, he went on. A quick look up from behind a bottle of unbelievably fizzy beer showed that his assessment was mostly right on the money. The place simply wasn't crawling with young lads on a party weekend; it was full of guys and women simply making the best of it in an economy that is hopelessly biased against the human condition and serves only the interests of the rich.

Later that evening we all split off and went our own ways. Marcin and I were tired but not tired enough to sleep, so we wandered down the side roads that housed endless arrays of bars with endless desperate girls barking at endless desperate men.

I saw a pool table in one, and we both agreed that it would be a nice change of pace from having ladyboys trying to grab our genitals. We went inside, and two girls offered to join us. We simply huffed in weary resignation and told them we just wanted a beer and a game of pool, nothing else. They served us a beer and asked if they could play against us.

We agreed and got very badly beaten at pool by two women who were barely large enough to reach the table. We bought them a beer and sat down, eventually settling into chatting with them. I was straight up from the outset, explaining I had a girlfriend, and she asked to sit and chat anyway, as it was rare to actually talk to someone who wasn't looking for something from her.

We talked, and I listened to her story. I heard how her husband had beat her, how her family had threatened to feed her son to the pigs unless she sent money home, and how trapped she was in the life she had. She was very open, seemed happy to just tell me her story, and glad to have someone listen to it. We spoke for hours, but then it was time to go.

She offered to take me to her home—no charge. I insisted that I couldn't, and she eventually got angry and walked off in a mood.

On the way home Marcin said I was a bastard. I told him to explain how I had done anything wrong to anyone. He said that I had talked with her; I had cost her some time when she could have been out finding a customer and making money. The thought had literally never occurred to me, but maybe he had a point. To be fair, though, I had been straight with her throughout. Maybe her experience told her I must have wanted something after all. When it comes to somewhere as deeply confused as Pattaya, maybe there are no right answers?

44

Falling Action

Date—November 29th
Location—Pattaya, Thailand
Mood—Knackered

It had been a fun time, but we were ready to leave Pattaya. It can be a nice place to visit, but we'd been pushing our livers since we'd arrived in Kathmandu, and I was starting to feel completely drained and totally washed out. I needed a rest.

We packed up to the usual attention from the staff, who were all very friendly and interested. The woman running the hotel made jokes about the bikes and our journey, as well as perfectly valid comments questioning our sanity and possibly our intelligence. She eventually explained, sounding exasperated at our choices, "I wouldn't marry you; you're fucking idiots." We laughed and grunted and pretty-much agreed with her and then headed for our bikes and off to look for a breakfast somewhere else.

We found a place nearby that looked good. We checked the menu, which had a variety of well-chosen things offered together in a selection of set menus. I have no idea why they bothered, because what we ordered was nothing even remotely similar to what we got. I asked for a cheese omelette and toast and got scrambled eggs and bacon. Marcin ordered a set American breakfast and got a pot of flowers with a shoe in it.

If you parked two valuable things in London, such as our bikes, which in Thailand were worth five or six times what they are back home, they would be gone by the time we returned, but they were left in the biggest and most questionable area in all of Thailand, and nobody touched them.

They were respectfully photographed and then simply left alone. In London I had once returned to the parking bay to find my motorcycle knocked over and just lying in the road. I once parked it behind my work and returned to it to find a screwdriver had failed to overcome the ignition, but the guy had given it a good enough try that there was no way to get it started myself.

The ride back was uneventful in the extreme. I had been noticing a slight pulsing through the power-train though. With a heavy heart, I came to consider that the vibrations from the clutch may have done some permanent damage. Under acceleration there was a shake, a slight shudder which she'd not had before. She had developed a slight power-wobble past sixty-five mph to go along with it. She was tired—we both were, in fact. It had been a hell of a trip for both of us, and we'd made great time all along the way, but we'd done it at the expense of not giving her the maintenance she needed. In a few days I was going to take her somewhere quiet to clean her up and give her the attention she so richly deserved. That, or she would likely break down and give me the punishment that I so richly deserved.

We had to go back to Bangkok and pick up our gear first. Marcin did, at any rate. For him, his life was about to continue back on the road. In only a few days he'd be crossing into Malaysia, and I wouldn't see him again until the next year, when he was planning to come over on a visit.

It was a strange feeling, knowing we'd be splitting off. We'd been together on the road for a long time—not a huge amount of time actually, but the busiest, most intense experience I'd had since

I dated a paranoid schizophrenic with an interest in sharp cutl We'd been through so much, and by some miracle, we'd survived

When we started out I wasn't at all sure we'd get along, but now we were like old friends. Perhaps we were more than that—li brothers, maybe. I had done more with him during this time thar had in years with any of my other friends. We were close by now we'd been forced to share a bed, socks, underwear, and even a toil while he had a stomach bug. You don't do that without getting to b close friends, or killing one another. It had proven to be a fine lin between the two, and more so than you might think. Years later, w would get together and both of us would casually refer to ourselve as family without a second thought. We had started to think tha way already.

We finally got back into Bangkok via the same roads that were perfectly adequate for us. Thai roads were built cheap; they're smooth sheets of concrete with reasonably good driving standards. Traffic is certainly bad in places, and there are plenty of people driving beyond their abilities, but it's generally better than most parts of Southeast Asia.

Marcin had slowed down a lot. His riding was less intense, and it seemed like he'd lost his edge. I could tell how much he was enjoying Thailand. The weather was treating us well, the roads were easy going, the scenery was great, and we'd been having a lot of fun together. His moaning and griping was a thing of the past, and everything just seemed pleasantly easy. I led the way along the roads, and he was edging behind, losing pace with my smaller, slower bike. That was unheard of.

Now that he was back on the road and his trip was truly back underway, he didn't seem so much like himself. Neither of us were well—the cold/flu bug we had was biting us both hard, and it had robbed us of a lot of our enthusiasm. He was coughing like I had been a few days ago, and his stomach was in a bad way, even by the standards of *his* stomach.

After we collected our gear, we hit the road out of Bangkok and began the ride to the border in earnest. We both had sufficient experience to know that it was going to be the hardest part of the day. City traffic was always the worst, and Bangkok was especially bad. It wasn't easy to get into or out of the massive city sprawl, which in places, was little more than a car-park.

had been lucky, and it hadn't been too bad getting in, but ic was starting to congeal as we left, and we had to fight for ch of distance we covered. The timing was against us, but s nothing we could do about that. It was a reality of the

ow, my trip was over, and I let Marcin do it his way without t from me. I had no interest in the pace or direction—I was observer from then on, and it left us both feeling oddly about everything. The mood was strangely unfamiliar, en. It was like, even under the beautifully clear blue skies, ad was following us closely along the way.

problems came back with the KTM, as could have been y predicted without supernatural abilities of any kind. a clean bill of health from a trusted KTM service centre, nning poorly, coughing and sputtering as we made our g. Marcin reported that the engine felt choked. He said lid it with the top box and panniers on, like maybe they nehow blocking the flow of air. I still suspected that it was t of being stuck in motionless traffic, but we were both just g really. Either way, it was far worse before, and it ran well n to get us out of Bangkok. We made it out eventually, but it hell of a slog, and neither of us were really in the mood for it.

e stopped off for fuel and got some water from the mart that et off at the side. By then, we were sweating buckets. The idity was horrible, and it wasn't even that particularly hot there It got up to thirty-five degrees, by my sensor, and I had been hailand while it had climbed to forty-five. At that temperature aps your will to live and your skin sizzles beneath the sun. otorcycle gear is heavy and hot, and it's not uncomfortable when u're moving along; but sitting stationary for any length of time nder a beating hot sun with your engine wafting hot air up to you s a whole different story.

I started to see things I knew as we edged our way awkwardly out of the city. The route was one I'd followed before with my partner, and it was nice to see things looking familiar, a sure sign we weren't doing anything too radically stupid, even by our incredibly low standards.

While we stopped at one point, I casually mentioned Hua Hin, a place I had been with my girlfriend before on the way back from a trip to the jungles down south. It must have hit a chord, because before I knew it, he was plotting it as a route. I didn't mind—the night was setting in, and I was tired, the heat was draining the last of my strength, and from the look of Marcin, he was suffering right along with me.

We did, indeed, head to the town, and we found a hotel pretty quickly that met our budget. You could get a place in a nice guesthouse for only £4, but we spent a bit more for a room with Wi-Fi and other little luxuries, including free breakfast, and it only came to £10 between us, which was still a bargain.

Dinner was a bowl of Thai noodles for me, and Marcin had almost everything else on the menu in various quantities. The food was good. It seemed to get better the further you travelled from Bangkok, not that there's anything wrong with it there. In Pattaya they cater too much to the tourists, and the food and the prices suffer. Out along this road it was still very tourist-oriented but still a bit Thai too, which was nice—a refreshing break from the gaudy glowing neon signs offering everything from alcoholic intoxication to unspeakable acts of human depravity, often involving ping-pong balls in places that were never designed to house them.

We had a beer on the beach after dinner and just sat there putting the world to rights under a clear sky with the sound of waves gently licking the sand in front of us. Mostly we discussed motorcycles and Marcin's growing dissatisfaction with the troublesome KTM. He had chosen it purely because of the power; I had chosen mine due to a more complex set of criteria, but neither of us were completely satisfied. I could have had a Honda XR650—a lighter, cheaper motorcycle that I could have rebuilt to whatever specifications I wanted for half the cost of the BMW, and it would have been a bit quicker besides. We both agreed that on the road all that mattered was simplicity and reliability. It was really all we cared about now.

There had been a stretch in Pakistan while we were riding to Quetta. It was muddy, rocky, and had no real road. It had been a dangerous region to ride through and one that was patrolled by police vans with fifty-calibre anti-aircraft guns bolted to the roof. Right then, realisation had struck us both.

At some point, if you're doing it right, then it all comes down to one thing with an adventure bike. On any trip there will come a time when adjustable suspension, flexible pegs, variable ignition, ABS, or any other pointless gadget won't matter in the slightest. If you're having an adventure and pushing yourself enough, then all that will matter is the ability of that back wheel to keep turning so that you have a good chance of getting out of the stupid situation you just managed to get yourself into. Everything else after that point is just extra weight, extra cost, and extra problems. Even Marcin agreed.

Stretching the extra power from the KTM motor had made the bike more complex, and therefore, larger and more troublesome. The BMW had come with a state-of-the-art engine-management system that could adapt to any environment. In practice it struggled a great deal, and I would have got better service from a good upgraded carb on a simpler, older engine.

You can't do a long trip without gaining a fresh perspective, and mine was that I wanted things to be cleaner and simpler.

We headed back and had an early night without any more alcohol. An early night was something both of us needed. I later regretted the fact that I wasn't completely intoxicated when Marcin had a bout of very loud explosive stomach problems in our shared toilet.

45

The Perfect Crime

Date—November 30th
Location—Hua Hin, Thailand
Status—Competent, for once

Breakfast was included, so we had some. It was a buffet, and between us we managed to essentially remove it from existence. It finished at ten, which was roughly the time we started eating. This was in stark contrast to our time through the Middle East, where we'd been stretching the hours as far as we could, starting early, riding into darkness, and taking barely any time between to even think, or whatever Marcin's version of thinking was. Mine was increasingly questionable.

Marcin's internal organs were not on our side. He went into the toilet and had a massive, noisy, and foul-smelling eruption on the pan, which almost shook the walls and definitely cracked the foundations of my faith in human biology. After the first of many explosions, he called out, "Oh, it doesn't smell like flowers in here!"

He was perfectly correct. The smell of flowers were nowhere to be found.

The little vent under the door let the sheer awesome power of his guts out to do battle with the very tenets of decency. After a bit more of that, we went to breakfast, hoping against hope that he could hold whatever evil remained inside back from the outside world. Sadly, breakfast was almost over by the time we got his anus under control, but what was left was very good. It was a buffet with rice and Thai dishes, toast, tea and coffee, and then two separate people asked if we wanted eggs and brought us them the way we liked them. It was all very nice, and the price was even nicer.

After breakfast, there was more unpleasantness from Marcin's foul innards behind closed doors, which went on long enough to have sacrificed an entire toilet roll to the gods of poor hygiene. He certainly does nothing without a certain style.

How either of us survived is anyone's guess, but he came out looking rather worse for wear, and we headed back to our bikes before the gas did permanent damage to our lungs. We loaded up and shipped out.

The road out of Hua Hin was familiar again, the same road I had followed the last time I was there. My girlfriend had taken me to visit the town with her best friend. I'm still not really sure why—it was just a lot of people selling key rings and expensive coffee. They thought I'd like it, but after the jungles, full of the a far more real and interesting side of Thailand, it all seemed a bit of a disappointment to me—like a silver artificial Christmas tree pretending to be the real thing. This time it seemed better—it was a nice place to stop on the road, but little more. What I did know was that the roads ahead were friendly, with plenty of places for fuel and food, and there was little that could go wrong and cause us problems.

At least, that's what I thought. I'm not sure why I kept thinking things like that, after the world had showed me so many times how resourceful it was at causing us problems. To be fair, we caused most of them ourselves, and what was coming for us was really more of the same.

Marcin started driving more like Marcin—his speed edged up, and he started overtaking everything. He made a lot of mistakes along the way though, which wasn't like him at all. He rides fast and thinks slow, but one thing you couldn't take away from Marcin is that he knows how to ride a motorcycle. He was born to it, and the KTM sat beneath him like an extension of his own body.

But this time he wobbled, he missed things by way too narrow a margin, and although it would be easy to say it's not like him to ride so dangerously—that would be a lie—it wasn't like him do those things quite so often. He wasn't well; whatever he had wrong with him was affecting his judgement.

We made it out onto the main road, which also looked familiar, and we plodded on, with me keeping a watchful eye on him in the mirror as I lead the way and tried to keep him under control. It was a hot day, but when we were moving it seemed okay. The wind blew through my vented jacked and trousers and kept me cool enough to feel quite comfortable.

Stopping was another issue. While stationary I could take off my helmet and jacket, but my trousers turned into a portable sauna, and my T-shirt became a wet rag on my back, which then became cold and clammy as soon as we started riding again.

Even worse, if we took off our gear, we had to put it back on. Our helmets were awash with a foul-smelling cold moisture, a blend of cooled-down sweat and rotting foam that you just don't want to put your head in. Sadly, and rather predictably, the heat stopped my fuel system from working properly, and she refused to siphon. That was no problem for us, since petrol stations were easy to find along the way.

We stopped for petrol, and I filled the main tank. That was when I saw it—the reason for the odd pulsing sensation from the drive train. The Super-Heavy-Duty DID bullet-proof chain that was guaranteed for 50k miles was knackered, quite completely and thoroughly. It had not just loosened but had finally given in to the abuse I had heaped upon it. The bearing between the two plates of the primary link was missing. That meant it had shattered and fallen out. I'd never heard of that happening before and was quite proud of myself.

That explained the twitching that I'd noticed since we'd arrived in Thailand. I had checked it over and lubricated the system quite carefully, but the cracks in the roller must have been too small to be seen. The damage had been done, and no amount of WD-40 was going to fix it. The sides were taking the strain but had bent. I couldn't carry on in good conscience, knowing she was that damaged. The chain wouldn't hold up—the link was wrecked.

We rolled to the side and bickered as we always did. In the end, I decided it needed to be fixed, and Marcin couldn't argue with that fact, even though he did try to.

Marcin was carrying a chain splitter, so we got the primary link away, hoping it could be reconstructed. Unfortunately, he was slightly heavy-handed, and the link was effectively destroyed in the process. Not only that, the splitter tool snapped too, and that was meant to be made from toughened steel, so I had no idea how the hell he managed to do that.

So, by then, we were slightly worse off than when we'd started, as my chain was now a long straight thing, instead of a long looped thing, and was only going to be capable of allowing me to ride twenty centimetres along at a time. Suddenly, the border looked a very long way away.

I tried using stainless steel bolts as pins to drift out a link, but they bent instantly, and the links refused to give way. I found one in my tools that just barely did the job, and it just managed to press out a pin and get another link off. We did the same trick and split another. With the wheel rolled all the way in, we could just reconnect the chain . . . in theory.

We had a bent pin and sealed it with two very knackered X-rings, and we then tapped the pin back in until it was just touching the other link plate. With much growling and shouting, mostly at one another, we got what was left of the clamp tool to push the bastard thing back into the link plate until it worked.

There was no getting it out; there would never be any way of getting it out, but that suited me perfectly. We adjusted it up, with Marcin sitting on the bike to get the tension right, and we were done. I spun the wheel, and our repair was seamless. It was a damn fine roadside bodge, and I was very proud of our resourcefulness. High fives were exchanged, and there was grinning all round.

A group of soldiers came up to us, but it was all friendly, and an exchange of warm, genuine smiles and happy nods was shared. We later got stopped by the police as well. They asked where we were from, noticing the UK plates on our machines. I told them London. He tapped the plate, and I nodded. He grinned and simply said, "Well done." That was it—we were on our way again.

We managed just thirty-five miles, and then it gave up. I lost all power to the back wheel. I rolled her into a petrol station, and this time the chain had come off the sprocket. I had assumed the repair had failed, but it was fine. I couldn't even find it, which speaks volumes to the quality of our work, but even greater volumes to how bad the rest of the chain was.

Luckily, the chain was just in need of adjusting. Clearly, the weight difference between Marcin and myself was considerably more than I had thought. I tightened it, and we rode another hundred miles with me gingerly accelerating, slowing carefully, and feeding gentle power into corners. Nothing. No hassle at all, and happily, no pulsing from the drive-train.

It gradually left my mind as we made our way along. The roads were long and generally straight, with slight, long curves into wide, sweeping bands. The verges had huge, green striking palm trees that served as constant reminders that we were in a place very far from home.

We found a hotel some time after dark, which was no mean feat on those roads, since apart from the trees, there was nothing much of anything about. We had to bump up onto a curb, which made me wince as I remembered the cobbled-together rear-end of my bike, but there was no problem, and the chain held up admirably. She would probably manage another 5,000 miles, but I was resolved to getting a new one as soon as I could find a suitable replacement. That was an issue I would deal with after we got Marcin off to the opposite side of the Malaysian border.

The motel was surprisingly decent, and everything there was even cheaper than usual. We had food from the local market—rice and two Thai dishes each, with water and a bowl of vegetables, and it came to £2 for both of us. The room was £10, but it was hard to find a motel out there, so we knew it would be slightly more expensive. That evening, we settled a hundred miles outside of Phucket.

We were still chatting about what to do next. There were only three BMW dealers in Thailand but probably dozens of places I could find a chain if I looked hard enough. We had no Internet at the motel, which cut down my options and reduced our conversations to conjecture.

We thought about going into Phucket, where I knew there was a BMW dealer. I knew that didn't, by any means, mean that they would have a suitable chain. I told Marcin that I was confident I could get to the border and that I was happy she would comfortably make it back to Bangkok in the condition she was in. I wasn't entirely confident, but that was now my problem, and I had neither the right nor the wish to make it his.

46

Goodbye

Date—December 1st
Location—Surat Thani, Thailand
Mood—Maudlin

This morning was the beginning of the end, or maybe the end of the beginning, depending on how you looked at it. This was to be our final day riding together, and it was a beautiful day indeed. The sun was high and hot, and there was hardly a cloud in the crystal blue sky, but we rode like we were back in India, in yellow smog, with everyone trying to kill us. There was definitely a gloom in the air. Marcin and I both felt it from the moment we got up and ate breakfast.

At one point along the way, he asked why I was riding so slowly. There were other things on my mind, and I hadn't even realised I had been.

Today was the day that Marcin was going to cross the Malaysian border, and I would be turning around and going back towards Bangkok to figure out what to do with the rest of my life.

It had been a slow day previously, thanks to the chain failure, so we had a fair bit of time to make up to get us back on Marcin's self-imposed schedule. We actually could have made the border the day before at the easy pace we had set ourselves, even after the problems we had. The weather was on our side, and we hoped to make the border at around 2PM. Apparently, that should have been no trouble, according to maps, GPS, and Google's best estimates.

So we headed off, and for a while, things still looked familiar. I knew my girlfriend's mother lived along that particular road somewhere, and I kept my eyes open for the turn-off, so I could use it as an estimate of our progress. I didn't manage to spot it. They all looked very much the same, and I had previously only been there at night. In fact, when we went together even she couldn't find it straight away, and she had grown up there.

Marcin wanted to make some videos, so I rode up front for a while so he could record me. I kept a steady line, but a cautious one. The driving standards dropped as we headed further south, as they did heading towards any of the borders we'd crossed. The driving had been fairly respectable in general, but it sure had its moments.

There were always a few idiots driving too fast and trying to nudge you out of the way. We saw many slow tucks that cruised along in the outside lane, making you pass on the inside while someone comes blasting up behind without looking where they're going.

On a long ride through Thailand I expected to see roughly three accidents a day. Usually it was someone driving off the road to wind up in the drainage gullies that ran alongside. Once I had seen a fuel-tanker that had crushed a row of cars against a motorway barrier, killing probably dozens of people, who were trapped in their vehicles. It was nothing compared to where we'd been, but it was still important not to relax for a moment, just in case.

The roads dragged on and on, but finally we saw a sign to the border, and we cut off at a hard ninety-degree angle and headed down the road on the final leg of the run to the border. According to the sign, it was only another forty miles to the exit. I was tired, not just because of a lack of sleep, an abundance of alcohol, flu, and stomach trouble, but because of the heat and humidity sapping what little strength I had left after all the other things did their share of the damage.

I had mentioned crashing-out at the border and maybe heading back in the morning, just hoping there would be a town there where we could have a proper send-off. As we travelled on there was less and less. Thailand tapered off into a few cluttered places selling junk-food and little pockets of increasingly bad driving. I had heard the last leg of the country was mostly occupied by Muslims, and it seemed to be true. Suddenly, women were covered in scarves, and there were signs for mosques along the roads. In retaliation, there were some of the biggest, boldest, brightest, and ugliest Buddhist temples I had ever seen.

We saw one that was particularly massive; it was a huge, pastel-covered thing with gilt paintwork and a giant statue on the roof, surrounded by a mass of gold statues laid out in front. It was one-upmanship of the gaudiest possible kind and laughable to see. Other religions were represented too—there was a Catholic cemetery and Christian symbols posted on fences.

Marcin was leading—his GPS was still the only one of the two that was barely holding itself together, although we'd learned some time ago not to rely on it, even if it appeared to be fully functional. He was getting slower and slower as we made our way along, barely making thirty mph at some points, even on wide open roads with nothing else about.

As we rode along, the signs began to contradict one another, so we didn't know how far we had left to go. Then, all of a sudden and without warning, we were there.

There was the border; nothing more than a fence in the middle of the road diverting traffic into a compound. We parked up briefly, and police tried to move us along. We knew this was it. I suggested heading back to the last half-decent place for a quick coffee, as there was nothing on the border—certainly nowhere to stay and nowhere to get a drink of a more adult kind.

The shop was just a shop, so our last drink together was a can of ice coffee and a bottle of ice tea. We chatted about the inevitability of this moment, which had been increasingly inevitable with every plodding turn of the wheel. We both knew I was staying in Thailand, and Marcin had to power on towards Australia—a force of nature brutally blundering into the unknown and trying to eat or crash into it, occasionally stopping to break down or moan that the speed wasn't fast enough.

With nothing else to give, I passed on the lucky pen—a silly little yellow piece of plastic. Marcin grumbled at first and gasped, as if I was handing him something of huge significance. "But it's the lucky pen!" he said, not quite touching it with his outstretched fingers. We both laughed at ourselves as we remembered it really was just a silly little plastic pen.

It was a difficult moment for us both. We had been through so much and done so many crazy things together that splitting up was a hard thing to do. We stopped for a few last pictures and were finally done. The time had finally arrived, the one we had both been dreading for the last few days, wringing out each second as we went along the way.

We had an awkward moment with some massively manly hugging and shaking of hands before Marcin rode off on his way, looking back sadly as he went.

It all brought a lump to my throat, I don't mind admitting. He told me the trip wouldn't have been fun without me, and he was right—we're very different in many ways, but we're a lot alike too. We play well together, and the trip had been immense fun, great fun for us both and for everyone who'd met us along the way. Marcin could be hard work, but he was a good man, and I felt that we'd forged a bond that would last us a lifetime.

I was really going to miss him, I thought, as I watched him ride to the compound. He looked back one last time as he vanished into the yard. The trip was hard, but I never once felt like quitting or turning back. I never felt like it was too much.

Marcin had made it fun for me too.

I stood there for some time, feeling like I'd made a mistake. My heart wasn't really in Thailand. I felt like I belonged on the road; that was where I felt truly alive, and for once, everything about my life had made sense.

On the way back my mind chewed over the times we'd had. In fact, I couldn't think of much else. I had to force myself to keep up the pace, since my heart wasn't in it at all, and I found myself creeping along at a snail's pace. The concept of forwards was fairly confused now. It had no real relevance, since there was suddenly nowhere I needed or really wanted to be.

And so I headed back, since there was nothing else to do. I was resolved to trying to get back to where we had stayed the previous night. I rode on into the dark, and then the temperature dropped. First I noticed my mirrors had steamed up, then my visor went white with mist. Suddenly, the roads were soaking wet, and the moon had vanished. I was worried about heading into a night-time tropical storm, but as I carried on it dried up a bit.

I figured out how far it would be to the same point, around 400 miles round trip, and I still saw nothing that reminded me of the same hotel. In the end, I found another of the super-petrol-stations with a mall and a hotel attached on the side. I decided to stay and get some rest; it was the same price, only £10, with free Internet, and was very decent, far better than I actually needed.

I had some dinner at the local place outside, alone for the first time I could remember. There was no vegetarian option, so I just had rice and eggs, which came with free water and a plate of veggies for only sixty pence. It was all quite good, but I was shattered and suffered instant celebrity status, which I could really have done without. For once, I just really needed to be alone and feel sorry for myself.

Being surrounded by people was bad enough when I was with Marcin, but to have to do it alone was no fun at all. I missed him already. It was suddenly very quiet on the road. I drank everything from the mini-bar and went to bed.

The End

That Was Then, This Is Now

After arriving back at Bangkok, I ended up only spending just a few short days there. I was in poor shape physically, so I just rested up in the cheapest guesthouse I could find until the worst of being ill was out of my system. I survived on a diet of Nepalese curry, coffee, and free Wi-Fi. Bangkok was very quickly proving expensive, so I waited for the return of my girlfriend in Pattaya, where I at least knew a few people, and where, with daily living expenses only around half that of Bangkok, I could stretch my resources that much further.

Marcin and I stayed in touch, of course. I had been reading his daily posts and watching as he got further and further away. From the boring confines of my room, I fixed his cutting out problems. I posted on various forums and spent a few hours searching the net for other signs of the same issue.

It turned out to be nothing more than a blocked fuel filter mesh in the tank. He ripped it out, and the bike was fine afterwards, in that respect at least. He did later admit that the KTM wasn't for him and sold it in Australia.

I had some time to myself while I waited for my girlfriend and hated every minute of it. When she finally did arrive, it was like she was a completely different person, and not in a good way.

I was riding high on emotion and decided to ask her to marry me on New Year's Eve at the stroke of midnight. She accepted, of course, and then before the ring was even slipped on her finger, she said, "That's great, now we can have children." Well, that was all news to me. I never wanted children, and we'd never spoken of such a thing. I presumed we were too old, and I thought she felt the same way. I was, of course, quite wrong, about everything, as usual.

With significant doubts firmly planted in my mind, I rode back down once again to her mother's house in the outer reaches of a jungle somewhere, almost exactly in the centre of nothing.

To say it didn't go particularly well is something of an understatement. Her mother never liked me from the moment she first asked me what I did for a living and I told her I'd just been made redundant. On this occasion, she asked for me to give her £20,000 for her daughter. Her younger brother then nearly accidentally shot himself in the head and tried to steal my BMW while I was asleep. It was one of those nights that you don't read about in romantic fiction.

All in all, this was something our relationship couldn't easily survive, and consequently, it didn't.

Also, Thailand increasingly became a place that I couldn't easily survive, and I was forced to leave while facing incarceration for the horrible crime of owning a motorcycle. A friend had called me up and asked how long I'd been there. Like me, he had ridden a 650cc BMW halfway round the world and had encountered an issue. If a bike remains in Thailand for longer than six months, it becomes a criminal offence, not that anyone tells you that at any point.

It was the final straw, after dealing with the people and bureaucracy for, what was then, almost a year. I decided it was time to get out and never look back, which is exactly what I did and with surprisingly few regrets.

The BMW did get the attention she deserved, but never quite enough of it. She was painted yellow, cleaned and fixed up, and lasted for many more thousands of miles around Asia, until eventually Marcin paid me a visit in my new home in Phnom Penh, Cambodia, where I had settled into working as a teacher and was struggling to become a writer.

I lent him the bike for him to do a trip around Cambodia, Laos, and Thailand. He called me from Bangkok with the happy news that my bike was on fire. She's currently having a major rebuild, and who knows what might come out the other end. Not a round-the-world tourer for sure, as in that respect, her useful days are over, and she's looking forward to semi-retirement as an urban scrambler or, more likely, a paperweight.

Marcin and I spoke of another trip, but sadly, both of us made our respective partners pregnant, which threw a bit of a spanner in the works and surprised both of us, since neither of us had any plans in that department. Marcin now has a daughter, and I have a son, and they became instant best friends as soon as they met.

Looking back after all this time, I felt rather empty at the conclusion of such an epic journey. I met several other riders—Ed, a young man desperately trying to prove something by riding a Honda C90 from Malaysia to England, and Damien, who finally caught up while I was living in Bangkok.

When he rode off into the traffic it brought it all back. The call of the road was very strong, and I struggled to fight the urge to head off into the wild unknown along with him.

I was very lucky to have done what I did. By now, Iran is quite a different place, I hear. Apparently, English travellers now require a guide, and the hostility is quite severe. Turkey has also descended into utter chaos, as a dark shadow crosses over the whole planet.

Adventures like I had may soon be confined to the history books, if the world goes the way it looks like it's going. Passports, as we know them, were introduced during wartime, with a promise that they wouldn't last beyond the hostilities. Of course, now they're considering micro-chipping whole populations, and people don't seem anywhere near as angry about that as they should be.

With a son running around my house making engine noises, my mind is filled with prospective journeys one day with him—teaching him to build a bike, how to ride, how to form his own opinions instead of adopting those of others.

I wonder what kind of world my son will have to ride around when it's his turn.

But, for now, it's still my turn, and I'm already building a bike and planning my next adventure. Marcin and I are considering a ride from Alaska to Argentina, but there are other, smaller adventures to be had along the way. Who knows where the road ahead might lead.

Also from Road Dog Publications

Bonneville Go or Bust*[1 2] *by Zoë Cano

A true story with a difference. Zoë had no experience for such a mammoth adventure of a lifetime but goes all out to make her dream come true to travel solo across the lesser known roads of the American continent on a classic motorcycle.

I loved reading this book. She has a way of putting you right into the scene. It was like riding on the back seat and experiencing this adventure along with Zoë.—★★★★ Amazon Review

Southern Escapades*[1 2] *by Zoë Cano

As an encore to her cross country trip, Zoë rides along the tropical Gulf of Mexico and Atlantic Coast in Florida, through the forgotten back roads of Alabama and Georgia. This adventure uncovers the many hidden gems of lesser known places in these beautiful Southern states.

. . . Zoë has once again interested and entertained me with her American adventures. Her insightful prose is a delight to read and makes me want to visit the same places.—★★★★★ Amazon Review

Chilli, Skulls & Tequila*[1 2] *by Zoë Cano

Zoe captures the spirit of beautiful Baja California, Mexico, with a solo 3 000 mile adventure encountering a myriad of surprises along the way and unique, out-of-the-way places tucked into Baja's forgotten corners.

Zoe adds hot chilli and spices to her stories, creating a truly mouth-watering reader's feast!—★★★★ Amazon Review

Hellbent for Paradise*[1 2] *by Zoë Cano

The inspiring—and often nail-biting—tale of Zoë's exploits roaming the jaw-dropping natural wonders of New Zealand on a mission to find her own paradise.

Motorcycles, Life, and . . . [1 2] *by Brent Allen*
Sit down at a table and talk motorcycles, life and . . . (fill in the blank) with award winning riding instructor and creator of the popular "Howzit Done?" video series, Brent "Capt. Crash" Allen. Here are his thoughts about riding and life and how they combine told in a lighthearted tone.

The Elemental Motorcyclist [1 2] *by Brent Allen*
Brent's second book offers more insights into life and riding and how they go together. This volume, while still told in the author's typical easy-going tone, gets down to more specifics about being a better rider.

A Short Ride in the Jungle [1 2] *by Antonia Bolingbroke-Kent*
A young woman tackles the famed Ho Chi Minh Trail alone on a diminutive pink Honda Cub armed only with her love of Southeast Asia, its people, and her wits.

Beads in the Headlight [1] *by Isabel Dyson*
A British couple tackle riding from Alaska to Tierra del Fuego two-up on a 31 year-old BMW "airhead." Join them on this epic journey across two continents.

A great blend of travel, motorcycling, determination, and humor.—★★★★★ Amazon Review

Chasing America [1 2] *by Tracy Farr*
Tracy Farr sets off on multiple legs of a motorcycle ride to the four corners of America in search of the essence of the land and its people.

In Search of Greener Grass [1] *by Graham Field*
With game show winnings and his KLR 650, Graham sets out solo for Mongolia & beyond. Foreword by Ted Simon

Eureka [1] *by Graham Field*
Graham sets out on a journey to Kazahkstan only to realize his contrived goal is not making him happy. He has a "Eureka!" moment, turns around, and begins to enjoy the ride as the ride itself becomes the destination.

Different Natures [1] *by Graham Field*
The story of two early journeys Graham made while living in the US, one north to Alaska and the other south through Mexico. Follow along as Graham tells the stories in his own unique way.

Thoughts on the Road [1 2] *by Michael Fitterling*
The Editor of *Vintage Japanese Motorcycle Magazine* ponders his experiences with motorcycles and riding and how they've intersected and influenced his life.

Northeast by Northwest [1 2] *by Michael Fitterling*
The author finds two motorcycle journeys of immense help staving off depression and the other effects of stress. Along the way, he discovers the beauty of North America and the kindness of its people.

. . . *one of the most captivating stories I have read in a long time. Truly a MUST read!!*—★★★★★ Amazon Review

Hit the Road, Jac! [1 2] *by Jacqui Furneaux*
At 50, Jacqui leaves her home and family, buys a motorcycle in India, and begins a seven-year world-wide journey with no particular plan. Along the way she comes to terms with herself and her family.

Asphalt & Dirt [1 2] *by Aaron Heinrich*
A compilation of profiles of both famous figures in the motorcycle industry and relatively unknown people who ride, dispelling the myth of the stereotypical "biker" image.

A Tale of Two Dusters & Other Stories [1 2] *by Kirk Swanick*
In this collection of tales, Kirk Swanick tells of growing up a gear-head behind both the wheels of muscle cars and the handlebars of motorcycles and describes the joys and trials of riding

Man in the Saddle [1 2] *by Paul van Hoof*
Aboard a 1975 Moto Guzzi V7, Paul starts out from Alaska for Ushuaia. Along the way there are many twists and turns, some which change his life forever. English translation from the original Dutch.

The Wrong Way Round[1,2] *by Andy Benfield*
The tale of the first westerner to cross into Burma from India on a motorcycle in over fifty years. It's also the story of a man coming to grips with his age and his romance with a woman twelve years younger. The story unfolds along some of the world's most stunning landscapes as the couple hurtle toward Burma among the Himalayas.

Shiny Side Up[1,2] *by Ron Davis*
A delightful compilation of articles ands essays on all things motorcycle by Ron Davis, writer, columnist, and associate editor for *BMW Owners News*, the largest magazine for BMW motorcycle owners on the planet.